THE LAYMAN'S GUIDE TO VIRGINIA LAW

Edited by

N. J. Bailes
J. L. Brown
D. B. Costello

THE MICHIE COMPANY

Law Publishers

Charlottesville, Virginia

COPYRIGHT 1977
BY
THE MICHIE COMPANY

Library of Congress Catalog Card No. 77-81626

TABLE OF CONTENTS

Chapter	Page
1. Introduction: Development of the Law	1
2. Relationship of Client and Attorney	12
3. Contract Law	30
4. Real Estate Transfers	45
5. Landlord and Tenant Law	59
6. Taxes	83
7. Wills: Distributing Property at Death	111
8. Insurance	133
9. Motor Vehicles	167
10. Liability for Harm to Persons and Property	187
11. Rights of Sick or Injured Workers	202
12. Family Relationships	229
13. Civil Liberties: Constitutional Rights	256
14. Women and the Law	277
15. The Criminal Justice Process	297
16. Procedure in Civil Suits	310
17. Federal Assistance	320
Index	333

FOREWORD

The Layman's Guide to Virginia Law is not designed to be a substitute for legal counsel. The goal of the Marshall-Wythe Law School's Student Bar Association and the editors has been to publish a book which will acquaint the Virginia resident with the procedures and substance of Virginia law in terms comprehensible to a nonlawyer.

The legal profession's increasing awareness of the need to educate the layman concerning basic legal rights is evidenced by the increasing number of legal aid societies and lawyer referral services. This book is designed to benefit layman and lawyer alike, by providing the average citizen with a ready reference to which he can turn for an explanation of legal rights and obligations. Hopefully, it will encourage individuals to seek legal advice; reluctance to approach an attorney, for whatever reason, often leads to situations in which legal aid is eventually a necessity — but then it is too late. Many legal problems could be avoided if people were more aware of the workings of the legal system.

The *Guide* should familiarize nonlawyers with the basic concepts of law, explain when an attorney is needed and why, how to select a lawyer, and what that lawyer can do for a client. As an additional benefit, it is hoped that the explanations contained herein will help to dispel some of the mistrust of the legal profession that seems abundant in today's society.

Much time spent by attorneys explaining basic concepts might be saved by presenting clients with an easily-read book which can be perused at leisure, allowing the attorney to take up where the *Guide* leaves off. A client will then have a better grasp of the situation, but, again, it must be warned that a client will not be prepared to conduct his own case. For example, the chapter on wills and decedents' estates will explain the rights of the decedent's heirs under state law, the advantages of having a will, and how an attorney can assist in planning an estate. It will NOT attempt to teach the reader how to draw a will or plan an estate competently on his own. It is for this reason that readers will frequently be cautioned in the following pages to consult legal counsel when it appears that they have incurred legal obligations, or when they wish to assert their rights under the law.

The Layman's Guide was written by students and graduates of the Marshall-Wythe School of Law of the College of William and Mary. Each chapter has been reviewed by one or more practitioners familar with the subject. The Student Bar Association of the law school has sponsored this project with the guidance and support of faculty members. Any profits from the sales of the *Guide* will be given to the law school for the improvement of its library.

ACKNOWLEDGMENTS

The editors wish to extend their gratitude to the large number of people whose generous voluntary contributions of time and effort made *The Layman's Guide* a reality. The Student Bar Association of the Marshall-Wythe Law School, under the leadership of Guice Strong, provided considerable labor and monetary assistance. Special thanks are also due to those members of the Marshall-Wythe law faculty who provided guidance and constructive criticism: Acting Dean Emeric Fischer, C. Harper Anderson, Richard E. Walck, Irma Lang, Dulcie Fowler, Tom A. Collins, Bolling R. Powell, Jr., Thomas H. Jolls, Ronald C. Brown, Douglas Rendleman, Kermit Dunahoo, and Jerome Leavell.

We also thank the Honorable J. R. Zepkin, general district court judge for the 9th district of Virginia, and attorneys Michael Geffen, Vincent Sapp, Tonita Warren, and Daniel Small for their advice and labor donated for the completion of the project.

Acknowledgment is also due the staff of the Oklahoma Law School's own *Layman's Guide* project, under the leadership of Michael Fought, for the suggestions and inspirations that assisted the work in Virginia.

Above all, Dr. William F. Swindler, professor of law at Marshall-Wythe, is due the major credit for completion of the *Guide*. His constant efforts in support of this work deserve the highest praise.

J. L. B.
N. J. B.
D. B. C.

CHAPTER 1

Introduction: Development of the Law

J. L. Brown

THE LEGAL SYSTEM GENERALLY

Law evolves in a piecemeal fashion, but it is always there to guide our relations with others. Twenty centuries before the Christian era Hammurabi promulgated a code for Babylonia; the Mosaic code for the Israelites was only eight centuries younger. Even primitive societies existing before these ancient codes were guided by customs and practices equivalent to laws.

The Anglo-American system of law is over one thousand years old. Revolutions have been infrequent in its experience; instead it has evolved through a slow process of change, but a process that has been ruthless and highly selective in what it has retained.

Every society has its own working legal system, for law is as natural to man as is religion. It is often said that when three or more persons are convened for any length of time they will elect a leader, enact laws and quarrel about both. Law is thus inevitable to society; and it follows that to have laws one must have a government. In a democracy, the government is one of laws and not of men. No man is above the law and it supersedes the men who enforce it, as has been seen during the Watergate era. The power of law comes from belief in it and reliance upon it. Without laws there would be anarchy. It can be said, then, that law arises out of necessity either real or imagined — sometimes wise, sometimes not.

To understand the law of today, one must look at its development in the context of its times. The roots of the American legal system lie in the English legal system, with some French influence (especially in Louisiana) and Spanish influence (evidenced by the community property laws of California). France and Spain are civil law jurisdictions which trace their legal systems back to Roman origin. The modern impetus of the civil law has been the French code drafted under Napoleon. The main distinction between civil law and common law is the source of law relied upon. Civil law is oriented towards a legislative code, which is an all-encompassing enactment of all basic law of a particular nation. For interpretation, the courts look to treatises on the law written by prominent legal scholars rather than to earlier judicial decisions, as is done in common law jurisdictions. Prior cases are not totally ignored, but neither are they binding.

Common law jurisdictions, however, do rely on statutes as well as cases, and the modern trend has been to enlarge the role of statutes. Courts interpret these statutes, giving consideration to the intent of the legislature in passing them. American courts have the unparalleled power of judicial review by which a court can declare a statute invalid because it conflicts with either the federal or a state constitution. Judicial review of the validity of legislation is foreign to the majority of civil law jurisdictions.

American law has evolved from American experience, but in the process it has been influenced by both civil and common law jurisdictions. This chapter will outline the evolution of the American legal system. An understanding of the roots and development of law is necessary, even though most common law has now been legislated into statutory form, because judges will still reach back a few centuries to examine statutes and decisions of old in order to aid their comprehension of modern American law, characterized as a system of legislation reviewed and interpreted by the courts subject to constitutional limitations.

Evolution of English Common Law

English history begins with the ancient Britons (known as Celts) in 30,000 B.C. The people of this society built Stonehenge and were important in a genetic sense as ancestors of the Welsh and of the Celtic population of Ireland. The Romans displaced the Celts, beginning their conquest in 55 B.C. and completing it a century later. During the Roman era the isles were known as Britannia. Roman contributions are mostly of archaeological interest, although Roman law may be said to have had some influence on the evolution of England's legal system.

Germanic peoples, who became known as the Anglo-Saxons, began their invasion during 449 A.D. and by about 700 A.D. had divided the isles into a heptarchy consisting of seven separate kingdoms. These kingdoms were consolidated under Alfred the Great with the Peace of Wedmore in 886 A.D. By the end of the ninth century the foundations of Anglo-Saxon civilization were laid.

Anglo-Saxon law was mostly custom, but was codified from time to time into "dooms" concerned primarily with prescribing certain penalties for listed crimes, which included treason, homicide, wounding, assault, rape and theft. These penalties were influenced by the Church, which attempted to temper violence by emphasizing compensation. For example, if a man murdered another he would be required to compensate the dead man's relatives rather than being killed himself. There were other crimes, such as killing the king, which could not be paid for with money. Then the punishment was the forfeit of all property and the maiming of the offender, *i.e.,* cutting off his ears or a hand. The concept of imprisonment for crime was unknown; jails existed, but their purpose was merely to house the accused until trial.

Trials took place in Hundred courts — a local government subdivision. If a crime was committed in open view a trial was deemed unnecessary, but if the parties were uncertain of what transpired a trial was held. Trials were public, and began with an oath by the defendant, who swore he did not commit the crime. This oath was standardized, and if the defendant was not letter perfect in his delivery of it the people believed God was interfering to show the accused was guilty. Oath helpers, who can be analogized to modern character witnesses, were acquired by each side to swear the party testifying was an "honest man." Thus, the tribunal was left with a set of conflicting oaths. At this point a trial by ordeal was permitted, and the accuser chose either a standard or a triple ordeal depending upon the nature of the crime and the reputation of the accused. The theory behind the ordeal was that God would protect the innocent but let the guilty perish in the ordeal. The cold water ordeal required the accused to be dunked in a pond; if he was being truthful the water would reject him, but if he was lying the accused would sink to his death. There was no appeal. The accused could escape trial by ordeal only through confession.

The next period of legal development began in 1066 with William the Conqueror and his Norman followers. Administrators by nature, the Normans began a process of centralization starting with the initiation of a full-fledged feudal system. At the top were William and his Norman lords, who together owned all of the land. William put his stamp upon the legal system, and consolidated the informal Anglo-Saxon structure into an arm of the King and state, so that a well-defined court system dispensed the King's justice.

Among the legal reforms introduced by the Normans was the concept of appeal of a local court judgment to a higher court. King William established the procedure for appeal by sending his own judges out to the localities. The principal functions of this *Curia Regis* (court of the King) remained the administration of criminal justice and settlement of other disputes, but the influence of the Norman judges prodded the Anglo-Saxon courts to a national standard of justice whereby judgment at the village court level was less subject to purely local variations.

Before long the need for recordation was recognized and scribes began to accompany judges on their rounds. Written opinions evolved, and these began to be utilized for consultation by judges deciding similar cases. Thus a body of law was created that judges could refer to for guidance. Labeled *stare decisis* (let the decision stand) this doctrine required the court to follow the law set forth in prior cases decided by the highest court of the given jurisdiction so long as the principle extracted from such case is logically essential to the decision and is both reasonable and appropriate to the situation at hand. *Stare decisis* added stability to law in that it was fairly certain the law would follow where the court had been. However, the doctrine of *stare decisis* has never been a straitjacket, for judges can overrule earlier cases if they feel such decisions were wrong or they can distinguish away unwanted precedents by making fine distinctions between the facts of the cases. Problems sometimes arose when the situation in question did not fit into a prior case. If it did not satisfy a specific form, the party could not maintain suit.

The Courts of Chancery were created to fill the gap left by the absence of an adequate legal remedy in those cases which did not fit the prescribed forms. Their primary purpose was to dispense justice in the absence of written law. However, where a legal remedy was adequate, the parties could not obtain such equitable relief. Therefore, a body of equitable principles evolved from the decisions of these Courts of Chancery which could be applied where the common law had no suitable remedy for a particular wrong, but these never became so rigid as the common law requirements.

Along with the substantive differentiation between equity courts and common law courts, there are some important procedural differences which concern judgments. In law courts, parties can obtain a favorable judgment, usually money or property, but they cannot order the parties to do a particular thing. Equity courts can order things not to be done *via* injunctions, or order them to be done *via* specific performance; but they have no jurisdiction over property and thus cannot give monetary judgments. In sum, equity has power over persons, but not over things.

The next major development in legal history was *Magna Carta,* or The Great Charter, signed in 1215 at Runnymede by King John. It was considered the first national English statute and severely limited the monarch's power by making judges independent of the king and by establishing a council of nobles which eventually evolved into Parliament's House of Lords. This marked the beginning of the chipping away of the monarch's absolute power.

English society was changing due to commercial development. Land ownership as the source of wealth and power was being displaced by a new mercantile class. A further sharing of power was necessitated by this development and by the wars of succession following the death of Henry VIII, which reappeared frequently during the ensuing 300 years. For survival as ruler, the monarch needed the nobles and the merchants as supporters. Through all of these wars and power struggles the influence and importance of Parliament grew — first the House of Lords developing from the *Curia Regis* and then the House of Commons, which reigned supreme after Oliver Cromwell. This supremacy in the government carried over to the law, so it fell to the Commons to change or repeal old laws and to draft new ones. Thus began the statutory law of England. In the beginning, courts looked at statutes with suspicion as unwelcome invaders; but soon they began to apply these statutes as well as the common law, using the principle of *stare decisis* to interpret the statutes. In order to determine the law in a particular instance one had to look at the statute itself and then the interpretation of it by the courts.

AMERICAN COLONIAL LAW

The 169 years between the settlement of Jamestown and the Declaration of Independence is said to be the dark age of American law. Necessity was the supreme lawmaker in the colonies, and laws in the early settlements were more like military orders. There were as many legal systems as there were colonies, not only because each colony was founded at a different point in the development of the English legal system, but also due to their different methods of origin (some being established by royal charter and others as joint stock ventures or proprietary colonies) and the fact that the colonies were populated by diverse people — religious dissidents, wealth-seekers, or criminals transported to the colonies to rid England of their presence.

Theoretically the English common law system was transplanted to her American colonies, though it was really unclear which laws and decisions were binding on the colonists. Many acts of Parliament were applied as a matter of course since most colonists considered themselves Englishmen entitled to the same rights and privileges as those in the mother country. In essence, the colonists borrowed from England what they wanted and accepted what they were forced to accept.

The colonies had no separation of powers as known today. Courts performed judicial, administrative, and quasi-legislative functions; while the legislatures heard appeals, they conducted few trials. The strings binding the colonies to England were more social and cultural than political; thus colonial law was more a child of English law than its subordinate, and was often a nonconforming child. For instance, equity and common law were administered side by side in the colonial courts, and rules of procedure and evidence were elastic rather than rigid as in England.

By the eighteenth century the English influence in colonial law became more prominent, partly as a result of natural development, partly by choice, and partly because England was becoming more aware of her colonies and serious about governing them. Appeals were taken from colonial courts to a special committee formed within the English monarch's Privy Council. This committee was more concerned that colonial law be in line with English politics and policies than that it conform to ordinary rules of law. For this reason, the committee was never an efficient overseer of the colonial courts, so the number of appeals remained small. In general, the committee was permissive and incompetent; even the colonial legislation was reviewed in a haphazard fashion, with many delays and a high tolerance for deviation. As a result, the orders of the council were not always obeyed and its influence was most strongly felt as a shadow during legislative debates over new laws.

The court system still formed a pyramid within each colony, with overlapping jurisdictions. Appellate and original jurisdictions were exercised in the same court. Judges were almost all laymen, but they were not totally ignorant; most knew a great deal about the relevant law of their own colony.

Colonial law also involved much codification. The colonies could not wait for their law to evolve as England's had. Custom and case law slowly seeped from colony to colony, but borrowing of statutes was a much faster process. Virginia was the model for the southern colonies, as Massachusetts was for the northern ones. By the eighteenth century wholesale code borrowing was largely ended and three patterns or models became evident: the colony's own system, that of its neighbors, and that of the mother country. It was the Revolution which ushered in the next significant event.

Constitutional Law

With the Declaration of Independence came the war and, finally, peace. The forming of a new nation was the uppermost problem and this called for lawmaking. Though defended by many, the reputation of the common law was badly tarnished, as was that of the legal profession since many lawyers had been Tories. What was needed was an Americanization of the common law system. The newly-independent states enacted a variety of statutes attempting to define what would be retained and what would be rejected of the English legal system. Essentially, England remained the major source of all law not strictly new or strictly American; the habits acquired during colonial rule were not easily overthrown. Then, too, American cases were not generally reported until a generation after the Revolution, so English ones were necessary to fill the gap. Borrowing was pervasive, but it was also selective, *i.e.,* the new states acquired only what they needed and wanted.

The Revolution had been a time of innovation. While colonial law had been paternal, emphasizing order and the struggle against sin, a new attitude developed during the Revolution which saw service rather than suppression as the primary function of law. This attitude was reflected in the instruments chosen to govern the new states.

The Articles of Confederation, the first of those instruments, were more a reaction against English rule than an attempt to create an American nation. They provided a very loose coalition of sovereign states, with no strong executive and no federal judiciary, although Congress was given some judicial power over disputes between states and concerning admiralty law. Due to the inherent weakness of such a structure, the Articles failed to govern well.

Faced with a breakdown of their confederation, Americans turned their attention to forming a stronger government — one which could effectively regulate commerce and provide for the common defense. As a result of their efforts and innovation, the Constitution was written. To create their new government, the new states had to waive certain powers, which they enumerated in the Constitution. In order to protect themselves from establishing a tyrannical federal government, they added a Bill of Rights which outlined what the new government could and could not do.

This written Constitution was a new idea, but has become very popular. A constitution has two basic functions: (1) to shape a permanent government, and (2) to enumerate the essential rights and limitations upon that government. The framers viewed the Constitution as reflecting the relations between the federal government and the states rather than establishing a direct relationship between the citizen and the central government, which was natural due to the territorial vastness and poor communications network of the new nation. Not until after the adoption of the Fourteenth Amendment and the creation of the "incorporation doctrine," which imposed many constitutional restrictions on the federal government on the state governments as well, did the direct relationship between citizen and federal government come into being.

At the time of its creation the Constitution was more than a mere framework. It even contained fragments of a code: a definition of treason, the guarantee of a jury trial, and a miniature code of criminal procedure provided by the Bill of Rights. The Constitution was the supreme law of the land, and would always take precedence over congressional legislation. The Supreme Court was created to settle all disputes arising under the Constitution, and over the years judicial power increased at the expense of the legislature. The concept of judicial review developed, whereby the Supreme Court reviews congressional legislation and has power to invalidate it if the law abridges the Constitution or if Congress did not have power to enact the particular law. Legislative supremacy declined as judicial power gained strength, partially because Americans were more afraid of too much law than of not enough.

The states also adopted constitutions, using the federal one as a model. Durability has been a feature of the federal constitution, but not of the majority of the states' constitutions: some states have had as many as ten constitutions, while only a few have had but one. The states did copy many other features of the federal constitutional development, however, *i.e.,* constitutional *stare decisis* and judicial review on a state level.

This book concerns itself with the substance and procedures of Virginia's law because most laws which directly affect the citizen are enacted on the state level, *e.g.,* property laws, wills, contracts, domestic relations, etc. These are state laws and are affected by federal law only if they violate constitutional limitations, or perhaps federal supremacy in some situations.

VIRGINIA LAW

Since this book concerns Virginia law it is important to examine briefly the state's history. The first Europeans to settle in Virginia were a group of Spanish Jesuits who established a mission, probably in the vicinity of the York River, in 1570. Indians destroyed their mission within a few months.

Early expeditions by Sir Walter Raleigh under Queen Elizabeth's rule led to the eventual creation of a charter colony in 1606 of Virginia, named for the "Virgin Queen." The first permanent English settlement was Jamestown in 1607. This colony was governed by Governor Dale's Code of 1611, which established a stern system of authority with a single ruling group controlling the colony. It concerned rules for soldiers' duties and for criminal law and it reflected the crudities of life in Virginia. On paper it seemed very severe, but it was deemed necessary at the time. Trivial crimes, such as stealing stores, were punished by death because of the importance of provisions in the early days of the colony.

Dale's Code disappeared by 1620. The colony was on a firmer footing by then and needed to attract more colonists, so a certain amount of self government was allowed, with the creation in 1619 of the first representative legislature in America — the forerunner of the House of Burgesses (now the General Assembly). By the late 1630s, the colonists were making laws in an organization which allowed local people a share of the power.

The settlement became a royal colony in 1624 and acquired governors appointed by the King. The royal governor and his council formed the highest court in the colony. County courts were established in 1623 as monthly courts manned by commissioners (usually local planters), who became known as Justices of the Peace by 1661. These courts handled administrative matters such as tax collection and road building as well as their judicial duties; they became the heart of colonial government in Virginia.

During the Revolution many Virginians played a prominent role — they had been loyal to the King, but at the same time they favored liberty and wished to govern their own affairs. Virginia adopted its first constitution in June of 1776, including a Declaration of Rights, which was the first of its kind in an American constitution. The Articles of Confederation were ratified in 1778; when the Constitution replaced them, Virginia became the tenth state by ratifying it on June 25, 1788.

Since that first Virginia constitution, there have been five more — 1830, 1851, 1870, 1902, and most recently, 1971. The General Assembly is the oldest representative legislature in America and still retains the essential structure of the House of Burgesses. The court system is topped by a Supreme Court with seven justices who serve twelve-year terms. Virginia's lower courts consist of Circuit Courts, which are courts of record, and General District Courts and Juvenile and Domestic Relations District Courts, which are courts not of record. Judges of the circuit courts are elected by the General Assembly for eight-year terms, and judges of the general district courts and the juvenile and domestic relations district courts for six-year terms. The functions and jurisdictions of these courts will be explained in Chapter 16 concerning legal procedure.

Through the remainder of *The Layman's Guide* the reader will find discussions of Virginia law as it applies to certain sets of facts and circumstances. Law is a process which is made to fit situations which arise. Where it does not fit, new laws are enacted and decisions interpreting them are made. Since it is a continuing process of legal evolution, even the lawyer who studies the system for three years before entering practice is only scratching the surface, but his training enables him to see what needs to be done and how to do it. The lawyer stands between the layman and the lawmaker; that is all that can be realistically expected of him in a legal system which is constantly growing and changing with the needs of society.

CHAPTER 2

Relationship of Client and Attorney

J. H. Klein

IN GENERAL

There are over 10,000 members of the Virginia State Bar,[1] yet the average citizen, in his everyday life, may have little or no contact with the members of the legal profession. Therefore, when he is faced with a situation in which he needs legal assistance, there is a good chance that he will not be familiar with the people to whom he must turn for help — attorneys. This chapter is designed to acquaint the average person with the legal profession in an introductory manner. Four important issues will be considered: (1) the training and qualifications of an attorney, (2) how the layman can select an attorney, (3) the responsibilities of the client and attorney in dealing with each other, and (4) costs of legal services. After examining each of these questions, the citizen will be more familiar with the role of the legal profession and better able to understand how lawyers function.

TRAINING AND QUALIFICATIONS OF AN ATTORNEY

In Virginia, the state supreme court has inherent authority over those who practice law in the state. The court has authority to define the practice of law, prescribe a code of ethics governing the professional conduct of attorneys, and to prescribe disciplinary procedures.[2] In an exercise of this authority, the Virginia State Bar was created, to which all attorneys in the state belong and pay dues. The State Bar acts as an administrative agency for the court in carrying out its supervision of the legal profession.

The state prohibits anyone from practicing law who has not been authorized to do so. This prohibition is made to protect the public

---

1. *Executive Director's Report*, 22 VA. BAR 23 (May-June 1974).
2. VA. CODE § 54-48.

from being advised by unqualified persons or by persons over whose conduct the judiciary has no control. Licensed attorneys, as members of a state bar, are subject to judicial supervision. Unauthorized practice is not proscribed as a means of reducing competition in the legal profession. The prohibition ensures that the public receives competent legal assistance, with the incompetent attorney subject to sanction.

The State Board of Bar Examiners is the agency set up to regulate the admission of attorneys to the bar. An applicant must meet the Board's requirements to be admitted. He must include in the application a certificate from the city or county court where he resides, or from his law school dean if he is a law student, that he is a person of honest demeanor or good moral character, is over the age of eighteen, was a resident of the state at the time the application was filed, and intends to continue as a resident until the time of the bar examination.[3] A student applicant must also submit certification that he will complete his degree requirements within three months of the exam. He also files a statement that he will complete all degree requirements.

The Board requires that an applicant be a graduate of a law school approved by the American Bar Association or by the Board. There are four approved law schools in Virginia: the Marshall-Wythe School of Law at the College of William and Mary, the T.C. Williams School of Law at the University of Richmond, the University of Virginia School of Law, and the Washington and Lee University School of Law. An applicant can also qualify for the exam by completing at least a three-year course at an accredited college and studying law for three years in the office of an attorney who practices law in Virginia full-time.[4]

Successful completion of the bar exam is then required for admission. The Board gives two exams a year, which must be four months apart. Presently they are offered in February and July. When one has successfully passed the exam and has met the other

---

3. *Id.* § 54-60.
4. *Id.* § 54-62.

requirements, the Board issues a license to practice law in Virginia. It sends a list of those licensed to the state supreme court.

It takes considerable study and effort to become a practicing lawyer. While this in itself is no guarantee that all lawyers are competent, successful completion of all the requirements listed above does indicate a certain degree of knowledge and preparation on the part of the lawyer.

It is also possible to be admitted to the bar without passing the Virginia bar examination. An attorney outside of Virginia who files an application, who has been licensed and practicing in another state for five years, and who pays the required fee, can be admitted without examination if the court decides he is a proper person to practice law in this state.[5] In addition, an attorney from another jurisdiction may be permitted to conduct a particular case in Virginia courts in association with a Virginia attorney, where such a privilege is allowed to Virginia attorneys in that lawyer's state. This type of arrangement is known as comity.

SELECTION OF AN ATTORNEY

After one knows how attorneys get to be attorneys, the question then becomes, How does one select an attorney to represent him? This decision is made a bit more difficult for the layman because, by the terms of the Code of Professional Responsibility,[6] the lawyer is not allowed to advertise or solicit business; Disciplinary Rule 2-101 (A) of the Code says a lawyer shall not use "any form of public communication that contains professionally self-laudatory statements calculated to attract lay clients." This includes use of such methods of advertisement as newspapers, magazines, radio, television, and other commercial advertisements. The lawyer may list himself or his firm in the alphabetical and classified sections of the telephone directory where he lives, has his office, or has a number of clients. He may also be listed in an approved law list or legal directory.

---

5. Rule 1A:1, Sup. Ct. (Va.).

6. The Code of Professional Responsibility, as adopted by the Supreme Court of Virginia in 1970, is set out in Volume 211 of Virginia Reports, at pages 295-358.

This limitation on advertising by attorneys may have the effect of leaving the layman in the dark about which lawyers are most reputable or most able in particular areas of the law. Nonetheless, it is the prospective client who must seek out the attorney; the attorney may not seek out clients.

If one is going to select a lawyer, there are several ways to proceed. One way is to sit down and randomly look through the yellow pages of the telephone book under "attorneys" or "lawyers." As noted above, attorneys may list themselves in this section. Thus, one can find listed together most of the attorneys in a particular area. Or one may turn to a "law list," which is a legal directory in which attorneys in different areas are listed, along with brief biographical sketches and other informative data. Some such directories undertake a rating system, which may be based upon such factors as years of practice, standing in the community, types of clients, etc. Or the prospective client may wish to rely on the suggestions and recommendations of friends and relatives who have had previous contact with attorneys.

Once one has reached a preliminary decision about a lawyer he is considering as his legal counsel, he should then consider the personal qualities and characteristics of that attorney. It is better to evaluate such qualities as his experience, intelligence, character, and reputation than the size of his legal fees, although cost may sometimes have to be a factor.

Another consideration is whether one wants the services of a sole practitioner (an attorney who works by himself) or of a firm (a group of lawyers working together). When a client uses a firm, he has the resources and prestige of the entire organization behind him, but the fees may be higher. With a sole practitioner, the client may get more personal attention, but the lawyer may not have such extensive resources to bring to bear on the case.

Finally, it may not always be best to look for the busiest lawyer who has been practicing the longest. While such an attorney will probably have experience with a broad variety of legal problems, if he is quite busy, the client might not get as much close personal attention as he desires. On the other hand, it is possible that a young lawyer, just building a reputation, will be able to give more personal attention and may even bring more spirit and enthusiasm to a case.

Selecting a lawyer should be far more than picking a name at random from the yellow pages. Sometimes, though, people feel unable to select a lawyer on their own. Perhaps the surest method is to use Virginia's new Lawyer Referral Service, established by the Virginia State Bar. By calling this toll-free number, 800-552-7977, a person seeking legal counsel may be referred to a member of the statewide lawyer referral panel who practices in the caller's area. The individual may then make an appointment with the suggested lawyer for up to half an hour of consultation for a fixed initial fee of $15.00. If financially eligible, the caller may be referred to a local Legal Aid office for free consultation. Any additional legal services and fees will be subject to agreement between the client and the attorney.

Clearly, in order for such a system to be of any use, the public must be made aware of its existence. So the referral service must be adequately publicized. Fortunately, this is possible, because a Disciplinary Rule of the Code of Professional Responsibility expressly permits attorneys to cooperate with a lawyer referral service operated, sponsored, or approved by a bar association of the local area.[7]

There are some limitations on the usefulness of this project. The system is not a means of reducing legal costs, for only the first visit with the attorney is at the low rate. After that, the cost will be determined by the attorney and the client. As a means of aiding in lawyer selection, the system has limitations. There is little guarantee that the lawyer designated is going to be competent to handle certain cases. Upon his application, and payment of a registration fee, he will be added to the referral list, with no attempt by the service to assess his ability to handle specific cases. Protection is afforded in the Disciplinary Rule stating a lawyer shall not "handle a legal matter which he knows or should know

---

7. DR 2-103 (D) (3).

that he is not competent to handle without associating with him a lawyer who is competent to handle it." [8]

There are other groups which provide assistance to their members in selecting attorneys. Some labor unions may have particular attorneys whom they recommend to their members who need assistance. Other groups, such as the American Civil Liberties Union or the National Association for the Advancement of Colored People, are interested in seeing that constitutional rights of individuals are secured and preserved. They may offer legal assistance to those with a problem in which the group takes an interest.

Persons who cannot afford to pay for the services of an attorney may have one appointed to aid them at the state's expense in certain circumstances. Virginia law provides that in civil matters the court *may* provide an indigent person with counsel.[9] In criminal matters, one accused of a crime has a constitutional right to legal counsel, even if he cannot afford to pay for it himself. Further details of this right can be found in Chapter 13 on constitutional rights.

Choosing an attorney can be accomplished through a variety of means. But in the attorney-client relationship it is important that both parties be able to trust each other. Therefore, it is important that the client select his attorney with some care.

RESPONSIBILITIES OF ATTORNEY AND CLIENT

After selecting an attorney, the next concern is how the client and his attorney will function together — that is, the division of their respective responsibilities.

The attorney occupies a unique professional position. He represents the client and is to act in the client's best interests; yet, at the same time, he is an officer of the court. That means he has responsibilities to the court as well as to his client. The Code of Professional Responsibility was adopted by the American Bar

---

8. DR 6-101 (A).
9. VA. CODE § 14.1-183.

Association as the set of principles established to govern the conduct of attorneys. In 1970, the Virginia Supreme Court adopted the Code as the Virginia Code of Professional Responsibility, and it is thus applicable to any attorney licensed to practice law in this state.

The Code of Professional Responsibility is organized into nine canons of principles. Each canon is followed by a number of "ethical considerations," which are goals that lawyers should strive to meet, and by "disciplinary rules," which are mandatory standards lawyers must meet or be subject to disciplinary action. It is impossible in this short article to consider any details of the "ethical considerations" (EC's) and "disciplinary rules" (DR's) which accompany the canons. However, it is at least useful to mention the subject matter of the canons themselves.

Under the canons, a lawyer should aid in maintaining the integrity of the profession, should help the profession meet its duty of making legal assistance available, should help prevent the practice of law by persons not authorized to do so, should keep the confidences of a client, should use his professional judgment in the interests of his client, should provide his client with competent legal representation, should represent his client zealously, should help to improve the legal system, and should avoid any action that even appears to be improper. This is of course only a summary of the provisions of the Code. Anyone interested in the full provisions of the Code can obtain a copy from the American Bar Association or can find the provisions as adopted by the Virginia court in Volume 211 of *Virginia Reports,* which is available in any law library and in many college and public libraries.

Turn now to a consideration of what these principles mean. What are the responsibilities of the attorney in actual practice?

When the client first meets with the attorney and begins to discuss the client's problem, a privileged lawyer-client relationship is created whether or not the attorney takes the case. The creation of this relationship is important, because it marks the time when certain responsibilities attach: responsibilities owed by the lawyer to the client and by the client to the lawyer. Sometimes an attorney will require, or a client offer, a retainer — that is, a part of the total fee which is paid when the attorney accepts the case. This then binds the attorney to act on behalf of his client and not to accept other business that conflicts with his client's interests, unless the client agrees to it after full disclosure by the attorney of the possible effects it might have upon him.[10]

Once the client entrusts his problem to the attorney, the attorney must act with a reasonable degree of care and skill in the conduct of the case. The attorney cannot and does not guarantee a settlement of the case that will satisfy the client. He undertakes only to represent the client and exercise reasonable care and skill in his representation. If he fails to meet that standard and the client is thereby injured, the attorney may be liable for that injury. However, the attorney acting according to his own professional judgment generally is not considered to have acted negligently. In other words, the attorney is generally not liable for an error in judgment.

Therefore, in a suit by a client against an attorney for negligence or malpractice, the client must prove four essential points: (1) that the attorney was employed by him, (2) that there was neglect by the attorney of a reasonable duty, (3) that this negligence resulted in (was the proximate cause of) loss to the client, and (4) the extent of the damages suffered by the client. The attorney would be liable only for injury actually received by the client. Fortunately for both the public and the legal profession, the great majority of attorney-client relationships do not result in problems that would call for such an action by the client.

Generally, once the attorney has accepted a case, he may take whatever legal actions he thinks proper in carrying on the case. He has authority to take the steps he considers necessary to protect the interests of his client. The attorney is the agent of the client, which means the client will be bound by the acts of the attorney. For example, the attorney may admit facts in a trial, which admission is then binding on the client. But this general authority is not unlimited. For example, the lawyer has no authority to compromise a client's claim without the client's consent. Nor may

---
10. DR 5-105.

he waive the constitutional rights of an accused client in a criminal case.

The lawyer-client relationship is one of trust and confidence, but for it to operate as such, the client must be able to have confidence that what he tells his attorney will remain confidential. It is only when the lawyer knows all the facts of the matter he is handling that he can function properly, yet only when the client trusts the attorney and can rely on his confidences being kept will he feel free to discuss with his attorney all the facts of his case. It is for this reason that the Code provides that a lawyer should preserve the confidences and secrets of his client.[11] This responsibility continues even after the lawyer-client relationship has terminated.

This ethical responsibility is carried over into the rules of evidence. A client is privileged from having offered into evidence what he disclosed to his attorney in confidence. However, the privilege is limited, in that actual concealment by an attorney of evidence of a crime is improper, where the attorney knows the police are seeking that evidence.

The client can expect that his attorney will do everything possible under the law to protect and further the client's interests. This is the meaning of the canon which says a lawyer should represent his client "zealously within the bounds of the law." [12] The attorney is expected to advocate his client's position through use of whatever means and methods in his professional judgment are proper and legal. Under our system "of laws, not of men" each person can expect to have his conduct judged according to the law. Therefore, he can expect his attorney to use the full extent of the law in presenting his claims.

Again there are limits. The attorney is not permitted to encourage his client to commit criminal acts or to counsel his client on how to commit criminal acts and avoid the penalty for them. His conduct is limited by the requirement that his representation be "within the law."

In summary then, the lawyer-client relationship, when created, establishes a relationship of trust and confidence in which the

---

11. Canon 4.
12. Canon 7.

lawyer owes his client a duty of reasonable care, of keeping his confidences, of representing him "zealously," and of not representing interests adverse to the client.

The attorney is also an officer of the court and a member of the legal profession. He therefore has responsibilities to both the court and the profession. As an officer of the court, an attorney must not abuse the processes of the court by bringing cases merely to harass, or cases which are simply frivolous. A lawyer who abuses his position by engaging in such conduct is subject to disciplinary action. Furthermore, as a member of the profession, a lawyer must conform to the provisions of the Code of Professional Responsibility, or he can be subjected to discipline. Therefore, a brief examination of the procedure for disciplining attorneys in Virginia may be of interest.

The Code of Virginia provides that, if a complaint, verified by an affidavit, is made to the state supreme court or any court of record of the state, alleging any malpractice or unlawful, dishonest, unworthy, corrupt or unprofessional conduct on the part of any attorney, or if the court itself notices such conduct, it may (if it deems it proper) issue a *rule* against such attorney, which means he must show cause why his license to practice law should not be suspended.[13] Such a complaint may also come to the court from the District Committee of the Virginia State Bar. This is a committee of lawyers in each Congressional District which is created to hear and investigate complaints of misconduct against members of the bar in that district. If a District Committee receives a complaint, it may decide either that the complaint is unfounded (and dismiss it) or that the complaint deserves a hearing. If, after a hearing, the Committee decides disciplinary action is necessary, it brings the matter to the courts. Then, where a verified complaint has come from the District Committee, the court *shall* issue a rule against the attorney. Two other judges of the circuit court, plus the judge who issued the rule then hear and decide the case. If the attorney is found guilty, his license may be suspended for a time or revoked. The court may also issue a reprimand, in which case

---

13. VA. CODE § 54-74.

the license is not suspended, but the attorney is advised that his conduct was improper. Either the complainant or the attorney may appeal the decision of the court to the supreme court of the state.

It should be clear then that the courts and the bar are serious about maintaining the standards and ethics of the legal profession. Indeed, that is the reason for the entire procedure outlined above. The courts are less interested in meting out punishment than in protecting the public, as the court itself said in a 1971 case.[14] The court also noted that, "The question is not what punishment may the offense warrant, but what does it require as a penalty to the offender, as a deterrent to others, and as an indication to laymen that the courts will maintain the ethics of the profession?"[15] The punishment dealt out by the Virginia courts to licensed Virginia attorneys found guilty of improper conduct in Watergate-related matters stands as evidence that the attorney's conduct is policed and that a failure to meet proper standards will be dealt with. So laymen who believe they have a grievance against an attorney, or who feel there has been improper conduct by an attorney, should bring the matter to the attention of the proper authorities. The legal profession, under the watchful eyes of the courts, will discipline itself.

Having considered the various responsibilities of the attorney to the client, it is only fitting to turn next to the responsibilities of the client to the attorney.

First, the client owes the attorney the truth. He should tell his attorney all the facts as he knows them, not just the ones he thinks might be advantageous to his position. Only when the attorney has all the facts, as they actually occurred, can he properly analyze the client's situation and make proper decisions about the conduct and management of the case. Remember that the lawyer will keep confidential what the client relates to him. The very reason for this is to encourage the client to disclose fully what he knows to his lawyer. Full disclosure is not just a moral or ethical necessity; it is good tactics as well. It is far better for a lawyer to know all the facts well in advance — even the ones that may seem damaging

---

14. Seventh Dist. Comm. v. Gunter, 212 Va. 278, 284, 183 S.E.2d 713 (1971).
15. Maddy v. First Dist. Comm., 205 Va. 652, 658, 139 S.E.2d 56 (1964).

to the case — than it is to have an opponent suddenly spring the damaging information on the attorney at a later date when he is least prepared for it.

Second, the client must recognize that the attorney functions within the terms of the Code of Professional Responsibility. Therefore, a client must not make demands upon the lawyer which will cause the lawyer to violate the terms of the Disciplinary Rules or to engage in improper conduct. Indeed, the Code provides that the attorney may seek to withdraw from the case where his client insists that the lawyer engage in conduct that is prohibited by the Disciplinary Rules or is illegal.[16] Where it is obvious that the continued employment of the attorney will result in violation of a Disciplinary Rule, the attorney's withdrawal from the case is mandatory.[17]

Third, the client, while retaining authority to terminate the attorney-client relationship at any time and retaining authority to compromise or settle the case without his attorney's approval, still is liable to the attorney for his fee. The client may discharge his attorney, even without good cause, but the attorney may then receive at least the value of his services which have already been rendered. Similarly, the client may agree to settle the case without his lawyer's consent, but the lawyer may still recover the reasonable value of his services rendered. Laymen should note that an attorney has a lien on property or money in his possession belonging to a client until his fees are paid. If necessary, the attorney may bring suit against his former client to recover his fee. This is an undesirable situation and one that is to be avoided when at all possible. The Code of Professional Responsibility says that a lawyer should strive to avoid controversies over fees and should try to settle amicably any disputes on the subject.[18] But it also allows the attorney to sue for his fee where that is necessary.

Cost of Legal Services

Many laymen, who have had little contact with the legal profession, seem to avoid initiating such contact because they fear

---
16. DR 2-110 (C) (1) (c).
17. DR 2-110 (B) (2).
18. EC 2-23.

it will be prohibitively expensive to them. While the cost of legal services can sometimes be substantial, in a number of cases the fees are not so large as might be feared. In any case, to put off seeking legal advice because the cost might be high is certainly short-sighted. All too often the layman only seeks legal assistance after the legal problems have been created. For example, a death may have occurred without a will having been drawn up, or title to land may be contested due to failure to have the title searched prior to acquisition. It is then too late for the attorney to provide advice about how to minimize costs, taxes, or liabilities. He must deal with the circumstances at hand, although the results may well have been different if proper legal advice had been sought at the outset. What this suggests is the importance of "preventive legal advice." It should be obvious that it is much cheaper to get proper advice early and thus minimize legal problems than to go to a lawyer only when a problem has already developed and the only solution is expensive action in the courts.

But in any case, once the client does come to the attorney, what can he expect the costs of legal services to be? The answer is that the cost varies. The fees charged by lawyers must be reasonable. Lawyers are prohibited from charging excessive fees. The Code says a lawyer shall not charge any "clearly excessive fee." [19] Among the factors the Code lists as guides in determining a reasonable fee are the following: the time and labor required by the case, the difficulty of the questions involved, the amount of the lawyer's time the case will take up, the customary fee in the locality, the amount of money involved in the case, and the experience, reputation, and ability of the attorney.[20] All these factors and others weighed together help determine what will be a reasonable fee in a particular case.

Often an attorney will have developed a system of scheduled fees. He may charge a certain amount per hour of his time, or so much per day in court, or so much for performing a particular task, such as drawing up a will. (A set fee suggested to the attorney, or required, by his state or local bar association in a so-called

---

19. DR 2-106 (A).
20. DR 2-106 (B).

"minimum" or "suggested" fee schedule has been declared illegal, as a violation of the federal antitrust laws.)

The attorney and client may properly contract for the services of the attorney, and fix the amount of compensation in the contract. Such a contract is valid and may be enforced just as other contracts. Where the contract for the services is made before the attorney has established any lawyer-client relationship, the courts will treat the contract for fees just as they would any other contract. But where such a contract calls for an exorbitant fee or is oppressive or fraudulent, it would be unenforceable in the courts. However, where the contract for fees was entered into after a relationship of trust and confidence was already established between the lawyer and client, the courts would scrutinize carefully any contract calling for additional compensation. The burden rests upon the attorney in such a case to show that the contract is fair and reasonable and that there was no undue influence on the part of the attorney.

Sometimes attorneys take cases on a "contingent fee basis," which means that they receive as compensation a portion of the recovery made in the case. If there is no recovery made, then the attorney receives no fee. The average contingency fee may range from about one-fourth to one-third of the recovery made, and even more in extraordinary cases. Contingent fees are used in cases where there may be a sum recovered — will contests, personal injury cases, workmen's compensation cases, stockholder's derivative suits, etc. It should be noted that the Disciplinary Rules prohibit charging a contingent fee for representing a defendant in a criminal case.[21] The contingent fee is criticized on several grounds. Some critics contend that the process can often lead to exorbitant legal fees, while others argue that lawyers often end up working for nothing at all. Critics complain that the procedure makes the lawyer essentially a partner in the suit, which may make him less able to give impartial advice and may even lead him to try to settle the case quickly in order to maximize his compensation for the number of hours he works on the case. Others complain that

---

21. DR 2-106 (C).

there is no relationship between the fee charged and the number of hours worked.

Despite these criticisms, there are important benefits from the contingent fee system. It enables people who otherwise might be unable to afford legal assistance to pursue their claims with competent legal help. So, even though a portion of the recovery is paid to the attorney, the client still realizes more than he would have without the assistance of trained legal counsel. Additionally, the system encourages the victims of accidents to seek legal advice early and thus to be aware of their rights. Despite the various criticisms, it would seem improvident to alter the contingent fee system until some other means is devised to provide the necessary access to the judicial system which the contingent fee route currently affords.

It should be clear by now that the matter of fees for legal services is a matter of some importance. There are times, unfortunately, when disputes arise between clients and their attorneys over the amount of fees due for legal services rendered. Such a development is unfortunate. It means there has been a breakdown of the close relationship that is supposed to exist between lawyer and client. Attorneys are expected to make every effort to settle in an amicable manner such disputes as may arise, though as noted above, they may sue for their fees if that is necessary. But such a suit is detrimental to the lawyer, to the legal profession, and even to the client. Therefore, one of the very first things that should be discussed fully between an attorney and a prospective client is the amount of the fee. The type of fee (hourly, contingent, etc.), the amount, and when it will be due, should all be discussed and settled early in the relationship. This should prevent any misunderstandings about fees later. Again, early preventive action is highly preferable to delay and perhaps significant problems later.

Despite all that has been said above, it is clear that the costs of legal services can sometimes be substantial. In inflationary times, the expenses the attorney must bear increase also, so there would seem to be little prospect of the cost of legal services being reduced in the near future. Nevertheless, there are a number of developments that could have an effect on the cost of legal services or on the services an attorney can render for a given fee. Without going into great detail on any of these, some potential developments should be noted.

First, a number of communities in Virginia have seen the establishment of some sort of legal aid society. This is an organization that renders various types of legal services to persons who are unable to pay. The society may be set up under the auspices of a law school, a local bar association, or even a local unit of government. Those who live in an area served by a legal aid society and who qualify for its assistance may receive important legal help that they might not otherwise be able to afford.

Second, the Virginia Supreme Court permits limited appearances in court by third-year law students, under the supervision of licensed attorneys. The third-year practice rule may enable certain people who would otherwise have been without legal assistance to receive certain aid from a student practitioner, under supervision of a licensed attorney.

The above programs would primarily benefit those who are not able to afford legal services under the present system. There are also developments that may aid persons of moderate income. The possible benefits to the consumer from any court decision making antitrust laws applicable to suggested fee schedules have already been noted. Another important development is the increasing interest in the use of "legal assistants" or "paraprofessionals." The idea is to train people to do some of the more routine everyday tasks of the attorney, which can then free the attorney to devote more time to detailed and complex matters that only a lawyer is trained to handle. The "paralegal" would be something less than an attorney, but something more than a legal secretary. Some of the tasks that might be properly performed by a trained paraprofessional could include obtaining factual histories of clients, making factual inquiries, and answering factual questions for the attorney or the client. An attorney could conceivably provide more services for the same legal fee or perhaps even pass along some savings to the client. In any case, the program does seem to have significant potential benefits for both the legal profession and for the public.

In Virginia, the Professional Efficiency and Economics Research Committee of the Virginia State Bar has for some years been promoting the use of paralegals in Virginia law firms.[22] This Committee has also been working with the Virginia Community College System in establishing a training program for paralegals. The possibilities are real that Virginians may see the benefits of this development.

Increasing use of group legal service plans is also noteworthy. In these plans, individual members of a group, such as a labor union, are provided with legal services by attorneys selected or recommended by the group. The plan is funded by dues paid by the group members. There are two types of group plans: Open Panel or Closed Panel. In Open Panel plans, the client may choose any attorney to represent him, and the cost will be borne by the group. The panel of lawyers from which the client may select is open and unrestricted. In a Closed Panel plan, the group chooses an attorney, or a list of attorneys, from which the member must choose his legal counselor.

There are several possible advantages to a group plan. It may be that as the number of cases increases, the cost per case may decrease, thus reducing somewhat the overall cost of legal services. The client may think it an advantage to have an attorney chosen for or recommended to him, especially if he is not familiar with any lawyers. Also, the attorney's salary would be determined ahead of time by the group, so the matter of fees would already be decided.

However, a number of questions about the propriety or advisability of such plans do remain. Closed Panels are criticized for the possible economic effects they could create for attorneys not in the panel. It is also feared that attorneys employed by a large group might lose their independence and might be unable to exercise their "independent professional judgment" in the interests of the client, especially if the client's interests ever

---

22. *Professional Efficiency and Economics Research Committee Annual Report,* 22 VA. BAR NEWS 53 (May-June 1974).

clashed with the interests of the group as a whole. That could happen, for example, where a union member was suing his union or its officers. Furthermore, some critics contend the group services system would lead to an increase in the number of cases brought to court. The fear is that easier access to legal assistance, with the costs paid by the group instead of the individual, would lead to more lawsuits. On the other hand, it can also be argued that a person who has a legitimate claim ought to be able to bring it before the courts. If the courts are overloaded, the proper solution would be to increase the ability of the judiciary to handle its workload, not to keep proper cases out of court. At any rate, if group systems can be set up so attorneys are not compromised, then it does seem that the members of the group have much to gain from such a system.

Finally, it should be noted that there are developments in the field of prepaid legal insurance. In this system, a client pays in advance for services he may need in the future, a system analogous to medical insurance programs. Some attorneys prefer this system to a group services plan because the attorney is selected by the client, not by the group. Legal expenses of the client would then be paid by the insurer as they were incurred, up to the policy limits. This kind of program can be difficult to set up because determining proper premium charges is difficult. Nevertheless, pilot programs of prepaid legal services have been undertaken. The American Bar Association sponsored such a plan in Shreveport, Louisiana, known as the Shreveport Plan, the results of which are now under evaluation. Plans such as this do show a potential for increasing the availability of legal services to the public, yet maintain the independence of the bar as well.

CHAPTER 3

Contract Law

R. T. Copeland

IN GENERAL

The body of the law of contracts is an overwhelmingly large area. Contracts are formed between individuals and companies almost daily whether for a purchase of gasoline with a credit card or a visit to a doctor's office for treatment. It is, therefore, only fit and proper that individuals should become more knowledgeable about what a contract is and how the laws of the State of Virginia and the United States affect and modify some of the more common contracts.

Perhaps the best place to start would be to answer the question, "What is a contract?" It has been defined in many different ways, but perhaps the best short definition is that a contract is "a promise or a set of promises, for the breach (or breaking) of which the law gives a remedy, or the performance of which the law recognizes as a duty." [1] While this may sound confusing, it can be looked at in a simpler way. That is, one who makes a legally enforceable promise has made a contract.

TYPES OF CONTRACTS

There are many different forms of contracts. The simplest of these is probably the oral contract: Buyer agrees to buy and Seller agrees to sell an article such as a lawn mower or a garden hoe. When each party has the intent to carry out his part of the bargain, a contract has been reached.[2] It should be noted at this point that certain types of things cannot be sold by an oral contract, such as land, goods, cars, boats, etc., where the sale price is over $500, but, these items will be discussed later in this chapter in connection with the Statute of Frauds. A written contract, on the other hand, is formed when the parties show their intent to contract by signing

---
1. RESTATEMENT OF CONTRACTS § 1.
2. 17 AM. JUR. 2d *Contracts* § 1.

a writing, which may or may not set forth all of the circumstances or "terms" surrounding their deal. When almost anything is bought from a dealer on an installment basis, such as a car or television set, a written contract is usually signed.

Sometimes the legally enforceable promises on which contracts are based are "express" (that is, by words or in the writings, the parties show quite clearly what they intend to do). In other cases, the contract is an "implied" contract. There are two types of implied contracts. One type is the contract implied in fact, wherein the actions of the parties themselves, but not the language of the agreement, show that they intended to form a contract. A good example of this type of contract would involve the furnishing of services for another at the request of the person served. The person receiving the services has given an implied promise to pay a reasonable sum for these services. Thus, when an individual takes his car to a mechanic and requests that work be done, he does not have to say to the mechanic, "I'll pay you for your work," because it is implied by his actions in taking the car to the mechanic that he will pay.

The other type of implied contract is the contract implied in law. These are not "true" contracts under the earlier definition. They are really contracts that the law makes, so that one party is not unjustly enriched at the expense of another. For example, if a person makes a payment in full for a product but the seller is not able to furnish the product due to no fault of his own, the law will imply that a contract exists between the parties, to the effect that if the product is not furnished, the money paid to the seller will have to be returned to the buyer. Suppose that a real estate agent tries to sell a house for a homeowner. After finding a buyer ready to pay the price, the homeowner decides that he will not sell the house, and revokes the authority of the agent to find buyers. Here, the law would require that the agent be paid a commission anyway, since he performed the agreed service.[3]

---

3. 4B MICHIE'S JURISPRUDENCE *Contracts* § 103 (1974).

ABILITY TO CONTRACT

The next pressing question is, "Who can make contracts?" The answer to this is that any competent adult is capable of contracting. The term "competent" means an individual over the age of majority (eighteen years old) who has not been adjudicated insane and is not otherwise incompetent, such as by being a convicted felon serving one year or more in the state penitentiary.[4] If a person is not capable of making a valid contract due to a disability, such as lack of age or other incompetency, but has entered into one anyway, disputes arise about the rights and obligations of the various parties. If a seventeen-year-old decides to buy a car and the dealer sells it to him knowing of his infancy, then the infant can, after reaching the age of majority, reject the contract and tender back to the seller what remains of the article taken under the contract.

Assume that an individual under the age of eighteen is mistakenly granted credit by an airline, and goes on an extended journey. Upon attaining the age of eighteen, he renounces the contract. What does he have left to tender back to the airlines, since they furnished services, instead of tangible goods? The answer is obvious: Nothing. The airline has, therefore, lost the fare that it expended transporting the infant. While this may seem unfairly to give individuals under the age of eighteen a great deal of freedom, the laws of Virginia are designed for the protection of the infant; an individual who contracts with an infant proceeds at his own risk.[5] However, there are many cases in which the infant has misrepresented his age and obtained goods from a seller. In these cases, the courts have allowed the seller to recover against the infant for the value of the goods taken. The law also allows a recovery for the seller when infants purchase necessities. Note, however, that an adult party to the agreement is not allowed to avoid the contract if the infant chooses to hold him to it.

---

4. VA. CODE § 53-305.
5. See generally, 42 AM. JUR. 2d *Infants* § 58 et seq.

Procedures for Contracting; Essential Steps and Elements

The next question to be answered is, "How does one make contracts?" Here the language of the law becomes important. Lawyers tend to speak freely in terms of offer and acceptance, consideration, bilateral or unilateral contracts, and other so-called "terms of art" when discussing contracts. An "offer" can best be defined as being a statement, written or oral, which expresses one party's willingness to form a contract with another or others.[6] It must be definite and certain. Simply stating, "I'd like to talk to you about buying your car," is not definite enough to constitute an offer. An offer is effective when received by the person or persons to whom it is addressed. In other words, offers are only effective as to those to whom they were addressed. If *A* says to *B*, "I offer to sell you my car for $5," *C*, standing nearby overhearing, cannot jump up and say, "I accept," since *A*'s offer was not directed to *C*. It is, of course, quite a different case when an individual places an advertisement in a newspaper offering to sell his car for a certain price. In that instance, he is effectively offering his vehicle to anyone who reads the newspaper.[7]

Simply because an offer has been made does not mean that a contract will be formed, since the individual who makes the offer can revoke it at almost any time until the other party accepts it. Therefore, if *A* wrote *B* a letter offering him his car for $5 and *B* hesitated about buying it, *A* could revoke his offer if he did so before *B* accepted it. Additionally, the death of the offeror (that is, the person who offers) revokes all of his offers that are unaccepted at the time of his death.

After an offer has been made, the other party can act to accept it or reject it. Acceptance often means simply signifying to the person who made the offer that one wishes to accept it. Generally, though, the best thing to do when accepting an offer is to accept it in the same manner in which the offer was made. If the offer was made by mail, it would be best to respond by mail. This type of acceptance has often been called the "mirror image rule." The Uniform Commercial Code, which is in effect in Virginia and in 48

---

6. 17 AM. JUR. 2d *Contracts* § 31.
7. *Id.* § 34.

other states and which governs most sales of goods, does not require this "mirror image" acceptance; in most cases a valid contract will be made even if an individual accepts an offer in a manner different from that in which it was made, provided the acceptance is made in such a manner that the person making the offer knows that it is being accepted.

Having capable parties desiring to contract, with one party making an offer and the other accepting it, the only element lacking is "consideration," the cement to bind the contract together. Consideration may be thought of as "some right, interest, gain, advantage, benefit or profit to one party, ... or some forbearance, detriment, prejudice, inconvenience, disadvantage, loss or responsibility, act, or service given, suffered, or undertaken by the [other party]." [8] If *A* and *B* contract for *A* to sell and *B* to buy *A*'s car for $500, the $500 would be the consideration to bind the contract. On the other hand, if *A* says to *B*, "*B*, give up your farm and come take care of me for one year and I will give you $5,000," and *B* accepts this offer and fulfills his part of the bargain, even though *B* has not parted with money or anything tangible of value, he has taken on responsibility which he was not otherwise obligated to take; it is services rendered which furnishes the binding element, the consideration, for the contract. There is seldom any inquiry by the courts about the adequacy of the consideration unless it was a token consideration that was obviously without value, or the consideration was a sham.

THE NEED FOR WRITTEN AGREEMENTS

Even when there are two parties or more who are all competent and capable of contracting, and who have completed the requirements of offer, acceptance and consideration, problems can still develop. For example, one party may refuse to perform his part of the bargain even though the other party has already performed his or her part of the bargain. When a contract fails, it must be examined to see whether or not an "enforceable" contract has been made. The laws of Virginia may affect a

---

8. BLACK'S LAW DICTIONARY 379 (Rev. 4th ed. 1968).

contract's enforceability. For instance, the statute in Virginia commonly called by lawyers the "Statute of Frauds" requires that certain contracts must be in writing.[9] The term "Statute of Frauds" refers to the fact that the purpose of the law is to prevent fraud in certain transactions: contracts for the sale of land, contracts to answer for the debts of another, and most importantly, contracts for the sale of goods over $500. Therefore, when a large amount of money is involved or an agreement concerns property or other matters important to life or livelihood, all of the terms of the agreement should be written and signed by all parties. It is generally unnecessary to notarize these documents. The Statute of Frauds is a very complex area of the law and the author can only reiterate that an individual should see a lawyer if he finds himself involved in an oral contract to which the Statute of Frauds may apply, because there are many exceptions to the rule: even if a buyer pays $600 for an automobile, for example, and the seller fails to deliver it or the title, the Statute of Frauds requirements do not mean the money is lost, because there are implied contracts or other remedies in law and equity to fall back on to obtain restitution of the money.

Governmental Protection or Modification of Contracts

As we have already seen with the Statute of Frauds, the laws of the various states and of the United States, and the United States Constitution, place certain restrictions on contracts by declaring certain types of contracts to be void, or ineffective. Note, however, that the United States Constitution states that, "No state shall ... pass any law impairing the obligation of contracts," and the Virginia Constitution follows that prohibition by stating in Section 11 of Article I that, "the General Assembly shall not pass any law impairing the obligation of contracts ...." These constitutional prohibitions do not prevent the legislature from enacting measures that modify contracts and protect Virginia citizens.[10] Perhaps one of the better known areas in which the state protects its citizens is in the area of gambling contracts. Virginia

---

9. VA. CODE § 11-2.
10. Hurley v. Hurley, 110 Va. 31, 65 S.E. 472 (1909); Kennedy Coal Corp. v. Buck Horn Coal Corp., 140 Va. 37, 124 S.E. 482 (1924).

law, and the courts' interpretation of it, is strictly against the enforcement of any gambling debts. The Code of Virginia voids "all wagers, conveyances, assurances, and all contracts and securities whereof the whole or any part of the consideration be money or other valuable thing, won, laid, or bet, at any game, horse race, sport or pastime, and all contracts to repay any money knowingly lent at the time and place of such game, race, sport or pastime, to any person for the purpose of so gaming, betting, or wagering or to repay any money so lent to any person who shall at such time or place, so pay, bet or wager." [11] Recent case law in Virginia has expanded this idea so that even a holder in due course (a person who holds a note from the person to whom it was made payable), the most protected individual in negotiable instrument law, cannot collect on the note because of the illegality of the note when it was made.[12]

The second type of contract that has been rendered unenforceable by statute in Virginia is the pyramid contract, commonly known as a chain letter or cumulative contract. A pyramid promotion scheme is a program wherein a person gives up a thing of value for an opportunity to receive compensation or other things of value in return for inducing others to participate in the program.[13] A recent national furor erupted over a cosmetics firm that did this type of recruiting and soliciting in order to build up its sales force and the sale of its products. In 1970, the General Assembly declared all such contracts and agreements to be against public policy, and therefore, void and unenforceable.[14] Thus, if a person signs up on a chain letter promising to pass along a fifth of alcohol in return for getting other fifths of alcohol, he cannot be sued if he breaks his promise, nor can he sue anyone else to enforce similar promises. That contract is void. Other such agreements, equally void, include contracts to break the law; contracts for immoral purposes; contracts to restrain trade; contracts in violation of zoning laws; contracts in derogation of

---

11. VA. CODE § 11-14.
12. Glassman v. FDIC, 210 Va. 173, 173 S.E.2d 843 (1970).
13. VA. CODE §§ 18.2-239, 18.2-240.
14. *Id.* § 18.2-239.

marriage so as to promote divorce; contracts to require certain religious beliefs; contracts to accomplish fraud; contracts detrimental to the state, such as those procured by force; contracts for the corruption of public officials; contracts for the sale of public offices; contracts to aid in the escape of criminals; contracts to obstruct justice; contracts to encourage the illegal sale of goods, and many more.[15]

Perhaps one of the most important unenforceable contracts to the consumer is the "unconscionable" contract, whereby an individual or company, through sharp dealing or fast trading practices, takes an immense advantage over another person. When this type of contract is formed, a court, finding it unconscionable, may render it unenforceable. One who has entered into a contract that is illegal or void and has lost money in making the contract, may or may not, depending upon the circumstances, be able to recover the money given to the other party. In such cases, it is always best to consult an attorney.

How Consumers Can Legally Break Contracts

There are two additional types of contracts that are modified and controlled by state statutes. In both of these, the statute does not render the contracts void, but it does require that one or both of the parties meet certain requirements so that the contract will be valid. The first of these laws is the Virginia Home Solicitation Sales Act.[16] In many areas of Virginia, individuals go from door to door selling encyclopedias, lifetime picture services, pots and pans, vacuum cleaners, or Bibles, and find many people who will sign a contract for these goods and services, though they later regret it and wish to cancel the purchase. Under the Virginia Home Solicitation Sales Act, the contract can be cancelled in some instances. The Act applies only to a consumer sale (not a business sale or lease of goods other than farm equipment) in which the seller or his agents try to sell or lease something at any residence other than the seller's, and the buyer then decides to accept the

---

15. 17 Am. Jur. 2d *Contracts* §§ 155-215.
16. Va. Code §§ 59.1-21.1 to 59.1-21.6.

offer. It does not apply to the cash sale of goods for less than $25, nor to leases or sales pursuant to existing accounts or pursuant to prior negotiations that have been carried on before elsewhere.

To void the contract under this statute, written notice of cancellation must be given to the seller at his address before midnight of the third day after the contract is signed; this notice must tell the seller of the desire to cancel the contract. Notice will be considered to be properly given when a properly addressed and stamped envelope is dropped into the mailbox. There are some limitations on this right to cancel: The right does not apply when a person has requested the seller to furnish these goods or services without delay because of an emergency, nor does it apply if the seller has made a substantial beginning in his performance of the contract. The meaning of the term "substantial beginning" has not been made clear under the Act through interpretation by the Supreme Court of Virginia, but it would likely include cases wherein a buyer has ordered goods that are specially made for him, such as personalized Christmas cards, and the seller has begun work on them or has substantially completed them. The Home Solicitation Act clearly states that the agreement or contract must state on its face that the buyer has the right to cancel the contract. If a contract does not have this section in it, in the proper size type, the right to cancel remains effective until this notice is provided. After cancellation, the seller must return to the buyer within 10 days of the cancellation any payments and any other evidence of indebtedness. If goods were traded in, they must be returned by the seller; if they are not returned, the buyer may elect whether or not to recover an amount equal to the trade-in allowance. If the seller refuses to give back the money, the buyer can obtain a lien on the goods to secure his recovery.

For his part, though, the buyer must, upon demand within a reasonable time, return to the seller any goods delivered to him, but he is under no obligation to deliver these goods to the seller at any place other than the buyer's residence. If the seller fails to demand the return of his goods within a reasonable time, by statute the goods then become the property of the buyer. The buyer must, however, take reasonable care of the goods for a reasonable time.

In the case of a service contract, even if the seller has performed his services for the buyer prior to the expiration of the time limit for cancellation, the seller is not entitled to compensation if the buyer cancels the agreement according to law.

A small chart can be made here of the steps to remember. First of all, the buyer must give notice of cancellation within three days after signing the contract if the contract has the clause which shows that the right exists. Second, the seller must return money or goods within 10 days and demand his goods back within 20 days or they become the buyer's property; if the seller does not pay the buyer back within 10 days, he can take legal action against the seller and retain the seller's goods as security for the money that the seller owes. Finally, in a service contract, if the seller furnishes services before the buyer cancels the contract, he may not recover for the services he has rendered.

The last area where the law modifies the contracts of the parties is in the area of employment agency contracts.[17] The Employment Agencies Act prohibits any agency from requiring, as a condition of rendering service, that an applicant sign any type of a promissory note or authorization to confess judgment before taking a job.[18] Other acts by employment agencies are also prohibited. An agency may not refer an applicant to an employer for a position that the employment agency does not know to be open, unless the employer specifically requested to see that particular applicant, or without making an appointment for the applicant with the employer. The employment agency may not refer an applicant to an employer for a position for which the employment agency knows that the applicant is not qualified. The agency may not employ any counselor who does not meet the proper standards and qualifications as set forth in the Act. Finally, the agency may not change the location of any office or establish a new office without giving proper notice to state officials.[19] The Employment Agency Act prevents an agency from knowingly

---

17. *Id.* §§ 40.1-12 to 40.1-21.
18. *Id.* § 40.1-16.
19. *Id.* § 40.1-17.

sending any help or servants to any place of bad repute, house of ill fame or assignation house or to any house or place kept for immoral purposes; the agency employee doing so may be punished by a fine of not less than $1,000, nor more than $5,000, or by imprisonment from one to ten years (or both).

THE SALE OF GOODS

Contracts involving the purchase and the sale of goods are controlled by the Uniform Commercial Code (UCC) which takes up an entire volume of the Code of Virginia. The term "goods," according to the Uniform Commercial Code, means generally all moveable articles other than money, investment securities, and similar items. Goods include the unborn young of animals and even things attached to realty that can be separated and removed from the real estate.[20] Entire books have been written on each of the various parts of the Uniform Commercial Code, so that it must be stressed that the following discussion is simply a condensation of the more important points of the Uniform Commercial Code as they effect the consumer.

An individual who is a consumer of products and who is going to buy or sell an item, such as an automobile, a television set, a boat or trailer, or other goods worth over $500, should make sure that a signed written contract or memorandum is drawn up. This writing need not be elaborate, but it should describe the goods being sold, including the quantity, and must be signed by the person against whom any suit is to be brought. Perhaps the greatest problem that arises under the Uniform Commercial Code is whether or not the contracts that were formed were intended to be complete writings, that is, whether or not both parties intended to look within the four corners of the document for all of the solutions to the problems that affect it. If the parties did intend that the contract hold all of the agreements or statements surrounding it within its body, should a dispute arise, a court will not look outside the contract nor into evidence of other agreements that cannot be found within it. Therefore, it is imperative that the

---

20. *Id.* § 8.2-105(1).

consumer be aware of and look out for such clauses as, "This agreement is intended to be the complete understanding between both parties and all oral understandings and agreements are merged into it." This type of clause or statement in a written contract is called a merger clause; its effect is to prevent an individual from bringing into court and introducing in evidence the statements made by the seller or the buyer that are not written down and included within the body of the contract. It would, therefore, serve the consumer to make sure, when he is purchasing a major piece of personal property, that all of the terms and guarantees are written down and incorporated into the contract.

The Uniform Commercial Code affects the ideas of offer and acceptance as earlier discussed, in that it completes incomplete contracts, (documents which omit certain terms, such as time or manner of delivery, or even price). In these cases, the Uniform Commercial Code permits the courts to supply the missing terms.

As might be expected, the Uniform Commercial Code outlines for both the buyer and the seller the remedies they have when their contract is not fulfilled. Basically, the buyer has the right to "cover," that is, to purchase the goods from someone else and then collect the difference between what he paid for the replacement goods and the price at which he agreed to buy from the seller. The buyer can also recover from the seller the difference between the market price of the goods he was going to pay and the prevailing market price he will have to pay if he tries to purchase the goods somewhere else. When a buyer breaches a contract, the Uniform Commercial Code provides that the seller may be able to sell to someone else the goods that he would have sold to the buyer, and recover either his lost profit or the difference between the market price of the goods he sold to the second party and what he would have gotten for them from the buyer. In certain unusual circumstances, the seller can even make the buyer take the goods. As stated many times in this chapter, when an individual has a problem which would fall under the Uniform Commercial Code he should seek the advice of a competent attorney in this field.

Perhaps the greatest thing that the Uniform Commercial Code provides to the consumer of goods is the law of warranties. A warranty is a statement, either express or implied, that represents a fact.

Express warranties are those that are specifically stated by the seller. For example, the salesman in a used car lot expressly warrants to a purchaser that what he is about to purchase is a car. The salesman may have breached his express warranty if the purchaser discovers, after purchasing the car, that it did not have wheels, tires, an engine, windshields or seats, and could scarcely qualify as a car. Express warranties are usually express direct representations of the value or worth of an object. One case has held that a salesman who states that a vehicle is guaranteed for 90 days and is of first rate quality has given an express warranty.[21]

An implied warranty, on the other hand, is presumed by the law to be made by the seller, unless he specifically *denies* that such a warranty is given. There are several types of implied warranties. A seller is presumed, first of all, to guarantee that he has good title to the goods he sells, that he has the right to sell them, and that there is no security interest attached to the merchandise unless the contrary is made clear by specific language or circumstances. Secondly, the implied warranty of merchantability requires that the goods being sold pass without objection under the terms of the contract, and that they be fit for the ordinary purposes for which such goods are made. A bowling ball which is flat on one side would not pass the test of merchantability. The serving for value of food or drink to be consumed either on the premises or elsewhere is also a sale, thus raising an implied warranty of merchantability that the goods must at least pass without objection into trade under the contract description.[22] Virginia courts generally recognize an implied warranty of merchantability in the sale of all kinds of goods.[23]

Another implied warranty is the implied warranty of fitness for a particular purpose. Where the seller at the time of the sale has reason to know of any particular purpose for which the goods are

---

21. C.E. Wright & Co. v. Shackleford, 152 Va. 635, 148 S.E. 807 (1929).
22. VA. CODE §§ 8.2-312, 8.2-314.
23. *The Implied Warranty of Merchantability — Smith v. Hensley,* 48 VA. L. REV. 152 (1962).

required, and knows that the buyer is relying on the seller's skill and knowledge to select or furnish these goods, there is, unless excluded or modified, an implied warranty that the goods should be fit for such purpose. As an example, shoes are normally goods which are used for walking on the ground, but there may be instances wherein a seller knows that his buyer wants a particular type of shoe, such as a climbing boot; since the seller knows that the buyer has entrusted him with the task of selecting a special climbing boot, the seller has, therefore, impliedly warranted that the boot would be fit for the particular purpose of climbing mountains.[24]

While the Uniform Commercial Code furnishes implied warranties to the buyer, it can also take these implied warranties away from the buyer.[25] The implied warranty of merchantability can be excluded or modified, but the statement that attempts to exclude or modify this warranty must be in writing and conspicuous.[26] Language of a disclaimer in print of the same size, style and color as that used in most of the other provisions, and immersed in the body of the contract, fails of its purpose and is not "conspicuous" within the meaning of the law, and is therefore ineffective.[27] If a seller wishes to exclude this implied warranty of merchantability, he must mention the term "merchantability," and must make the writing that excludes the warranty conspicuous. However, the warranty of merchantability can be excluded by the use of such expressions as "as is" or "with all faults" or other language which in common understanding "calls the buyer's attention to the exclusion of warranties and makes it plain that there is no implied warranty."[28] Furthermore, when a buyer, before getting the goods, has examined the goods, or the sample or model, as fully as he desires, or has refused to examine them, there can be no implied warranty with regard to the defects which an examination under the circumstances should have revealed to

---

24. VA. CODE § 8.2-315, comment 2.
25. Id. § 8.2-316.
26. Id. § 8.2-316(2).
27. Lacks v. Bottled Gas Corp., 215 Va. 94, 205 S.E.2d 671 (1974).
28. VA. CODE § 8.2-316(3)(a).

him.[29] So, while there may be implied warranties available under the Uniform Commercial Code, a buyer must make sure in reading a contract before purchasing the goods whether or not these warranties are disclaimed.

In fact, there is no substitute for the careful reading of any document before signing it. By reading the proposal, buyers and sellers alike can be made aware of potentially disadvantageous terms contained in the writing, and will have an opportunity to demand a careful explanation of any terms that are unclear. If the other party's explanation is unsatisfactory, legal counsel should be sought *before* a person enters into an agreement. Waiting until after the contract is in force before asking an attorney for advice is usually too late.

---

29. *Id.* § 8.2-316(3)(b).

CHAPTER 4

Real Estate Transfers

N. J. Bailes

In General

The purchase of a dwelling is, for the average person, the largest investment that he will make in his lifetime. Despite the magnitude of this venture, it is frequently commenced without sufficient expertise or the aid of competent advisors who are specialists in such transactions.

An overview of the entire process of purchase and sale of a residence may best be begun by a brief explanation of the roles of those advisors who are equipped to aid in this most important transaction. Assume that two unrelated parties, Mr. Buyer and Mr. Seller, respectively, decide to buy and sell a residence. Mr. Buyer will initially need someone to aid him in finding a house that suits his needs and his ability to pay. Mr. Seller, on the other hand, will need someone to find a buyer for his house. Either can undertake this "finding" role on his own. However, there are numerous competent individuals with a wealth of information and experience who can both save time for the parties and help to ensure that important factors are not overlooked. The most common intermediary is the real estate broker, or his employee, the real estate salesman. Attorneys are also entitled to perform the "finding" function and sometimes do engage in this practice, but they act more often in large commercial transactions than in the average residence purchase and sale.

Often the buyer will not have the cash with which to purchase the residence. In this situation he will have to seek financing from one of many sources available. Again, the real estate agent or an attorney may help in this search, although it is not essential that assistance be obtained. Traditionally, this is handled by the real estate representative, who has knowledge of the lending institutions available, their rates of interest, and the readiness of mortgage money. It may be that the seller will be willing to help in the financing, if he does not need the cash immediately, or if he wants to take advantage of the tax benefits of an installment sale.

If Buyer is willing to accept Seller's assurances that the title being transferred is "clear," title assurance may not be necessary. However, if the benefits of title search and assurance and the risks involved in neglecting these matters are thoroughly explained to Buyer, he will usually decide that the title should be searched, and he will require assurances that it is "clear." Many lenders require title search and title insurance as a protection of their interest in the property. Title work is usually handled by an attorney.

The closing of a real estate transaction is apt to be the most complicated portion of the entire procedure. Existing mortgages may have to be discharged or transferred; taxes, insurance and the like must be prorated; fees and charges must be paid; and the proper signatures must be obtained. Unless Buyer and Seller are extremely knowledgeable in the area of real estate transfers, they will need an attorney to guide them through closing, and to protect their interests.

Through all of these steps, both Buyer and Seller should have competent advice as to the legal, financial and practical consequences of the transaction. An attorney can advise them in most of these matters. Although the majority of people involved in such transactions would agree that an attorney is a necessary participant in the closing activities, few realize that obtaining legal advice prior to undertaking any of the steps in a purchase and sale of real estate would not only cost them little more, but in many cases would prevent expensive errors that occur long before closing.

Prior to seeking advice, there are certain determinations which should be made by Buyer and Seller. Buyer should decide what his priorities are for specific characteristics of a residence. For example, he may need a large house if he has several children. He may need special types of accommodations for hobbies or pets. He may feel that it is of prime importance to live in an area which provides all of the city utilities, or he may prefer to forfeit such conveniences for the advantage of living in the country. He should assess his financial situation carefully and make a realistic decision as to how much he can afford for a down payment and how much he can spend monthly for mortgage payments, utilities, and other regular expenses. These decisions will help him to determine what price house he can afford to purchase, and will save the time he would waste looking at houses above or below his price range. If he intends to pay the entire price of the house in a lump sum, his decision will be somewhat simpler, but he still must know exactly how much he can afford to pay.

Seller will also need to evaluate his financial position as regards the value of the house. If he has kept records of the purchase price and the improvements he has made on the house, he can more easily determine his investment and how much he needs to realize from the sale. He will need to know the current value of the property and will have to determine what items he is willing to include in the sale (for example, appliances, drapes, rugs, carpets, special decorative items). In determining the current value of a residence, it is often beneficial to employ an appraiser. Appraisals are required for certain types of financing, and they help to give both parties an idea of the value of the house.

In making the financial determinations, both parties could be aided by the advice of an experienced real estate agent. Under current practice, the buyer will not have to pay the real estate representative for his services, but the seller will. Realtors charge a percentage of the selling price of a house for their services in locating a buyer. These services include advertising and showing the house, advice as to financing, value of the property, and various other incidents of the transaction.

LISTING CONTRACT

Before undertaking the chore of finding a buyer, the realtor will require that the seller sign a contract. Under Virginia law a broker may be employed by oral contract,[1] but as an added protection the broker will require that the seller sign a "listing contract." There are various types of listing contracts, but in a given area the realtors have usually agreed upon a particular form, and the seller

---

1. 3A MICHIE'S JURISPRUDENCE *Brokers* § 6 (1976).

will not be offered a choice as to the terms of the contract. Before signing the contract, it would be wise for the seller to discuss it with his lawyer and determine exactly what his obligations and those of the realtor are under the proposed contract. If the contract amounts to an offer by the seller that he will pay a commission if the purchaser is found within a specified time, the offer will only be accepted and become a binding contract if a purchaser is found within that time.[2] At any time before a purchaser is found, the seller may withdraw the offer.[3] However, if the contract amounts to a contract of employment for the fixed time period, or a binding contract that a commission will be paid if a purchaser is found within the specified time, the broker will be entitled to payment even though the seller has already sold the property to someone else, or withdrawn it from the market.[4]

Upon delivery of title and payment for the property, the duty and agency of a real estate agent ceases.[5] If the agent does not find a purchaser, he receives no compensation.[6] His duty is to find a purchaser who is ready, willing and able to enter into a contract on the terms specified by the seller.[7] The agent does not have the authority to bind the owner unless he has expressly been given such authority.[8] The ordinary listing contract does not give the realtor the power to sign a contract of sale.[9]

If the real estate agent finds a buyer and the sale is not consummated due to some fault of the owner of the property, the owner will be obligated to pay the commission. If the sale fails due to the fault of the prospective buyer, he may be liable to the broker for the commission. However, if the fault is that of the broker, no commission will be due.[10]

---

2. Atlantic Coast Realty Co. v. Townsend, 124 Va. 490, 507, 98 S.E. 684, 689 (1919).
3. *Id.*
4. *Id.*
5. Board of Trustees of Oberlin College v. Blair, 45 W. Va. 812, 32 S.E. 203, 206 (1898).
6. 3A MICHIE'S JURISPRUDENCE *Brokers* § 7 (1976).
7. Voyentzie v. Ryan, 154 Va. 604, 611, 153 S.E. 688, 690 (1930).
8. *Id.*
9. Halsey v. Monteiro, 92 Va. 581, 583, 24 S.E. 258, 259 (1896).
10. Reiber v. James M. Duncan, Jr. & Associates, Inc., 206 Va. 657, 660, 145 S.E.2d 157, 160 (1965).

Certain listing contracts provide that the broker will be due his commission if the house is sold during the specified time, even though the realtor was not instrumental in obtaining the purchaser.[11] This type of contract is common today. Even in situations in which the commission is dependent upon the agent being the "procuring cause" of the sale, it is very difficult, as a practical matter, to prove that the realtor was not the procuring cause, as he has usually advertised the listing and placed a sign in a conspicuous place on the property.

When the contract of sale is signed, the buyer will be expected to give a purchase money deposit, often called "earnest money," to guarantee his performance. This amount varies according to the wishes of the parties and the value of the property involved. Earnest money is held by the buyer, or by the broker if one is involved. At closing, it is included in the purchase price of the property. If the seller fails to perform, the deposit must be returned to the purchaser. The broker is not allowed to retain it as part payment for his services unless the buyer defaults.[12]

CONTRACT OF SALE

The contract of sale is an agreement to sell and to buy the title to land. Therefore, the nature of that title is of prime importance. Unless otherwise specified in the contract, the seller is bound to deliver "marketable title," which is one free from reasonable doubt as to its validity. It must be title which could be sold to a reasonable purchaser. In order to be marketable, the title need not be free from every technical criticism, but it must be free from defects which would subject the purchaser to the hazards of litigation. Marketable title includes both legal and equitable title. Equitable title is the right of a party to have legal title transferred to him upon the performance of certain conditions, while legal title is that which is created by written deed as provided by statute.

If Buyer and Seller have not contacted an attorney for advice

---

11. W.D. Nelson & Co. v. Taylor Heights Dev. Corp., 207 Va. 386, 389, 150 S.E.2d 142, 145 (1966).
12. Hicks v. Howell, 203 Va. 32, 36, 121 S.E.2d 757, 759 (1961).

prior to agreement on the purchase, it is imperative that they do so before signing the contract of sale. The attorney will examine the contract carefully to determine whether there are unfavorable provisions that seriously affect his client. For instance, it should be determined who will bear the risk of loss between the time of the signing of the contract and the closing. If the purchaser is to bear the risk, he must obtain hazard insurance immediately. In Virginia, upon execution of the contract of sale by all parties, equitable title to the property passes to the buyer.

It is the duty of the attorney to determine whether the contract is properly executed by both parties, and whether the parties are competent to execute such contract. Frequently the parties involved are strangers to each other and to the attorney. In such situations, the attorney must be careful to establish the correct identities, particularly that of the seller.

The contract of sale must contain an adequate description of the property. It must specify what, if any, personal property is to be included in the sale (*e.g.,* major appliances, window air conditioners) and give exact descriptions. If there is any property which might be assumed to be a part of the sale, but is not included, the contract should specify that such property is not included. Also included in the contract must be a clear statement of the consideration which is to be paid for the property. If the buyer is to borrow a portion of the money for the purchase, the contract should specify that the purchase is contingent upon the buyer's ability to obtain a specific type of loan (*e.g.,* F.H.A. or G.I.) or a certain amount, with a definite rate of interest, and for a specific term of years.

Form contracts often state that the conveyance is to be made subject to "existing conditions and restrictions of record." Although these restrictions and conditions often will not adversely affect the buyer's intended use of the property, there are situations in which they could render the property useless for the purpose which the buyer intends. Copies of existing conditions and restrictions should be furnished to the buyer as an integral part of the contract, or, if this is not done, the seller should warrant the property to be suitable for the use the buyer intends to make of it. The contract should specify which party is to pay for "points," if such are to be charged. Points will be explained in the discussion of financing.

Often the specified date of closing will be of utmost importance to one of the parties to the contract. For instance, the buyer may need to move in on a particular date, or the seller may need the proceeds which he will receive at closing in order to make the down payment on another house. In Virginia, unless it is expressly stated in the contract that time is of the essence, the parties will not be strictly held to a particular date.

Other miscellaneous provisions which should be included in the contract are provision that the seller will obtain, at his expense, a termite inspection and will repair any termite damage; provision for plumbing and heating inspection; provision guaranteeing that the premises will be in the same condition on the date of closing as they were at the time of execution of the contract of purchase and sale; provision stating the specific use to which the property is to be put; provision concerning the risk of loss; and provisions concerning closing costs, closing date, possession date and recordation of the deed.

TITLE SEARCH

One of the areas of greatest controversy in the field of real estate transactions is the title examination. The importance of this search is minimized by many people, but certainly not by anyone who has suffered because of a faulty title, the defects of which were not discovered in time to protect him from severe loss. Although the title examination is generally done by the attorney for the buyer, it can be done by other trained personnel. If, however, it is undertaken by a layman with no training, not only will it take an inordinate amount of time, but factors may be overlooked which would be of extreme importance in protecting the prospective purchaser. The records which must be examined will be located in the clerk of the circuit court's office in the proper jurisdiction, which is usually where the real estate is situated. These records consist of the grantor and grantee index, the index to wills, the judgment lien index, the index to financing statements, deed books, miscellaneous lien books, will books, judgment lien dockets, plat or map books, and the land books.

Usually the seller will furnish the buyer with a complete legal description of the property to be conveyed. This description should be compared with the recorded description of the subject property when it was conveyed to the seller, any plat of record, and any plat which is to be recorded at the time of the conveyance. If no plat exists, the description should be carefully examined to ensure that the described boundaries meet or enclose the area to be conveyed.

The first step in a search of title is the construction of the "chain of title." The deed which conveyed the property to the seller should lead to the seller's source of title, which, in turn, will lead to the previous source of title. Each deed, then, will lead to the next precedent deed, and, if there is no break in the chain, the examiner will be able to go back the customary sixty years in the chain of title. If there is a break in the chain, the examiner must go to other records to determine the source of title of the last grantee. Often the property will be found to have been obtained by devise or inheritance.

After the chain of title has been established, the title examiner must "adverse" the persons named in the chain of title. This consists of examining the grantor index to ensure that the property was not conveyed out of the chain of title, thus rendering the deed ineffective to pass title.

The next step to be taken is to examine the judgment lien index. A recorded judgment is an effective lien on presently held and subsequently acquired property. Unless a judgment lien has been revived, it can be enforced for only twenty years from the date of the judgment. Any recorded judgment less than twenty years old and not marked satisfied is a valid existing lien on the property.

The examiner must also check the index to financing statements. Anyone who holds a security interest in "fixtures" must file his financing statement in the appropriate clerk's office (the jurisdiction where the real estate is located). Therefore, this index must be searched to determine if any individual in the chain of title has given a security interest in any of the fixtures on the real estate in question.

Having successfully completed the above steps, the examiner should abstract the conveyances affecting the property, meaning he must write down simple digests of the links in the chain of title. These digests should include the identity of the grantor, grantee, type of deed, date of deed, date of acknowledgement by each person executing the deed, date of recordation, deed book and page number, consideration, description of property, conditions, easements, restrictions, encumbrances, covenants, signatures and seals of all grantors, judgments, and financing statements.

Further, the examiner must check to see that all taxes on the property have been paid. This can be determined with respect to local property taxes by examination of the records in the office of the treasurer or commissioner of revenue (for current taxes) and the clerk's office for tax records more than three years old. No public records will reveal whether federal gift and estate taxes have been paid, so the examiner will have to use other methods of making that determination. Records will be found of the Virginia gift and inheritance taxes in the Wills Book. If the examiner is unable to find record of payment of any of these taxes, he must note an exception on the certificate of title.

Another factor which should be investigated by the title examiner is the possibility of bankruptcy of any of the parties in the chain of title. Under Virginia Code, § 55-141, certified copies of bankruptcy proceedings may be recorded in deed books and indexed in the grantor index. However, this is not always done and the examiner must determine local custom. He may have to examine the bankruptcy records in the appropriate Federal District Court. There are many other special problems which may arise, and the examiner must be alert to all of them, including special commissioner's deeds and decrees for alimony and child support which may constitute a lien on real estate.

If title insurance is desired, the examining attorney will certify title to the insurance company on the forms provided. The title insurance company will then issue a title insurance policy to the owner or mortgagee. The buyer should request that the attorney explain exactly what the policy insures against. Typically these policies do not insure against every possible loss, and the purchaser often believes that, once he has purchased title insurance, he is insured in every situation. The system of title insurance was instituted because no system of title searching is perfect. Errors could occur due to the complications of a title search, and forgeries and other factors that cannot be guarded against could cause a loss. The person who desires to have title insurance must apply to the title insurance company (often through an attorney) for an examination of title. He pays the company a fee, in return for which the company agrees to make an examination of the title and to insure against defects.

After the examination, the person requesting the search should insist upon being given a report of title, which is a statement that sets forth a description of the property, the name of the owner, and a detailed list of all encumbrances and defects found in the records. This report enables the prospective owner to know the exact condition of the title to the property. Any objections to title which were not agreed upon in the contract must be removed by the seller. After this is done, and after closing, the title company will issue its policy of title insurance. The property may be subject to encumbrances which were agreed upon (*e.g.*, mortgages) and these will be noted in the policy. The policy should be checked carefully to determine that the property is properly insured and that no other exceptions are included except those agreed upon.

TYPES OF OWNERSHIP

Prior to closing, the seller's attorney will draft the deed. In order to do this, he must know precisely how the buyer wants the title to be taken. By statute in Virginia, unless the deed states otherwise, there is a presumption that the buyer takes a fee simple title.[13] The attorney must know also what type of estate is to be created. In Virginia there are basically five types of estates.

The first, individual ownership, needs little explanation. The person who takes individual ownership has full and sole control

---

13. VA. CODE § 55-11.

over the property. The second type of ownership is joint tenancy, which is created when two or more persons take title at the same time, by the same instrument, with the same interest, and with the right to individual possession. Virginia statute provides that, in order for there to be survivorship between joint tenants, the instrument must specifically so provide.[14]

The third type of estate is the tenancy by the entirety, which can only be created in husband and wife, and is the most common type of tenancy used in transferring residential property to husband and wife. The prevalence of this type of tenancy is probably due to a desire to provide for survivorship.[15] One of the major benefits of this type of ownership is that the estate is immune from claim of individual creditors of either the husband or the wife.[16] However, neither husband nor wife alone can transfer his or her interest in any estate owned by the entirety.[17] Only by joining in a conveyance can they dispose of the estate in whole or in part.[18] This type of ownership also simplifies the administration of a decedent's estate,[19] although it does not excuse the survivor from filing inheritance tax returns.

The fourth type of tenancy that may be created is the tenancy in common. It is formed by the co-ownership of property by persons (with equal or varying proportions of ownership). Their title may have been acquired from the same or different sources. The tenants may convey their individual interests without the consent of the other(s). There is no survivorship unless specified in the deed, and the interests are subject to the claims of the individual creditors.

The last type of tenancy is that of the tenant in partnership. This is simply the interest that a partner has in the partnership property.

---

14. *Id.* §§ 55-20, 55-21.
15. Spies, *Some Considerations in Conveyancing to Husband and Wife*, 34 VA. L. REV. 480, 481 (1948).
16. Vasilion v. Vasilion, 192 Va. 735, 740, 66 S.E.2d 599, 602 (1951).
17. Ritchie, *Tenancies by the Entirety in Real Property With Particular Reference to the Law of Virginia*, 28 VA L. REV. 608, 616 (1942).
18. *Id.* at 617.
19. *Id.* at 620.

Financing

There are various methods by which the sale may be financed if the buyer does not choose to pay cash. The seller may finance the sale by taking back a note secured by a deed of trust, or a lending institution may finance the purchase price. In either of these situations, the necessary instruments are drawn by the appropriate attorneys. If the buyer is to assume the seller's existing loan, the assumption is included in the deed of bargain and sale. A distinction is made between assumption of a loan and taking "subject to" an existing loan. In an assumption, the buyer personally assumes the obligation of the note which is secured by the deed of trust. Taking "subject to" an existing deed of trust note carries no personal obligation on the part of the buyer. Therefore, the party taking "subject to" an existing deed of trust is not liable for a deficiency judgment in case of a foreclosure where the proceeds are not sufficient to pay off the note. In Virginia, the original maker of the deed of trust continues to be primarily liable for the payment of the note when the obligation is "assumed" by the buyer unless the original noteholder releases the original maker. Therefore the original maker could be made to pay a deficiency after foreclosure, even though the property had been sold several times under an assumption.

Points are another expense which arise during the financing of a house. This is a charge assessed by the lender which serves the purpose of increasing his return on the loan. One point equals one percent of the mortgage amount, two points equals two percent of the mortgage amount, and so on. On ninety and ninety-five percent conventional loans, the points will be charged to the purchaser as a premium for obtaining such a high loan. On FHA and VA loans, the seller must pay the points. The points fluctuate according to the money market and range from as low as one to as high as nine. As mentioned previously, the contract of sale should specify who is obligated to pay the points.

Closing

To the novice, closing is probably the most confusing part of the entire real estate transaction, since the experienced parties to the transaction usually do not take the time to explain the process and the entire complicated matter is handled in one very short meeting. Present at this time may be the seller and his spouse, buyer and spouse, attorneys of both parties, real estate brokers of both parties, any lienholders to be paid, any contractors and materialmen, representatives of lending institutions involved, and insurance agents. Often one or more of these will not be present, and they rely on the attorneys to protect their interests. It is a fairly common practice in Virginia, although frowned on by some, to have the same attorney representing both the buyer and the seller. This presents no problem so long as no conflict of interest arises.

The purposes of closing are many, but the goal is to transfer the title to the property as efficiently as possible while protecting the interests of all the parties concerned. Delivery of the deed in exchange for the promised consideration is a primary purpose, along with prorating certain expenses, such as taxes which may have been prepaid or are owing, and giving the parties credit for payments which may have been advanced.

It is preferable to have the deed of bargain and sale and deed of trust (if any) prepared prior to closing so that the attorneys can examine them carefully for errors. Arrangements should also be made in advance for releasing any deeds of trust or other security instruments which may be necessary. Both the buyer and the seller should check with their attorneys prior to closing to determine whether they have all of the necessary documents for closing.

For tax purposes, it is very important that each party to the transaction keep an accurate record of the financial arrangements made in relation to the purchase and sale. The settlement statements are of great benefit in this regard if they are logically and simply designed so that all may understand them. Settlement statements must be furnished to both buyer and seller to show the credits and prorations mentioned earlier.

Although the form of a settlement statement will vary depending upon the complexity of the transaction and the skill of the attorney drawing the statement, the seller will generally be expected to pay the following costs, where applicable: drawing the deed of bargain and sale and/or assumption, conveyancing tax, real estate commission, attorney's fee, termite warranty and corrective work, and his share of taxes, insurance, rent, water and electric bills, fuel oil, escrow account, interest, assessments and release fees. The buyer will, where applicable, pay the following: title examination and closing fee, drawing the deed of trust and note, assumption fee, recordation of deed of bargain and sale and deed of trust (including Virginia tax of 15¢ per $100 in value on the purchase price plus the amount of the deed of trust and 5¢ per $100 to the local unit of government), appraisal and inspection fee, title insurance, physical survey, and the prorations mentioned above.

After the closing, in order to protect his title, the buyer should be sure that his attorney records the deed immediately. This is the final link in the chain of protective measures which the buyer must be careful to observe in order to protect this, his largest and most important investment.

CHAPTER 5

Landlord and Tenant Law

K. M. King

IN GENERAL

The law of landlord and tenant has been slow to change. It has remained very close to the common law which the feudal system spawned, and which became the basis for most of American landlord and tenant laws. As a nation of urban and suburban dwellers, many Americans must look to a landlord as the only source of shelter for themselves and their families. They are no longer seeking a plot of ground from which to make their living, but simply a clean, comfortable apartment to live in. Many state legislatures such as the Virginia General Assembly have realized the need to modernize the laws in this area. In 1974, the General Assembly passed the Virginia Residential Landlord and Tenant Act.[1] The purpose of this Act was to "simplify, clarify, modernize and revise the law governing the rental of dwelling units and the rights and obligations of landlords and tenants; to encourage landlords and tenants to maintain and improve the quality of housing; and to establish a single body of law relating to landlord and tenant relations throughout the Commonwealth."[2]

This chapter will discuss the obligations the law puts on both the landlord and the tenant and the remedies that are available to the tenant or the landlord if either party fails to meet his duties under a lease or the duties imposed by law. Readers are cautioned that this chapter can only point out landlord and tenant rights under the Act, and if they think they have a possible cause of action under the Act they should consult an attorney. Solutions to cases turn on facts as well as law, and an attorney will be able to evaluate all the facts of an individual situation and advise his client on the best course of action. An attorney will also be aware of any other statutes or court decisions that either expand or limit the meaning of the Act as it relates to an individual situation. Since the Virginia

---
1. VA. CODE §§ 55-248.2 to 55-248.40.
2. *Id.* § 55-248.3.

Residential Landlord and Tenant Act did not become effective until July 1, 1974, the Virginia courts have not decided many cases involving the Act. Therefore, it is still subject to judicial interpretations at future dates which could restrict or expand the application of the Act or any of its provisions — another important reason to consult an attorney in a situation in which the Act may apply.

The Residential Landlord and Tenant Act is designed to cover the typical landlord and tenant relationships, such as the rental of an apartment in a multi-unit dwelling. This Act applies to all rental agreements entered into after July 1, 1974.[3] However, to be applicable the tenancy must not be exempt under the statute. There are a number of tenancies which are specifically excluded from the Act, but they are all situations which are not normally considered in the landlord and tenant classification. These include residence in a private or public hospital, nursing home or educational institution; occupancy in a home which is under a contract of sale; occupancy in a building run by a fraternal or social organization; residence in a hotel, motel or vacation home for less than thirty days; occupancy under a rental agreement in which the primary purpose of the lease is business, commerce or agriculture; residence in a public housing unit; and occupancy by an owner of a condominium unit.[4] All of these types of tenancies are regulated by other local and federal statutes. Another major exemption from the Act is occupancy of a single-family residence. If the owner of a single-family residence owns in his own name no more than ten single-family residences which are subject to rental agreements, such a single-family residence is excluded from the coverage of the Act.

THE LEASE

The law does not specify a form for a lease of a residential dwelling. The landlord and tenant may include in a rental agreement any terms and conditions which are not prohibited by

---

3. *Id.* § 55-248.10.
4. *Id.* § 55-248.5.

law. The lease should generally include the rent, the terms of the agreement, and the rights and obligations of the parties. If the lease does not specify the rent, the tenant shall be obligated to pay only the fair rental value for the use and occupancy of the dwelling. Rent shall be payable without demand or notice at the time and place agreed upon by the parties, such as the rental office of an apartment complex. Unless the parties make a different arrangement, the periodic rent is due at the beginning of each month, or in equal installments at the beginning of each term. For example, one-fifth of the total rent for a five-year lease term would be due at the beginning of each new rental year.

If the parties do not fix a definite lease term, the tenancy shall be week to week in the case of a roomer who pays weekly rent, and in other cases month to month. It is important to establish the length of the lease term if it is not already in the agreement, because the length of the term determines (in most cases) the amount of notice one must give before he can terminate the tenancy. A tenant from week to week need only give one week's notice of his intent to vacate. Correspondingly, the landlord must give the tenant one week's notice to vacate. In the case of a month to month tenancy, the tenant must give at least a month's notice of intention to vacate and the landlord must give the tenant one month's notice of termination of the lease. Tenancy must always terminate at the end of a rental period.

Several provisions are specifically prohibited by the Virginia Residential Landlord and Tenant Act from inclusion in rental agreements. The tenant cannot be made to agree to waive or forego his rights or remedies under the Act. The landlord cannot include a provision in the lease which authorizes a tenant to confess judgment. Confession of judgment bars the tenant from contesting any suit the landlord may bring against him on any matter arising out of the tenancy. Such a provision — often termed a "cognovit" — permits the landlord or other appointed agent to appear in court, instead of the tenant, and "confess" the justice of the action, admitting the truth of any and all claims asserted by the landlord. The tenant does not have to agree to pay the landlord's attorney's fee except where specifically allowed by the Act. The rental agreement cannot include a provision in which the tenant "agrees to the exculpation or limitation of any liability of the landlord to the tenant arising under law or to indemnify the landlord for that liability or the cost connected therewith." [5] This section of the Act is a significant change from previous landlord and tenant law: under the construction of leases which contain such an exculpatory clause, tenants would be unable to recover damages for injuries which were due to the landlord's negligence or that of his agents. If any of these prohibited provisions are included in a rental agreement, they are unenforceable. If the landlord brings a suit to enforce any of these provisions, the court may award to the tenant any actual damages suffered by him and reasonable attorney's fees which are required for his defense against the landlord's suit.

Even without a written rental agreement, a tenant can still benefit from the Act. If the landlord does not sign and deliver a written rental agreement, his acceptance of rent without reservation gives the rental agreement the same effect as if it had been signed and delivered by the landlord. Also, when the tenant does not sign and deliver a written rental agreement but accepts possession of the dwelling or pays rent, the rental agreement becomes effective. If a rental agreement is given effect in such a way, it is only effective for one year, regardless of the length of the lease term contained in the rental agreement, because the ancient Statute of Frauds requires that a lease for more than one year must be in writing.

Landlord's Obligations

The Virginia Residential Landlord and Tenant Act specifies obligations that every landlord who is not exempted from the Act must comply with. One of the major provisions relates to the security deposit that most landlords require a tenant to pay before he can move into the leased premises. The law defines a security deposit as "any deposit of money or property, whether termed security deposit or 'prepaid rent,' however denominated, which is

---

5. *Id.* § 55-248.9(a)(4).

furnished by a tenant to a landlord, lessor or agent of a landlord or lessor to secure the performance of any part of a written or oral lease or agreement, or a security for damages to the leased premises." [6] The law provides that the amount or value of the security deposit cannot exceed two months of periodic rent. When the lease terminates, the landlord may apply any part of the security and accrued interest held by him to the payment of accrued rent and the amount of damages which the landlord has suffered by the tenant's noncompliance with his duty under the law and any other damages specified in the original rental agreement. But the landlord cannot deduct for the usual reasonable wear and tear on the dwelling which is a consequence of normal living. The landlord must give his tenant a written itemized list of damage deductions, and the amount due to the tenant from the security deposit within forty-five days after termination of the tenancy. If the landlord willfully fails to comply with the law dealing with security deposit, or if he fails to return any deposit and interest, the tenant may recover such security due him together with actual damages and reasonable attorney's fees.

The landlord must also "accrue interest in six month increments, at a rate of three percent per annum, on all property or money held as security ...." [7] Interest is not required to be accrued on the deposit unless the landlord has held the security for a period exceeding thirteen months after the date of the rental agreement. The interest is only payable at the time of termination of the tenancy. The landlord is also required to keep an itemized record for public inspection of all deductions from the security deposit by reason of the tenant's noncompliance during the preceding two years. The law also requires the landlord to submit a record to all tenants within five days after occupancy of all damages to the dwelling existing at the time of occupancy. The record is considered correct unless the tenant objects to it in writing within five days after receiving it. If the tenant desires to be present when the landlord inspects the dwelling unit at the termination of the tenancy to determine the amount of security to be returned, he

---
6. *Id.* § 55-248.4(l).
7. *Id.* § 55-248.11(b).

must advise the landlord in writing. Then the landlord must notify the tenant of the date and time of inspection, which must take place within seventy-two hours of the termination of occupancy.

The landlord or his agent is required to disclose to the tenant in writing at the beginning of the tenancy the name and address of the person or persons authorized to manage the premises, and of the owner of the premises or any other person authorized to act for the owner for the purpose of service of process and receiving notices and demands. If the premises are sold, the landlord must notify the tenant of the sale and disclose to the tenant the name and address of the purchaser and a telephone number at which the purchaser can be reached. The information that the landlord is required to furnish must be kept current. This provision applies to and is enforceable against any successor landlord, owner or manager, and they are required to keep permanent records.

The law requires the landlord to maintain fit premises. The landlord must comply "with the requirements of applicable building and housing codes materially affecting health and safety." [8] Virginia has no statewide housing or building codes, so one must look to county or city ordinances to see what requirements the landlord must meet. In addition to those requirements, the landlord must make all repairs and do whatever is necessary to put and keep the premises in a fit and habitable condition. He is required to keep all common areas shared by two or more dwelling units of the premises clean and safe. It is the duty of the landlord to maintain in "good and safe working order and condition all electrical, plumbing, sanitary, heating, ventilating, air-conditioning and other facilities and appliances, including elevators, supplied or required to be supplied by him." [9] The landlord must provide and maintain receptacles in the common area for the collection and removal of waste and garbage, and must arrange for their removal. The landlord is also obligated to "supply running water and reasonable amounts of hot water at all times and reasonable heat in season except where the dwelling unit is so constructed that heat or hot water is generated by an

---

8. *Id.* § 55-248.13(a)(1).
9. *Id.* § 55-248.13(a)(4).

installation within the exclusive control of the tenant or supplied by a direct public utility connection." [10]

Some of these duties are not absolute. The landlord and tenant may agree in writing that the tenant perform the landlord's duties to keep the common area in a clean and safe condition, to provide for trash removal, or to supply running water, hot water and heat. They may also agree to have the tenant perform "specified repairs, maintenance tasks, alterations and remodeling." [11] These types of agreements which allow the landlord to assign his statutory duties to the tenant require special negotiations between the landlord and tenant. They are not automatically part of a lease. The law requires that this type of transaction must be "entered into in good faith and not for the purpose of evading the obligations of the landlord," and that the agreement must not "diminish or affect the obligation of the landlord to other tenants in the premises." [12]

When the landlord notifies the tenant of any change in the terms or provisions of a tenancy, that notice constitutes a notice to vacate the premises. Such notice must be given in accordance with the terms of the rental agreement or as otherwise required by law.

TENANT'S OBLIGATIONS

The Virginia Residential Landlord and Tenant Act enumerates specific obligations and duties of the tenant as well as those of the landlord. Unless otherwise agreed upon, the tenant shall occupy his dwelling unit only as a dwelling unit. He must comply with all obligations "primarily imposed upon tenants by applicable provisions of building and housing codes materially affecting health and safety." [13] The tenant must look to local ordinances to find out these duties as they vary from locality to locality. The law requires the tenant to "keep that part of the premises that he occupies and uses clean and safe as the conditions of the premises permit." [14] He is required to remove trash from his dwelling unit

---

10. *Id.* § 55-248.13(a)(6).
11. *Id.* § 55-248.13(c).
12. *Id.* § 55-248.13(c).
13. *Id.* § 55-248.16(a)(1).
14. *Id.* § 55-248.16(a)(2).

in a clean and safe manner and dispose of it in the appropriate receptacles that the landlord provides. The tenant must keep all plumbing fixtures in his unit as clean as possible. He must "use in a reasonable manner all electrical, plumbing, sanitary, heating, ventilating, air-conditioning and other facilities and appliances including elevators in the premises." [15] He must "not deliberately or negligently destroy, deface, damage, impair or remove any part of the premises or permit any person to do so whether known by the tenant or not." [16] The law requires that he conduct himself, and require other persons on the premises with his consent, whether known by the tenant or not, to conduct themselves, in a manner that will not disturb his neighbors' peaceful enjoyment of the premises.

Another important tenant obligation is to abide by all reasonable rules and regulations imposed by the landlord, who has the right to regulate the tenant's use and occupancy of the premises, within reason. Such rules or regulations are enforceable against the tenant only if they meet certain standards. The purpose of the rule must be to

> promote the convenience, safety or welfare of the tenants in the premises, preserve the landlord's property from abusive use or make a fair distribution of services and facilities held out for the tenants generally. [17]

The rule must be reasonably related to the purpose for which it was adopted and apply to all tenants in the premises in a fair manner. It must be sufficiently explicit to fairly inform the tenant of what he must or must not do in order to comply with the rule, and it must not be for the purpose of evading the landlord's obligations under the law. The rule or regulation will only be enforceable against the tenant if the tenant has notice of it at the time he enters into the lease or when the rule is adopted. If the rule is adopted after the tenant enters into his lease, it is enforceable against him only if he has reasonable notice of its adoption and it does not work a substantial modification of his bargain. For

---

15. *Id.* § 55-248.16(a)(5).
16. *Id.* § 55-248.16(a)(6).
17. *Id.* § 55-248.17(a)(1).

example, a new rule which made the tenant responsible for the cost of repainting his unit if he vacated the unit before two years had expired would materially affect his bargain, since it would force him to assume financial obligations that he had not agreed to pay when he entered into his rental agreement. It would also penalize him for remaining on the premises less than two years, when his original lease agreement may only have obligated him to a lease term of one year. A rule adopted after the tenant enters into the rental agreement that works a substantial modification of his bargain is not valid unless the tenant consents to it in writing.

The tenant is required to grant access to his dwelling unit to the landlord or his agent. The tenant cannot unreasonably refuse the landlord access to the unit to make necessary or agreed repairs, decoration, alterations or improvements. The landlord cannot be denied reasonable access to the unit when he desires to exhibit it to prospective or actual purchasers, mortgagees, tenants or workmen. The landlord has the right to enter the dwelling without consent in case of emergency. The law does not allow the landlord to abuse the right of access or use it to harass a tenant. Except in case of emergency, the landlord must give the tenant reasonable notice of his intent to enter and may enter only at reasonable times. The law denies the landlord any other right of access except by court order, unless the tenant has abandoned or surrendered the premises.

The tenant is allowed to install burglary-prevention and fire detection devices within his apartment if he believes that they are necessary to ensure his safety, provided the installation does not permanently damage any part of the premises. The landlord or his agent must be given a duplicate key or instructions on how to operate all devices. Upon termination of the tenancy, the tenant shall remove all devices and repair all damages if the landlord requests him to do so.

The tenant is required to vacate the premises promptly at the termination of the term of occupancy, whether by expiration of the rental agreement or by reason of a default by the tenant. The tenant must remove all of his personal property from the premises and leave "the premises in good and clean order, reasonable wear and tear excepted. If the tenant fails to vacate, the landlord may bring an action for possession and damages, including reasonable attorney's fees." [18]

TENANT'S REMEDIES FOR WRONGFUL ACTS

The law specifies the remedies the tenant may use if the landlord breaches his obligations under the rental agreement or obligations imposed by law. If there is a material noncompliance by the landlord with the rental agreement, or nonperformance by the landlord of his duties under the Virginia Residential Landlord and Tenant Act, which materially affects health and safety, the tenant may deliver a written notice to the landlord specifying the acts and omissions constituting the breach, and giving notice that the rental agreement will terminate upon a date not less than thirty days after receipt of the notice if such breach is not remedied in twenty-one days. If the landlord remedies the breach by making repairs prior to the date specified in the notice, the rental agreement will not terminate. The tenant may not terminate the rental agreement if the condition which constituted the breach was caused by the deliberate or negligent act or omission of the tenant, a member of his family or some other person on the premises with his consent. The law allows the tenant to recover damages and obtain injunctive relief if the landlord fails to comply with his obligations. If the landlord's noncompliance is willful, the tenant may recover reasonable attorney's fees. If a rental agreement is terminated in this manner, the landlord must return all security plus accrued interest, if any, which is recoverable by law.

A landlord is required to deliver to the tenant only the legal possession of the leased premises, that is, the *right* to possession of the dwelling unit. The landlord is not required to deliver actual possession to the new tenant if that involves ousting the prior holdover tenant so the new tenant can move in. The Virginia courts have held that the new tenant has a remedy (under the unlawful detainer statutes) which allows him to bring suit against the

---
18. *Id.* § 55-248.20.

holdover tenant once the new tenant has received the legal right to possession from the landlord.

If the landlord willfully fails to deliver legal possession of the dwelling unit to the tenant, the rent abates, meaning it need not be paid until possession is delivered. Under Virginia case law, the term "possession" as used in this statute is limited to legal possession as it relates to a landlord. If the landlord fails to deliver this right to possession, the tenant may terminate the rental agreement upon at least five days' written notice to the landlord; upon termination, the landlord must return all prepaid rent and security deposits. The tenant, at his option, may file suit for possession of the dwelling unit against the landlord or any person wrongfully in possession, and may recover damages. This action is called unlawful entry or detainer. It may be used when there has been any forcible or unlawful entry upon property or, if the entry is lawful and peaceful, when the tenant retains possession of the property after his right to possession has expired. The law allows the person who has the right to possession of the premises, but who is not allowed actual possession, to sue the person who wrongfully remains in possession of the premises. The injured party may institute the action by filing "a motion for judgment in the circuit court alleging that the defendant is in possession and unlawfully withholds from the plaintiff the premises in question." [19] When the action is commenced in the circuit court, the summons is returnable thereto and, upon application of either party trial by jury shall be had.

In any case when possession of any house, land or tenement is unlawfully detained by the person in possession thereof, the landlord or the person entitled to possession may present to any magistrate or judge of the general district court a statement under oath of the facts which authorize the removal of the tenant or other person in possession. After receipt of this statement, the magistrate or judge shall issue a summons against the person named in the affidavit. When the summons is issued by a magistrate it may be returned to and the case heard and determined by the judge of the general district court.

---

19. *Id.* § 8.01-124.

The verdict or judgment is rendered for the plaintiff if it appears he "was forcibly or unlawfully turned out of possession, or that it was unlawfully detained from him ...."[20] The unlawful detainer statute also provides for damages sustained by the plaintiff due to the unlawful detainer. The Residential Landlord and Tenant Act also provides that "if a person's failure to deliver possession is willful and not in good faith, an aggrieved person may recover from that person the actual damages sustained by him and reasonable attorney's fees."[21]

If the landlord wrongfully or negligently fails to supply the tenant with heat, water, hot water, electricity, gas, or other essential services required by the rental agreement, the landlord has breached his part of the rental agreement and the law gives the tenant a right to redress against the landlord. The rights of the tenant do not arise, though, until he has given written notice to the landlord; no right arises if the condition that caused the breach is caused by the negligence or deliberate act or omission of the tenant, a member of his family or person on the premises with his consent. After the tenant has given written notice to the landlord specifying the breach, and the landlord has been given a reasonable time to correct the breach, the tenant at his election may recover damages equal to the amount by which the fair rental value of the dwelling unit is reduced, or he may procure reasonable substitute housing during the period of the landlord's noncompliance, in which case the tenant will be excused from paying rent for the period of the landlord's noncompliance, as determined by the court.[22] If the tenant brings this type of action he is entitled to reasonable attorney's fees which will be awarded to him by the court.

If one's dwelling unit or premises are damaged or destroyed by fire or other casualty to an extent that enjoyment of the dwelling is substantially impaired, the tenant may immediately vacate the premises and notify the landlord in writing within fourteen days afterwards of his intention to terminate the rental agreement. The

---

20. *Id.* § 8.01-128.
21. *Id.* § 55-248.22.
22. *Id.* § 55-248.23(a).

rental agreement will then terminate as of the date of vacating the premises. If the tenant chooses to remain in the damaged premises, the law requires that the rent be reasonably reduced in order to compensate the tenant for loss of the use of the damaged premises as long as they are not restored or repaired. If the lease is terminated because of damage or destruction the landlord is required to return all security and prepaid rent plus accrued interest, which is recoverable by law to the tenant. An accounting of rent is necessary in order to return prepaid rent to the tenant in the event of termination or apportionment made as of the date of the casualty or fire.

The law also provides tenants a specific remedy if the landlord unlawfully removes or excludes the tenant from his apartment or if the landlord willfully diminishes services to the tenant by interrupting the supply of gas, water or other essential services. In either of these cases, the tenant may recover possession of the dwelling unit by an action at law or may terminate the rental agreement. He may also receive the actual damages sustained by him and reasonable attorney's fees. If the rental agreement is terminated in this manner the landlord shall return all security and any accrued interest.

The Residential Landlord and Tenant Act establishes a new remedy for the tenant if a condition which constitutes a material noncompliance by the landlord exists upon his leased premises or there is a serious threat to health and safety which the landlord refuses to remedy. This remedy is referred to as rent escrow. The tenant can pay the rent he owes to the court in trust for the landlord and then bring the landlord into court to determine how the unsafe or unhealthy condition can best be remedied. Conditions that permit rent escrow include (but are not limited to) lack of heat; lack of hot or cold running water, except where the tenant is required to pay separate utility charges; failure to provide electricity or adequate sewage disposal facilities; infestation of rodents, except if the property is a one-family dwelling; or the existence of paint containing lead pigment on surfaces within the dwelling, provided the landlord has notice of such paint.[23]

---

23. *Id.* § 55-248.27.

The tenant commences such an action by filing in the general district court in which the premises are located a declaration detailing the undesirable conditions and asking for one or more forms of relief as provided by the statute. Before the tenant can be granted relief, he must prove that he has notified the landlord in writing by certified mail of the condition, or that the landlord was notified of such condition by a violation or condemnation notice from an appropriate state or local agency. He must also show that the landlord refused or has failed within a reasonable time to remedy the condition. A period in excess of thirty days from the date of the receipt of the notice by the landlord will be considered by the court to be unreasonable, unless the landlord introduces evidence to the contrary. The tenant must have paid into the court the amount of the rent owed to the landlord under the rental agreement within five days of the date on which it is due. The statute also requires the tenant to prove he has not been behind in his rental obligations to the landlord. The landlord can defend such an action on the grounds that the alleged condition does not exist, that the tenant caused the condition, or that the tenant has refused the landlord or his agent entry into the premises for the purpose of correcting such conditions.

The initial hearing must be held within fifteen calendar days after the service of the complaint upon the landlord or his authorized agent. When emergency conditions are alleged to exist, "such as failure of heat in winter, lack of adequate sewage facilities or any other condition which constitutes an immediate threat to the health or safety of the inhabitants of the leased premises," the court must order an earlier hearing.[24] If either party desires a preliminary hearing the court may hold such a hearing. The escrow money can be distributed only by court order after a hearing of which both parties had legal notice, or upon motion of both the landlord and tenant, or "upon certification by the appropriate inspector that the work required by the court to be done has been satisfactorily completed." [25]

The court has a variety of other remedies that may be ordered

---

24. *Id.* § 55-248.30.
25. *Id.*

after making findings of facts on the issues of the case. Some of the orders the court can issue include, but are not limited to, termination of the lease or ordering the premises surrendered to the landlord; ordering all money already accumulated in escrow disbursed to the landlord or to the tenant; or ordering that the escrow be continued until the conditions are remedied. The court can order an abatement of the rent in such an amount as may be equitable to represent the existence of the condition. The court can order the amount of money in escrow disbursed to the tenant when the landlord refuses to make repairs after a reasonable time, or to the landlord or a contractor chosen by the landlord in order to make repairs.[26] The court in its discretion can also order escrow funds disbursed to pay a mortgage on the property in order to stop a foreclosure, or to pay a creditor to prevent or satisfy a bill to enforce a merchant's or materialman's lien on the property. Finally, where the escrow account has been established for six months and the landlord has not made reasonable attempts to remedy the condition, the court will award all accumulated money to the tenant. If this occurs, the escrow is not terminated, but a new six-month period begins which can have the same result if the landlord does not remedy the condition.

Landlord's Remedies for Wrongful Acts

Landlords have specific remedies under the Virginia Residential Landlord and Tenant Act. The landlord has an action and remedy against the tenant who fails to comply with the rental agreement or violates his duties imposed by the Act that materially affect health and safety. When such a breach occurs the landlord may deliver to the tenant a written notice of the breach. The notice must specify the acts or omissions of the tenant that constitute the breach and that the rental agreement will terminate at a specific date not less than thirty days after the tenant's receipt of the notice. The tenant must be given twenty-one days to remedy the breach; if he does not comply with the rental agreement or his duties imposed by law, the rental agreement will terminate as the

---

26. *Id.* § 55-248.29.

notice provides. If the breach can be remedied by means of repair or payment of damages to the landlord, the tenant will be deemed to have remedied the breach if he makes the repairs or pays the damages prior to the date specified in the notice and the rental agreement will not terminate. But if the tenant's breach is due to failure to pay rent, and the tenant fails to pay the rent within five days after written notice by the landlord of nonpayment and the landlord's intention to terminate the rental agreement, the landlord may terminate the lease. If the tenant fails to vacate at the time specified in the notice, the landlord may regain possession of the premises by means of an action for unlawful entry and detainer.

If the tenant violates any of his statutory duties or contractual duties, the landlord may recover damages and obtain injunctive relief for noncompliance by the tenant, including reasonable attorney's fees if the breach was willful.[27]

Once the tenant has defaulted in payment of his rent (*i.e.*, failed to pay the rent within five days from the date it is due), the landlord has a right to recover the amount of damages due him. The landlord has a number of options. He can proceed under the provisions of the Residential Landlord and Tenant Act as already described. The landlord can also avail himself of the remedy of distress for rent. Distress, an ancient common law remedy, is "the taking [of] a personal chattel out of the possession of a wrong-doer into the custody of the party injured, to procure a satisfaction for a wrong committed; as for non-payment of rent, or injury done by cattle." [28]

Virginia retains distress as a statutory remedy and a means of enforcing the landlord's lien on the tenant's property for unpaid rent. According to the Virginia statute, "Rent of every kind may be recovered by distress or action." [29] "Rent may be distrained for within five years from the time it becomes due, and not afterwards, whether the lease be ended or not." [30] Distress is made by a sheriff or sergeant of the county or city where the premises are, or where the goods liable to distress are being kept. The sheriff or other officer acts under a distress warrant issued by the judge or clerk

---

27. *Id.* § 55-248.31.
28. BLACK'S LAW DICTIONARY 561 (Rev. 4th ed. 1968).
29. VA. CODE § 55-227.
30. *Id.* § 55-230.

of the local general district court or the local magistrate. This distress warrant is issued by the judge or magistrate only after the person claiming the rent, the landlord or his agent, makes an affidavit "that the amount of money or other thing to be distrained for (to be specified in the affidavit), as he verily believes, is justly due to the claimant for rent reserved upon contract from the person of whom it is claimed." [31] After the judge issues the distress warrant based on the affidavit, the sheriff must deliver the warrant to the tenant and levy on the tenant's goods.

The statute provides that "distress may be levied on any goods of the lessee, or his assignee, or undertenant, found on the premises, or which may have been removed therefrom not more than thirty days. A levy within such thirty days shall have like effect as if the goods levied on had not been removed from the leased premises." [32] Goods removed from the premises thirty days prior to the lien are treated the same as goods found on the premises to avoid letting the tenant remove all his tangible goods from the property before the landlord has an opportunity to enforce his lien for the rent owed him. The landlord can only levy for an amount equal to not more than six months' rent if the premises are used for residential purposes and not for farming, and for not more than twelve months' rent if the lands or premises are used for farming.

When a sheriff levies on goods, he takes legal possession of the goods either by actual levy or by constructive levy by merely listing the goods. If the distress is not contested by the tenant, the sheriff will post a notice of the sale of the property in a conspicuous place, usually the courthouse, for ten days. This notice must include the date, time and place of the sale. After the ten-day period a sale of the property under the normal procedure for a judicial sale of property will be carried out. This sale is usually accomplished by an auction. After the sheriff deducts his expenses, the proceeds from the sale are turned over to the clerk of the court, who pays the landlord the amount due to him for rent. Any amount remaining is turned over to the tenant.

---

31. *Id.* § 55-230.
32. *Id.* § 55-231.

The tenant has the right to contest the distress, by procuring a forthcoming bond, which is a surety bond "with sufficient surety, payable to the creditor, reciting the service of such writ or warrant, and the amount due thereon, including the officer's fee for taking the bond, commissions and other lawful charges, if any, with condition that the property shall be forthcoming at the day and place of the sale." [33] If the tenant gives bond, he retains possession of the property and the sheriff does not levy on the goods. The tenant who cannot procure such a bond can still retain possession of the property if he makes an affidavit stating that "he is unable to give the bond required ... and that he has a valid defense." [34] The tenant's valid grounds for defense are "that the distress was for rent not due in whole or in part, or was otherwise illegal." [35] The sheriff cannot take possession of the property if the tenant states in an affidavit that he is unable to give bond and he has a right to remove the action from the general district court to the circuit court because the amount in controversy is greater than $500.[36] If the tenant contests the distress, the property remains in his possession at his risk. The sheriff will then return the warrant and the tenant's affidavit to the court which issued the original warrant. The landlord, after ten days' written notice to the tenant, may ask the court for judgment for the amount of the rent and for the sale of the property levied on.[37] The tenant may defend against this motion using any defense allowed to him under law.

The landlord or his agent can avoid the effects of the tenant's forthcoming bond by posting a double indemnifying bond which has sufficient surety, in a penalty double the value of the property levied on, with condition to pay all cost and damages which may accrue to anyone by reason of his suing out such warrant. In that case, the officer takes possession of the property, and holds it subject to the order of the court.[38] The sheriff will retain

---

33. *Id.* § 8.01-526.
34. *Id.* § 55-232.
35. *Id.*
36. *Id.* §§ 16.1-92, 55-232.
37. *Id.* § 55-232.
38. *Id.* § 55-232.

possession until the court has rendered judgment on the landlord's motion for judgment on the rent alleged to be due. After judgment is rendered, the sheriff will retain the property until ordered by the court to sell the property to satisfy the landlord's lien, or to return the property to the tenant.

As stated previously, the sheriff or officer generally will not take actual possession of the property to be distressed, but there are special cases under which the officer will be required by court order to take actual possession of the property. The judge or magistrate has the authority to issue an ex parte order to the officer commanding him to take possession of the property in question only if the landlord or his agent by evidence proves the probable validity of the underlying claim and also proves that he knows of no valid defense to the suit, that there is an immediate danger that the property will be destroyed or concealed, and that "the person whose property is to be taken has clearly, intelligently, and voluntarily waived in writing in a document other than, and not contingent upon the lease, his right to a hearing prior to the taking of possession." [39] In all other cases in which the landlord requests a court order that the officer take actual possession of the tenant's property, the order or process may issue only after reasonable notice to the person whose property is being taken and after a hearing before a judge or magistrate on the probable validity of the underlying claim.[40] The judge or magistrate may receive evidence in the form of affidavits or oral testimony which shall record the name of each witness and a brief summary of his testimony.[41] After the officer takes possession of the property pursuant to an ex parte order, or after denial of an application to issue such order by a magistrate, "upon application of either party, and after reasonable notice, a judge of the general district court having jurisdiction shall conduct a hearing to review the decision to issue the ex parte order or process and in the event such judge finds such order or process should not have been issued, the court

---

39. *Id.* § 55-232.1(a)(ii).
40. *Id.* § 55-232.1(b).
41. *Id.*

may award actual damages and reasonable attorney's fees to the person whose property was taken." [42] One must be cautioned that the procedure just described does not apply to the levy or distress on property by the officer if the officer does not take actual possession of the property subject to distress.

Distress and attachments for rent are considered a drastic remedy. In order to safeguard the tenant's right to his property, Virginia law provides for an action for wrongful distress:

> If property be distrained for any rent not due, or attached for any rent not accruing, or taken under any attachment sued out without good cause, the owner of such property may, in an action against the party suing out the warrant of distress or attachment, recover damages for the wrongful distraint, seizure, or sale.[43]

So the landlord acts at his peril if he sues an attachment or obtains a distress warrant for invalid reasons. But when distress can be made for rent justly due and any irregularity or unlawful act shall be afterwards done by the party distraining, or his agent, the distress itself shall not be deemed to be unlawful, nor shall the party making it be therefore deemed a trespasser. The party aggrieved by such irregularity or unlawful act, by action, recovers full satisfaction for the special damages he shall have sustained thereby.

One other matter should be pointed out in regard to attachment and distress: the power conferred upon the officer delivering the distress warrant or attachment. The officer, "if there be need for it, may, in the daytime, break open and enter into any house or close in which there may be goods liable to distress or attachment, and may, either in the day or night, break open and enter any house or close wherein there may be any goods so liable which have been fraudulently or clandestinely removed from the demised premises." [44] This statute gives the officer much greater rights than he would have if he were delivering an ordinary summons or process. The officer is also allowed to levy such distress warrant

---
42. *Id.* § 55-232.2.
43. *Id.* § 8.01-41.
44. *Id.* § 55-235.

or attachment on property liable for the rent found in the personal possession of the party liable therefor.

The landlord can also bring an action at law to receive rent due him for the reasonable use and occupation of his property. He can also sue the tenant for breach of contract.

In addition to the remedies provided by the Virginia Residential Landlord and Tenant Act to the landlord in the case of the tenant's failure to pay rent, the Act also provides for other specific remedies for the landlord in the case of other acts or omissions of the tenant. One of these is a remedy for the tenant's failure to maintain the premises. When the tenant violates his duties under the law or the rental agreement, materially affecting health and safety, the tenant may be forced to remedy the breach by repair, replacement of a damaged item or cleaning, as promptly as conditions require (in case of emergency) or within fourteen days after written notice by the landlord specifying the breach and requesting that he remedy it within that period of time. If the tenant fails to comply within the period of time specified in the notice, the landlord may enter the dwelling unit and have the work done in a workmanlike manner. The landlord may submit an itemized bill for the actual and reasonable cost or the fair and reasonable value of the repairs as rent on the next date when periodic rent is due. If the rental agreement has terminated, the landlord may demand immediate payment.[45]

If the rental agreement requires the tenant to give notice to the landlord of an anticipated extended absence in excess of seven days and the tenant does not notify the landlord, the landlord may recover actual damages from the tenant. If the tenant's absence exceeds seven days, the landlord may enter the dwelling unit at times reasonably necessary to protect his possessions and property.

If the landlord rents an abandoned dwelling unit for a term beginning prior to the expiration of the rental agreement, the old lease is deemed to be terminated as of the date the new tenancy begins,[46] meaning that the old tenant is relieved of his obligation

---
45. *Id.* § 55-248.32.
46. *Id.* § 55-248.33.

to pay rent and the new tenant takes over the obligation. It is up to the landlord to elect to accept the abandonment as a surrender of the premises. If the landlord does make that election the old rental agreement terminates as of the date that the landlord has notice of the abandonment. The landlord is not required to accept the abandonment of the premises. He is free to leave the premises vacant for the duration of the lease term, and then sue the tenant for all back rent.

The law considers that the landlord waives his right to terminate the tenancy of a defaulting tenant if he accepts periodic rent payments from a tenant. This waiver also applies if the landlord accepts performance by the tenant that varies from the terms of the rental agreement or the rules or regulations subsequently adopted by the landlord. The receipt by the landlord of *part* payment of past due rent, however, does not constitute a waiver.

The landlord also has a specific remedy to recover back rent or damages after termination of the rental agreement. After the end of the lease term, "the landlord may have a claim for possession and for rent and a separate claim for actual damages for breach of the rental agreement and reasonable attorney's fees, . . . which claims may be enforced, without limitation, by the institution of an action for unlawful entry or detainer." [47]

Virginia law provides that a landlord may not recover or take possession of the dwelling unit by willfully interrupting services or causing the interruption of electric, gas, water or other essential services required by the rental agreement.[48]

If the landlord or tenant desires to terminate a week to week lease, he must give the other party written notice at least seven days prior to the next rent due date. A month to month tenancy may be terminated by either party giving written notice to the other at least thirty days prior to the next rent due date. "If the tenant remains in possession without the landlord's consent after expiration of the term of the rental agreement or its termination, the landlord may bring an action for possession and if the tenant's

---

47. *Id.* § 55-248.35.
48. *Id.* § 55-248.36.

holdover is willful the landlord may also recover the actual damages by him and reasonable attorney's fees." [49]

When the tenant refuses to allow the landlord lawful access to the premises, the landlord may obtain injunctive relief to compel access or to terminate the rental agreement. If either of these situations occurs, the landlord may recover actual damages and reasonable attorney's fees. If the landlord makes an unlawful entry of the leased premises, or a lawful entry in an unreasonable manner, or makes repeated demands for entry which may be lawful but which have the effect of unreasonably harassing the tenant, the tenant may obtain an injunction to prevent such conduct or he may terminate the rental agreement.[50] The tenant can also recover actual damages and reasonable attorney's fees.

The Virginia Residential Landlord and Tenant Act strictly prohibits retaliatory action by the landlord against a tenant who complains to a governmental agency about the landlord's violation of the local housing or building code; who makes a complaint or files a suit against the landlord for his violation of the law or their rental agreement; or who organizes or becomes a member of a tenants' organization. The landlord may not retaliate against such a tenant "by increasing rent or decreasing services or by bringing or threatening to bring an action for possession or by causing a termination of the rental agreement except as otherwise provided by law." [51]

If the landlord attempts to take any retaliatory action against a tenant the "tenant is entitled to the applicable remedies provided [by law] and may assert such retaliation as a defense in any action against him for possession." [52] The landlord *is* allowed to bring an action for possession against the tenant, however, if the tenant caused the violation of the housing or building code through his lack of reasonable care; if the tenant is in default in rent; if

---

49. *Id.* § 55-248.37.
50. *Id.* § 55-248.38.
51. *Id.* § 55-248.39.
52. *Id.*

compliance with the building or housing code requires alteration, remodeling or demolition which would deprive the tenant of the use of the dwelling, or if the tenant is in default of a provision of the rental agreement materially affecting the health and safety of himself or others.

The Virginia Residential Landlord and Tenant Act of 1974 clarifies the respective duties and obligations of landlords and tenants, and provides both landlord and tenant a way to enforce their rights.

> Any person adversely affected by an act or omission prohibited under this chapter may institute an action for injunction and damages against the person responsible for such act or omission in the circuit court in the county or city in which such act or omission occurred. If the court finds that the defendant was responsible for such act or omission, it shall enjoin the defendant from continuance of such practice, and in its discretion award the plaintiff damages as herein provided.[53]

The law gives easier access to the courts by either landlord or tenant, and relieves some of the financial burden by providing that the landlord or tenant may recover reasonable attorney's fees. This means that the losing party will have the reasonable attorney's fees of his opposing party included in the judgment that he will have to pay. This provision is helpful to both parties because it means they will have an easier time obtaining, and paying for, the aid of an attorney, since the attorney's fees will be awarded by the court to the prevailing party. This should encourage both sides, especially the tenant, to seek the legal counsel they really need to help them vindicate their rights.

---

53. *Id.* § 55-248.40.

CHAPTER 6

Taxes

D. W. Bender

IN GENERAL

Taxes consume a large percentage of each American's earnings. They are the topic of the day three months each year. The number of different taxes can be staggering, especially if the taxpayer incurs tax liability in several states. Fortunately, the tax laws were designed to make compliance almost automatic. Many taxes are added to the cost of goods and services. Others are assessed by local commissioners of revenue, some with and some without the requirement that the taxpayer file a return. The income tax, which is the most difficult to calculate, is paid by individuals primarily through withholdings from their paychecks. Very little conscious effort is required for compliance; for this reason most taxpayers do not engage in prospective tax planning.

Opportunities for effectuating significant tax savings abound. The more one understands about the tax system, the better is his position to realize tax savings and to benefit from the use of tax counsel. Ordinarily the individual can acquire the expertise necessary for filing his own tax returns and can obtain assistance if necessary by dialing the toll-free number (800-552-9500 in Virginia) maintained by the Internal Revenue Service (IRS). The IRS also distributes a booklet entitled "Your Federal Income Tax" (Publication number 17 which is as good as any available for sale on newsstands.

In some instances, however, professional tax counsel will prove most beneficial. At the very least, every taxpayer should have an attorney prepare an estate plan to accord with his wishes in a way that will mitigate the tax burden on his estate. Divorce and separate maintenance agreements can have a great impact on tax liability. Significant tax savings may also be realized through proper timing and structuring of large transactions and employment contracts, and by choice of the proper form of business organization.

Adequate recordkeeping is a prerequisite for IRS recognition of any statement or claim. The IRS distributes a booklet entitled "Recordkeeping Requirements" (Publication number 552). The records which must be kept will vary among taxpayers. The businessman will want to have his accountant or attorney establish a bookkeeping system for him at the outset. It is considerably more difficult, often impossible, to compile the proper records after memories have faded and documents have been filed away. Different methods of accounting can produce significantly different tax consequences. Lack of adequate records has both adverse tax and adverse business management consequences. Improper recordkeeping is commonly associated with the failure of new enterprises.

A word of caution is in order. The law permits income tax preparers to hang out their shingles without any formal training or licensing. In recent years the IRS and other concerned groups have tried to publicize the inadequacies of these services.[1] Many good guides are available at newsstands. The taxpayer who feels uncomfortable filling out his own return with the assistance of a good guide would be best advised to seek the free services offered by the IRS or to consult a licensed professional, either a Certified Public Accountant (C.P.A.) or an attorney.

A basic understanding of the system of federal, state, and local taxes will enable the taxpayer to realize greater savings and make more effective use of professional counsel. The remainder of this chapter is devoted to summary explanations of the income, social security, estate, gift, inheritance, property, and sales and use taxes as they affect the Virginia taxpayer. The taxpayer who wants the best, most up-to-date source of instructions on year-end filing will find numerous income tax manuals available from the IRS or at newsstands during the tax season. Many good books on specific areas of interest are also available. Note, however, that tax materials of a specific nature become outdated very rapidly.

---

1. B. C. IND & COM. L. REV. 13:895, 13:896 to 13:898 (1972).

Federal Income Tax

(a) *An Overview*

All taxpayers, including individuals, partnerships, associations, corporations, and fiduciaries for trusts and estates, must file a federal income tax return and pay an income tax, unless specifically exempted by IRS Regulations. The income tax is levied only on *taxable income* earned during the tax year. The marginal rate of tax, or the taxpayer's tax bracket, is not the effective rate of tax. Certain items are exempted, deducted, or treated in a preferential manner, and the marginal rate only applies to the last increment of taxable income. The marginal rate is approximately twice the effective rate of the tax.

Individuals, fiduciaries, and partnerships must file federal income tax returns by April 15, or the fifteenth day of the fourth month following the close of a tax year other than the calendar year.[2] Taxpayers with significant amounts of income not subject to withholding are required to file estimated income tax returns by April 15 for the current tax year and to make quarterly estimated income tax payments.[3] Individuals, trusts, and estates are taxed at progressive rates varying from fourteen to seventy percent of taxable income,[4] with the rate of tax on personal service income limited to fifty percent unless the taxpayer elects income averaging for the current tax year.[5]

Partnerships are not income taxpaying entities; however, they are required to file annual informational returns. The partnership return shows partnership taxable income and lists separately various items of gross income and deductions, and assigns each partner a *distributive share* of each. These must be shown as items of income, business expense, or itemized deductions on the partners' personal income tax returns.[6] Partners are taxed on their distributive shares whether or not they actually receive them. Whenever a partnership retains earnings for use in the business,

---
2. INT. REV. CODE § 6072(a).
3. *Id.* §§ 6015, 6073(a).
4. *Id.* § 1.
5. *Id.* § 1348.
6. *Id.* §§ 701, 702.

the partners are taxed on income which they did not actually receive. The method of determining taxable income is one of the critical differences between being a member of a partnership and being a shareholder in a corporation.

Corporations must file federal income tax returns by March 15, or the fifteenth day of the third month following the close of the tax period.[7] All corporations with estimated annual tax liabilities of $40 or more are required to file estimated income tax returns by the fifteenth day of the fourth month and may pay the tax in equal quarterly installments.[8] Special amendments to the Internal Revenue Code provide that corporations are taxed at the rate of twenty percent on the first $25,000 of taxable income, twenty-two percent of the second $25,000, and forty-eight percent of taxable income in excess of $50,000 through December 31, 1977.[9] Unless these provisions are extended, corporations will thereafter be subject to taxation at the rates of twenty-two percent of the first $25,000 of taxable income and forty-eight percent of taxable income in excess thereof. Since dividends to shareholders are not deductible from corporate taxable income, all corporate income is, in a sense, taxed twice: first to the corporation as earnings, and then to the shareholder when distributed as dividends.

Pursuant to Subchapter S of the Internal Revenue Code, certain small business corporations may elect to be taxed as partnerships except as to certain items of capital gains income in excess of $25,000. Like partnerships, "Subchapter S corporations" are required to file informational returns. Most small corporations are eligible for this treatment. An election must be made early in the tax year and various qualifying requirements must be met.

(b) *Computation of Taxable Income*

The beginning point in calculating federal income tax liability is *gross income*, which consists of "all income from whatever source derived...," except certain items of exempt income. Gross income includes, but is not limited to, wages, salaries, tips, bonuses, commissions, fees, dividends, interest, rents, royalties, profits,

---

7. *Id.* § 6072(b).
8. *Id.* § 6154(a), (b).
9. *Id.* § 11.

pensions, annuities, endowments, profits from sales or exchanges, some life insurance proceeds, distributive shares of partnership income, alimony, and income from an estate or trust.[10] It includes not only cash, but also the cash value of goods and services received as compensation. And it includes items which the taxpayer could have collected during the tax year, but which he voluntarily deferred until a subsequent tax period, or assigned to the benefit of another.

The following items of *exempt income* do not constitute a part of gross income: Social security and workmen's compensation benefits,[11] veterans benefits,[12] most lump sum life insurance payments received at the insured's death,[13] interest on most state and local government bonds,[14] gifts, inheritances, bequests,[15] some compensation for injuries and sickness,[16] amounts received under accident and health plans,[17] the first one hundred dollars of dividend income from domestic corporations,[18] scholarships and fellowship grants received without obligation,[19] meals and lodging furnished by the employer for his convenience,[20] a portion of the gain from the sale or exchange of the residence of a taxpayer over age 65,[21] certain living expenses received under insurance contracts,[22] and many employee fringe benefits.[23]

The first intermediate step in determining taxable income is *adjusted gross income* (AGI), gross income less trade and business expenses and certain other items.[24] AGI is the basis for calculating the standard deduction and the floor under medical expense

---

10. *Id.* § 61.
11. *Id.* §§ 105, 106.
12. 38 U.S.C. § 3101.
13. INT. REV. CODE § 101(a)(1).
14. *Id.* § 103.
15. *Id.* § 102.
16. *Id.* § 104.
17. *Id.* § 105.
18. *Id.* § 116.
19. *Id.* § 117.
20. *Id.* § 119.
21. *Id.* § 121.
22. *Id.* § 123.
23. *Id.* §§ 101, 106, 107, 119.
24. *Id.* § 62.

deductions. Nonbusiness deductions, or the standard deduction, and personal exemptions are subtracted from AGI in determining *taxable income* for individuals.[25]

Although wage earners are not as likely to have them as other taxpayers, trade and business deductions are available to individuals as well as to business taxpayers.[26] Since individuals may claim some deductions either as trade and business expenses or as personal deductions, such deductions need not be forfeited by the election of the standard deduction. If taken as business expense deductions, rather than as personal deductions, AGI will be lower and will result in a lower floor for deductible medical expenses. In general, trade and business expense deductions are allowed for all "ordinary and necessary expenses paid or incurred during the taxable year in carrying on any trade or business...." [27] Even if the taxpayer has no trade or business, he may deduct "all the ordinary and necessary expenses paid or incurred during the taxable year (1) for the production or collection of income; (2) for the management, conservation, or maintenance of property held for the production of income; or (3) in connection with the determination, collection, or refund of any tax." [28] However, as a matter of public policy, no deduction is allowed for fines or penalties or other illegal payments.[29] Employees may have trade and business expense deductions for meals, lodging, and other travel expenses incurred while away from home overnight on business, transportation expenses incurred in connection with the performance of services as an employee (but not for commuting expenses unless incurred while traveling directly from one place of employment to another), for employee moving expenses, and for legitimate business expenses reimbursed by the employer.[30] Individuals may also have trade and business expenses as

---

25. *Id.* § 63.
26. *Id.* § 62.
27. *Id.* § 162.
28. *Id.* § 212.
29. *Id.* § 162(c), (f).
30. *Id.* §§ 62, 217.

self-employed taxpayers, and for private pension plans.[31] Not all expenditures are currently deductible in the year incurred.[32] Business expenses which are *ordinary and necessary* are, of course; but the cost of acquiring assets used for trade or business is not considered an "expense" but is deductible over the asset's estimated useful life as an annual allowance for depreciation. Various methods of accounting for depreciation may be used. The basic straight-line method allocates the same amount of depreciation to each year. Accelerated depreciation methods permit a greater proportion of the depreciation allowance to be claimed during the earlier years of the asset's useful life. However, if the asset is sold prematurely, any excess depreciation will be recaptured as ordinary income. If the asset will still have an appreciable salvage value at the end of its useful life in the trade or business in which it is being used, this amount will not be included in the depreciation allowance. The rate of depreciation allowed depends upon the type of property involved and is never allowed for property which does not decline in value.[33] Natural resources being depleted are generally subject to an allowance for depletion based upon their cost basis or upon the income they produce, rather than a depreciation allowance.[34]

Nonbusiness (or itemized) deductions are granted to individual taxpayers to equalize the incidence of the income tax with the taxpayer's ability to pay vis-a-vis others at the same income level, and for reasons of social policy, such as encouraging home ownership. The taxpayer may elect the standard deduction (provided his spouse also so elects) of sixteen percent of AGI, with maximum $2,800 for married taxpayers filing joint returns or $1,400 each if filing separately, and $2,400 for single taxpayers. There is a minimum standard deduction or Low Income Allowance of $2,100 for married taxpayers filing joint returns or $1,050 each if filing separately, and $1,700 for single taxpayers, provided that

---

31. *Id.* § 62.
32. *Id.* § 261.
33. *Id.* § 167.
34. *Id.* §§ 611-613.

if one spouse elects the Low Income Allowance the other must do likewise.[35]

It may be beneficial to itemize deductions, especially if the taxpayer owns a home. An individual may claim as deductions expenses incurred on behalf of anyone claimed as a dependent for income tax purposes. Itemized deductions are allowed for medical and dental expenses, including insurance premiums and transportation;[36] interest;[37] taxes;[38] charitable contributions;[39] contributions to candidates for public office up to $100 per taxpayer;[40] casualty and theft losses;[41] alimony or support payments which are not designated for child support;[42] private pension plans (if the taxpayer is not eligible for coverage under an employer-sponsored plan);[43] and expenses incurred for the production of income (if not claimed as a trade or business expense deduction).[44]

Personal exemptions are another form of nonbusiness deductions. The taxpayer is entitled to exemptions for himself, his spouse, and each dependent and to an additional exemption if either he or his spouse are blind or over age sixty-five. Each exemption reduces taxable income by $750.[45]

Almost all taxpayers will be entitled to income tax credits for tax year 1977. Credits are more valuable than deductions because each tax credit dollar reduces tax liability by one dollar, whereas a one-dollar tax deduction would reduce taxable income by only ten cents if the taxpayer were in the ten percent bracket, or at most by seventy cents in the highest bracket. Each taxpayer will be entitled to a tax credit of thirty-five dollars for each personal exemption (excluding exemptions for age and blindness) he claims,

---

35. *Id.* § 141.
36. *Id.* § 213.
37. *Id.* § 163.
38. *Id.* § 164.
39. *Id.* § 170.
40. *Id.* § 218.
41. *Id.* § 165(c)(3).
42. *Id.* § 215.
43. *Id.* § 219.
44. *Id.* § 212.
45. *Id.* § 151.

or two percent of his taxable income up to $9,000, whichever is higher, for the years 1976 and 1977 only, with the additional condition that the credit may not exceed the tax liability for the year (*i.e.,* the tax credit is not subject to refund). In addition, low income households, in which the husband and wife file a joint return, or which include at least one dependent child, will be entitled to a tax credit of ten percent of personal service income or AGI, whichever is higher, if the joint income is $4,000 or less; or a smaller credit if such income is between $4,000 and $8,000. Taxpayers over age 65 or receiving benefits under a retirement plan for public employees may be eligible for a Credit for the Elderly of up to $375 if social security, railroad retirement, and other tax exempt annuity or pension benefits plus a portion of earned income do not exceed $2,500 per annum.

A credit of fifty percent of contributions to candidates for public office is allowed, limited to $25 per individual or $50 per joint return, and further limited to the amount of the tax due.[46] There is also a credit for employers who participate in the Work Incentive (WIN) Program,[47] and an on-again, off-again Investment Credit to encourage business investment in depreciable assets.[48] Individuals who maintain a household which includes as a member one or more qualifying dependents are allowed a credit for a percentage of household and dependent care expenses necessary to enable the taxpayer to work.[49]

Not all income is treated alike for tax purposes. Capital gains income and losses, that is, the gains and losses realized from the sale of capital assets, are singled out for differential treatment. Capital assets subject to capital gains treatment are all items of property held by the taxpayer with the exception of the following: inventory or stock in trade; depreciable property or real estate used in trade or business; copyrights, literary, musical or artistic compositions, letters, or memorandums created by or for the taxpayer or received as a gift from the creator; receivables

---

46. *Id.* § 41.
47. *Id.* § 40.
48. *Id.* § 38.
49. *Id.* § 44A.

acquired through obligations in business or property; noninterest bearing government securities maturing within one year;[50] and government publications received by a taxpayer other than by purchase at the public sale price.

Capital gains and losses are distinguished as either short term or long term (more than six months for taxable years before 1977; nine months for taxable years beginning in 1977; and one year for taxable years beginning after December 31, 1977) by the length of holding period. Long term capital gains are set off against long term capital losses to produce net long term capital gains or losses for the year; and likewise for net short term capital gains or losses. *Net capital gain* is what is accorded "favorable capital gains treatment." Net capital gain is net long term capital gains minus net short term capital losses.[51] For individuals, net capital gain is taxed at one half the rate at which ordinary income is taxed, limited to a maximum rate of twenty-five percent on the first $50,000 of net capital gain.[52] The corporate tax on net capital gain is limited to a maximum rate of thirty percent.[53]

Net short term gains and losses are treated as ordinary income except that net long term capital gains and losses offset net short term capital gains and losses on a dollar for dollar basis. Individuals may offset up to $1,000 of ordinary income with capital losses for taxable years before 1977, $2,000 for taxable years beginning in 1977, and $3,000 for taxable years beginning after 1977.[54]

The taxpayer who understands the capital gains rules can use them to his benefit by advance tax planning. For instance, if the taxpayer wants to sell his residence and move into an apartment, any gain realized from the sale would be long term capital gains subject to favorable treatment as net capital gain. However, a loss on the sale of a residence or other property held for personal use would not be deductible. If the sale of his residence would result

---

50. *Id.* § 1221.
51. *Id.* § 1222.
52. *Id.* § 1201(b).
53. *Id.* § 1201(a)(2).
54. *Id.* § 1211.

in a loss, the taxpayer could convert the property into business property which is not subject to the capital gains rules by renting it out and then selling. Such a loss would be an ordinary loss completely deductible from ordinary income in the year it is incurred.

Some of the complex provisions of the Internal Revenue Code applicable to taxpayers engaged in business activities allow the taxpayer more favorable treatment then do the general capital gains rules. Consequently, it is practically impossible for most taxpayers engaged in business activities to compute their tax liabilities without risking sacrifice of the benefits of these and other provisions unless they consult with accountants or attorneys who are well versed in the tax laws.

However, every taxpayer should know that there are a few ways to dispose of an appreciated capital asset without realizing taxable income. One way is to make a gift of the appreciated asset, preferably to a taxpayer in a lower tax bracket.[55] The gain on the sale will be taxed to the donee as if he had acquired the asset at the donor's cost.[56] The taxpayer could make a charitable contribution of the capital asset.[57] In many cases he would be entitled to a tax deduction for the current market value of the asset, but would not be taxed on the gain[58] (nor would the tax-exempt charity). On the other hand, if the asset has depreciated in value below cost, the donee will be treated for tax purposes as if he had acquired the asset at the market price prevailing on the date of the gift. A taxpayer cannot make a gift of a tax loss.[59] Unless the donor himself sells the asset, the tax loss will not be realized by anyone. If the taxpayer is in contemplation of death, all capital assets which have declined in value should be sold to realize the nontransferable tax losses.

(c) *Subsidiary Concepts*

Relief is provided for individuals whose income varies greatly from year to year and which subjects them to unusually high rates

---

55. There is no income because there is no "sale or exchange of an asset."
56. INT. REV. CODE § 1015(a).
57. *Id.* § 170.
58. *Id.* § 170(e). See note 55 *supra*.
59. *Id.* § 1015(a).

of tax during the peak years. If the individual's taxable income for the current year exceeds one hundred and twenty percent of the average taxable income for the previous four years (average base period income) by at least $3,000, he may be eligible for *income averaging*. No provision is available for averaging income for the current year if it is unusually low. Generally, an individual is ineligible for the benefit of this provision if he (and his spouse) furnished less than one-half of his support during any one of the years in the base period. Individuals electing this provision must forfeit the benefit of a few other provisions for the tax year of the election, most notably the fifty percent maximum rate of tax on personal service income, and the twenty-five percent maximum rate of tax on the first $50,000 of net capital gain (capital gains).[60]

Technically speaking, the *Withholding Tax* is separate and distinct from the income tax toward which it is credited. The employer who fails to collect it from his employees' wages is liable for the withholding tax if the employee subsequently fails to pay the income tax on the wages toward which it would have been credited.[61] Otherwise, failure of the employer to collect and pay the tax results in liability for a fine or penalty only.[62] The withholding tax is roughly equivalent to income tax liability calculated on the basis of exclusions claimed for dependents and the presumption that the remuneration for the payment period is representative of the employee's annual income.[63] Employees who incurred no income tax liability during the preceding taxable year and who anticipate that none will be incurred during the current tax year can request their employers not to withhold the tax from their wages.[64]

All taxpayers whose income exceeds certain amounts and whose federal income tax liability is expected to exceed withholdings by $100 are required to file an estimated income tax return and to make quarterly estimated income tax payments.[65] If withholdings

---

60. *Id.* §§ 1301-1304.
61. *Id.* § 3403.
62. *Id.* § 3402(d).
63. See generally *id.* § 3402.
64. *Id.* § 3402(n).
65. *Id.* § 6015(a).

plus estimated income tax payments constitute less than eighty percent of the tax due, penalties and interest may be assessed on the deficiency from the dates that the quarterly payments were due,[66] unless the prepaid taxes equal or exceed the tax liability for the preceding year.[67]

To prevent regular avoidance of the income tax, there is a *Minimum Tax* on items of tax preference in addition to the regular income tax liability. It is imposed at a rate of fifteen percent on items of tax preference, such as accelerated depreciation or capital gains treatment, which are in excess of $10,000 ($5,000 if married and filing separately) plus income tax liability otherwise incurred in excess of tax credits, and carryovers of prior years' income tax liability in excess of tax preference items.

The Internal Revenue Code imposes two additional taxes on corporations which are used to avoid income taxes on shareholders. An *Accumulated Earnings Tax* is imposed on unreasonable accumulations of earnings beyond the needs of the business at confiscatory rates. A confiscatory *Personal Holding Company Tax* is assessed on undistributed income of closely held corporations which receive primarily passive investment income and amounts received under contracts for the personal services of the principal shareholders.

(d) *Reference to Other Sources of Material*

The Internal Revenue Code alone is several times as long as this book. The summary treatment provided here is not intended as a detailed statement of the law, which changes frequently. Rather, its purpose is to impart to the reader a very basic understanding of the mechanics involved. The rules stated omit mention of minor exceptions or special conditions which may be relevant to the reader. The taxpayer with a tax problem will need to refer to much more intensive sources of material or, in many cases, consult a tax expert.

VIRGINIA STATE INCOME TAX

The Virginia State Income Tax incorporates the provisions of the

---

66. *Id.* §§ 6601(a), 6654, 6655.
67. *Id.* § 6654(d)(1).

Internal Revenue Code by reference.[68] Calculations are based on federal adjusted gross income (AGI) with modifications to account for several differences in coverage.[69] The amount of itemized deductions or the standard deduction or low income allowance claimed for federal income tax purposes applies for state income tax purposes as well, except that no itemized deduction is allowed for state income taxes, and except also that the state allows an itemized deduction of five times the amount allowable as a credit for federal income tax purposes for expenses for household and dependent care services necessary for gainful employment.[70] A deduction of $600 is allowed for each personal exemption claimed for federal income tax purposes, plus an additional $400 for each exemption allowed by reason of age,[71] (*i.e.,* a taxpayer over age sixty-five is entitled to exemptions amounting to $1,600, or $2,200 if blind). Virginia income is taxed pro rata to nonresidents and part-year residents.[72] Credit is given for taxes paid on out-of-state income up to the amount of the Virginia income tax.[73]

Individuals must file state income tax returns for the previous year by May first [74] with the commissioner of revenue for the city or county in which he resides or directly with the State Department of Taxation in Richmond.[75] Corporations and partnerships must file by April fifteenth or the fifteenth day of the fourth month following the close of the taxable year, with the Department of Taxation in Richmond.[76] The rates for individuals vary progressively from two to five and three-quarters percent of Virginia taxable income.[77] Corporations are taxed at a flat rate of six percent.[78] Virginia employers are required to withhold the state income tax from wages.[79]

---

68. VA. CODE § 58-151.01.
69. *Id.* § 58-151.013(a), (b), (c).
70. *Id.* § 58-151.013(d)(1), (2).
71. *Id.* § 58-151.013(d)(3).
72. *Id.* § 58-151.013(f).
73. *Id.* § 58-151.015.
74. *Id.* § 58-151.062(a).
75. *Id.* § 58-151.064(a).
76. *Id.* § 58-151.078.
77. *Id.* § 58-151.011.
78. *Id.* § 58-151.031.
79. *Id.* § 58-151.2.

An individual who reasonably expects to receive income not subject to withholdings in excess of exemptions plus $400 must file a declaration of estimated income by May first of the taxable year, unless he is a farmer or will have an estimated tax of $40 or less, in which case he must file by January fifteenth of the succeeding year.[80] Estimated state income tax payments from individuals are due in four equal installments.[81] Individuals send declarations and payments of the estimated tax to the local commissioner of revenue.[82] Corporations must file declarations of estimated taxes by the fifteenth day of the fourth month of the taxable year if the estimated tax due can reasonably be expected to exceed $1,000.[83] Declarations and payments of estimated corporate taxes are to be made to the Department of Taxation.[84]

SOCIAL SECURITY TAXES

All individuals and their employers covered by the Federal Insurance Contributions Act must pay social security taxes in 1977 on the first $16,500 of remuneration to the employee,[85] or the first $16,500 of net earnings from self-employment plus remuneration as an employee; but no tax is imposed on self-employed income if it amounts to less than $400.[86] Employers are required to deduct the taxes from wages paid,[87] and in addition to match the employees' contributions.[88] The rate of tax is 5.85 percent (through the year 1977; thereafter increasing to 6.45 percent by 2010).[89] Accordingly, the employer paying an individual $16,500 or more per year in wages must contribute $1,930.50 on his behalf, half of which is deducted from the employee's wages, and half of which is taxed to the employer. Self-employed individuals are taxed at the

---

80. *Id.* § 58-151.21(a), (e), (f), (g).
81. *Id.* § 58-151.22(a)(1), (a)(4), (b).
82. *Id.* § 58-151.24.
83. *Id.* §§ 58-151.36(a), 58-151.37, 58-151.38.
84. *Id.* § 58-151.39.
85. INT. REV. CODE § 3121(a)(1); see P-H PAYROLL GUIDE ¶ 6013.
86. INT. REV. CODE § 1402(b).
87. *Id.* § 3102.
88. *Id.* § 3111.
89. *Id.* § 3101.

rate of 7.90 percent of self-employment income,[90] with no matching of withholdings.

The Federal Insurance Contributions Act does not cover agricultural workers receiving non-cash wages or receiving cash wages of less than $150 covering less than twenty working days per year. Nor does it cover non-cash tips or cash tips amounting to less than twenty dollars in any calendar month.[91] Various other forms of employment are also exempt from coverage.[92]

Employees who work for more than one employer may have more than $965.25 deducted from their wages for social security taxes. Each employer must deduct and match a contribution up to that amount. However, the employee is entitled to a refund of any excess amount deducted from his wages. Refunds are obtained through a credit against federal income tax liability.[93]

GIFT, ESTATE, AND INHERITANCE TAXES

Both the Federal Government and the Commonwealth of Virginia tax transfers of property at death or by gift during the taxpayer's lifetime. When dealing with the estate of a decedent, it is important to remember that the estate is also subject to federal and state income taxes.

The mechanics of the *Federal Estate Tax* are similar to the income tax. A Federal Estate Tax Return must be filed for every estate with property valued at $120,000 or more. The *gross estate* is the value of everything owned by the decedent at death,[94] including the value of gifts made within three years of death,[95] transfers with possession or income reserved for the life of the decedent,[96] revocable transfers,[97] annuities,[98] and life insurance[99]

---

90. *Id.* § 1401.
91. *Id.* § 3121(a).
92. *Id.* § 3121(b).
93. *Id.* § 31(b).
94. *Id.* § 2031(a).
95. *Id.* § 2035(a).
96. *Id.* § 2036(a).
97. *Id.* § 2038.
98. *Id.* § 2039.
99. *Id.* § 2042.

in which the decedent has an interest, and interests in jointly held property unless the decedent acquired his interest in the property as a gift from the co-owner.[100] The *adjusted gross estate* (AGE) is the gross estate less funeral expenses, administrative expenses, claims against the estate, mortgages and other indebtedness in respect of property which is valued in the gross estate without reference thereto,[101] and fortuitous losses incurred during settlement which are not compensated by insurance or otherwise.[102]. From AGE, bequests for public, charitable and religious uses,[103] and transfers to a surviving spouse up to $250,000 or fifty percent of AGE, whichever is higher,[104] are deducted in determining the *taxable estate*. The rate of tax varies from eighteen to seventy percent of the taxable estate.[105] A unified credit against the estate and gift tax is allowed,[106] and credits are allowed up to certain amounts for state inheritance taxes paid,[107] for gift taxes paid on property given away by the decedent during lifetime but taxable by the Estate Tax because the gift was considered to be in contemplation of death,[108] for a portion of federal estate taxes paid on bequests to the decedent's estate by a person who died within ten years before or two years after the decedent's death,[109] and for foreign death taxes.[110]

The *Virginia Inheritance Tax* is a combination inheritance and estate tax. It covers all of the decedent's property within the jurisdiction of the Commonwealth which passes by will or intestate succession, by grant or gift conveying possession or enjoyment at or after the grantor's death, by gift made in contemplation of death, by transfer with possession or enjoyment reserved to the grantor for life, and jointly held interests in property.[111]

---

100. *Id.* § 2040.
101. *Id.* § 2053(a).
102. *Id.* § 2054.
103. *Id.* § 2055.
104. *Id.* § 2056(c)(2).
105. *Id.* § 2001.
106. *Id.* §§ 2010, 2505.
107. *Id.* § 2011.
108. *Id.* § 2012.
109. *Id.* § 2013.
110. *Id.* § 2014.
111. VA. CODE § 58-152.

With respect to all property within his control, the executor or administrator of the estate must pay the tax within nine months of the decedent's death and withhold the same from the shares of the beneficiaries.[112] With respect to property over which he has no right of control, the devisee must pay the tax directly to the Department of Taxation.[113] The tax is the greater of the credit for state inheritance taxes allowed against the federal estate tax, or the progressive state inheritance taxes based upon the relationship of the beneficiary to the deceased.[114]

Class A beneficiaries consist of spouses and all lineal ancestors and dependents of the decedent. Bequests to Class A beneficiaries are exempt up to $5,000 and are taxed at rates varying from one to five percent. Brothers, sisters, nephews, and nieces constitute Class B beneficiaries. Bequests to them are subject to a $2,000 exemption and are taxed at rates varying from two to ten percent. All other beneficiaries are in Class C. The first $1,000 of bequests by the decedent to any Class C beneficiary is exempt, and the balance is taxed at rates varying from three to fifteen percent.[115] Bequests to charities are exempt.[116]

The *Federal Gift Tax* is imposed upon the donor. The tax is calculated on a quarterly basis by figuring the tax on all gifts made since 1932 and deducting the tax which would be due under the same schedule on gifts for all previous periods.[117] Thus, if the taxpayer makes a $1,000 gift during the current quarter, having previously made $1,000,000 in taxable gifts, he will incur a gift tax liability at the rate of forty-one percent of the $1,000 gift. The first $3,000 of gifts to any donee during the calendar year are excluded from taxable gifts.[118] A gift by one spouse to a third party may be treated as having been made one-half by him and one-half by his spouse if both spouses consent.[119] There is a Unified Credit

---

112. *Id.* §§ 58-159, 58-166, 58-176.
113. *Id.* §§ 58-160, 58-161.
114. *Id.* § 58-162.
115. *Id.* § 58-153.
116. *Id.* § 58-154.
117. INT. REV. CODE § 2502.
118. *Id.* § 2503(b).
119. *Id.* § 2513.

applicable against federal estate and gift taxes. The $30,000 credit in effect in 1977 is equivalent to a $120,666 exemption. The credit will increase each year until it reaches $47,000 (the equivalent of a $175,625 exemption) in 1981.[120] In addition, gifts to charities and the like,[121] and the greater amount of $100,000 or fifty percent of the value of gifts to one's spouse [122] are deducted from taxable gifts. Married couples may make joint gifts of up to $6,000 per year to each donee without using their Unified Credits or incurring any tax liability. Consequently very few taxpayers incur gift tax liability.

The *Virginia Gift Tax* is computed in an entirely different manner. The tax is imposed on an annual,[123] rather than an aggregate, sum of gifts to one donee. The tax is imposed on the donor using the same rates and exemptions as the state inheritance tax.[124] Any person liable for the payment of the state gift tax must file a return with the Department of Taxation in Richmond and pay the tax due by May first following the calendar year of such gifts. Any person required to file a federal gift tax return is required to report the results of the final audit thereof within ninety days of receipt to the Department of Taxation.[125]

SALES AND USE TAX

The Commonwealth of Virginia imposes a three percent tax on sales and use of most personal property within the state.[126] Most local governments impose an additional one percent sales and use tax.[127] The sales tax is imposed on retail sales, including rentals, and the services of fabricating tangible personal property and furnishing, preparing, or serving tangible personal property consumed on the merchant's premises.[128] Excluded from coverage

---

120. *Id.* §§ 2010, 2505.
121. *Id.* § 2522.
122. *Id.* § 2523.
123. See P-H EST. PLAN. (Va.) ¶ 4004, n.1.
124. VA. CODE §§ 58-219, 58-220.
125. *Id.* §§ 58-223, 58-238.
126. *Id.* § 58-441.4.
127. *Id.* §§ 58-441.49, 58-441.49.1.
128. *Id.* § 58-441.2(b).

are inconsequential sales without separate charge involved in professional, insurance, or personal service transactions; agricultural supplies purchased by farmers; motor vehicles and trailers (which are subject to the two or three percent Motor Vehicle Sales and Use Tax);[129] motor vehicle fuels; gas, electricity, or water delivered to consumers through mains, lines or pipes; newspapers delivered to consumers; school lunches subsidized by the government and textbooks sold by educational institutions for use of their students; occasional sales; alcholic beverages sold in government stores; sales to certain businesses and governmental units; sales of goods for use outside the state; and medicines and medical supplies dispensed by prescription.[130] The use tax is imposed on goods purchased in other states and brought into Virginia for use.[131] A credit is allowed for sales and use taxes paid in other states on the same article.[132] The use tax does not apply to nonresident taxpayers who move into the state to establish a *permanent* residence or business and who bring into the state personal property acquired at least six months previous thereto for use out-of-state.[133] The state collects the tax from dealers [134] who *must* state it separately and pass it along to customers.[135] Dealers are allowed a "discount" of three percent of the state tax due in return for collection of the state sales tax.[136] The purpose of the dual sales and use tax system is to prevent the avoidance of the sales tax by means of purchases from out-of-state merchants and to place nonresidents doing business in Virginia on an equal footing with local businessmen.

PROPERTY TAXES

(a) *Generally*

Property taxes are distinguished from most other taxes by their

---

129. *Id.* §§ 58-441.6(f), 58-685.10 et seq.
130. *Id.* § 58-441.6.
131. *Id.* § 58-441.9.
132. *Id.* § 58-441.8.
133. *Id.* § 58-441.10.
134. *Id.* § 58-441.12.
135. *Id.* §§ 58-441.18, 58-441.19.
136. *Id.* § 58-441.25.

tax base. Property taxes are based upon the ownership of property rather than upon specific transactions or special privileges. Virginia's Constitution reserves real estate and tangible personal property for local taxation only.[137] These constitute the prime revenue sources of city and county governments in Virginia.[138] Intangible personal property is taxed by the state government only,[139] except merchants' capital which is only taxed locally.[140] The property of various civic and religious organizations is exempted from taxation by statute.[141]

(b) *Real Estate Taxes*

Real estate is reassessed for tax purposes every few years. Intermittent adjustments are made for new grants, improvements, and easements.[142] Landowners must be notified of any changes in assessment and of the time and place to present objections thereto.[143] If no general assessment is made within four years, the owner of overassessed real estate may seek judicial relief.[144]

Local governments *may* exempt or defer taxes on the principal residence of certain elderly persons. The property must consist of a residence owned and occupied by a person over age sixty-five. The combined income of all of the owners and their relatives living therein may not exceed $10,000, excluding the first $4,000 of the income of each of the owner's relatives living there other than the owner's spouse. The net worth of the owners and their spouses may not exceed $35,000 excluding the exempted residence and adjoining lot up to one acre.[145]

Local governments with land use plans *may* adopt ordinances providing that property used for agricultural, horticultural, forest, or open-space purposes may be assessed on the basis of its value

---

137. VA. CONST. art. X, § 4.
138. William H. Sager, *Property Classification for Taxation*, 43 VA. L. REV. 1325 (1957).
139. VA. CODE §§ 58-405, 58-441, 58-830.
140. *Id.* §§ 58-9, 58-10, 58-420.
141. *Id.* § 58-12 et seq.
142. *Id.* § 58-763.
143. *Id.* § 58-792.01.
144. *Id.* §§ 58-764, 58-774.1.
145. *Id.* § 58-760.1(a), (b).

for such use. Property so taxed is assessed by both methods; and if it is ever converted to a nonqualifying use, the balance of the back taxes assessed on the fair market value becomes due.[146]

(c) *Tangible Personal Property*

Tangible personal property is taxed locally.[147] The chief items subject to the tax are mobile homes,[148] motor vehicles and trailers, airplanes, boats, and commercial and agricultural property.[149] The assessments are made by the local commissioners of revenue, based partially upon Personal Property Tax Returns which are due on May first[150] or as otherwise provided by local ordinance.[151] Local commissioners of revenue have access to local automobile registrations. They may also require operators of apartment houses, trailer camps and parks, marinas and boat storage facilities, and airports to supply lists of tenants[152] to assist them in identifying taxable personal property. Generally property tax assessments are based on property held within the Commonwealth as of January first of the tax year.[153] However, any local government may opt to base its assessments on property held as of July first.[154]

(d) *Intangible Personal Property*

Shares of bank stock, monied capital in competition with banks, and capital of a trade or business are taxed as intangible personal property.[155] These items of property are taxed only by the Commonwealth, except merchants' capital which is taxed only by local governments.[156]

Merchants' capital consists of inventory of stock on hand, the excess of accounts receivable over accounts payable, and other

---

146. *Id.* §§ 58-769.4 to 58-769.10.
147. *Id.* § 58-829.
148. *Id.* § 58-829.3.
149. P-H STATE & LOCAL TAXES (Va.) ¶ 31,280.
150. VA. CODE § 58-837.
151. *Id.* § 58-847.
152. *Id.* §§ 58-863, 58-863.1.
153. *Id.* § 58-835.
154. *Id.* § 58-847.
155. *Id.* §§ 58-410, 58-420, 58-465, 58-485.
156. *Id.* §§ 58-9, 58-10, 58-832.

intangibles.[157] Note that inventories, which are in fact tangible property, are included with intangible personal property for purposes of taxation.[158] The tax on capital is thirty cents per hundred dollars of *actual value*.[159] Property is assessed as of January first, unless the taxpayer elects to have his assessments based on the average value of property held on January first and the preceding August first.[160] Intangible personal property tax returns and tax payments are due May first at the place where the taxpayer files his state income tax return.[161]

Banks and competing institutions [162] are taxed on the value of the shares of their corporate stock outstanding [163] as of January first.[164] The tax is levied against shareholders, but payable by the institution out of shareholders' funds.[165] The tax on bank stock is one dollar per hundred dollars of the stock's value,[166] which excludes the assessed value of real estate.[167] Returns are due March first [168] and the tax is payable on or before June first.[169]

(e) *Liability of Taxpayer for Taxes*

The taxpayer is personally liable for all property taxes assessed against him.[170] Alternatively, personal property belonging to the taxpayer or the estate may be seized and sold for payment of delinquent taxes on any property.[171] When taxes on real estate are delinquent on December thirty-first following the third anniversary of the due date, the real estate may be sold to collect all delinquent taxes on said property. Published notice of judicial

---

157. *Id.* §§ 58-411 (trade or business), 58-833 (merchants' capital).
158. See *id.* § 58-412.
159. *Id.* § 58-418.
160. *Id.* § 58-423.
161. *Id.* §§ 58-424, 58-429, 58-432, 58-441.
162. *Id.* § 58-420.
163. *Id.* § 58-471.
164. *Id.* § 58-470.
165. *Id.* § 58-480.
166. *Id.* § 58-473.
167. *Id.* § 58-471.
168. *Id.* § 58-470.
169. *Id.* § 58-480.
170. *Id.* § 58-1014.
171. *Id.* § 58-1001.

sale in a newspaper of general circulation is required thirty to sixty days prior to judicial sale.[172] The owner may redeem his property prior to the judicial sale by payment of taxes, penalties, interest, costs of publication of notice, and attorney's fees into court.[173]

TAX PLANNING

Tax planning for the purposes of minimizing liability will focus primarily on the income, gift, and estate taxes. Yet the prospective employer needs to consider the costs of payroll taxes in calculating the cost of labor. And the prospective businessman must consider property and other taxes affecting his business in evaluating the probability of success. A more extensive list of federal, state and local taxes affecting the Virginia taxpayer is provided in graphic form in the appendix which follows.

---

172. *Id.* § 58-1117.1.
173. *Id.* § 58-1117.10.

APPENDIX

Federal Taxes
Federal Income Taxes, *see* pp. 85-95.
Accumulated Earnings Tax, *see* p. 95.
Personal Holding Company Tax, *see* p. 95.
Estate and Gift Taxes, *see* pp. 98-101.
Social Security Taxes (FICA), *see* p. 97-98.
Railroad Retirement Tax [174]
Federal Unemployment Tax [175]
Tax on Transfers to Avoid Income Tax [176]
Withholding Taxes, *see* pp. 94-95.
Estimated Income Tax, *see* pp. 85, 86, 94-95.
Minimum Tax, *see* p. 95.
Excise Taxes:
    Special Fuels [177]
    Motor Vehicles and Parts [178]
    Tires and Tubes [179]
    Petroleum Products [180]
    Lubricating Oil [181]
    Sporting Goods [182]
    Firearms [183]
    Communications Facilities (telephone service) [184]
    Transportation by Air [185]
    Foreign Insurance Policies [186]
    Wagering [187]

---

174. INT. REV. CODE §§ 3201-3233.
175. *Id.* §§ 3301-3310.
176. *Id.* § 1491.
177. *Id.* § 4041.
178. *Id.* §§ 4061-4063.
179. *Id.* §§ 4071-4073.
180. *Id.* §§ 4081-4084.
181. *Id.* §§ 4091-4094.
182. *Id.* § 4161.
183. *Id.* §§ 4181-4182.
184. *Id.* §§ 4251-4254.
185. *Id.* §§ 4261-4282.
186. *Id.* §§ 4371-4375.
187. *Id.* §§ 4401-4414.

Occupation Tax on Coin-Operated Gaming Machines [188]
Tax on Use of Certain Vehicles (trucks) [189]
Tax on Use of Civil Aircraft [190]
Oleomargarine [191]
White Phosphorus Matches [192]
Adulterated Butter and Filled Cheese [193]
Cotton Futures [194]
Interest Equalization Tax [195]
Certain Activities of Private Foundations [196]
Alcohol [197]
Tobacco [198]
Machine Guns and Firearms [199]

State and Local Taxes
State Income Taxes, *see* pp. 95-97.
Sales and Use Taxes, *see* pp. 101-102.
Motor Vehicle Sales and Use Tax [200]
Property Taxes, *see* pp. 102-106.
Inheritance Tax, *see* pp. 99-100.
Gift Tax, *see* p. 101.
Estimated Income Tax (credited toward income tax) [201]
Withholding Tax (credited toward income tax) [202]
Unemployment Insurance Tax [203]
County Capitation Tax (optional) [204]

---

188. *Id.* §§ 4461-4464.
189. *Id.* §§ 4481-4484.
190. *Id.* §§ 4491-4494.
191. *Id.* §§ 4591-4597.
192. *Id.* §§ 4801-4806.
193. *Id.* §§ 4811-4846.
194. *Id.* §§ 4851-4877.
195. *Id.* §§ 4911-4931.
196. *Id.* §§ 4940-4948.
197. *Id.* §§ 5001-5691.
198. *Id.* §§ 5701-5763.
199. *Id.* §§ 5801-5871.
200. VA. CODE §§ 58-685.10 to 58-685.25.
201. *Id.* §§ 58-151.21 to 58-151.28.
202. *Id.* §§ 58-151.1 to 58-151.20.
203. P-H PAYROLL TAXES ¶ 8000.
204. VA. CODE § 58-851.1.

TAXES: APPENDIX   109

Recordation Tax (deeds) [205]
Tax on Wills and Administration [206]
Writ Taxes [207]
Corporate Charter, Registration, Entrance, and Franchise Taxes [208]
Local Telephone Service Tax [209]
Local Utility Tax [210]
Tobacco Products Tax [211]
Severance Tax (minerals) [212]
Building Permits [213]
Motor Fuels Tax [214]
Forest Products Tax [215]
Occupation and Privilege Taxes: Architects, Attorneys, Auctioneers, Bondsmen, Bowling Alleys, Savings and Loan Associations, Collection Agencies, Dentists, Dry Cleaners and Laundries, Engineers, Fortune-Tellers, Garages, Horse and Mule Sales by Nonresidents, Hotels and Lodging Houses, Itinerant Vendors and Auctioneers, Shows and Sales of Nonprofit Organizations, Junk Dealers, Labor and Emigrant Agents, Medical Doctors, Mercantile Agencies, Merchants on Trains, Patent Medicine Salesmen, Pawnbrokers, Photographers, Pistol Dealers, Police and Firemen's Associations, Pool Halls, Pulpwood Suppliers, Real Estate Brokers, Coin-Operated and Vending Machines, Small Business Investment Companies, Soft Drink Manufacturers, Storage and Impounding Companies, Tobacco Dealers, Undertakers, Veterinarians, Livestock Dealers.[216]

---

205. *Id.* §§ 58-54 to 58-65.1.
206. *Id.* §§ 58-66 to 58-70.
207. *Id.* §§ 58-71 to 58-76.
208. *Id.* §§ 58-442 to 58-464.
209. *Id.* § 58-587.1.
210. *Id.* § 58-617.2.
211. *Id.* §§ 58-757.1 to 58-757.28.
212. *Id.* § 58-774.
213. *Id.* §§ 58-766, 58-766.1.
214. P-H STATE & LOCAL TAXES (Va.) p. 202.
215. *Id.*
216. VA. CODE §§ 58-239 to 58-404.01.

Insurance Company License Tax [217]
Public Service Corporations Franchise and License Taxes (regulated industries) [218]
License Taxes
    Amusements [219]
    Auctioneers [220]
    Brokers, Commission Merchants, etc.[221]
    Contractors [222]
    Peddlers [223]
    Trading Stamp Suppliers [224]
    Slot Machines [225]

---

217. *Id.* §§ 58-486 to 58-502.10.
218. *Id.* §§ 58-503 to 58-685.
219. *Id.* §§ 58-268 to 58-284.2.
220. *Id.* §§ 58-286 to 58-289.
221. *Id.* §§ 58-290 to 58-296.
222. *Id.* §§ 58-297 to 58-303.1.
223. *Id.* §§ 58-340 to 58-354.
224. *Id.* §§ 58-354.1 to 58-354.7.
225. *Id.* §§ 58-355 to 58-369.1.

CHAPTER 7

Wills: Distributing Property at Death

K. A. Emden

IN GENERAL

Modern American rules governing the transfer of private wealth after death have their origin in the early English law. The disposition of land was within the jurisdiction of the common law courts and was governed by their rules. Canon law and church courts were utilized to distribute the personal property of the deceased. If a man died intestate (without a will), his land was taken by his eldest son and his personal property divided equally among all of his children;[1] his widow was also entitled to a share of the land; she received a dower interest in one-third of her husband's real property for the duration of her life.[2]

Wills were used extensively by the English middle class. Great statutes such as the Statute of Wills (1540) were enacted to regulate their use. The formal will had to be signed by the deceased and attested by witnesses. Oral wills were less widely used.[3] Probate of wills was administered by the ecclesiastical courts.[4]

The structure which evolved under the English legal system provides a point of departure for the analysis of modern Virginia rules regulating the transfer of property after death. It is the purpose of this chapter to outline and define the current status of intestate succession, wills, and estate administration (probate) with reference to the applicable Virginia Code provisions.

INTESTATE SUCCESSION (What Happens If One Does Not Make a Will)

The law of intestate succession is governed primarily by statutes. These statutes are utilized when an individual fails to execute a will, when his will directs that his property be passed *via*

---
1. L.M. FRIEDMAN, A HISTORY OF AMERICAN LAW 57 (1973).
2. *Id.* at 59.
3. *Id.* at 58.
4. *Id.* at 48.

the intestate succession laws, or when his will is ineffective to pass all or part of his property and the state courts must resort to the statutes to properly dispose of his estate.

The Statute of Descent was originally written by Thomas Jefferson and became law in 1785; it displaced the system of primogeniture [5] (whereby the eldest son inherited all real property). The statute has been amended many times since its original enactment and currently sets up an order in which real estate passes to heirs after a person dies intestate. (It is important to note that the law in effect at the time of the intestate's death is the law which governs the passage of his property.) The order of inheritance dictated by the present statute is (1) to the children of the intestate and any descendants of such children subject to any dower or curtesy interest of the surviving spouse of the intestate; if there be no child, nor descendent of any child, (2) to the intestate's surviving spouse; if none, (3) to the intestate's father and mother or the survivor; if none, (4) to brothers and sisters, and their descendants; if none, (5) one-half to the nearest maternal relatives and one-half to the nearest paternal relatives of the intestate in the following order: (a) grandfather and grandmother or the survivor, (b) aunts and uncles, and their descendants, (c) great-grandparents, (d) brothers and sisters of grandparents, and their descendants. If there are neither maternal nor paternal relatives of the intestate, then the relatives of the intestate's spouse would be entitled to the property in the same order as shown in number five above.[6]

The Statute of Distributions [7] plans the way in which personal property is passed to the distributees. If the spouse of an individual survives him, and he had no children, then the surviving spouse is entitled to all of the personal property remaining after the payment of funeral expenses, administration charges and debts. If the intestate had any children, whether illegitimate (if the intestate was a female), by adoption, by marriage to the surviving spouse, or from a previous marriage, these children are entitled to

---

5. *Id.* at 58.
6. VA. CODE § 64.1-1; Newton v. Newton, 199 Va. 785, 102 S.E.2d 312 (1958).
7. VA. CODE § 64.1-11.

two-thirds of the personal property and the surviving spouse is entitled to only one-third after payment of funeral expenses, administration expenses and debts. Otherwise, personal property is distributed in the same proportions and to the same persons in the same order as real estate descends (the Statute of Descent above).[8]

At common law there was no procedure for the adoption of children; the concept is purely statutory. Therefore, at common law a child always inherited from his natural parents. The Virginia statute treats a child, once adopted, as the natural child of his adoptive parents when the adoptive parents die intestate, and also when there is a will except where the will specifies that "issue" inherit.[9] An exception to this rule occurs where the natural parents are living and divorced, one remarries, and the step-parent adopts the child. Here the adopted child is considered to be the natural child of his natural parents and the natural child of his adoptive parents for the purposes of inheritance; he inherits from both his natural parents and his adoptive parents.[10]

An adopted child is also treated as the natural child of his adoptive parents when he dies intestate. If he has no children who survive him, his property passes as if he were the natural child of the adopting parents.[11] If the adopted child has a spouse who survives him, the spouse or any person in a prior class would be entitled to all of his real property and personal property.[12]

Virginia will normally recognize the validity of an adoption proceeding in another state, but will not treat as valid such proceedings in a foreign country where they are conducted in a manner considered to be contrary to Virginia public policy.[13]

Illegitimate children could not inherit from their natural parents or other ancestors at common law. The present rule in Virginia is that a child who is born illegitimately inherits only from his natural

---

8. Newton v. Newton, 199 Va. 785, 102 S.E.2d 312 (1958).
9. VA. CODE § 63.1-234.
10. *Id.*
11. *Id.*
12. *Id.* §§ 64.1-1, 64.1-11.
13. Doulgeris v. Bambacus, 203 Va. 670, 127 S.E.2d 145 (1962).

mother [14] unless the natural father marries the natural mother and acknowledges that the child is his own either prior to or after the marriage.[15] If the natural father fulfills these requirements, then the child inherits from his natural father as well as from the natural mother.

The heirs and distributees of an illegitimate child include his children, his spouse, his natural mother and his maternal relatives.[16] The natural father and the paternal relatives would not be his heirs or distributees unless the child is legitimized. Therefore, if the child is deemed legitimate at his death, there is inheritance to the natural father.

Children who are born of a void marriage or of one which is annulled by judicial action are considered to be legitimate,[17] including children born of a common law or bigamous marriage.[18] There is a strong presumption of legitimacy if at the time of a child's birth the natural mother is married. It is presumed that such a child is the child of the husband.[19] Children born to a married woman who are conceived by artificial insemination performed by a properly licensed physician at the request and with the consent in writing of the mother and her husband are considered to be legitimate.[20] Posthumous children of an intestate inherit from him if they are born within ten months of the intestate's death.[21]

Persons descended from common ancestors are relatives of the whole blood; persons descended from only one common ancestor are relatives of the half blood. Half blood relatives could not inherit land at common law. The Virginia rule is that half blood relatives inherit half as much as the whole blood relatives.[22] For example, if the intestate had the following relatives — John, a whole blood relative, Mary, a whole blood relative, and Sam, a half blood

---

14. VA. CODE § 64.1-5.
15. Hoover v. Hoover, 131 Va. 522, 109 S.E. 424 (1921); VA. CODE § 64.1-6.
16. Fitchett v. Smith, 78 Va. 524 (1884).
17. VA. CODE § 64.1-7.
18. McClaugherty v. McClaugherty, 180 Va. 51, 21 S.E.2d 761 (1942).
19. VERNIER, AMERICAN FAMILY LAWS 241 (1936).
20. VA. CODE § 64.1-7.1.
21. *Id.* § 64.1-8.
22. *Id.* § 64.1-2.

relative — John would get two-fifths of the intestate's estate, Mary would get two-fifths of the estate and Sam would get one-fifth of the estate.

The concept of representation (taking *per stirpes* or by stocks) and inheritance *per capita* are utilized in the intestate statutes. Representation is generally defined to provide that the children of the deceased children of an intestate inherit as representatives of their deceased ancestors.[23] To determine the number of representative shares, count those relatives who are living and those relatives who have predeceased the intestate but who are survived by living relatives. *Per capita* distribution requires that the total number of takers be counted and each receive an equal fractional share of the whole.[24] Virginia requires that if the takers are in the same degree of kindred to the deceased they take equally; if they are in different degrees of kindred to the intestate they take the fractional shares that their deceased parents would have taken.[25]

An advancement is defined as "... an irrevocable gift *in praesenti* of money or property, real or personal, to a child by a parent to enable the donee (child) to anticipate his inheritance to the extent of the gift ...."[26] The doctrine is based on the presumption that a parent who dies intestate intends equality among his children in the division of his property. In Virginia when a person has received such a gift, he must put the gift into hotchpot if he wishes to share in the remainder of the intestate's estate.[27] For example, if an advancement of $5,000 was made to one of the intestate's children, and the intestate has two other children, if he leaves an estate of $19,000, the child who received the $5,000 would be required to put his money into the hotchpot bringing the total to $24,000. Each child would then receive $8,000. If the child who received the gift refused to put his gift into hotchpot, he would be barred from receiving a share of the intestate's estate. The child

---

23. Vashon v. Vashon, 98 Va. 170, 35 S.E. 457 (1900).
24. *Id.*
25. VA. CODE § 64.1-3.
26. Nobles v. Davenport, 183 N.C. 207, 209, 111 S.E. 180, 181 (1922).
27. VA. CODE § 64.1-17.

116 LAYMAN'S GUIDE TO VIRGINIA LAW

is only required to bring the advancement into hotchpot if he wishes to share in intestate property.

Specific offense or acts may prevent an individual from taking an intestate share of an estate. A person who is convicted of the murder of the intestate is barred from taking by life insurance, by will and by intestacy.[28] When the intestate's spouse deserts him, such spouse forfeits her share in the intestate's estate unless they reconcile and live together prior to the intestate's death.[29]

WILLS (The Exercise of the Right to Decide Where One's Property Will Go and How to Accomplish the Distribution)

The individual who wishes personally to plan for the disposition of his property makes a will. A will is of no legal consequence until the testator is dead. Several technical terms are normally used with reference to wills and will provisions. The following definitions will aid the reader's understanding of the material which follows: A *devise* is a disposition of real property by will; the person who receives the devise is called a *devisee*. A *legacy* is a disposition of cash by will; the person who receives the legacy is the *legatee*. A *bequest* is any other disposition of personal property by will including cash. An *attested will* is one that complies with all of the requisite state formalities including witnesses who subscribe to it. A *codicil* is an instrument which amends or supplements the will. *Probate* is the procedure whereby it is judicially proven that a will is valid. A *residuary clause* disposes of any property which remains in the estate after all bequests, devises, and legacies have been satisfied.[30]

There are several requirements for executing an effective will: the testator must have testamentary capacity and testamentary intent, and must comply with certain formalities prescribed by law.

Testamentary capacity is determined at the time the will is executed and not at the time of the death of the testator. The test of mental capacity which must be present at the time of

---

28. *Id.* § 64.1-18.
29. *Id.* § 64.1-23; Eyber v. Dominion Nat'l Bank, 249 F. Supp. 531 (W.D. Va. 1966).
30. Sanborn v. Sanborn, 14 N.J. Misc. 260, 184 A. 400, 402 (1936).

execution [31] involves two elements: a fourfold test of intellectual capacity and a test of mental capacity without intellectual capacity known as the insane delusion test. The test of intellectual capacity is a test of capacity only, not a test of what one knows. This test consists of the following elements: the testator's capacity to recollect his property; the testator's capacity to recollect the natural objects of his bounty and their claims upon him; the testator's capacity to know the business he is about; and the testator's capacity to interrelate the previous elements.[32] The insane delusion test determines whether the testator began his deductive reasoning process from something which was grounded in fact and was not a figment of his imagination.[33] If a will provision is shown to be the product of an insane delusion, the provision will be disqualified. Another requirement of testamentary capacity is that the testator must be eighteen or older when he signs the will.[34]

Testamentary intent is defined as the testator's intent to have his property pass at his death or the intent to direct distribution to be made at death (as opposed to a transfer during his lifetime); this intent must be found within the four corners of the will.[35] The intent to make a will can be vitiated in several situations when it is shown that the making of the will was not in fact the act intended by the testator. Such factors include undue influence upon the testator, fraud in the inducement or the factum, and mistake in the factum; the will can be invalidated if these factors are present.

Undue influence involves the subordination of the testator's intent to the intent of a dominant person. When undue influence upon the testator is shown, those will provisions which were the result of such influence will be invalidated. In order to show undue influence, the following factors must have been present at the time of the execution of the will: a testator who has the propensity to

---

31. VA. CODE § 64.1-47.
32. Tucker v. Sandidge, 85 Va. 546, 8 S.E. 650 (1888).
33. Eason v. Eason, 203 Va. 246, 123 S.E.2d 361 (1962).
34. VA. CODE § 64.1-47.
35. First Church of Christ, Scientist v. Hutchings, 209 Va. 158, 168 S.E.2d 178 (1968).

be dominated, a person who is capable of dominating the testator (anyone who is in a confidential relationship with the testator is considered to be capable of dominating), some activity on the part of the dominant person aimed at making the testator act according to the dominant person's wishes, and a will provision which results from such activity which is in favor of the dominant party or a natural object of the dominant party's bounty which is greater than such person would have gotten under the intestate statutes. If there is competent intervening advice given to the testator prior to the execution of the will, then the claim of undue influence may be defeated.

Mistake in the factum refers to a mistake concerning the nature of the instrument or its contents. When this is shown, the mistaken provision may be deleted. If the mistake involves the identity of the entire will, then the entire will fails. If a fraudulent misrepresentation induces the testator to include a particular provision in his will, or the misrepresentation relates to the entire will, the provision or the whole will can be invalidated.

Fraud and mistake in the inducement occur when the testator executes a will or includes a provision in the will based upon his belief that certain facts are true when they are not. For example, suppose a testator decides to leave $10,000 to his son. He later has reason to believe that his son has been killed, and therefore writes a codicil which revokes the $10,000 gift. The son is not in fact dead. If such a provision were induced by fraud, it should be invalidated; a provision included due to mistake can be corrected if it is obvious from the provision what the testator would have done had he been aware of the true facts.

The third requirement of executing an effective will is compliance with certain statutory formalities. Three types of wills are permitted under the Virginia statutes: attested wills, holographic wills, and soldiers' and sailors' wills. An attested will requires the presence of witnesses at the signing of the testator. A holographic will is one entirely in the handwriting of the testator; it does not require the presence of attesting witnesses, but the testator's handwriting must be identified by two witnesses.[36] A soldier's and sailor's will is an oral will which can, under certain circumstances, dispose only of personal property.[37]

The formal requirement of a writing may be satisfied by some type of permanent recording for an attested will, and by a writing entirely in the handwriting of the testator and proved as the testator's handwriting by two witnesses for a holographic will. Since the soldier's and sailor's will is an oral will, the requirement of a writing is inapplicable.

Holographic wills must be signed by the testator. An attested will can be signed by the testator himself or by his proxy. A proxy signature must meet two tests: the signature must be made in the presence of the testator, and must be made at his direction.[38] A signature as such is not an absolute requirement of an attested will: the testator's mark or stamp can be a signature if the testator intends it to be his signature. The testator's signature must be made in a "manner as to make it manifest that the name is intended as a signature."[39] The signature may appear anywhere on an attested will[40] but must be signed at the logical end of a holographic will to demonstrate the finality of the testator's intent.[41]

Attestation of witnesses is required for nonholographic wills. Two witnesses[42] who are competent must attest. Competency for attestation requires that the witnesses be able to testify to the facts of the will's execution.[43] An attestation clause is often inserted for this purpose; it recites all of the formal steps that were

---

36. VA. CODE § 64.1-49.
37. *Id.* § 64.1-53.
38. Chappell v. Trent, 90 Va. 849, 19 S.E. 314 (1893).
39. Meany v. Priddy, 127 Va. 84, 102 S.E. 470 (1920).
40. Murguiondo v. Nowlan, 115 Va. 160, 78 S.E. 600 (1913); Presbyterian Orphans' Home v. Bowman, 165 Va. 484, 182 S.E. 551 (1935).
41. Perkins v. Jones, 84 Va. 358, 4 S.E. 833 (1888); Warwick v. Warwick, 86 Va. 596, 10 S.E. 843 (1890); Dinning v. Dinning, 102 Va. 467, 46 S.E. 473 (1904); Hamlet v. Hamlet, 183 Va. 453, 32 S.E.2d 729 (1945); McElroy v. Rolston, 184 Va. 77, 34 S.E.2d 241 (1945).
42. Ferguson v. Ferguson, 187 Va. 581, 47 S.E.2d 346 (1948); French v. Beville, 191 Va. 842, 62 S.E.2d 883 (1951).
43. Ferguson v. Ferguson, 187 Va. 581, 47 S.E.2d 346 (1948).

taken in executing the will and is presumed correct. Competent witnesses include the testator's spouse, the executor appointed by the will, or a trustee appointed by the will,[44] as well as disinterested parties.

A testator must sign or acknowledge the will in the presence of the two witnesses although the witnesses may sign the will at separate times.[45] Each witness must, however, sign the will while in the presence of the testator.[46]

There are three methods by which a will may be revoked: by a physical act to the will,[47] by a subsequent instrument,[48] or partially by a divorce *a vinculo matrimonii* (since 1968).[49]

To revoke a will by a physical act, the testator or someone in his presence and at his direction must do one of the following: cut, tear, burn, obliterate, cancel or destroy the will itself, or the signature of the testator, with the intent to revoke the will.[50] When a will cannot be found at the testator's death but can be traced to his possession prior to his death, it is presumed that the testator destroyed the will with the intent to revoke it; if a will is found in the testator's possession after his death and it is defaced or mutilated, it is presumed that the testator intended to revoke it.[51]

A will may be revoked by a subsequent instrument which expressly states that the testator intends the revocation of his prior will; a will may be revoked by an instrument subsequent to the will which contains provisions which are inconsistent with the will provisions. Such instrument must meet the formal requirements previously outlined.[52]

If the testator is divorced after making his will, the provisions

---

44. VA. CODE § 64.1-51.
45. Parramore v. Taylor, 52 Va. (11 Gratt.) 220 (1854).
46. Chappell v. Trent, 90 Va. 849, 19 S.E. 314 (1893).
47. VA. CODE § 64.1-58.
48. *Id.*
49. *Id.* § 64.1-59.
50. *Id.* § 64.1-58.
51. Ballard v. Cox, 191 Va. 654, 62 S.E.2d 1 (1950); Franklin v. McLean, 192 Va. 684, 66 S.E.2d 504 (1951); Sheltering Arms Hosp. v. First & Merchants Bank, 199 Va. 524, 100 S.E.2d 721 (1957).
52. VA. CODE § 64.1-58; Bradshaw v. Bangley, 194 Va. 794, 75 S.E.2d 609 (1953).

in the will made in favor of his divorced spouse are automatically revoked.

One may wish to revive or republish his will after he has revoked it. This cannot be accomplished by a revocation of the revoking instrument.[53] Rather, the testator is required to either reexecute his will or republish it by a codicil.[54] To republish by codicil, the codicil has to identify the will in question and must show that the testator considered the will to be in effect at the time the codicil is made. A nonholographic attested will may be republished by a holographic codicil.[55] Such a revived or republished will is considered to have been made at the time that it is reexecuted or republished.[56]

A person who is provided for in a will may die before the will is executed or he may die before the testator's death; this situation is referred to as a lapse. When this occurs, the children of the person so named take the estate devised or bequeathed, unless the will itself directs a different disposition.[57]

Pretermitted heirs are children who are born to the testator after the execution of his will. There are two situations in which a pretermitted heir is affected by the will. The first occurs when there is another child of the testator who is alive at the time of the execution of the will and who has a provision made in his favor in that will. If a child born after the will's execution has neither been provided for by the will nor excluded by it, and the parent has not in his lifetime provided for such child, then the afterborn child may claim a share of the deceased parent's estate. This share would be limited to the lesser of the following amounts: what he would have been entitled to if the parent had died intestate or the value of the provision made in favor of the living child. If there is more than one child living and provided for, then the pretermitted heir may claim the value of the largest amount given to any one child.[58] The

---

53. Timberlake v. State-Planters Bank of Commerce & Trust, 201 Va. 950, 115 S.E.2d 39 (1960).
54. VA. CODE § 64.1-60.
55. *Id.*
56. *Id.* § 64.1-72.
57. *Id.* § 64.1-64.
58. *Id.* § 64.1-71.

second situation occurs when no other child was living when the will was executed. The afterborn child can take an intestate share as long as he was not mentioned or provided for in the will.[59]

There are several interests which a spouse surviving the testator may have in the property of the deceased spouse in addition to or in lieu of will provisions in the surviving spouse's favor. These interests of the surviving spouse can be classified in eight categories: (1) The spouse may be an heir to all real property if the testator had no children or if there are no living descendants of any children which he may have had; [60] (2) the spouse may be entitled to all of the deceased testator's personal property if he had no children or if there are no living descendants of his children; if there are such children or their living descendants, the surviving spouse is entitled to a one-third share of the personal property; [61] (3) the spouse may be entitled to one-third of the real estate in fee simple in the form of a dower or a curtesy interest; [62] (4) the spouse may be entitled to interests granted under homestead and other exemption laws; [63] (5) the spouse may be entitled to a forced share; [64] (6) the spouse may obtain title to the family automobile; [65] (7) the spouse may obtain the contents of joint bank accounts and of certain savings accounts in the deceased's name; [66] (8) the spouse may be entitled to money owed the deceased by the State, the United States, or his employer, and certain small amounts of stock owned by the deceased.[67]

At common law neither spouse was an heir; neither had a claim to intestate realty except through dower or curtesy. The husband had an interest known as the marital right: upon marriage the husband had an estate for life in all of his wife's real estate. The term curtesy was used to refer to the husband's life estate in all

---

59. *Id.* § 64.1-70.
60. *Id.* § 64.1-1.
61. *Id.* § 64.1-11.
62. *Id.* §§ 64.1-19, 64.1-41.
63. *Id.* §§ 64.1-127; see also *id.* 34-4, 34-12 to 34-15, 34-26, 34-27.
64. *Id.* § 64.1-16.
65. *Id.* §§ 46.1-96; see also *id.* 46.1-92, 46.1-93.
66. *Id.* §§ 6.1-73, 6.1-195.26.
67. *Id.* §§ 64.1-123, 64.1-123.1.

of his wife's realty after her death. The wife had an interest known as dower, which was a one-third life estate in all of the real property of which the husband had been seized at any time during their marriage. The Virginia statutes provide for both dower and curtesy, and by statute the terms are made synonymous;[68] the interest provided is a one-third fee simple interest. The spouse can take dower or curtesy but must waive any devise in lieu of curtesy made in the wife's will or any jointure provision in the husband's will for the wife;[69] a jointure provision is a devise or conveyance in the will in the wife's favor made to take effect at the death of the husband and which will last at least for the wife's life. Such provision made by either spouse would bar dower and curtesy rights[70] but would not bar the spouse's intestate share of real property where the deceased dies intestate and with children. Where the deceased dies intestate and without children, dower and curtesy have no application.[71]

According to present statutes, in the case of complete intestacy, where the intestate has no children, the surviving spouse gets an absolute interest in all of the personalty; if there are children, then the surviving spouse gets an absolute interest in one-third of the personalty.[72] Where the spouse's will makes provision for the surviving spouse, the spouse may renounce the provision and take a forced share of the estate. Where the spouse's will fails to provide for the surviving spouse, the spouse may also take a forced share of the deceased spouse's estate. When such an election is made, the surviving spouse gets one-half of the personal property where there are no children or descendants of these children and one-third if there are children or descendants of the children.[73]

A partial intestacy occurs when some, but not all, of the deceased person's property is disposed of by his will. When there is a partial intestacy, the surviving spouse is entitled to an intestate share of

---

68. *Id.* §§ 64.1-19, 64.1-19.1.
69. *Id.* §§ 64.1-22, 64.1-30.
70. *Id.* §§ 64.1-22, 64.1-29.
71. Newton v. Newton, 199 Va. 785, 102 S.E.2d 312 (1958).
72. VA. CODE § 64.1-11.
73. *Id.* § 64.1-16.

the real property as well as anything given by the will. If the spouse accepts a devise in lieu of curtesy or a conveyance or devise in lieu of dower, dower or curtesy rights would be barred but not the intestate share of realty.[74] When the deceased's will makes provision for the spouse of a bequest of personal property, if the spouse accepts the bequest under the will, the spouse cannot receive one-half of any intestate personal property; the spouse must either take the bequest of personal property made by will or must take one-half of the intestate personal property.[75]

In addition to the forced share, a surviving widow or minor children of the testator have rights to certain specified items of personal property, such as the family Bible.[76]

A family is extended some protection against creditors by a homestead allowance of personal or real property not to exceed the sum of $5,000.[77] This allowance cannot be claimed by a surviving spouse if there are no creditors unless the deceased claimed homestead prior to his death. The surviving spouse cannot choose to take a homestead allowance if there has been an election to take either jointure or dower,[78] and their value will be subtracted from the value of the homestead allowance.[79] Minor children may secure a homestead allowance even if the surviving widow has taken jointure or a downer interest.[80]

The spouse may obtain title to the family automobile which may have been registered solely in the name of the deceased spouse or in the names of the surviving spouse and deceased spouse jointly. Upon the death of a spouse in whose name the automobile was registered, the registration of the vehicle remains in force for the remainder of the period for which the license plates or decals are issued or until the ownership of the car is transferred before the end of such period by the executor or administrator of the

---

74. *Id.* § 64.1-19; Newton v. Newton, 199 Va. 785, 102 S.E.2d 312 (1958).
75. VA. CODE § 64.1-16; Newton v. Newton, 199 Va. 785, 102 S.E.2d 312 (1958).
76. VA. CODE §§ 64.1-127, 34-26, 34-27.
77. *Id.* § 34-4.
78. *Id.* § 34-12.
79. *Id.* § 34-15.
80. *Id.* §§ 34-12, 34-15.

deceased's estate, or by the surviving spouse if the car was owned jointly.[81] To transfer title when the car was registered in the name of the deceased spouse, the surviving spouse must fill out an application to the Division of Motor Vehicles requesting a transfer of the registration. The Division of Motor Vehicles will register the car and issue a new registration card, license plates and a certificate of title to the surviving spouse.[82] When the vehicle is registered to both persons or when the vehicle is distributed by the will, the surviving spouse or beneficiary under the will must apply to the Division of Motor Vehicles for a certificate of title, provide the Division with his or her name and address, and accompany such application with the registration card and certificate of title previously issued. The Division of Motor Vehicles, upon such application, will cancel the deceased's registration and issue a new certificate of title to the surviving spouse or beneficiary.[83]

A joint bank deposit, one made in the names of both spouses, payable to either or payable to the survivor, automatically becomes the property of the survivor upon the death of either spouse.[84] The surviving spouse may also receive the payment of the balance of a savings account in a savings and loan association in the name of the deceased spouse when no personal representative has qualified to administer the estate. When the balance in such an account does not exceed $5,000, the association may upon application and within one hundred and twenty days of the death, pay the balance to the surviving spouse or, if there is no surviving spouse, to the next of kin.[85] The balance of a savings account may also be paid to the personal representative of the deceased upon presentation by the personal representative of his certified letter of qualification.[86] When a savings account of the deceased is made payable to the named survivor or survivors, and if the survivor named by the deceased is his spouse at the time of this death, the association may pay the balance to the surviving spouse immediately. When the

---

81. *Id.* § 46.1-96.
82. *Id.* § 46.1-92.
83. *Id.* § 46.1-93.
84. *Id.* § 64.1-73.
85. *Id.* § 6.1-195.29.
86. *Id.* § 6.1-195.28.

survivor named is not the spouse, the association may pay the balance within sixty days.[87]

When a sum of money not exceeding $5,000 is owed the deceased by the State (a tax refund), or when a sum not exceeding $5,000 is owed the deceased by the United States (pension money, burial expenses of soldiers, or black lung benefits), or a sum is owed the deceased by his employer, or corporate securities owned by the deceased with an aggregate market value of $3,000 or less, these sums are payable to the surviving spouse, or if there is no surviving spouse then to those entitled to distribution under the intestate laws, after one hundred and twenty days if no personal representative has qualified to administer the estate.[88]

One may disclaim any interest which passes to him through intestate succession or by will. The disclaimer must be in writing and executed within ten months of the deceased's death in the same way as a deed to land.[89]

ESTATE ADMINISTRATION

Probate is the procedure by which a will is judicially proven to be the deceased's last will and testament. The will must be proved prior to the appointment of a personal representative since the will provisions determine the disposition of the deceased's property. Probate is also required to prove the title to any real estate which is disposed of by will.

In early English law, probate jurisdiction was vested in the ecclesiastical courts. The American colonies had no courts comparable to the church courts and probate jurisdiction was placed in the regular courts or in specially created branches of such courts.[90] The Virginia courts which have jurisdiction to probate a will are circuit courts.[91] The court will have jurisdiction if it is in the county or corporation which is the testator's last known place of residence, if it is where the testator had real property, or if it

---

87. *Id.* § 6.1-195.30.
88. *Id.* §§ 64.1-123, 64.1-123.1.
89. *Id.* §§ 64.1-188, 64.1-189, 64.1-196.
90. FRIEDMAN, *supra* note 1, at 48.
91. VA. CODE § 64.1-75.

is the place where the testator dies or where he has personal property.[92]

In order to probate a will or distribute an estate by intestacy, it must be shown that the testator is dead; death is a prerequisite for jurisdiction to probate. Where the testator has died in a hospital with an attending physician present to sign a death certificate, proof of death presents no problems. Where the testator has disappeared, proof of death is much more difficult. In cases where the testator is away from his domicile for at least seven years without having been heard from, he is presumed to be dead.[93] In addition to proving these facts, there are requirements which must be met before the court has jurisdiction to probate: Notice of the intent to probate the absent person's will must be published once a week for four successive weeks in a newspaper of general circulation in the city or county in question; a hearing must be held in not less than two weeks after the last publication; if the court believes that the presumption of death has been adequately shown, it will issue an order to that effect; this order must be published once a week for two successive weeks in a newspaper in a city or county where the will is sought to be probated and in the city or county where the testator was last heard from. Within twelve weeks of the last publication of the order, the testator's will may be admitted to probate in the absence of any evidence which would rebut the presumption of the testator's death. When there is a hearing on the order and evidence is presented which shows that the testator has been away for twenty years or more, a will can be admitted for probate without publication of the court's order or a twelve-week waiting period. A distribution by intestacy follows the same type of procedure as required for the admission of a will to probate.[94] No time limitation is placed upon submission of a will for probate [95] but one who destroys or fraudulently conceals a will may be sentenced from two to five years in the state penitentiary.[96]

---

92. *Id.*
93. *Id.* § 64.1-105.
94. *Id.* §§ 64.1-108 to 64.1-113.
95. *Id.* §§ 64.1-94 to 64.1-96.
96. *Id.* § 18.2-504.

Probate procedure is of two types: *ex parte* and *inter partes.* An *ex parte* proceeding is informal and may be held before the clerk of the court, a duly qualified deputy clerk [97] or before the court.[98] The probate of a will based on the presumption of death may be held only before the court.[99] When the proceeding is held before the clerk and the clerk refuses to admit the will to probate, there is an appeal to the court as a matter of right. Such appeal must be made within six months after the entry of the clerk's order.[100] If someone believes that an invalid will is being offered for probate, he may file a caveat with the clerk. The person filing the caveat will be notified of any attempt to probate such a will so that he may contest it if he chooses.

An *inter partes* proceeding is a formal proceeding which can only be held before the court. This type of proceeding may be instituted initially or on appeal from the clerk's order.[101] There is a right to a jury trial in this proceeding.[102]

Each estate requires the appointment of a personal representative. If a person dies intestate, the representative is referred to as an administrator; if a person dies with a will, the person is referred to as an executor. The personal representative performs a variety of functions: He has to collect any assets which the decedent may have, pay debts and taxes, and distribute the remainder to those persons who are entitled to receive them. A curator may be appointed by the court pending the appointment of an administrator or in the case of a will contest.[103] When no executor is appointed by the will or an appointed executor declines to serve, fails to post the required bond, dies or is removed, the court appoints an "administrator c.t.a."[104] Persons entitled to appointment by the court as administrators are the deceased's

---

97. *Id.* § 64.1-77.
98. *Id.* § 64.1-85.
99. *Id.* § 64.1-107.
100. *Id.* § 64.1-78.
101. *Id.* §§ 64.1-80 to 64.1-82.
102. *Id.* § 64.1-83.
103. *Id.* § 64.1-93.
104. *Id.* § 64.1-116.

surviving spouse or any person who is declared to be competent and suitable by the clerk of the court or the court where no person entitled to distribution under the intestate statutes has applied within thirty days of the intestate's death.[105] When there is no contest and no executor or administrator has been appointed within two months of the death, any person may move the court to appoint the sheriff as administrator. The person who moves for the sheriff's appointment is responsible for the state tax on the estate.[106] When a nonresident personal representative is appointed as administrator, a resident personal representative must be appointed to act with the nonresident.[107]

An executor of an executor has no authority over the estate of the first testator, but he may be appointed as the executor of this first estate;[108] this executor may be sued for any waste or destruction of the first estate by the deceased executor.[109]

A personal representative has duties to perform and powers conferred upon him. An administrator's duties and powers are prescribed by law; an executor's duties and powers are both prescribed by law and conferred upon him by the instrument creating his office. An executor has the power to bury the deceased, pay a reasonable price for the funeral, and preserve the estate from waste and destruction prior to taking his oath and posting a bond.[110] The representative must post a bond equal to the value of the gross personal estate; if he has been authorized to sell real estate, or receive the rents and profits thereof, the bond must cover the value of both the personal estate and the real estate which he is authorized to sell or the rents and profits he is authorized to receive.[111] It is customary in Virginia to post a bond for approximately twice the value of the personal estate when an individual surety is given and in a sum somewhat greater than the

---

105. *Id.* § 64.1-118.
106. *Id.* § 64.1-131.
107. *Id.* § 26-59.
108. *Id.* § 64.1-137.
109. *Id.* § 64.1-145.
110. *Id.* § 64.1-136; Scott Funeral Home, Inc. v. First Nat'l Bank of Danville, 211 Va. 128, 176 S.E.2d 335 (1970).
111. VA. CODE § 64.1-120.

value of the gross personal estate when a surety company is involved. In a number of situations a bond may not be required: if the will directs that an executor not post bond (the clerk or the court in its discretion may require a bond), or when the amount for which the personal representative is responsible is $1,000 or less.[112]

The personal representative is required to pay a probate tax as a prerequisite to his qualification [113] if the estate exceeds the sum of $100, including both real and personal property. If the value of the estate is under $1,000, the tax is $1.00; if the estate exceeds the value of $1,000, there is an additional tax of ten cents for every $100 or fractional amount in excess of $1,000.[114] An executor and an administrator are required to furnish a list of the heirs to be recorded in the Wills Book at the time of qualification.[115] The personal representative should inventory the assets of the estate and may request an appraisal of them.[116] He should marshal the assets of the estate other than land which pass directly to heirs and devisees. When the personal representative is required to sell the real estate, the proceeds from such sale pass as part of the personal estate.[117] The representative is empowered to execute a deed of conveyance of land subject to a sales contract by the decedent,[118] and pay the rents, profits, and proceeds of any sale of land to those entitled to receive them.[119]

The personal representative has many specific powers prescribed by law. He can sue and be sued on the deceased's contracts and for damages, whether direct or indirect, to any estate of or by the decedent.[120] He may renew the deceased's notes for a sum not greater than the amount due (including principal and interest) on the original note when the note is payable not later than

---

112. *Id.* §§ 26-1, 26-4.
113. *Id.* § 58-68.
114. *Id.* § 58-66.
115. *Id.* § 64.1-134.
116. *Id.* § 64.1-133.
117. *Id.* §§ 64.1-146, 64.1-147.
118. *Id.* § 64.1-148.
119. *Id.* § 64.1-151.
120. *Id.* §§ 64.1-144, 64.1-145.

two years after the representative's qualification.[121] He may maintain a suit for the wrongful death of the deceased.[122]

The personal representative is required to pay the deceased's debts. The order of preference of creditors is referred to as the order of abatement. The statutes set up classes of property. Each class is to be used before the next class becomes subject to creditors' claims; property in each class abates ratably. The order presently is as follows: intestate personalty, property charged by the will with payment of debts, residuary personalty, general legacies and bequests, specific legacies and bequests, intestate realty, and realty devised by will.[123] This order may be modified if the testator requests that a different order be utilized.[124] When a pretermitted heir asserts a valid claim, devisees and legatees contribute ratably to his share.[125] The federal estate tax and the state inheritance tax are prorated among the persons who are interested in the estate to whom property has been transferred which is includible in the gross estate in the proportions which the value of the particular property bears to the total estate.[126] The testator may request by will or by lifetime instrument that the taxes be paid or apportioned in a manner different from the statutory plan.[127]

The personal representative is normally allowed to be reimbursed for the reasonable expenses incurred by him and for compensation in the form of a commission.[128] Where authorized to sell land, the executor or commissioner is allowed a commission of five percent of receipts from the sale.

The personal representative is required by law to account for the assets which are within the estate, as well as the settlement of

---

121. *Id.* § 64.1-143.
122. *Id.* §§ 8.01-50, 8.01-244.
123. *Id.* §§ 64.1-153 to 64.1-159, 64.1-181 to 64.1-187.
124. *Id.*
125. *Id.* §§ 64.1-70, 64.1-71.
126. *Id.* §§ 64.1-161 to 64.1-164.
127. *Id.* § 64.1-165; Baylor v. National Bank of Commerce, 194 Va. 1, 72 S.E.2d 282 (1952); Bickers v. Pinnell, 199 Va. 444, 100 S.E.2d 20 (1957); Simeone v. Smith, 204 Va. 860, 134 S.E.2d 281 (1964).
128. VA. CODE § 26-30.

debts, within sixteen months of the court order conferring his authority.[129] A legatee can compel a distribution of the estate within six months from the date of the court order; the representative may have his bond refunded if this occurs.[130] The personal representative may obtain a show cause order directed to creditors and other persons within six months of his qualification; creditors who have claims against the estate must show cause why the estate should not be distributed at this time, thereby cutting off their claims.[131] The procedure normally follows this pattern: Before the six months elapse, the personal representative accounts, posts notice of settlement, posts and publishes notice of taking proof of debts, takes debts and demands, and files the commissioner's report upon debts and demands with a settlement of the account. After the six months have passed, a show cause order is issued, publication of the order is made, and after the expiration of a twenty-eight-day waiting period, the order of distribution of the estate is made. With the completion of distribution, the personal representative is discharged and the estate is closed.

---

129. *Id.* § 26-17.
130. *Id.* § 64.1-177.
131. *Id.* § 64.1-179.

CHAPTER 8

Insurance

R. C. Palamar

IN GENERAL

Life itself necessarily entails certain risks, some much greater than others. When, only half-awake, one struggles out of bed to turn off the alarm at 6:30 A.M., he risks breaking his toe on the corner of the dresser; when one drives to work, he risks his life (and the lives of others); and when one buys or builds a home, he risks losing it by fire or losing some of its contents through burglary. Financial protection against these events (and countless others) may be procured through insurance.

The basic concept of insurance is readily understandable to the layman: The insured protects whatever interest he desires to protect (life, health, property, business, financial security) by having an insurance policy on that interest. If one suffers a loss caused by one or more of the specific risks covered in the policy, the policy provides that the insurance company will compensate for that loss. In return for such protection, the insured pays certain monies (premiums) to the company. In effect, he is hedging against an occurrence which will cause him to suffer a loss. A quasi-legal definition can now be stated: Insurance is a contract by which one party (the insurance company — the *insurer*), for a compensation called the *premium,* assumes particular risks of the other party (the *insured)* and promises to pay to him or his nominee (beneficiary) a certain or ascertainable sum of money (or other thing of value) upon the happening of a specified contingency. Unfortunately, it is not entirely that simple. To understand the law of insurance, it is necessary to understand basic principles of contract law, the legislative policy toward regulation of insurers and their dealings with individuals, the law of agency, the nature and function of corporations and the laws applicable to them and much, much more.

It is, therefore, not the aim of this chapter to attempt to inform the reader of *the* law of insurance. It will instead attempt to give a general awareness of the following: (1) What insurance is, and how it works; (2) the kinds of risks against which one can obtain insurance protection; (3) how the law (both statutory and decisional) protects one by imposing strict regulations on insurance companies and the ways in which they can deal with the public and its money; (4) the basic relationship between the insured, the company and the insurance agent with whom he deals; (5) what the law dictates as the general obligations of the parties under the contract of insurance; and (6) particular kinds of insurance the *individual* is most likely to need and will benefit from.

This chapter is not an exhaustive treatment of the law. Neither will it be an advertisement for lawyers or insurance companies. Attorneys are forbidden publicly to solicit the use of their services. However, attorneys and insurance agents are trained professionals whose continued business existence depends on satisfied clients. So from time to time throughout this chapter when it is suggested that an attorney or insurance agent be consulted, such suggestion is made solely for the reader's benefit — so that he may have his interests protected and his legal rights explained and enforced.

State Regulation of Insurance Companies

The general aim of regulation of insurance companies is to assure, as much as possible, the safety and preservation of the monies they receive from their policyholders. Insurers are a kind of "public trustee" of funds, and Virginia, like all other states, has taken great pains to make certain that insurance companies will be managed so as always to be able to pay legitimate claims when they are filed.

There are basically two different kinds of insurance companies: *stock* companies and *mutual* companies. Stock companies have a fixed amount of capital stock, just like any other public corporation, which is owned by the shareholders who *are* the corporation and who elect its board of directors. A policyholder has no relation with such a corporation except by his insurance contract itself. He has no ownership in the company nor any right to share in its profits. The majority of fire and other casualty insurance in the United

States today is written by stock companies. With mutual companies, on the other hand, the *policyholders* are the company. The company acts through agents selected by its policyholders, the premiums paid in make up a fund out of which claims are satisfied, and a policyholder has a right to share in the profits of such a company, usually in the form of dividends. The vast majority of life insurance is written by such mutual companies.[1]

The law of Virginia imposes a regulatory scheme on all insurers. The kinds of insurance business a company can transact are specifically limited. For instance, a *title insurance company* may only transact title insurance, a *life insurance company* can only deal in life insurance, annuities, and accident and health insurance (unless it had been transacting other types of insurance continuously since 1932, in which case it may continue to do so), while all other companies are permitted to transact all other types of insurance.[2] One obvious aim of this restriction is to engender specialization among companies; a company forced to concentrate in one area must develop expertise in that area, to the ultimate benefit of its policyholders.

The State Corporation Commission is charged with the regulation, supervision and inspection of insurers.[3] Among other specified duties, the Commission oversees the trade practices of insurance companies (*i.e.*, its advertising),[4] has the power to examine and investigate every person engaged in the business of insurance to determine if he has been or is engaged in unfair competition or deceptive practices,[5] and, most importantly, oversees the regulation of premium rates which companies can charge.[6] While all such rates are determined with great mathematical precision, the public is protected by a statute which spells out the only factors companies can consider in formulating

---

1. VANCE, INSURANCE 123 (3d ed. 1951).
2. VA. CODE §§ 38.1-2 to 38.1-24.
3. *Id.* § 38.1-29.
4. *Id.* §§ 38.1-51, 38.1-52.
5. *Id.* § 38.1-53.
6. *Id.* §§ 38.1-218 to 38.1-279, 38.1-279.29 to 38.1-279.57.

their rates.[7] There are laws that dictate that such rates can be annually reviewed,[8] at which time the Commission can inspect the books of the company.[9]

All insurance companies must be licensed in Virginia if they transact business here.[10] A company's license is renewed annually [11] and rather steep deposits are required by the company before such license is issued or renewed.[12] Again, the purpose here is to protect the monies deemed held "in trust" by these insurers.[13]

The scope of investments which insurers can make with the money obtained from its policyholders is strictly defined, both as to variety and amount.[14] Finally, the law states that a company cannot, in any one policy, expose itself to a risk of more than ten percent of its surplus.[15]

The above regulations, and many others not detailed herein, all serve to police insurance companies with the ultimate goal in mind of preserving the money to satisfy legitimate claims as they arise — to make sure that policyholders always *do* get the protection they are paying for.

THE INSURANCE AGENT: HIS RELATIONSHIP TO THE INSURED AND TO THE COMPANY

An "agent" or "insurance agent" is defined in Virginia as one who is "authorized by any insurance company to solicit ... contracts of insurance ... and, if authorized to do so, to collect

---

7. *Id.* §§ 38.1-252, 38.1-279.33. Section 38.1-252, in part, provides that rates are made in accordance with the following provisions: (1) Rates cannot be excessive, inadequate or unfairly discriminatory; (2) due consideration is given to (a) past and prospective loss experience within Virginia and outside Virginia, (b) hazards, (c) reasonable profit margin, (d) dividends, (e) administrative expenses, and (f) investment income; and (3) all such rates are approved by the State Corporation Commission.
8. *Id.* § 38.1-255.1.
9. *Id.* § 38.1-265.
10. *Id.* §§ 38.1-85 to 38.1-98.1.
11. *Id.* § 38.1-98.
12. *Id.* § 38.1-108.
13. Shepherd v. Virginia State Ins. Co., 120 Va. 383, 91 S.E. 140 (1917).
14. VA. CODE §§ 38.1-179 to 38.1-217.
15. *Id.* § 38.1-32.

premiums on such contracts." [16] A "life agent" or "life insurance agent" is one "authorized to solicit ... *applications* for life insurance ... or for accident and sickness insurance, or for both." [17] A "resident agent" is an insurance agent who is a resident of Virginia.[18] For the protection of the policyholder, no company except a mutual company (*i.e.*, a company in which one has ownership rights) can conduct insurance business in Virginia except through "resident agents." [19] The purpose of these definitions and legal requirements is to see that the policyholder deals with someone taking a real interest in the performance of the company's obligations.[20] Such agents, licensed by the Commonwealth,[21] are members of the community where their clients live and must meet rigid legal qualifications.[22]

A recurring problem involving the agent, the company and its policyholder is that of the *authority* of the agent. A Virginia statute provides, "No agent ... shall make any contract of insurance or agreement with respect thereto other than that which is plainly expressed in the policy or contract issued," [23] meaning that no "side agreements" can be made between the insured and the agent. The real legal controversy can arise, however, when an agent (who, except for life insurance, *has authority* actually to *issue* the policy, rather than just take an application for it), at the insured's request, explains the meaning of a clause in the policy. For example, assume that one is applying for a fire policy (with the usual extended coverage associated with a homeowner's policy) which states, as a *condition* to coverage, "The building must not be unoccupied for more than sixty consecutive days." Suppose he explains to the agent that within a short time he will be taking an extended vacation, leaving the house for more than sixty days. Assume

---

16. *Id.* § 38.1-280.
17. *Id.*
18. *Id.*
19. *Id.* § 38.1-282.
20. Osborne v. Ozlin, 29 F. Supp. 71 (E.D. Va. 1939).
21. VA. CODE § 38.1-302.
22. *Id.* §§ 38.1-296, 38.1-301.1.
23. *Id.* § 38.1-294.

further that the policy states, "No one (including the agent) can waive any condition in this policy." Yet, when the customer tells the agent of his proposed vacation, he says: "That's O.K. The word 'unoccupied' in that clause means gone away with no intent to return, and you'll be back in four months, right?" While the policyholder is away, the house burns. The legal question here is: Is the insurance company bound by the action of its agent, or did the agent act outside of his authority in "explaining" the meaning of the word "unoccupied"? The Virginia courts have generally bound the company to the statements of its agents in a situation like this,[24] explaining that, from a commonsense point of view, the agent *did* have "apparent authority" to give the explanation he gave, and that the insured, uneducated in the law of insurance, should be able to rely on what the agent tells him.[25] Thus, the company is bound by an agent's acts if such acts are within the real or apparent (to the customer) authority of the agent.[26] But there is a commonsense limitation to this principle: If it is obvious that the agent has made a mistake or has done something which he has no authority to do, then the company generally *will not* be bound by the action of the agent. For example, assume that, in the previous hypothetical situation, instead of explaining the meaning of "unoccupied," the agent had said, directly contradicting the policy provision: "Oh, that's alright. Those little clauses don't mean anything anyway. You can disregard them anytime you want to. So what if you go away for a few months?" An "explanation" like this would sound doubtful to anyone, and the courts would be much more reluctant to allow recovery for a subsequent loss if anyone dared to rely on such a ridiculous "explanation."

The example is extreme in order to illustrate this point: When going to see an insurance agent, know exactly what is to be insured and be prepared to answer questions about that which is to be insured. Also *ask* questions about the type of coverage desired, and, most importantly, READ THE APPLICATION and, once received, READ THE POLICY. This is where an attorney can be

---

24. Royal Indem. Co. v. Hook, 155 Va. 956, 157 S.E. 414 (1931).
25. Maryland Cas. Co. v. Craig, 213 Va. 660, 194 S.E.2d 729 (1973).
26. Boykin & Tayloe v. Columbia Fire Ins. Co., 90 F. Supp. 647 (E.D. Va. 1950).

of service, *before* any loss is suffered necessitating a claim under the policy. If the insured does not understand any terms, he should see a lawyer and have them explained. If their meaning is not what was expected, or the coverage is not correct for what is to be insured, or some condition in the policy, based on what one thought he and the agent agreed to, is not as it should be, he should go back to the agent and straighten it out *before* something happens. This can and should be done because, within certain limits to be discussed later, insurance is available on just about anything imaginable, against just about any risk imaginable. But to provide proper coverage the agent has to know exactly with what he's dealing. Do not take the chance that the agent had authority to do something when indeed such authority did not exist.

THE INSURANCE CONTRACT IN GENERAL

(a) *Insurable Interest*

As noted in the introductory discussion in this chapter, an insurance policy is a contract, by the terms of which the risk of loss is passed from the insured to the insurance company. Because of the special relationship between a policyholder and the company, the law automatically imposes certain conditions and restraints on the form and content of the insurance contract. This discussion deals with some of the most important of these restrictions.

Basic to the understanding of how insurance works, and the special nature of an insurance contract, is the concept of *insurable interest*. This notion can best be illustrated by the following examples: (1) Suppose John Doe, who is a complete stranger to Evel Knievel, could take out a $1 million life insurance policy on the life of the motorcycle daredevil. It seems like a good bet that within a short time he'll splatter himself all over some canyon and John Doe would collect a handsome profit. However, John cannot take out such a policy because he does not have an insurable interest in Evel Knievel's life. (2) Suppose someone, again a complete stranger, could take out fire insurance on his neighbors' houses. He might watch joyfully as they burned a few months later, knowing he would collect. However, he cannot take out such policies because he has no insurable interest in property which he does not own.

With respect to life insurance there are three possible parties to the contract: the *owner* of the policy; the person *insured;* and the *insurer* (company). The legal rules of insurable interest which follow are extremely important: (1) One can *always* buy a life insurance policy on his own life (*i.e.*, the *owner* and the *insured* are the same). (2) If one desires to own a life insurance policy on the life of another, he may do so if, and only if, (a) the proceeds of the policy are payable to the estate of the person insured; (b) they are payable to someone designated by the person insured; or (c) they are payable to someone with an insurable interest in the individual whose life is insured. Thus, a close relative of the person insured, related to him or her by blood or marriage, can be the owner and/or beneficiary of life insurance on such person's life. He can also be the owner and/or beneficiary of a life insurance policy on the life of *anyone* so long as he has an economic interest in having the life of the insured continue.[27] However, one cannot have a life insurance policy taken out on his own life, which policy is unknown to him, except that (1) a husband or wife can so insure each other without the knowledge of the other; and (2) anyone having an insurable interest in the life of a minor (under eighteen in Virginia) can so insure that minor's life.[28]

Once the valid life insurance policy is purchased, however, the owner can always sell it, assign it, and/or change the beneficiary, and the company must comply with his request to do so. Just be sure to read the policy carefully and follow instructions on how to effect a change of beneficiary.

A detailed treatment of buy/sell agreements and stock redemption plans for small businesses, funded with life insurance, is beyond the scope of this article. However, the small businessman should be aware of these options in the context of estate planning as well as for purely business reasons. An attorney should be consulted by all participants in a "family" or "closely-held" (no

---

27. VA. CODE § 38.1-329.
28. *Id.* § 38.1-330.

public trading of shares) business at their *earliest* opportunity to determine the feasibility of such arrangements.

The insurable interest doctrine is even simpler with respect to insuring any type of property. The law says that one cannot be the beneficiary of insurance on property unless he has "substantial economic interest in the safety or preservation of the subject of insurance free from loss, destruction or pecuniary damage." [29] This does not mean one has to own the property, however, in order to be able to insure it. If one holds a mortgage on it, has it entrusted to himself as a bailee, or otherwise has an economic interest in the *preservation* of the property, he can insure it.

(b) *Mandatory Provisions*

For the protection of policyholders, the law recognizes the inequality of knowledge and bargaining power between the individual and the insurance company, and therefore mandates that *every* insurance policy *must* contain the following: (1) The names of the parties to the contract; (2) the subject of the insurance (*i.e.,* the life of John Doe, or the structure at 1001 Elm Street, Fairfax); (3) the specific risks insured against (*i.e.,* fire, hurricane, water damage, explosion, etc.); (4) the time when coverage begins and the duration of the policy; (5) a statement of the premiums to be paid; (6) the *conditions* pertaining to the insurance (*i.e.,* the house must not be unoccupied for more than sixty consecutive days), and (7) any other provision required by statute (see specific provisions required under the succeeding headings of this chapter on different types of insurance).[30]

(c) *How Property Insurance Is Procured; the Application*

Nearly all property insurance is procured in the following manner: One goes in to see an agent, tells him what he wants insured, and he agrees to take the application. The agent asks questions about the applicant and the property, and he fills out the application. He has the prospective policyholder sign the application, from which time he is "covered," and he sends it to the company. The company then reads the application and issues the

---

29. *Id.* § 38.1-331.
30. *Id.* § 38.1-334.

policy. This procedure may vary somewhat. The applicant may want "immediate coverage" and therefore will telephone the agent, and the agent will tell him "O.K., you're covered." Then a few days later the client will drop by to have the formal application filled out.

Again, this all sounds rather simple and devoid of legal problems. Unfortunately, there are a great number of problems which can arise because of the application procedure. If the policy comes back with the application attached to it, that application is legally deemed to be part of the policy and policyholder is responsible for all answers given in that application (because the company relies on these answers to issue the policy).[31] More importantly, if an answer in the application is untrue and *material to the risk*, the policy can be *avoided* by the company. For example, in an application for fire insurance on a warehouse and its contents, one question might have been, "Describe the exact nature of contents to be stored therein." If the applicant stated to the agent (or if he mistakenly wrote down) that steel cable was to be stored there when in fact he knew that drums of gasoline were to be stored there, the company can legally refuse to pay off on the policy if a fire occurs there,[32] even if the fire was caused by lightning rather than by one of the gasoline drums exploding,[33] because at the time of loss there existed an erroneous statement which, obviously, was material to the risk.

The rationale behind the law here is that the insurance company has the right to know with whom and with what kind of property it is dealing. An insurer can and will insure a person and his property against almost any conceivable risk (for the right premium) if he knows what that risk is.

How, then, can one avoid problems with the application and policy? First of all, be sure to know all the *facts* about what is to be insured and make these facts clear to the agent. Second, because the agent is the one who fills out the application based on the

---

31. Union Indem. Co. v. Dodd, 21 F.2d 709 (4th Cir. 1927).
32. VA. CODE § 38.1-336.
33. *Id.* § 38.1-342.

answers, make sure to *read it* before signing it, and make any necessary corrections. Third, when the policy comes back (usually with the application attached), be sure to read it and verify that the answers in the application are accurately reflected in the description of the property and conditions with respect thereto now contained in the policy. Again, if unsure of the meaning of policy terms, take the time to consult with an attorney. A little effort at this stage can save much grief later on should a loss be suffered. Finally, if the status of the insured property *changes* after the policy is in effect, the original answer may now be untrue; if loss occurs after the change, the company may be able legally to avoid payment (assuming again that the change was material to the risk). Therefore, one should immediately report any such change (*i.e.*, the property is moved, the slate roof on the house is replaced with wood shingles, or other kinds of property are now stored with the original property) to the agent. Most often a *rider* or *endorsement* (additional clause) can and will be put into the policy covering such changed conditions, usually at little or no extra premium cost.

FIRE INSURANCE

The heading of this discussion is designated "Fire Insurance" only because the statutes of Virginia on all property insurance come under this heading. The discussion really relates to all types of "hazard" insurance, including, but not limited to, fire, on real property (residential or business) and personal property.[34]

In general, the legal principle of "freedom of contract" applies to property insurance; that is, for the right price (premium) one can insure just about any type of property against just about any type of risk. With the new standard homeowner's policy and its extended coverage features, for instance, anyone can insure his home and its contents against a great variety of hazards, and insure himself against liability if someone is injured while on the premises. The same is true with a small business establishment. But this very breadth of available coverages can lead to problems if one fails to take the required steps. The insurance company, in

---
34. *Id.* § 38.1-373.

determining its premium rates and being able to fulfill its obligations under the policy (contract), has a right to know the specifics involved with each policyholder and his property.

Thus, in discussing such insurance with the agent, be sure to point out specifically: (1) The type of property to be insured; (2) its location; (3) what one's interest is in such property; (4) its value; (5) the kinds of coverage desired (if the agent is doing his job he will explain the multitude of coverages available), and (6) how much insurance is wanted.

For the protection and information of policyholders, any fire insurance policy and homeowner's policy containing fire protection issued in Virginia must contain the following provisions: (1) It must state the amount of insurance coverage, the rates and premiums thereon, tell that the amount of insurance cannot be more than the value of the insurable interest in that property, and inform one that the insurance will remain in effect *only* while the property is "located or contained as described in the policy" [35] (thus arises the obligation to inform the company of all changes); and (2) it must contain all endorsements (*i.e.*, the special coverages or special restrictions or exemptions the company wants).[36]

It must also contain the so-called "165 lines" provision, the highlights of which are as follows: (a) that the policy is *void* for fraud or willful concealment on the part of the insured of any material fact or circumstance concerning the property or his interest therein; (b) that without special endorsements, a fire policy alone will not cover certain property (accounts, cash, securities); (c) that without special endorsement, certain hazards are excluded (enemy attack, invasion, *theft*); (d) that the company has no liability for any loss occurring "while the hazard is increased by any means within the knowledge or control of the insured" (*e.g.*, one cannot store gasoline in bottles in his garage), or "while a described building ... is *vacant* or *unoccupied* beyond a period of sixty consecutive days" (to be safe, if going away for a long vacation or if the business is closed because of a strike, ask or hire someone to inspect the premises periodically); (e) that any other peril

---

35. *Id.* § 38.1-365.
36. *Id.*

(hazard) shall be (and thus *can* be) insured against by *endorsement in writing;* (f) that no policy provision can be waived by the agent; (g) that in case of loss, *notice of loss* and *proof of loss* must be given to the company in detail (thus pointing out the necessity of keeping accurate records in a safe place, like a bank vault, so that one can prove what was lost); and (h) that if the company refuses to pay the claim after a loss, one cannot sue the insurer later than two years after such loss and unless *all* policy provisions have been complied with.[37] Because the possibility of fraud and collusion exists in the property insurance field, the insurer must have the opportunity to investigate all claims. The importance of provision (h) above is illustrated by one Virginia case in which the court stated that a failure to file a proof of loss statement within the two-year period barred a court action by the insured even though his claim turned out to be legitimate.[38]

The law of Virginia also imposes strict limitations on the company's rights either to cancel a policy or to refuse to renew it at the end of each term, for a policy is of no benefit unless it can continue to protect the designated property as long as one owns it. Once a homeowner's policy on a home owned and occupied by him has been in effect for ninety days (a fair length of time to permit the company to conduct an investigation), it can be cancelled by the company *only* for one or more of the following reasons: (1) failure to pay the premium; (2) conviction of a crime arising out of acts which increase the hazard insured against (*e.g.*, arson); (3) the company discovers fraud on the part of the insured; (4) the insured commits willful or reckless acts which increase the hazard (*i.e.*, knowingly leaving the house unlocked when no one is home and suffering a loss by theft); (5) physically changing the property or allowing its deterioration, which leads to its becoming uninsurable upon physical inspection (*e.g.*, allowing electrical insulation to rot away without making repairs).[39] Moreover, the insurer cannot refuse to renew such a policy except for one or more of the above

---

37. *Id.* § 38.1-366.
38. Eden Corp. v. Utica Mut. Ins. Co., 350 F. Supp. 637 (W.D. Va. 1972).
39. VA. CODE § 38.1-371.2.

reasons. In addition, if the company desires not to renew, it must give notice of such intent at least thirty days before the current policy is to expire. Such notice must state the proposed date of termination and the reason or reasons for termination, and must advise that, within ten days after receipt of such notice, the policyholder has an absolute right to request the Commissioner of Insurance of the state to review the company's action.[40] If ever faced with the threat of cancellation or nonrenewal, one would be well advised to see an attorney quickly.

Because the company has the general right to control the risks it is insuring, within the limits allowed by law it will place many *exclusions* and *conditions* in property insurance policies. As the old saying goes, "the policy giveth and the policy taketh away." An *exclusion* is a specifically designated hazard or class of hazards to which coverage does not apply. For instance, damage due to earthquake, nuclear reaction or contamination, flood waters, sewer backups, and power failures is normally excluded from coverage. Depending on where one lives (on the beach or on top of the Blue Ridge), he may or may not be able to obtain such coverage by special endorsement. Of equal importance are *conditions*, those terms of the policy which must be complied with for whatever coverage one has to remain valid. Some conditions (the house not being "vacant" for a specified period, there being no "increase in the hazard" during the life of the policy, the necessity of reporting changes in the property, and the necessity to furnish a notice of loss and proof of loss) have already been discussed. Other common conditions in a homeowner's policy include: (1) a prohibition against "other insurance" on the same property (why should you collect $1,000 from each of three companies when your loss is only $1,000?); (2) for a loss from theft to be covered, there must be visible evidence of forced entry; (3) a prohibition against assignment of the policy without the consent of the company.[41]

---

40. *Id.*
41. Morotock Ins. Co. v. Rodefer Bros., 92 Va. 747, 24 S.E. 393 (1896); Virginia Fire, etc., Ins. Co. v. Lennon, 140 Va. 766, 125 S.E. 801 (1924); Daniel v. Bedford County Ass'n, 157 Va. 79, 160 S.E. 11 (1931).

These provisions are important to the company in controlling its risks. However, they are even more important to the policyholder who should be aware of the exclusions in order to take other steps besides insurance to try to protect against these excluded hazards, or to attempt, by special endorsement, to bring these hazards within the policy's coverage. Most importantly, one must be aware of the conditions before he can comply with them; if he does not know that an assignment (transfer) of the policy is prohibited, he will not know that he must get the company's permission to do so. The importance of reading the policy, understanding its terms, and consulting with an attorney to have them explained *before* suffering a loss, cannot be overemphasized.

LIFE INSURANCE

(a) *Definitions and General Introduction*
 (1) *Contract of life insurance*

A contract of life insurance "is not a contract of indemnity, as a policy against fire [or other hazards to property], for a definite period; but it is a contract to pay a certain sum of money [in exchange for the payment of premiums] upon the happening of an event [death] which is inevitable, and only uncertain as to the time it may transpire." [42] This definition, rendered over 100 years ago by the Supreme Court of Virginia, is still applicable today to one of the two major varieties of life insurance, that which is popularly known as "whole life" or "straight life." Under such an arrangement, premiums are paid over a fixed period (either the whole life of the insured or a fixed number of years agreed on when the policy is taken out), and the proceeds of the policy are paid out when the insured person dies (or reaches age 100). However, the other major type of life insurance — "term" — operates a bit differently: Like property insurance, one pays a premium to insure a life *only* for a stated period of time, and this time is the "term" during which the policy is in effect. The coverage *expires* at the end of the stated term. In between these extremes are a vast number of different types of life insurance coverages which are

---
42. Manhattan Life Ins. Co. v. Warwick, 61 Va. (20 Gratt.) 614 (1871).

available, a detailed discussion of which is well beyond the scope of this chapter. Depending on age, health, family situation, income and personal desires, a life insurance package can be custom-tailored. There is little "law" involved here, and the range of life insurance available can best be described by a life insurance agent.

(2) *Annuities*

An annuity contract is just the reverse of a life insurance contract. That is, a sum of money (either in one lump sum or in installments) is paid to the company; then starting at a date specified in the contract (say at age 65 when one retires) the company pays him a fixed (or sometimes variable) amount at certain intervals (monthly, quarterly, etc.) *while he lives*, with the additional possibility (if written into the contract) of that same amount or a percentage thereof being paid to the surviving spouse (or other designated beneficiary). To oversimplify: With an annuity one is betting he will live a long time; whereas with life insurance he is betting he will die more quickly.[43] Thus, an annuity contract may be a viable "hedge" to guarantee retirement income. Again, see an attorney and life insurance agent to discuss its feasibility.

Unlike other forms of insurance, the owner of a life insurance policy has certain rights in that policy. For example, once an insurable interest is established and the policy is issued, the owner can assign (sell) the policy,[44] change the beneficiary [45] and change any settlement option. A policy will normally provide (unless otherwise agreed that the original designation of a beneficiary is irrevocable) a *procedure* for changing the beneficiary. Virginia law clearly states that the company must accede to a formal request to make such a change, but it also states that clear notice must be given to the company in the manner provided in the policy.[46] Therefore, one must be sure that if his position as policy owner changes (*i.e.*, the beneficiary originally designated is, for whatever

---

43. VANCE, INSURANCE § 200, pp. 1019-21 (3d ed. 1951).
44. VA. CODE § 38.1-442.
45. *Id.* § 38.1-442.1.
46. Carter v. Carter, 202 Va. 892, 121 S.E.2d 482 (1961).

reason, no longer the one desired to receive the proceeds), one must take prompt action to make the change according to the method dictated by the policy.

(3) *Settlement options*

A possible, but somewhat unusual, alternative to having the company pay out the face value proceeds of the policy to the beneficiary at the death of the insured, is to have the company *retain* the proceeds after such death occurs and, for example, pay out interest on this lump sum to the spouse of the insured during his or her life, with the proceeds themselves then being paid to children or grandchildren at the spouse's death. One may wish to discuss this possibility with an attorney and/or life insurance agent.

Another unique feature of life insurance is that the "whole life" policy builds a "cash surrender value" after a relatively short time (usually about three years).[47] That is, the longer one pays premiums, the more *equity* he has in the policy (compare this feature to paying off the *principal* on a mortgage), and that equity *must* be returned if the policy is cancelled for any reason.[48] One may also borrow against that value. In no real sense, however, is a life insurance policy an investment; it is one particular device for providing financial security for the beneficiary, especially since the beneficiary generally does not pay any federal income tax on life insurance proceeds.[49] Other income and estate tax consequences with respect to life insurance are beyond the scope of this discussion, but an attorney should be consulted for estate planning advice with respect to the uses of life insurance.

(b) *How Life Insurance Is Procured*

The normal procedure for procuring life insurance is first to apply for it, and then to submit to a medical exam. The application and medical report are then sent to the company, which decides on issuing the policy based on the information therein. Unlike property insurance, a life policy is effective only "when delivered."

---

47. VA. CODE § 38.1-462.
48. *Id.* § 38.1-461.
49. INT. REV. CODE § 101(a)(1).

However, an important exception has arisen in recent years — the use of the "binder." Under this procedure, one makes application and pays the first premium simultaneously, at which time he is issued a "temporary coverage binder receipt." Under the law, this means that he is covered (retroactively) from the date of application and issuance of the binder, *so long as* the company finds (by looking at the application and medical report and making any other investigation it wants) that the holder was insurable at time of application.[50] Thus, if the applicant happens to die after making application and receiving a binder, but even before taking the medical exam, the company must pay unless *it* can prove he was uninsurable when he applied. Furthermore, in making this judgment after it has learned of the death, the company must use the "rules and practices of the company at the date of the application" and cannot presume uninsurability from the death itself nor unduly delay acting on the application.[51]

(c) *Mandatory and Prohibited Policy Provisions*

As it does with all other types of insurance contracts, Virginia law dictates that certain clauses must be contained in a life insurance policy.[52] The policy must tell the holder: (1) that premiums are to be paid in advance [53] (usually the policy will require "payment at the home office," but this requirement can be, and often is, waived by the agent who accepts a premium payment; however, be sure to make certain of this practice in the discussion with the agent to whom the premium will be paid); (2) that, after the policy is in effect for one year, there is a one month, but not less than thirty days, grace period within which to pay the premium after its due date without the company being able to cancel the policy; [54] (3) that statements made in the application become part of the policy only if the application is attached to it when it is

---

50. Wright v. Pilot Life Ins. Co., 379 F.2d 409 (4th Cir. 1967), *rev'g* 254 F. Supp. 1018 (W.D. Va. 1966).
51. Evers v. Standard Sec. Life Ins. Co., 345 F. Supp. 1162 (W.D. Va. 1972), *aff'd*, 490 F.2d 1407 (4th Cir. 1974).
52. VA. CODE § 38.1-390.
53. *Id.* § 38.1-391.
54. *Id.* § 38.1-392.

received;[55] (4) that after the insured has lived for two years after the effective date of the policy, the company cannot contest its validity except for nonpayment of premiums [56] (however, the company can always contest on the basis that there was no coverage of the particular risk which caused the death;[57] for example, if on the application past heart trouble was concealed and yet the ensuing medical exam failed to disclose it and the policy was issued, if the insured died of a heart attack two years and one day after issuance the company must pay; but even if he lived for twenty years after the policy was issued and died as a result of the crash of a military aircraft, a permissible *exclusion*, there is no coverage and the company does not pay); (5) that if one misstates his age in the application, the amount payable by the company will only be that amount that the premium actually paid in *would* have purchased at the correct age at the time the policy was issued;[58] (6) that (with mutual companies) one has a right to share in the surplus of the company (through dividends whose method of payment one has a right to choose);[59] (7) that after the policy is in effect for three years, the holder can borrow from the company with the policy serving as security for the loan;[60] and (8) exactly how much the current cash surrender value is (since if the policy is cancelled this amount is returned).[61]

The following provisions are prohibited by Virginia law from appearing in a life insurance policy issued in this state: (1) any clause attempting to limit rights to sue on the policy to a period shorter than one year after the death of the insured; [(2) if the holder has chosen an alternative settlement option as previously discussed, the company cannot pay out less than the face value of the policy;] (3) any clause providing for a forfeiture of the policy because of a loan outstanding against it, or (4) a clause saying that the insurance company's agent is the insured's agent (such is not

---

55. *Id.* § 38.1-393.
56. *Id.* § 38.1-394.
57. United Sec. Life Ins. & Trust Co. v. Massey, 159 Va. 832, 164 S.E. 529 (1933).
58. VA. CODE § 38.1-395.
59. *Id.* § 38.1-396.
60. *Id.* § 38.1-397.
61. *Id.* § 38.1-398.

true; the agent is the company's employee, not the policyholders').[62]

Other than the above provisions mandated or prohibited by statute, the general principle of freedom of contract does apply to life insurance contracts. The company has the right to exclude certain risks from coverage and to impose certain conditions which the owner/insured must meet in order to keep coverage valid.

(d) *Rights and Duties Under the Contract*

The law imposes a duty on the prospective policyholder at the time of application to make full disclosure "in good faith" of his known medical history. Since the company has the opportunity to check that condition through a medical exam and any other investigation, one is not required to make an exhaustive search on his own for any ailments previously unknown.[63] But if he does conceal something known to him and dies within the two-year period specified, the company can and will contest the claim if the untruth was "material to the risk."[64] Moreover, if one becomes aware of a change in his condition after the application and before issuance of the policy, he has a legal duty to inform the company of such change.[65]

Suicide is not a defense to a claim on a life insurance policy unless it is committed within two years from the effective date of issuance, in which case the company does not pay off on the face amount of the policy but will only return all premiums paid.[66] Moreover, there is a legal presumption against suicide in the case of an otherwise unexplained death, and the company must prove suicide to avoid the policy;[67] it cannot force the beneficiary to prove death was not suicide.

An important condition to payment of a claim is the furnishing to the company of notice, and proof, of death.[68] This can be easily

---

62. *Id.* § 38.1-406.
63. Talley v. Metropolitan Life Ins. Co., 111 Va. 778, 69 S.E. 936 (1911).
64. Chitwood v. Prudential Ins. Co. of America, 206 Va. 314, 143 S.E.2d 915 (1965).
65. Combs v. Equitable Life Ins. Co., 120 F.2d 432 (4th Cir. 1941).
66. VA. CODE § 38.1-437.
67. Cosmopolitan Life Ins. Co. v. Koegel, 104 Va. 619, 52 S.E. 166 (1905).
68. Metropolitan Life Ins. Co. v. Rutherford, 98 Va. 195, 35 S.E. 361 (1900).

accomplished through whatever local officials are charged with the keeping of death records (coroner, medical examiner, bureau of vital statistics, etc.) who will furnish a death certificate. The requirement is readily met, but often overlooked in the midst of grief and attention to the deceased's other affairs after death.

As with all other insurance, one should take care to note the exclusions in a life insurance policy, some of which may be as follows: suicide within the first two years of the policy; death in war or military service; death within two years as a result of a specified hazardous occupation; death while living in specified foreign countries; death while in a military aircraft; death resulting from a violation of the law by the insured (*i.e.*, being shot by a policeman during a robbery attempt).

A provision contained in most life policies is a "waiver of premium during total disability" clause, whereby if the insured becomes disabled and is consequently unable to work and earn money to pay the premiums, the premiums will be waived by the company during this period without interrupting coverage. The financial security acquired for the beneficiary by purchasing the policy will thus not be impaired by inability to pay premiums while disabled. The only requirement here is that the insured furnish proof of disability, and the company has the right to have him submit to a medical exam to verify his claimed condition.[69]

(e) *Group Life Insurance*

A relatively recent phenomenon is group life insurance available through employers. This insurance device differs from an individual policy in that the employee does not make a contract with the insurance company; instead, the contract (called the "master policy") is made between the company and the employing entity. Under such a policy, the employer, as one of the group insured, does not get to choose the amount of coverage. The amount usually is automatically determined by job class, salary level, length of service with employer, etc. The premium is significantly less than what each individual insured would have to pay for the same

---

69. Johnson v. Mutual Life Ins. Co., 70 F.2d 41 (4th Cir. 1934), *aff'd*, 293 U.S. 335 (1934).

coverage on an individual policy. The insurance itself is usually of the "term" variety, and such term is almost always the length of employment with the organization, coverage under such policy ending with the termination of employment.

The advantages of coverage under a group policy are that, since no medical exam is usually required, one may be able to get life insurance protection even though he may be uninsurable, and the employer may pay part or all of the premiums.[70]

While the employee does not receive a copy of the master policy, Virginia law mandates that he does receive a *certificate* setting forth the scope of insurance protection (*i.e.*, coverage), the person to whom the benefits are payable (designated beneficiary), and all the insured's rights under the law.[71] Such rights include: (1) If the policy is other than a "term" plan, it must contain nonforfeiture provisions (*i.e.*, if premiums are paid by the insured and for any reason employment is discontinued, he has a right to a refund of at least part of those premiums, just as with an individual policy); (2) the right to designate (and change) the beneficiary (who can be anyone except the employer)[72] and (3) the right to a grace period of thirty-one days for payment of premiums (unless the "policyholder" — the employer — gives the company written notice of a termination of employment before such termination occurs).[73]

Virginia law also mandates that the group policy itself (*not* coverage of any one individual) is incontestable after it has been in effect for two years. Furthermore, with respect to an insured under such policy, the company cannot contest coverage on the basis of any statement made relating to insurability after the policyholder has lived for two years from the time he first came under the coverage of the master policy.[74] As a practical matter, the insurance company does not often check each individual through a medical exam. But if it wants to do so, the policy itself (and the certificate) must spell out "the conditions, if any, under

---

70. VANCE, INSURANCE § 203 (3d ed. 1951).
71. VA. CODE § 38.1-428.
72. *Id.* § 38.1-424.
73. *Id.* § 38.1-424.1.
74. *Id.* § 38.1-425.

which the insurer [the company] reserves the right to require a person eligible for insurance to furnish evidence of individual insurability satisfactory to the insurer as a condition to part or all of his coverage."[75]

Another very important feature of group life coverage is the right to *convert* it, *without proof of insurability*, to individual coverage after employment ceases. Thus, so long as application is made within thirty-one days after group coverage has terminated, the insured automatically can qualify for individual coverage. The amount of such coverage cannot exceed what it was under the group policy, the company can limit such amount to $2,000, and the premium rate is determined solely by age at this time.[76] The law further protects one during the process of such conversion: If he dies after termination of group coverage but before the individual policy has been issued (*i.e.*, during the thirty-one days if he has not applied, or after the thirty-one days if he has applied and the individual policy has not been issued yet), the beneficiary is entitled to a claim under the *group* policy for the *amount* of coverage that would have been issued under the individual policy, "whether or not application for the individual policy or payment of the first premium therefor has been made."[77]

To summarize, group life coverage can be a relatively cheap method of life insurance protection obtainable through an employer, and because of the conversion privilege one can continue this protection even after his employment ceases. If presently covered under a group plan, be sure to have the certificate and read it. If not presently under a group life plan, one may wish to check with his employer about the possibility of obtaining such coverage.

Accident and Sickness Insurance

(a) *Generally*

This type of insurance, generally obtained from life insurance companies, protects one from loss resulting from sickness or from

---

75. *Id.* § 38.1-426.1.
76. *Id.* §§ 38.1-428.1, 38.1-428.2.
77. *Id.* § 38.1-428.3.

bodily injury or death by accident.[78] The coverage permitted under such a policy is very broad under Virginia law. An individual can procure coverage for himself and his dependents guaranteeing payments for direct and indirect results of sickness or accident. Besides medical payments and reimbursement for hospital costs, he may get coverage which pays for any disability when he cannot work, and for expenses of rehabilitation.[79] While not available under Blue Cross/Blue Shield, Medicaid, or any state insurance plan, one can contract with a private insurer for payments for medical care not performed by a physician (chiropractor, optometrist, optician, psychologist, podiatrist, etc.) and for dental care.[80] Naturally the broader the coverages, the higher the premiums. It thus becomes important to analyze thoroughly insurance needs and to tailor the coverage to them.

What has already been said about the application for a life insurance policy applies with respect to sickness/accident insurance. There is a good faith obligation to disclose the age, present health, and known preexisting conditions of all those individuals seeking to be insured. The policy can be avoided by the company for false statements if material to the risk.[81] Of special importance in accident policies is the obligation to report to the company any change in occupation.[82] Becoming a quarry worker setting dynamite charges after having been a bricklayer is obviously an increase of risk of accident, and the company has a right to know of such change.

Among other primary obligations under Virginia law is the requirement to disclose all other insurance which one may have covering the same risks (since one cannot recover more than his actual loss). If there are two separate policies, each with a $5,000 limit on hospitalization benefits and the actual hospital bill after an illness is $1,000, under Virginia law each company will pay its

---

78. *Id.* §§ 38.1-5, 38.1-347.
79. *Id.* § 38.1-348.
80. *Id.* §§ 38.1-347.1, 38.1-348.5.
81. *Id.* §§ 38.1-348.4, 38.1-361.1.
82. *Id.* § 38.1-350(1).

INSURANCE 157

pro rata share ($500) of the loss.[83] As with a life insurance application, one must correctly state the ages of those to be covered; if not, the amount payable by the company after a loss will be only that amount such as the premium paid in would have purchased at the correct age(s).[84]

Because of the emphasis on consumer protection and because health insurance is much more a necessity than a luxury today, Virginia's lawmakers have mandated that the following be printed in every accident/sickness policy: "If for any reason you are not satisfied with your policy, you may return it to the Company within ten days of the date you received it and the premium you paid will be promptly refunded." [85] However, this protection is of no benefit if one fails to read the policy promptly upon receipt. Be sure to do so, and if unsure of the meaning of any of its terms call the agent and have him explain them; also be sure that the application accurately reflects the statements made and the coverages desired and paid for.

Take special note of the following provisions, the substance of which must be printed in the policy itself, under the heading of "Required Provisions:" (1) There can be no changes made by the agent in any policy provisions, nor can the agent waive any such provisions; changes can only be made on approval by an executive officer of the company; [86] (2) although the company does not have to provide for automatic renewal, if it does so the policyholder's rights to renewal must be specified; [87] (3) the length of the grace period within which to pay premiums after they are due must be stated (7 days if premiums are paid weekly, 10 days if paid monthly, and 31 days for all other premium payment arrangements); [88] (4) if the company reserves the right not to renew, it must notify of its intent at least five days before the current period of coverage expires; [89] (5) the insured has at least twenty days to file his claim

---
83. *Id.* § 38.1-350(4).
84. *Id.* § 38.1-350(2).
85. *Id.* § 38.1-348.4.
86. *Id.* § 38.1-349(1).
87. *Id.* § 38.1-349(2).
88. *Id.* § 38.1-349(3).
89. *Id.*

after the loss (more time if reasonable); [90] (6) the insured has the right to change the beneficiary, so long as he notifies the company of his desire to do so; [91] and (7) the policy must state that, although the insurance company can cancel for any reason so long as it gives notice and returns unearned premiums, if it cancels after a loss covered by the policy is incurred it must pay that claim.[92]

It is just common sense that, in order to recover for loss due to accident, the event causing the loss must indeed have been an accident. The Supreme Court of Virginia has defined "accident" as "an event that takes place without one's foresight or expectation; an event that proceeds from an unknown cause, or is an unusual effect of a known cause, and therefore not expected." [93] Thus, if the lawnmower throws up a pebble which strikes someone in the eye, or if anyone slips in the shower and injures his back, such are clearly accidents — being unusual effects of a known cause. But the usual exclusion in an accident policy is "voluntary exposure to unnecessary danger"; the insured may be protected from thoughtlessness or carelessness, but not from an intentionally hazardous undertaking. The law draws the line here and it makes good sense: Why should an insurer pay for injuries resulting from conscious disregard for one's own safety? The Supreme Court of Virginia has held that the company did not have to pay under an accidental death policy under the following circumstances, deeming the event causing the loss a "voluntary exposure to unnecessary danger": A divorced husband went to his ex-spouse's house where they argued fiercely; he saw a gun on a table and, fearing she would use it, reached to snatch it away; erroneously believing he was about to use the gun against her, she grabbed it and, seeing him lunge at her, shot him to death.[94] The point of all this is that although one may be insured, the law does not permit him to take ridiculous chances with complete disregard for safety

---

90. *Id.* § 38.1-349(5).
91. *Id.* § 38.1-349(12).
92. *Id.* § 38.1-350(8).
93. American Nat'l Ins. Co. v. Dozier, 172 Va. 376, 2 S.E.2d 282 (1939).
94. Wooden v. John Hancock Mut. Life Ins. Co., 205 Va. 750, 139 S.E.2d 801 (1965).

and expect to collect from the company for the consequences of his actions.

A word of caution: If one suffers a loss covered by the policy, be very wary of signing a release in exchange for the company's offer to pay part of the claim. Very often the full extent of the losses may not be apparent until long after the original accident or illness, and some insurers may try to pressure the policyholder into signing such a release from future payments in exchange for "prompt" payment of initial bills. This practice is not widespread in the insurance industry, but it can and does occur. If it happens, see an attorney immediately to assure that the legal rights to full payment under the coverages contracted for are rendered. Do not in any case just sit back and hope the insurer will eventually pay all claims, for long delay could result in legitimate claims being cut off by the statute of limitations.

(b) *Group Health Insurance*

Many employers offer some kind of health insurance plan (as well as a life insurance plan) to their employees and their families. The same advantages of reduced premiums and convertibility apply to this type of coverage. If not under such group health coverage, inquiry should be made of the employer as to the possibility of his instituting such coverage.

(c) *Airline Single-Trip Accidental Death Insurance*

If you travel by air, you probably have seen vending machines or small booths at airports offering flight insurance.[95] These policies are worthwhile in that they offer a large amount of accidental death insurance for a very small premium. If you use such insurance, be sure that, if possible, someone else fills out the application and pays the premium (*i.e.*, becomes the "owner" of the policy on your life). If such is the case and a fatal accident does befall you, the proceeds of the policy will not be included in your estate. However, if you (the insured) are the "owner" of such policy, the policy proceeds, although payable to your designated

---

95. VA. CODE § 38.1-356.1.

beneficiary, will be included in your estate with adverse tax consequences.[96]

AUTOMOBILE INSURANCE

(a) *Generally*

One need only glance at the statistics to see the losses incurred in this country each year through the operation of motor vehicles — about 50,000 lives, millions of injuries, and billions of dollars in property damage. Most important are the statistics showing unbelievably large court verdicts in favor of those injured through the fault of other motor vehicle operators, verdicts which, if not insured against, could wipe out a lifetime of savings. Even in so-called "no fault" states (of which Virginia is not one at present) an individual's right to sue is preserved if his claim is above a very low threshold amount. Hence, the need for insurance protection.

Under Virginia law a person is not required to have insurance as a prerequisite to driving an automobile, but everyone should have such protection because a court judgment against him is valid for at least twenty years and is renewable for another twenty years by the judgment creditor. So while present assets may be small, without insurance one can be financially enslaved to his judgment creditor for a long, long time.

When contracting for automobile insurance the principal coverage sought is *liability* coverage, under which the insurance company agrees to indemnify for loss occurring as a result of legal liability to a third party for personal injuries and/or property damage inflicted on that third party. Such third party is the *beneficiary* of the liability insurance part of the contract between the insured and the insurer.[97] Moreover, the "loss" incurred need not have already come out of one's pocket before the insurer is obligated to pay; in effect, once a court renders judgment, that judgment "fixes the loss" and, assuming coverage lies, by its contract the company is obligated to pay at this point. The Virginia Supreme Court has expressed the nature of liability insurance, in

---

96. INT. REV. CODE § 2042.
97. Davis v. National Grange Ins. Co., 281 F. Supp. 998 (E.D. Va. 1968).

substance, as follows: When the company is bound by the terms of the policy to indemnify the insured by paying any loss sustained by him by reason of the liability imposed by law in case of injury to or the death of third persons, and to pay as well the court costs in any suit against the insured and also the interest on any judgment in the suit, the *cause of action of the insured* (the contractual right against the company to have it pay) is complete and he can recover on the contract as soon as the liability has become fixed and established by a judgment against him, even though he has sustained no actual pecuniary loss at the time he seeks to recover (from the company).[98]

Virginia law also permits, among others, the following types of automobile insurance coverages: (1) medical payments to the insured, all members of his household and all passengers, even if he has other health insurance; [99] more specifically, medical payments, hospitalization payments, compensation for disability, rehabilitation expenses, funeral expenses (up to $2,000 per person), and payments for lost income (up to $100 per week) for up to one year; [100] the availability of such coverages must be brought to one's attention by being printed on the front of the policy; [101] (2) collision insurance on one's own vehicle(s); and (3) "comprehensive" or "extended" coverage on the vehicle and its contents (against loss by theft, vandalism, the elements, etc.). While these coverages are important, they are far less so than liability protection. For this reason, the rest of the discussion will focus on Virginia's treatment of automobile liability insurance.

Because of the special nature of the automobile liability insurance contract (a contract for the ultimate benefit of an innocent third party who may be injured) many special features are required by law in all such contracts. Despite these broad requirements, however, the applicant for automobile insurance still must make certain he carefully explains to the agent his particular circumstances and insurance needs. For example, suppose he is

---
98. Indemnity Ins. Co. v. Davis' Adm'r, 150 Va. 778, 143 S.E. 328 (1928).
99. VA. CODE § 38.1-381.
100. *Id.* § 38.1-380.1.
101. *Id.* § 38.1-380.2.

married, his spouse drives, he has two children living at home who are licensed drivers, and he has two vehicles, both registered in his name. He may then be asked, and he must be sure to answer completely and truthfully: who the principal drivers of each vehicle are; where the vehicles are garaged; what the driving records of each of the four drivers are; approximately how many miles per year each driver puts on each vehicle; and to what uses (business use or not) the vehicles are put. Then he must be sure to discuss the dollar limits of liability coverage desired (the increase in premiums is quite small between that required for mimimum liability coverage and that which will purchase much greater coverage). Once this process is complete, all four drivers will be "named insureds" in the policy and the maximum family protection possible will be achieved. Then if any of the four, while operating either of the two insured vehicles, injures a third party, all are covered against a judgment of liability obtained by that third party. Besides this "normal" situation, however, Virginia law also makes it mandatory that the following liability coverages appear in the policy.

(b) *The Omnibus Clause* [102]

Basically this clause provides that coverage will lie, under the policy, with respect to anyone driving the car with express or implied permission of the insured. Thus, if any one of the covered parties lends either of the vehicles to anyone else who subsequently injures another while operating the vehicle, the company will pay for any loss resulting from a judgment against the permissive driver of the car. While the Virginia courts have liberally construed this omnibus coverage (since it is for the benefit of innocent third parties), there are at least two possible areas of danger: (1) where the applicant knows that he will regularly be lending his vehicle to a driver with a poor driving record and fails to disclose such a fact; and (2) where the person to whom the vehicle is loaned drives it to a place and in a manner so far beyond the permission given that he is deemed to have been on a "frolic of his own" rather than within the permission granted. In the former

---

102. *Id.* § 38.1-381.

case, the company may successfully avoid payment based on the misstatement in the application,[103] and in the latter by arguing that the deviation was so great as to characterize the operation as not with permission at all.[104]

(c) *Uninsured Motorist Coverage* [105]

This mandatory coverage provides that if any "named insureds" are injured personally or suffer property damage caused by an uninsured motorist, they can collect from their company under the policy up to $25,000 for bodily injury to or death of one person, $50,000 for bodily injury to or death of two or more persons, and $5,000 for injury to or destruction of property in any one accident.[106] These are the minimum mandatory coverages; for an additional premium a person can contract for higher uninsured motorist limits, up to the maximum regular liability coverage of his own policy. Moreover, the availability of such optional coverage must be made known by being printed on the front of the policy or as an attachment to the premium notice.[107]

Under all such uninsured motorist coverage, only a "named insured" under the policy is so covered by it. Thus, someone outside the family to whom the vehicle was loaned is *not* so covered if injured by an uninsured motorist. The courts simply draw a line here based on the fact that the insured, rather than the permissive driver, paid the premium for such uninsured motorist coverage.[108]

(d) *Unknown Motorist Coverage* [109]

If any named insured is injured or suffers property damage caused by a hit-and-run driver, or if there is no contact at all with another vehicle which simply forces him into a ditch causing injuries and/or property damage, he is entitled to the same

---

103. Bernstein v. Nationwide Mut. Ins. Co., 458 F.2d 506 (4th Cir. 1972).
104. Jordan v. Shelly Mut. Plate Glass & Cas. Co., 51 F. Supp. 240 (W.D. Va. 1943), *aff'd*, 142 F.2d 52 (4th Cir. 1944).
105. VA. CODE § 38.1-381(b).
106. *Id.* § 46.1-1(8).
107. *Id.* § 38.1-382.1.
108. Cunningham v. Insurance Co. of North America, 213 Va. 72, 189 S.E.2d 832 (1972).
109. VA. CODE § 38.1-381(d).

coverages as exist under the uninsured motorist section. However, as an absolute precondition to collecting on such a claim, the insured must report such an accident.[110] The reason for this requirement is to give the police and insurance company an opportunity to track down this unknown driver who was responsible for the loss.

(e) *Conditions and Exclusions in Policy*

At the risk of being overly repetitive, the warning is again given here that one carefully read his policy to determine the conditions and exclusions contained therein and to consult with an attorney if the meaning is not fully understood. Typical *exclusions* (risks not covered at all) under liability coverage include: losses incurred by someone while carrying passengers for hire, while driving a nonowned automobile (see the discussion of the omnibus clause *supra*), while the car is driven in violation of law (such as running a stop sign) if the violation causes the accident,[111] and if the loss is incurred because of an intentional act on the part of the insured.

Typical *conditions* which one must meet in order for the coverages to remain in effect include informing the company of any change in the "principal place of garaging" of the vehicles (since premium rates are at least in part determined by where one lives), being truthful on the application, and "cooperating" with the company in any lawsuit. By law, the company not only must pay any judgment but has the contractual duty to defend the insured in any lawsuit based on his operation of the insured vehicles. However, coextensive with the company's duty to defend is the insured's duty to cooperate in the defense.[112] This duty begins immediately at the time of accident: As soon as it is feasible to do so (*i.e.*, after the police are called and medical attention is given to anyone requiring it), be sure to obtain the names and addresses of other drivers involved, the license and registration number of all vehicles involved, the company and local insurance agent of these other drivers, and, if possible, the names and addresses of any witnesses to the accident. It is only fair that the insurer be

---
110. Nationwide Mut. Ins. Co. v. Clark, 213 Va. 666, 194 S.E.2d 699 (1973).
111. Maryland Cas. Co. v. Hoge, 153 Va. 204, 149 S.E. 448 (1929).
112. Hunter v. Hollingsworth, 165 Va. 583, 183 S.E. 508 (1936).

given notice of the accident [113] in order to be able to adequately prepare a defense to any suits, especially since the company must pay for the legal expenses of even groundless suits.[114]

Normally an insurer is only obligated to pay a judgment up to the policy limits of liability. However, in extreme circumstances the company will be made to pay more than these limits because of a lack of good faith on its part in settlement negotiations.[115] For instance, if the injured party sues for $300,000 and the policy limit is $100,000, if such party offers to settle his claim for $80,000 (within the policy limit) the company must carefully consider such an offer and cannot cavalierly disregard the insured's potential $200,000 exposure in the hope that a jury will bring in a verdict for less than $80,000.

Again on public policy grounds (the liability coverage being principally for the benefit of injured third parties), Virginia law tightly restrains the insurer's ability to cancel automobile insurance. The company *cannot* cancel or refuse to renew on the basis of age, sex, residence, race, color, creed, national origin, ancestry, marital status or lawful occupation (but *can* refuse to renew if a change in occupation materially increases the risk). Aside from these prohibitions, the company can cancel for any reason within the first sixty days of the effective date of the policy (that period being deemed sufficient time to afford the company an opportunity to investigate the applicant). After this time, however, there can be no cancellation except for failure to pay premiums and/or suspension or revocation of the driver's license of the insured. Even if such is the case, the company must give notice of its intention to cancel and the insured has the right to a hearing before the Commissioner of Insurance to determine the validity of the company's proposed cancellation.[116]

TITLE INSURANCE

When purchasing a home one is probably making the largest investment of his life. Common sense dictates that he wants to

---
113. Temple v. Virginia Auto Mut. Ins. Co., 181 Va. 561, 25 S.E.2d 268 (1943).
114. Rowe v. United States Fid. & Guar. Co., 375 F.2d 215 (4th Cir. 1967).
115. Davis v. National Grange Ins. Co., 281 F. Supp. 998 (E.D. Va. 1968).
116. VA. CODE § 38.1-381.5.

protect such an investment, and title insurance can offer one form of such protection against defects in the title. As stated by the Supreme Court of Virginia: "It is the lack of knowledge of the condition of a title that prompts insurance. The policy insures the policyholder that what he does not know about the title so far as liens and defects are concerned, does not exist." [117] The insurer also bears the responsibility for a mistake in the description of the property.[118]

The reader would be well advised to get his own attorney when he buys a home, even though the seller and real estate broker may tell him that he does not need one. Their interests may not coincide with his, the cost of an attorney is relatively small in comparison with the investment, and an attorney will know exactly how to protect the buyer's interest, including obtaining a title insurance policy. Irrespective of when the property was last sold and/or surveyed, there may be discoverable defects in the title which an attorney (or a trained title searcher he employs) can uncover and, hopefully, correct.

---

117. Title Ins Co. v. Industrial Bank, 156 Va. 322, 157 S.E. 710 (1931).
118. Marandino v. Lawyers Title Ins. Corp., 156 Va. 696, 159 S.E. 181 (1931).

CHAPTER 9

Motor Vehicles

K. T. Rye

IN GENERAL

Over the years, the automobile has changed from a luxury item to a necessity in almost every home and business. It provides increased services and greater mobility, and has generated a unique life-style complete with shopping centers, and chains of drive-in restaurants. Unfortunately, the automobile has also produced thousands of deaths, countless injuries, and an explosion of lawsuits over its operation and maintenance.

Before beginning this chapter, it might be helpful to clarify what is meant by the term "motor vehicle." Theoretically, any machine-propelled vehicle falls within this category. Thus, automobiles, buses, motorcycles and trucks, as well as golf carts and tractors, are all technically motor vehicles. However, for the purposes of this *Guide* and the laws of Virginia, motor vehicles include "every vehicle which is self-propelled or designed for self-propulsion and every vehicle drawn by or designed to be drawn by a motor vehicle and includes every device in, upon or by which any person or property is or can be transported or drawn upon a highway, except devices moved by human or animal power and devices used exclusively upon stationary rails or tracks, and vehicles used in this State but not required to be licensed by the State."[1] Since legislative enactments exempt golf carts and tractors from state licensing requirements,[2] they are not legally motor vehicles. Also exempted from the definition of a motor vehicle are pedal bicycles with helper motors, provided the motors are rated at less than one brake horsepower, and produce only ordinary pedaling speeds up to a maximum of twenty miles per hour.[3] However, when driven on the public roadways, their

---

1. VA. CODE § 46.1-389.
2. *Id.* §§ 46.1-45, 46.1-45.2.
3. *Id.* § 46.1-1(1a), (15).

operators are subject to the same road regulations which govern the drivers of other motor vehicles.[4]

Although federal and local laws also pertain to motor vehicles, this chapter focuses on those of the Commonwealth of Virginia. Since federal standards control vehicular equipment, interstate commerce, and other areas having a small impact on the average driver of this state, they will not be discussed. Local laws aim primarily at traffic control within particular jurisdictions and vary accordingly.

Virginia's motor vehicle statutes regulate most administrative and operational aspects on a statewide basis. All licensing and registration of drivers and vehicles remain a prerogative of the state. Other areas where the Commonwealth intervenes include traffic accidents and citations for violations of the motor vehicle laws.

Although each of these areas will be covered within this chapter, it is merely a brief overview of the subject matter. Should a question remain unanswered, consult (1) the local office of the Division of Motor Vehicles (hereinafter referred to as DMV), (2) the main office of DMV (located at 2220 West Broad Street in Richmond), or (3) the motor vehicle laws contained in Title 46.1 of the Code of Virginia.

THE REGISTRATION PROCESS

(a) *Title Certificate and Registration*

Upon acquisition of a motor vehicle and prior to its operation on the public roadways, it must be registered with the DMV and a certificate of title secured in the owner's name.[5] In all cases, the new owner must complete certain forms requiring a brief description of the vehicle, its identification or engine number, the owner's name and address, Social Security number, and the names and addresses of all persons holding liens upon the vehicle.[6] Failure to register the vehicle, or the knowing inclusion of a false

---

4. *Id.* § 46.1-171.
5. *Id.* § 46.1-41.
6. *Id.* §§ 46.1-52, 46.1-53.

statement on the registration application,[7] or failure to pay the registration fee, can subject the owner to a penalty of up to six months in jail and/or a fine of $500.[8]

On payment of the registration fee and pending final approval of the application, the owner receives a temporary registration certificate permitting operation of the vehicle.[9] Currently, the registration fee is fifteen dollars for all automobiles and trucks weighing 4,000 pounds or less, and twenty dollars for all such vehicles exceeding 4,000 pounds, while the charge for motorcycles and trailers is somewhat less.[10] A certificate of title may be secured for any vehicle for a fee of seven dollars.[11]

In certain cases, registration fees or the registration requirements themselves have been waived by special enactments. For example, all motor vehicles used exclusively in farming or horticulture do not require registration. A farmer can move his tractor from one portion of his land to another, transport his crops to market, or secure equipment repairs by using the public roadways, provided the distance traveled does not exceed ten miles. Similar exemptions are also applicable to motor vehicles employed exclusively in sawmill and mining operations.[12] In certain cases, disabled veterans are eligible for a waiver of the registration fee on their vehicle. To determine whether an individual qualifies for this or other exemptions, consult the local office of DMV.[13]

Upon approval of the application, a certificate of title and permanent registration are issued and mailed to the owner within several weeks. However, where the vehicle has been pledged as security to cover a debt, the registration goes to the owner and the certificate of title to the lienholder. The title certificate lists all persons having liens upon the vehicle in order of repayment.[14] Until the debt is paid in full, some creditor retains the title certificate.

---

7. *Id.* § 46.1-64.
8. *Id.* §§ 46.1-16.01, 46.1-152.
9. *Id.* § 46.1-42.
10. *Id.* § 46.1-149.
11. *Id.* § 46.1-78.
12. *Id.* § 46.1-45.
13. *Id.* § 46.1-149.1.
14. *Id.* § 46.1-69.

Since an automobile or truck cannot be lawfully purchased, traded or exchanged without this title certificate, the owner is unable to dispose of the vehicle until the listed creditors either give their consent or are paid. Once the first creditor is satisfied, the title certificate passes to the next lienholder and so on, until all have received their money.[15]

Should the vehicle be pledged as security to cover a subsequent debt, this new lienholder must be reflected on the title certificate. On payment of a five dollar fee,[16] DMV will cancel the incorrect certificate and issue an updated one.[17]

Once the registration and title certificate are obtained, each must be signed in ink by the owner in order to be validated. Although the Motor Vehicle Code states that all individuals "shall have in [their] possession [their] registration card ... [and] license" while driving, conviction does not automatically result if discovered without them. In such an event, the operator must subsequently produce these documents either to the arresting officer or to the court at the time of his appearance. Failure to produce them on these occasions is a misdemeanor punishable by a fine.[18]

When the title certificate is lost or damaged, DMV will replace it for a nominal fee.[19] If an individual moves or changes addresses, he must inform DMV within thirty days. Prompt notification permits the agency to correct its records and saves a five dollar fee for noncompliance.[20] Similar provisions apply for replacement of lost or damaged registration cards, but no fee is charged.[21]

When selling, purchasing or exchanging a motor vehicle, the title certificate is vital in the transaction. All transfers between private individuals require an exchange of the vehicle's title certificate to consummate the deal. Without this proof of ownership, an individual may unknowingly receive a stolen car (or one with numerous liens against it) and lose his entire investment.

---

15. *Id.* § 46.1-74.
16. *Id.* § 46.1-78.
17. *Id.* § 46.1-70.
18. *Id.* § 46.1-7.
19. *Id.* § 46.1-55.
20. *Id.* § 46.1-52.1.
21. *Id.* § 46.1-55.

A certificate of title is not required when the vehicle is purchased new from an authorized dealer. Here, the dealer issues a temporary certificate which remains in effect until DMV mails out a permanent one. If a used car is purchased and lacks a title certificate, the dealer may still complete the sale and issue a thirty-day temporary certificate. However, failure to produce the old certificate within this period or to apply for a replacement empowers the buyer to repudiate the sale and recover his purchase price.[22]

Assuming the seller possesses a valid certificate of title, he then completes the sale by delivering a list of all liens presently held on the vehicle, endorsing title over to the new owner on the back of the certificate,[23] and recording the current mileage in the proper space.[24]

A word of caution is appropriate concerning the mileage. Federal and state law demand an accurate reading and deal harshly with any alteration of the odometer.[25] If the seller knows the figure is incorrect, the law requires written disclosure of this fact to the buyer.[26] However, nothing in these statutes prevent necessary repairs or replacement of the mechanism provided the mileage remains the same as before the work. If this cannot be done, one simply readjusts the odometer to zero and attaches a notice specifying the number of miles prior to repair to the left door frame of the vehicle.[27] Thus, the buyer knows the correct mileage and true worth of the vehicle. Once the mileage is accurately recorded and the certificate properly endorsed, the purchaser writes his name and address on the front of the certificate and forwards it to DMV for a new certificate.[28]

(b) *Insurance*

The second step in obtaining a registration card requires the owner to secure sufficient auto insurance or its equivalent. Should

---

22. *Id.* § 46.1-90.1.
23. *Id.* § 46.1-87.
24. *Id.* § 46.1-89.1.
25. 15 U.S.C. §§ 1984, 1989; VA. CODE § 46.1-89.1.
26. 15 U.S.C. § 1988.
27. 15 U.S.C. § 1987.
28. VA. CODE §§ 46.1-89, 46.1-91.

an accident happen, this theoretically guarantees that the innocent party will recover his expenses. To comply, an owner must demonstrate his financial responsibility in case of a mishap. This may be done by (1) producing evidence of a current insurance policy from a company licensed to do business in Virginia; (2) obtaining a duly executed bond; (3) depositing $35,000 in cash or securities with the state,[29] or (4) paying the uninsured motor vehicle fee of $150 to DMV.[30]

Most Virginians select the first alternative and obtain an insurance policy having a minimum coverage of $25,000 for the bodily injury to or death of one person, $50,000 for the bodily injury to or death of two or more persons, and $5,000 for injury to or destruction of property in any one accident ($25,000/$50,000/$5,000), as required by law.[31] Those electing to pay the uninsured motorist fee should realize that this is not insurance and offers no financial protection in the event of an accident. The $150 fee merely exempts the individual from the insurance requirement for registration purposes.[32]

(c) *Inspection*

Once the title certificate has been transferred and adequate proof of financial responsibility produced, the owner must have his vehicle inspected to ensure safe operation. If the vehicle meets the minimum standards, the owner receives an inspection sticker and will not have to repeat this safety check for approximately six months.

By law, all motor vehicles (including trailers) seeking registration or currently registered in this state must be checked every six months at a state-approved inspection facility.[33] Each inspection includes an examination of the lights, windshield wipers, brakes, horn, steering and suspension, tires and the exhaust system to ensure their proper functioning,[34] and the official

---

29. *Id.* §§ 46.1-468, 46.1-485.
30. DIVISION OF MOTOR VEHICLES, VIRGINIA DRIVER'S MANUAL 1976-77, p. 47.
31. VA. CODE § 46.1-1(8).
32. DIVISION OF MOTOR VEHICLES, VIRGINIA DRIVER'S MANUAL 1976-77, p. 47.
33. *Id.* at 61.
34. *Id.*

inspection station may make a charge of four dollars for each such inspection.[35] If a vehicle fails to meet the minimum standards, the owner must immediately have the defect repaired. Once the old inspection period expires and the problem remains uncorrected, further operation of the vehicle is prohibited except to secure repairs.[36] Parts and labor are not included in the inspection fee, and repairs necessitate a reinspection if done by any establishment other than an official inspection facility.[37]

Although inspections normally occur twice a year, the superintendent of state police may compel motor vehicles to be examined at any time. Owners who refuse to comply or repair defects subsequently discovered subject themselves to a penalty for each day of unlawful operation.[38]

(d) *License Plates*

The fourth and last step in the registration process is the acquisition of license plates. Presently, the law requires that all vehicles registered in Virginia display valid state license plates prior to operation on the public roadways. Motorcycles and tractor trailers must have a single plate affixed to the back of the vehicle, while passenger cars and trucks must display one front and rear.[39] Emblems, insignias or trailer hitches which obstruct or render the plates illegible must be removed.[40]

Unknown to many Virginians, the state offers special license plates available on application and payment of an extra fee. For example, any owner may request a particular letter-number combination on his license tags on payment of an additional ten dollar fee.[41] Members of volunteer fire departments or rescue squads have the opportunity to secure distinctly marked plates indicating their emergency function.[42] Vehicles which are twenty-five years old or more and meet the criteria of an exhibition

---

35. VA. CODE § 46.1-321.
36. *Id.* § 46.1-315.
37. *Id.* § 46.1-322.
38. *Id.* § 46.1-315; see also § 46.1-16.01.
39. *Id.* § 46.1-99.
40. *Id.* § 46.1-107.
41. *Id.* § 46.1-105.2.
42. *Id.* §§ 46.1-105.3, 46.1-105.4.

vehicle are eligible for permanent "antique" plates for a mere five dollar fee.[43] For the physically handicapped, distinctive license tags affording a free parking privilege in municipal lots and publically metered areas are also available. Although this privilege applies on a statewide basis, it has no effect where parking is expressly prohibited or in areas which restrict parking during periods of heavy traffic.[44]

Upon the sale or disposal of a motor vehicle, the former owner may surrender the plates to DMV and receive a refund of a portion of the fee paid.[45] Where this individual has already purchased another vehicle or intends to do so in the near future, the law permits him to retain them for his new acquisition and avoid the additional expense of new plates. To qualify for this savings, the DMV requires the owner to file a new application and pay all transfer fees.[46]

Securing, Renewing, and Losing a Driver's License

All individuals wishing to drive must be tested and certified by the state. The Commonwealth offers two basic licenses — the operator's and the chauffeur's. Each type allows special endorsements for the use of vehicles that may not otherwise be operated on a regular license.[47] In most cases applicants seek a standard operator's license which authorizes the driving of passenger cars, trucks, and other vehicles not used for hire. Anyone under eighteen years of age will not be issued an operator's license unless the individual has successfully completed a state-approved driver education course.[48] Learner's permits are available to applicants over the age of fifteen years, eight months. These permits allow beginning individuals to operate a motor vehicle only when accompanied by a licensed driver who is actually

---

43. *Id.* § 46.1-104.
44. *Id.* § 46.1-104.1.
45. *Id.* § 46.1-97.
46. *Id.* § 46.1-95.
47. *Id.* § 46.1-373.
48. *Id.* § 46.1-357.

seated beside him. Each permit costs three dollars and remains valid for one year.[49]

To receive an operator's license, an applicant must demonstrate his ability to operate a motor vehicle and pass the written and visual portions of the examination.[50] Assuming the individual satisfies all criteria and pays the nine dollar fee, an operator's license will be issued to him and remain valid approximately four years.[51] However, a license is not permanent, nor does the law consider it a right to which all are entitled. Rather, it is a privilege which is subject to revocation for violation of the traffic rules and regulations.[52] For the protection of the general public as well as the individuals themselves, anyone found mentally or physically incompetent to drive will not receive a license.[53]

A chauffeur's license permits the operation of a common carrier of passengers or any vehicle driven by an employee for a living. The local cab driver, delivery service, and Good Humor man are examples of those who must secure this type of license. All applicants must be eighteen years of age and pass the visual, written, and road portions of the examination.[54] Unlike an operator's license, it is subject to further regulation by the local unit of government,[55] costs twelve dollars and remains effective for approximately two years,[56] and permits the operation of other passenger vehicles (including the family car) as well as vehicles operated for hire.[57]

Individuals already possessing either type of license and desiring to drive a bus, motorcycle or other motor vehicle having three or more axles with a weight in excess of 40,000 pounds need not obtain an additional license. After successfully completing all examinations and payment of a small fee, one's current license

---

49. *Id.*
50. *Id.* §§ 46.1-357.2, 46.1-369.
51. *Id.* §§ 46.1-380.1, 46.1-380.2.
52. Prichard v. Battle, 178 Va. 455, 17 S.E.2d 393 (1941).
53. VA. CODE §§ 46.1-357.2, 46.1-359 to 46.1-361.
54. *Id.* §§ 46.1-357.2, 46.1-369.
55. *Id.* § 46.1-353.
56. *Id.* §§ 46.1-380.1, 46.1-380.2.
57. *Id.* § 46.1-374.

receives an endorsement permitting operation of these vehicles. Thus, if a person wants to drive a motorcycle but has no license, an operator's permit with the proper endorsements will allow him to drive it.[58]

Although the Motor Vehicle Code normally demands state certification and licensing, certain drivers are specifically exempted. All military personnel currently stationed in Virginia, their spouses and their dependent children not less than sixteen years of age, are not considered to be state residents for licensing purposes. Therefore, if they possess a valid driver's license from their home state or country, they may operate a motor vehicle without obtaining a Virginia license.[59] Similar reasoning applies to nonresidents presently enrolled as full-time students at accredited educational institutions within the Commonwealth.[60] Any nonresident who temporarily lives and works in Virginia may drive with a home-state driver's license for no more than sixty days.[61] However, all nonresidents who have not been licensed either as an operator or chauffeur in their home state or country, and all new residents of Virginia who have been licensed under the laws of their home state or country, are required to obtain a Virginia driver's license within thirty days.[62] In addition to these exemptions, state licensing requirements do not apply to the operation of vehicles entirely on private property[63] or to the movement of farm machinery along the public roads within a short distance of the homestead.[64] If one is unsure about his status, consult the local office of DMV *prior* to operation.

If one moves to a new location or misplaces or damages his license, the authorities require prompt notification. Duplicates for lost or destroyed ones will be issued for three dollars.[65] When an individual has relocated or otherwise changed his status, the

---

58. *Id.* § 46.1-373.
59. *Id.* §§ 46.1-354, 46.1-354.1.
60. *Id.* § 46.1-355.
61. Division of Motor Vehicles, Virginia Driver's Manual 1976-77, pp. 6-7.
62. Va. Code §§ 46.1-355.1, 46.1-456.
63. *Id.* § 46.1-349.
64. *Id.* § 46.1-352.
65. *Id.* § 46.1-379.

proper procedure involves notifying the DMV within thirty days either by a personal visit to any DMV branch office or by attaching the address change stub from his license, filling in the correct information, and mailing it to the main DMV office in Richmond. An updated license will then be issued at no additional cost. A fee of five dollars may be imposed for failure to notify the DMV of a change of address.[66]

A summary of the expiration periods and fees for driver's licenses and permits [67] follows:

Type	Expiration Period	Original	Renewal	Duplicate
Operator's license	4 years	$9.00	$9.00	$3.00
Operator's with endorsements	4 years	$12.00	$12.00	$3.00
Chauffeur's license	2 years	$12.00	$12.00	$3.00
Chauffeur's with endorsements	2 years	$15.00	$15.00	$3.00
Instruction permit	1 year	$3.00		No fee

Issuance of a license is only the first half of the battle. All licensees must then comply with the rules governing operation and maintenance of the vehicle, and submit to periodic retesting to have their licenses renewed. Generally, a renewal requires the applicant to appear at DMV, fill out the appropriate forms, undergo an eye examination,[68] and pay the license fee. A more extensive procedure including a visual and written test is mandated by statute in the renewal years most immediately prior to the year of the applicant's thirtieth, thirty-eighth, and forty-second birthdays, and every four years thereafter. No road test is normally required for renewal, and careful drivers often discover the written test has been waived because of their operating record.[69] However, DMV always

---

66. Id. § 46.1-368.1.
67. Id. §§ 46.1-380.1, 46.1-380.2 (operator's and chauffeur's licenses), 46.1-357 (instruction permits), and 46.1-379 (duplicate licenses).
68. Id. § 46.1-357.2.
69. Id. § 46.1-380.1.

reserves the option to order a complete examination before granting a renewal if it deems one appropriate.[70]

Retesting will also be ordered whenever the state believes one is incompetent to drive.[71] Frequently, a series of minor traffic violations, involvement in an auto accident or conviction for a serious breach of the Motor Vehicle Code may justify an immediate reexamination. Since an unfit driver poses a danger to the public and himself, the failure to report for reexamination is grounds for the suspension or revocation of his license.[72]

Loss of license may also occur for violations of the Motor Vehicle Code. The length and severity of the punishment generally increases proportionally with the nature of the offense and the frequency of its occurrence. Where the violation is a serious one, such as manslaughter involving a motor vehicle, leaving the scene of an accident, or perjury in connection with applications to DMV, a guilty verdict can mean a one year license revocation.[73] Other offenses resulting in loss of license encompass driving while under the influence of drugs or intoxicants,[74] reckless driving,[75] or failure to attend a driver improvement clinic.[76] Although suspension or revocation often inflict personal hardship, the act is not intended as a penal measure, but is designed "to protect the ... highways from those who are not qualified to operate motor vehicles...."[77] Usually, this loss of the driving privilege occurs in addition to other fines and penalties imposed as punishment for the offense.

Continued violations which menace lives and property may result in stiffer penalties. Under Virginia's Habitual Offender's Act, anyone convicted of any three of the following, singularly or in combination, within a ten-year period is branded as an "habitual offender" and automatically forfeits his license for ten years: (1) manslaughter resulting from the operation of a motor vehicle; (2)

70. *Id.*
71. *Id.* § 46.1-383.
72. *Id.*
73. *Id.* § 46.1-417.
74. *Id.* § 46.1-421.
75. *Id.* § 46.1-422.
76. *Id.* § 46.1-514.16.
77. Prichard v. Battle, 178 Va. 455, 461, 17 S.E.2d 393, 395 (1941).

MOTOR VEHICLES 179

driving while under the influence of intoxicants or drugs; (3) operating a vehicle with a suspended or revoked license; (4) lying on the DMV's applications, and (5) leaving the scene of an accident in which property damage occurs in excess of $250, or in which death or bodily injuries result.[78]

In cases where the Motor Vehicle Code mandates an automatic loss of license upon conviction, a judicial appeal is not permitted except as to questions of identity.[79] Those claiming such a mistake in identity encounter the burden of proving otherwise.[80]

When an individual faces the possibility of losing his license, the commissioner of the DMV will give appropriate notice to the parties to appear and settle the matter.[81] If this preliminary hearing renders a decision adverse to the licensee, a court appeal is possible if initiated within thirty days of the commissioner's ruling.[82] However, merely appealing the decision does not restore the driving privilege. Until the court actually reinstates the license, the commissioner's decision remains in force and unconditionally bars the individual from operating a motor vehicle on the public roadways.[83] Those discovered driving with a suspended or revoked license face a jail sentence of at least ten days, an additional period without the privilege of driving, and/or a fine upon conviction.[84]

Virginia residents may forfeit their licenses for failure to pay traffic tickets, fines or judgments arising out of a motor vehicle accident. As an implied condition to receiving a license or operating a vehicle in Virginia, all drivers "shall be deemed ... to have consented to pay all lawful fines and court costs assessed against [them] for violations of the motor vehicle laws ...." [85] Therefore, a failure to pay justifies a license suspension until the offender complies.[86]

---

78. VA. CODE §§ 46.1-387.2, 46.1-387.7.
79. 2B MICHIE'S JURISPRUDENCE *Automobiles* § 10 (1970).
80. VA. CODE § 46.1-387.3.
81. *Id.* § 46.1-430.
82. *Id.* § 46.1-437.
83. *Id.* § 46.1-367.
84. *Id.* § 46.1-350.
85. *Id.* § 46.1-423.3.
86. *Id.*

Involvement in an accident in another state, territory or Canada also subjects Virginians to this law.[87] Regardless of where the mishap occurs, if the court determines fault and renders a monetary judgment for the other party, and thirty days elapse without payment of the amount, when the Virginia DMV receives notification of this failure to pay, the commissioner may suspend the offender's driver's license, registration, and license plates.[88] In certain cases this thirty-day requirement may be temporarily waived upon consent of the creditor or if the court agrees to payment on an installment basis.[89] Once a suspension occurs, it remains effective until the judgment is satisfied and the offender supplies proof of his financial responsibility in the future.[90]

Although the rationale behind license suspensions and revocations is to eliminate the unsafe driver, they take effect only after the accident or fatality has already occurred. New legislation, entitled the Virginia Driver Improvement Act, focuses on prevention of these problems rather than a subsequent cure. By rating all Virginia drivers, it seeks to identify the unsafe driver and help him before he loses his license or causes a traffic mishap.[91]

Beginning January 1, 1975, the commissioner of the DMV will assign point values to convictions for traffic offenses occurring within the Commonwealth, other states or Canada. The more serious the offense the larger number of demerits given, but in no event is the number to exceed six demerit points for any single conviction. For example, a driver convicted of speeding twenty miles per hour or more above the posted limit, reckless driving, or racing would receive the maximum of six demerit points. One who is found guilty of failing to yield the right of way, speeding between ten and nineteen miles per hour above the posted limit, or failure to stop at a stop light receives four demerit points, while speeding between one and nine miles per hour above the posted

---

87. *Id.* § 46.1-443.
88. *Id.* § 46.1-442.
89. *Id.* § 46.1-445, 46.1-448.
90. *Id.* § 46.1-459.
91. COMMONWEALTH OF VIRGINIA DIVISION OF MOTOR VEHICLES, OUR DRIVER IMPROVEMENT PROGRAM IS A NEW WAY OF KEEPING SCORE FOR SAFE DRIVING 1.

speed limit, improper driving or passing, or failure to obey a highway sign results in three demerit points. When a person is convicted of two or more offenses committed on a single occasion, points will only be assessed for the one having the greater point value.[92] An example is Mr. Reck Less who attempts to pass another car while driving through a stop light at an intersection. Although convicted of reckless driving, running a red light, and improper passing, he gains points only for the one offense having the greater value. Thus, Mr. Reck Less has six points assessed against him for purposes of the Driver Improvement Act. Had these same offenses occurred on separate occasions, he would have received six points for reckless driving, four for failure to stop at the stop light, and three for improper passing, making a total of thirteen demerit points.

All demerit points remain in effect for a period of two years from the date of the offense and are utilized in determining what form of sanction will be imposed against the driver.[93] When a driver accumulates six demerit points in a twelve-month period, or nine demerit points in twenty-four months, DMV sends him an advisory letter warning that additional violations may endanger his driving privilege. As additional demerit points accumulate, the operator will be ordered to attend a group interview where his problem is discussed and attempts are made to avert subsequent offenses. Further convictions and more demerit points result in a personal interview with an agency official. After considering various factors, the interviewer recommends to the commissioner that he impose one of the following actions: (1) suspend the offender's driver's license for a period not to exceed six months, and upon termination of the suspension place him on probation for a period of not less than three nor more than twelve months, or (2) place the offender immediately on probation for a period of not less than three nor more than twelve months, and require him to attend a driver improvement clinic.[94]

---

92. VA. CODE § 46.1-514.6.
93. *Id.* § 46.1-514.7.
94. *Id.* §§ 46.1-514.9 to 46.1-514.11, 46.1-514.19.

Assuming that the latter alternative is imposed on the offender, the clinic costs twenty dollars and attendance is mandatory. Meeting one night per week for a two-hour session, the course runs four consecutive weeks and seeks to rehabilitate the person's driving habits. At the successful completion of instruction, DMV subtracts five demerit points from the individual's point total.[95] Failure to attend the interviews and/or clinic without good cause results in an indefinite loss of license until the individual reenters these activities and completes them.[96]

Driver Improvement Act

Sanctions	Number of Points Points
Advisory Letter	6 points during 12 months, or 9 in 24 months
Group Interview	8 " " " " " 12 " " "
Personal Interview	12 " " " " " 18 " " "
Formal Hearing After Clinic	6 " " " " " 12 " " "

Although the Driver Improvement Act focuses on the problem driver, it also rewards careful operators with a safe driving point. To qualify, one must maintain a driving record free of suspensions and convictions of traffic offenses for a calendar year. Each year of careful operation warrants a safe driving point, and up to five points may be accumulated. Thereafter, these credits are used to offset any demerits incurred.[97]

Despite advisory letter, interviews, and clinics, certain drivers continue to violate the law and accumulate demerits. If six points in one year or twelve in two years are incurred within twenty-four months of attendance at an improvement clinic, DMV charges this driver as habitually negligent and conducts a formal hearing to determine his fitness (or lack of it) to drive.[98]

---

95. *Id.* § 46.1-514.12.
96. *Id.* § 46.1-514.16.
97. *Id.* § 46.1-514.8.
98. *Id.* § 46.1-514.19.

Accident and Aftermath

Auto accidents involving injury, death, and property damage occur frequently in Virginia and throughout the country. More than 52,378 injuries and 1,220 deaths resulted from motor vehicle mishaps in the Commonwealth during 1973 alone.[99] When an accident happens, the law requires all drivers involved to "stop as close to the scene of the accident as possible without obstructing traffic...." [100] Assistance should be given to the injured, including transportation to the hospital if necessary or if they request it. Once the injuries have been treated (or if none occurred), the drivers are then required to exchange certain information, including their names, addresses, driver's license numbers and vehicle registration numbers,[101] and, if known, the names of their insurance carriers.[102]

To protect oneself against future litigation, one should always attempt to get the names and addresses of witnesses to the occurrence.[103] Arguments with the other driver should be avoided, and one should not admit liability regardless of feelings about personal responsibility. Though later investigations may exonerate the conduct, inadvertent admissions of guilt may hinder the chances of recovery. If the other driver refuses to furnish the necessary information or the situation appears to be getting out of hand, police should be called in to handle the matter. In all cases involving injury or death, the police must be notified promptly. Although not required by law, the insurance carrier should be contacted immediately so that a representative can institute appropriate action. Prompt notice is required by most insurance policies as a condition of coverage.

Where the mishap involves an unattended vehicle, the Motor Vehicle Code requires that a reasonable effort be made to locate its owner. If he cannot be found, the driver is required to leave a

---

99. COMMONWEALTH OF VIRGINIA DIVISION OF MOTOR VEHICLES, *supra* note 91, at 8.
100. VA. CODE § 46.1-176.
101. *Id.*
102. DIVISION OF MOTOR VEHICLES, VIRGINIA DRIVER'S MANUAL 1976-77, p. 53.
103. *Id.*

note in a conspicuous place at the scene of the accident providing all necessary information, and must report the incident to the police within twenty-four hours. If, as a result of injuries sustained in the accident, the driver is unable to comply with these requirements, he shall, as soon as reasonably possible, make the report to the police and make a reasonable effort to find the owner of the vehicle and report the required information to him. Regardless of the amount of damage or the public or private location of the accident, the law requires that this report be promptly filed.[104] Under no circumstances should one ever leave an accident without first rendering aid to victims and giving the specified information. Hit-and-run drivers who leave the scene of an accident resulting in the injury to, or death of, any person face penalties of up to five years in prison and/or a fine.[105] And even where no death or injury results but damage to property exceeds $250, a failure to stop renders the driver liable to a six-month license suspension in addition to other penalties.[106]

Drivers involved in accidents causing injury to or death of any person, or property damage in excess of $250, have a legal duty to file an accident report with DMV within five calendar days.[107] This does not mean the agency must receive it within this period, but only that the report be mailed by the close of the fifth day. Failure to file or an intentional falsification of information subjects the offender to a license suspension until he supplies the correct answers or enters the report.[108] All parties involved, their lawyers or agents may inspect the report of the other driver and may use it in preparing their claims.[109] Accident reports made by investigating officers are confidential, and cannot be used as evidence in any trial, civil or criminal, arising out of any accident.[110]

Virginia currently has a two-year statute of limitations regarding legal action over a vehicular mishap involving personal

---

104. VA. CODE § 46.1-176.
105. *Id.* § 46.1-177.
106. *Id.* § 46.1-177.1.
107. *Id.* § 46.1-400.
108. *Id.* § 46.1-405.
109. *Id.* §§ 46.1-407, 46.1-408, 46.1-410.
110. *Id.* § 46.1-409.

injuries, meaning that legal action must be instituted within two years of the accident or all claims are forever waived.[111] A person may be entirely innocent of fault, but lose by waiting too long before taking action. Any uncertainty regarding the statute of limitations or when a claim must be initiated can be resolved by obtaining legal assistance.

THE CITATION

Police officials have the authority to stop any motor vehicle for the purpose of inspecting its equipment and operation, its engine or identification number or its contents or load, if the motor vehicle is a property carrying vehicle, or for the purpose of securing such other information as may be necessary,[112] and may stop the driver of any motor vehicle for the violation of a statute or ordinance. Assuming a driver has been stopped for speeding, the officer will typically ask to see the driver's license and vehicle registration card, and issue a summons for the infraction. The citation orders the operator to appear at a hearing at a specified time (at least five days later) and location. After pledging his appearance, the officer generally allows the individual to proceed.[113]

This procedure will not be followed where the driver desires an immediate hearing, refuses to guarantee his later appearance or seems likely to disregard the summons.[114] Any driver may request an immediate hearing (within twenty-four hours) and go before the local magistrate to resolve the controversy.[115] When a driver's future appearance at the hearing seems highly suspect, he, too, goes directly before the magistrate and has bail set to ensure his presence at the later date.[116]

Once bail is posted, the driver is released from custody. Failure to appear as scheduled forfeits the entire sum as the cost of the individual's fine and may prompt a warrant for his arrest. If the

---

111. *Id.* § 8.01-243.
112. *Id.* § 46.1-8.
113. *Id.* § 46.1-178.
114. *Id.* §§ 46.1-178, 46.1-179.
115. *Id.* § 46.1-178.
116. *Id.* §§ 46.1-178, 46.1-179.

individual cannot be located, DMV suspends his license until notified of his full compliance.[117]

Should an individual be halted for driving under the influence, he has the option of refusing blood and breath tests. However, a refusal can result in the suspension of his license for ninety days on the first offense and for six months on the second and each subsequent offense.[118] If a driver consents to the tests, has them administered, and is later convicted of driving while under the influence, his license will be revoked for six months to one year on the first offense. (A second or other subsequent conviction within ten years results in an automatic three-year license revocation.[119]) In either situation, the driver receives a citation and is removed from the roadway.

---

117. *Id.* § 46.1-178.1.
118. *Id.* § 18.2-268.
119. *Id.* §§ 18.2-271, 46.1-421.

CHAPTER 10

Liability for Harm to Persons and Property

E. J. Passarelli

D. B. Costello

TORT DEFINED

Torts are civil wrongs or injuries for which the law attempts to provide remedies, usually in the form of money payments, or damages. As distinct from a criminal act, which is a violation of statute, a tort involves the violation of a legal duty imposed on an individual either by statute or court decision. The elements of the action require that there be a duty owed by the defendant to the plaintiff, a breach of that duty, with damage as a proximate result.[1] It may be a direct invasion of some legal right of the individual, or the infraction of a public duty with special damage accruing to the individual, or the violation of some private obligation with resulting damage.[2]

NEGLIGENCE GENERALLY

Negligence is the most common tort, frequently encountered by individuals in their daily dealings with others. The application of negligence law has many practical consequences for Virginians. Careless acts which injure people or property can result in lawsuits seeking damages ranging into the millions of dollars. It may mean financial gain to some, or economic ruin to others. Knowledge of the law of negligence may enable one to avoid negligent acts and potential liability for those acts. It may also increase awareness of the fact that the law has a remedy in damages for an injury to a person caused by the negligence of another. As this chapter will demonstrate, negligence law tends to be complicated and

---

1. Mobile v. McClure, 221 Ala. 51, 127 So. 832, 835 (1930).
2. BLACK'S LAW DICTIONARY 1660-61 (4th ed. 1951).

confusing. It is to be stressed that only an attorney trained to recognize the finer points of the law should be entrusted with affairs of this nature.

WHAT IS NEGLIGENCE?

One who commits a negligent act causing injury may be liable to others for the harm caused by that negligence. The liability for negligence exists, however, only where one violates a legal duty which he owes to another to exercise due care for the safety of that person or his property,[3] and the violation of that duty causes harm to another. The violation of duty can be the result of a failure to act as a reasonable and prudent person would ordinarily have acted under the circumstances of the situation.[4]

THE DUTY OWED TO OTHERS

The law imposes duties upon men according to the circumstances in which they are called on to act. One has a duty to conduct his everyday activities so that he will not injure others.[5]

Duties may be created by statutes and ordinances specifying particular kinds of conduct, and the failure to comply with these legal requirements may be negligence in and of itself.[6] For instance, traffic codes are designed to protect the general public from the hazards of the automobile.[7] When John Driver exceeds the speed limit, he has breached a duty of care prescribed by the legislature for the safety of other drivers and pedestrians. No matter how well he can handle his car at high speeds, the law declares that he is endangering the safety of the public. If, while exceeding the speed limit, he has an accident which results in an injury, the driver could be sued by the injured party.[8] In general, all violations of statutes enacted to prevent injury to persons or

---

3. Virginia Ry. & Power Co. v. Winstead, 119 Va. 326, 89 S.E. 83 (1916).
4. Norfolk & Portsmouth Traction Co. v. Daily, 111 Va. 665, 69 S.E. 963 (1911).
5. Overstreet v. Security Storage & Safe Deposit Co., 148 Va. 306, 138 S.E. 552 (1927); Rice v. Turner, 191 Va. 601, 62 S.E.2d 24 (1950).
6. Lavenstein v. Maile, 146 Va. 789, 132 S.E. 844 (1926).
7. Prichard v. Battle, 178 Va. 455, 461, 17 S.E.2d 393, 395 (1941).
8. Carroll v. Miller, 175 Va. 388, 9 S.E.2d 322 (1940).

property can be negligence *per se*,[9] if the injury which results from the wrongful act is the type of harm the law intended to prevent, and the person injured is one the law was designed to protect.[10]

Special duties to others may arise from one's own actions. Normally, a person is not under a duty to help another in an emergency, but this is not the case when a person (the victim) was placed in peril through the fault of the wrongdoer. When John Citizen causes an emergency, he is under a legal duty to aid any persons endangered by his actions, *and* must also exercise due care in rendering assistance.[11] Even without a legal duty to help, if a bystander at an accident renders any help at all, he is obligated to act like a prudent and reasonable person.

THE STANDARD OF CARE REQUIRED

Each person has a duty to conduct himself as the average reasonable person would have conducted himself in similar circumstances; the amount of care will vary, though, depending upon the situation.[12] A reasonable man is expected to be considerably more careful where the degree of danger as a result of his actions is higher. One who deals with explosives must exercise greater care than a person handling sacks of oranges. People who lawfully create a fire on their property must exert a degree of care that demonstrates a reasonable respect for the dangerous potentials of fire, so as to avoid injuring others.[13] The duty to exercise ordinary care extends to sports activities where there is a risk of injury to others. Golfers, for example, must recognize the dangers they present to others in golfing. The Virginia Supreme Court has ruled that golfers should use ordinary care in warning others that they are about to shoot.[14]

---

9. Richardson v. Lovvorn, 199 Va. 688, 101 S.E.2d 511 (1958).
10. Smith v. Virginia Transit Co., 206 Va. 951, 147 S.E.2d 110 (1966).
11. Safety Motor Transit v. Cunningham, 161 Va. 356, 171 S.E. 432 (1933).
12. Boggs v. Plybon, 157 Va. 30, 160 S.E. 77 (1931).
13. Collins v. George, 102 Va. 509, 46 S.E. 684 (1904).
14. Alexander v. Wrenn, 158 Va. 486, 164 S.E. 715 (1932).

Must the Negligent Act Cause Injury?

A person may be wronged by a negligent act of another and yet not be compensated, if no actual damage resulted from the negligence. To sue someone for a lawful but negligently performed act, one must be able to demonstrate that he was injured in his person or property, or the lawsuit will fail. Without injury, there can be no recovery.[15]

Causation can be direct, where the injury results from an uninterrupted series of events, without any external intervening force; or it can be indirect, where some force intrudes after the defendant's act and contributes to the plaintiff's injury.[16] If the intervening force is foreseeable in the risk created by the defendant's negligence, he may still be held liable for the resulting harm. In the case of an automobile accident, for example, it is generally considered foreseeable that someone may try to rescue the victim and may be negligent in the attempt, thus adding to the injuries. The original negligent motorist will still be liable for the added injuries caused by the negligent would-be rescuer. Likewise, injuries resulting from, or aggravated by, the malpractice of physicians who may treat the victim are deemed reasonably foreseeable and may result in further liability on the part of the negligent driver. On the other hand, unforeseeable intervening forces, such as criminal or intentionally wrongful acts of other parties, acts of God, or gross negligence, may break the chain of events between the defendant's first wrong act and the resulting harm, and may even save the defendant from any liability for his initial negligence.

As a general rule, if a reasonable man could anticipate *any* injury from his negligent act, he may be held responsible for *all* the direct consequences,[17] even if he could not foresee the precise type or extent of the harm.[18] For example, assume that John Driver negligently causes an automobile collision in which Paul Pedestrian

---

15. Sides v. Richard Mach. Works, Inc., 406 F.2d 445 (4th Cir. 1969).
16. Wallace v. Jones, 168 Va. 38, 190 S.E.2d 82 (1937).
17. Tripp v. Norfolk, 129 Va. 566, 106 S.E. 360 (1921).
18. *Id.*; Cox v. Mabe, 214 Va. 705, 204 S.E.2d 253 (1974).

is cut by flying glass. Bacteria, to which Paul is particularly susceptible, enter an open wound and infect it, leading to Paul's death. Although Driver may not have anticipated the precise injury, he would be liable for the consequences of his act, since he should have foreseen some injurious result.[19]

THE EFFECTS OF THE VICTIM'S WRONGFUL CONDUCT

Contributory negligence is careless conduct on the part of the complaining party (plaintiff) which is a contributing cause of his own injuries. The plaintiff's lack of due care concurs or cooperates with negligent acts of the defendant to cause harm to the plaintiff.[20] Normally, if the plaintiff in a lawsuit for negligent injuries or other harm is guilty of any contributory negligence, he is barred from recovery,[21] even though his own negligence may be minor compared to the defendant's.[22] Virginia law does not attempt to allocate damages according to the degree to which each party is at fault in an accident.[23] If Pedestrian in the foregoing example is twenty percent to blame for the accident involving Driver, despite the fact that his own negligence contributes slightly to the accident, he will recover nothing from Driver for his injuries.

One doctrine softens the harshness of contributory negligence: the doctrine of last clear chance, which is applied so that an injured person's contributing negligence will not bar recovery *if* the other party, immediately prior to the accident, had the last clear chance to avoid it and failed to do so.[24] For the rule to apply to a Virginia case, the injured party must be physically unable to remove himself from the danger to which he negligently exposed himself, or he must be unconscious that the danger exists. Recovery will not be barred if the defendant saw or, if exercising due care, should have seen the injured party in time to avoid the accident.[25]

---

19. Houston v. Strickland, 184 Va. 994, 37 S.E.2d 64 (1946).
20. Western Union Tel. Co. v. Virginia Paper Co., 87 Va. 418, 12 S.E. 755 (1891).
21. Washington v. Schuyler, 433 F.2d 362 (4th Cir. 1970).
22. Etheridge v. Norfolk Southern Ry., 143 Va. 789, 129 S.E. 680 (1925).
23. Yeary v. Holbrook, 171 Va. 266, 198 S.E. 441 (1938).
24. Craighead v. Sellars, 194 Va. 920, 76 S.E.2d 212 (1953).
25. Simmers v. DePoy, 212 Va. 447, 184 S.E.2d 776 (1971).

Negligence in Automobile Accidents

Automobile accidents account for the great number of the negligence claims and injuries in America. As a result, state statutes and local ordinances extensively regulate the operation of vehicles. Highways are open to public use, but cannot be lawfully abused. Recognizing the obvious dangers of automobile travel, one must operate a car with the degree of care that a reasonable and prudent person would use under each circumstance.[26]

Violations of traffic laws may become the cause of an accident, and violators may be guilty of negligence for that reason alone. But compliance with traffic regulations will not always guarantee that a driver will not be charged with negligent operation of a vehicle. Depending on the circumstances, it may be necessary to be far more careful than traffic regulations demand. Speeds which are acceptable on dry, sunny days may be unreasonably reckless under conditions of ice and snow. Therefore, drivers must not only comply with traffic laws, but must also use common sense on the roadways.

There are no firm rules as to what may constitute negligence in the operation of a motor vehicle, but past cases in Virginia courts, along with some state statutes, can provide a guide for operating automobiles so as to avoid endangering life and property in certain common situations. Driving a car with known defects in any of its operating mechanisms or safety devices can constitute negligence *per se.*[27] The brakes, tires, headlights and safety equipment must meet state inspection standards at all times. Tires which pass inspection in September, but are unsafe in November, must be changed in November, even though inspection would not be required for another four months. Violating speed limits is negligence, also, and may even cause a driver to forfeit the right-of-way to which he would have been entitled had he not been speeding.[28]

People who do not drive defensively can be liable for negligence.

---

26. Richmond Greyhound Lines, Inc. v. Brown, 203 Va. 950, 128 S.E.2d 267 (1962).
27. Martin v. Penn, 204 Va. 822, 134 S.E.2d 305 (1964).
28. Va. Code § 46.1-221.

LIABILITY FOR HARM TO PERSONS AND PROPERTY

It is the general duty of drivers to maintain a lookout to prevent injury to others,[29] and a proper lookout includes watching for stopped cars, for people changing tires, and for pedestrians using the street.[30] Certain other specific acts and omissions have been held by Virginia's Supreme Court to give rise to liability:

(1) A driver attempting to pass must signal the car ahead of him so that the other is aware of the attempt.[31]

(2) Passing on the right will constitute negligence *per se*, unless the driver of the other vehicle has signaled his intention to turn left.[32]

(3) One is usually considered negligent if he stops his car in such a manner as to impede traffic or to make the highways dangerous.[33] Even in case of emergencies, caused by accident or mechanical breakdown, it is necessary to remove a disabled vehicle from the highway as quickly as possible.

(4) Choosing an inappropriate unsafe place in which to change a flat tire can be considered a negligent act.[34]

Who Is Liable for Negligence?

Generally, the person held liable for negligent acts is the person who committed them. There are exceptions, however:

(1) An owner who knowingly permits his car to be driven by an incompetent person will be held liable for the injuries caused by the incompetent.[35]

(2) An owner who knows, or has reason to know, that someone is exceedingly reckless, drinks heavily, or is inexperienced as a driver, should not allow that person to drive his car.[36]

---

29. Stillman v. Williams, 181 Va. 863, 27 S.E.2d 186 (1943).
30. Green v. Ruffin, 141 Va. 628, 125 S.E. 742 (1924).
31. Poole v. Kelley, 162 Va. 279, 173 S.E. 537 (1934).
32. Gary v. Artist, 186 Va. 616, 43 S.E.2d 833 (1947).
33. Birtchard Dairy, Inc. v. Edwards, 197 Va. 830, 91 S.E.2d 421 (1956).
34. Davis v. Scarborough, 199 Va. 100, 97 S.E.2d 731 (1957).
35. Denby v. Davis, 212 Va. 836, 188 S.E.2d 226 (1972).
36. Crowell v. Duncan, 145 Va. 489, 134 S.E. 576 (1926).

(3) Anyone who knowingly permits an unlicensed minor to drive his car will be held responsible for the negligent injuries caused by such minor, even though the minor will also be liable.[37]

(4) Where an employee is negligent in the use of an automobile while performing his employer's business, the employer can be held liable for any injuries caused by the employee, in addition to the employee's liability. In order for the employer to be held liable, the employee must have committed the negligent act while in the course of his employment; however, the employer will not automatically be held liable merely because the act was done during the time of employment.[38]

Liability of Owners and Occupiers of Real Estate

People who own or lease property are required to maintain it in such a condition that others are not put in danger. Injuries caused by abandoned pits or wells, slippery flooring, dangerous staircases, or any other unsafe conditions could result in liability to those who maintain control over the property.

Different degrees of care may be required of the landowner and the renter, depending upon which outside or third parties use certain areas. The duty toward undiscovered trespassers is slight: one must only avoid deliberately injuring them. Strangers who go onto private lands without permission or invitation cannot recover for injuries caused to them by unsafe conditions on the property. However, if the trespassers are known, or reasonably should be known, by the landowner to be on the property, he must use ordinary care to avoid injuring them.[39] Furthermore, where a landowner maintains a dangerous object likely to attract children, such as a swimming pool or a dangerous electrical installation, the owner or occupier must take precautions to prevent injuries to children even if they should be trespassing.[40]

---
37. Va. Code § 8.01-64.
38. Barnes v. Hampton, 149 Va. 740, 141 S.E. 836 (1928).
39. Norfolk Southern Ry. v. Fincham, 213 Va. 122, 189 S.E.2d 380 (1972).
40. Taylor v. United States, 326 F.2d 284 (4th Cir. 1963).

"Licensees" have a higher status in law than trespassers. A licensee is a person who is expressly or impliedly granted permission to be on property. Social guests are licensees. There is no duty to keep property safe for them, but when one knows of a dangerous condition which is unlikely to be discovered by the guest, it is necessary to warn the licensees about the condition or to make it safe.[41]

Business visitors and people who are invited to enter public property are called "invitees" in negligence law, and are due greater protection than licensees. The owner or renter must take affirmative action to ensure that the premises are reasonably safe.[42] A shopkeeper must use reasonable diligence in clearing the floors of dangerous objects, or must give warning of their presence.[43] In general, wherever invitees use property, the possessor of the property must make reasonable positive attempts to discover any dangerous conditions and make arrangements so that they will not cause injury.[44]

NEGLIGENCE INVOLVING LANDLORDS AND TENANTS

A landlord is generally not liable to his tenants for injuries resulting from conditions not known, or from conditions of which he had no reason to be aware. Dangerous conditions, obvious to the tenant only, will not become grounds for a negligence suit against the landlord. If the tenant knows about some danger, Virginia law provides that he must avoid it or find some way to make the condition safe.[45] A landlord must warn his tenant about dangerous conditions known to the landlord, but he has no duty to maintain the property he rents, except to the extent provided by the Virginia Code. Recently enacted statutes require that landlords maintain all electrical, plumbing, sanitary, heating, ventilating, air-conditioning and other facilities and appliances, including elevators, supplied or required to be supplied by him in

---

41. Busch v. Gaglio, 207 Va. 343, 150 S.E.2d 110 (1966).
42. Raven Red Ash Coal Co. v. Griffith, 181 Va. 911, 27 S.E.2d 360 (1943).
43. Colonial Stores, Inc. v. Pulley, 203 Va. 535, 125 S.E.2d 188 (1962).
44. Richmond & M. Ry. v. Moore, 94 Va. 493, 27 S.E. 70 (1897).
45. Revell v. Deegan, 192 Va. 428, 65 S.E.2d 543 (1951).

good and safe working order and condition.[46] If the landlord takes it upon himself to repair things that he has no duty to repair, he must still use reasonable care in his work so that items he fixes will not injure others.[47]

Common areas are the responsibility of the landlord to maintain. Common areas are places where tenants use the property along with other tenants. Such places as sidewalks, stairways used by two separate apartments, and swimming pools, are normally under the control of the landlord, and it is his duty to inspect such areas and keep them in a safe condition for the general use of his tenants.[48] One example of his potential liability can be seen in snow removal from sidewalks. Sidewalks are commonly used by many residents of apartment dwellings; therefore, it is the duty of the landlord to use reasonable care to eliminate dangerously slick conditions on sidewalks. Failure to act in a reasonable manner to remove the hazard caused by a snowstorm can be considered negligence on the part of the landlord.[49]

INTENTIONAL INJURIES

Liability may result from intentional acts which cause harm, as well as from negligent acts. These acts, called intentional torts, may be directed against a person or his property. Liability arises when a person acts with intent to cause specific consequences or is substantially certain these consequences will result. Fraud, libel and slander, assault and battery, and invasion of privacy are some of the more common intentional torts. These and others will be examined in the following pages.

(1) Assault results when a defendant intentionally acts toward another so as to cause in that other person a reasonable expectation of immediate harmful or offensive touching. Most simply put, an assault embodies a threat of bodily harm. Simply pointing a gun at a person can be an assault, whether

---

46. VA. CODE § 55-248.13.
47. Luedtke v. Phillips, 190 Va. 207, 56 S.E.2d 80 (1949).
48. Gumenick v. United States, 213 Va. 510, 193 S.E.2d 788 (1973).
49. Langhorne Rd. Apts., Inc. v. Bisson, 207 Va. 474, 150 S.E.2d 540 (1966).

or not the gun was loaded. All that is needed is the apparent ability to harm the plaintiff, not actual ability. Throwing a punch and missing can be an assault, as can an unsuccessful attempt to kiss a stranger or anyone else who might find that conduct offensive.

Note, however, that words can never constitute an assault, no matter how threatening. When the words are accompanied by action, though, an assault can be the result. Consider the difference between these situations: (a) Defendant, a giant of a man, stands with his hands in his pockets and rages at plaintiff, "I'm going to kill you! I'm going to knock your head off!" (b) Defendant, the model of a 98-pound weakling, clenches his puny fist at plaintiff and warns, "I'm going to belt you." The first example does not have all the elements needed to constitute an assault. There is no attempt and, therefore, no apparent ability to make good the verbal threat. The second example, however, contains all the necessary elements, including the immediate threat of some harm, regardless of the seeming lack of strength on the part of the defendant.

Words alone can *negate* an assault by removing any reasonable grounds for belief in immediate contact. For example, defendant advances on plaintiff, swinging a baseball bat, and saying, "If you weren't my next-door-neighbor, I'd pulverize you!" The qualification of the threat removes any apprehension of immediate contact.

(2) When harmful or offensive contact actually results from the defendant's intended act, a battery has been committed. A punch in the jaw can be a battery; so can a pat on the rear from one not privileged to deliver it. It is not even necessary that the victim know of the touching at the time it occurs: Prince Charming's kiss delivered to Sleeping Beauty could have been grounds for an action for battery, if the lady had been inclined to pursue the matter and if the Prince's intentions had been offensive. In some cases, when a doctor performs an unnecessary operation (such as, without permission or emergency conditions, removing the patient's appendix "since he was having a tonsilectomy anyway"), it is a battery, even though the patient was unconscious at

the time and had consented to the one operation; he had not consented to have his appendix removed.

(3) False imprisonment requires that the defendant intentionally confine or restrain the plaintiff to a bounded area, either by imprisonment within physical barriers or by threats of force directed at him or a family member, or at plaintiff's property. Imprisonment includes the failure to provide an escape from a situation which the plaintiff has voluntarily entered, as where a driver refuses to let a hitchhiker get out of the car. A type of false imprisonment is false arrest of an individual for a criminal offense without a warrant or other justification. A law enforcement officer may arrest without a warrant where he has reasonable grounds to believe that a felony was committed and that the arrested person committed it, or where a misdemeanor breach of the peace was committed in his presence. A private citizen may make an arrest for a felony only where a felony has actually been committed and he reasonably believes the arrested person committed it. A private citizen may arrest for a misdemeanor only on the same basis as law enforcement officers.

(4) Libel and slander, both forms of defamation, involve the defendant's use of language which is injurious to plaintiff's reputation, which identifies the plaintiff to any reasonable third party, and is in fact communicated to some other party resulting in actual injury to the victim's reputation. The method of defamation encompasses verbal remarks, written words, cartoons, and any other form of communication capable of conveying the injurious information. Libel is that type of defamatory statement recorded in some permanent form (usually, but not always, the written or printed word). Slander involves only verbal remarks which lack the physical permanence of libelous material.

Certain types of communications are considered to be slander *per se,* meaning they are presumed to have injured the plaintiff's reputation regardless of the extent of the actual damage. Statements to the effect that the plaintiff is incompetent in his business or profession, has a loathsome disease (usually confined to mean venereal disease or leprosy), has been guilty of an infamous crime (one involving moral turpitude), or is unchaste (a category applicable only to unmarried female plaintiffs) are slander *per se.*

Where public officials or public figures are plaintiffs in an action for defamation, they can usually recover damages for libel or slander only when they prove that the defendant acted maliciously, *i.e.,* with knowledge that the statement was false or with a reckless disregard for its truth or falsity. Politicians, athletes, and show business personalities commonly fit this category, since they are considered by the courts to have ample opportunity to refute any allegations publicly.

Furthermore, where the allegations appeared in a news medium which is made defendant in an action, the plaintiff must prove that the medium was negligent in allowing the defamatory matter to be published, meaning that the harm to the plaintiff must be visible in the material to a reasonably prudent person having editorial control.

Truth is always a defense to an action for libel or slander, regardless of the degree of harm to the plaintiff's reputation. Consent is also a defense. In addition, many remarks made during legislative, judicial or executive governmental proceedings are absolutely privileged, meaning that for reasons of public policy (allowing a full and free exchange of information in important proceedings), the defendant cannot be called to account for his statements no matter how outrageously defamatory they may be. Other so-called "qualified privileges" exist, meaning the privilege will be available only when used in a reasonable and proper manner, and without malice. An attorney should be consulted, however, to determine properly when the lengthy list of privileges may apply in a given case.

(5) Where a statement is true, but nevertheless damaging to plaintiff's reputation, damages may be sought for invasion of privacy — specifically, the unwarranted public disclosure

of private facts about the plaintiff. The right to privacy includes protection against the use of the plaintiff's name or picture by the defendant for commercial advantage; malicious publication by the defendant of facts about the plaintiff which would be objectionable to a reasonable person under the circumstances; or intrusion by the defendant into the plaintiff's private affairs or seclusion, such as by "bugging" the plaintiff's house.

Liability for Defective Products

The liability of manufacturers, distributors and merchants for defective products which injure members of the public can be based on theories of negligence, strict liability, or breach of warranty.

Damages may be awarded to an injured plaintiff if the defendant was negligent in making or selling the product. Ordinary rules of negligence law apply here. However, if the plaintiff sues on a strict liability theory, he must prove that the defendant is engaged in the business of making, selling or otherwise distributing the product and that the product reached the plaintiff substantially unchanged from the condition in which it left the defendant. In addition, the product itself must be unreasonably dangerous, such that ordinary care on the part of the user cannot eliminate the risk of substantial harm.

Liability can also be based on three types of warranty, or on misrepresentation of the qualities of the product. The *implied warranty of merchantability,* as contained in the Uniform Commercial Code (which governs most, if not all, business transactions) requires that a seller warrant the goods he sells to be of "merchantable quality," meaning they must be fit for the ordinary purposes for which such goods are normally used.[50] A similar theory of liability is the *implied warranty of fitness,* which is deemed to have been given when a seller knows, or reasonably should know, the particular purpose for which the product is required and knows that the buyer is relying on the seller's skill or judgment to select a suitable product. Before damages can be

---

50. Va. Code § 8.2-314.

awarded, however, it must be proven that the buyer did, in fact, rely on the seller's skill or judgment in making the purchase.[51]

Different from the implied warranty is the *express warranty*, which is an affirmative statement of fact about the nature of the goods made by the seller or manufacturer. The plaintiff must prove that the product failed to conform to the warranty description.[52]

Finally, *misrepresentation* can be the basis for an award of damages where the defendant knowingly makes a false and material representation about the quality, nature or proper use of the goods, on which the buyer was intended to rely and on which he did in fact rely.[53]

Conclusion

The foregoing discussion has been a simplified explanation of a complex subject. The number of torts, their essential elements, and the possible defenses or excuses for each could — and do — fill many books. The safest course in any situation in which a person causes harm to another, or is accused of causing harm, is to consult legal counsel. The essence of tort law is to attempt to provide a remedy for every injury, and a lawyer is best able to analyze the facts of each situation to determine the respective rights and liabilities of the parties.

---

51. *Id.* § 8.2-315.
52. *Id.* § 8.2-313.
53. *Id.* § 8.2-721.

CHAPTER 11

Rights of Sick or Injured Workers

D. W. Heileman

Joe Brown was a bank official away from home on a business trip. While having a drink in the cocktail lounge, he was joined by a charming little brunette. One drink led to several more and they soon retired to his hotel room.

Joe Brown never woke up. A cigarette carelessly discarded by him or his girlfriend burned them both to death. Brown's widow, seeking consolation for her loss, decided to sue someone; but it was difficult to think of a sound legal theory on which to proceed. Mrs. Brown could hardly bring suit against the cigarette manufacturer for placing dangerous products on the market. Likewise, the hotel could not be sued for failing to protect its guests from cigarette fires. Since the only party at fault in this case seemed to be Brown himself, Mrs. Brown appeared to be out of luck.

Still determined to ease her loss, Mrs. Brown sued her husband's employer, claiming a work-related death. The Supreme Court of California ruled that the death of Joe Brown was compensable under the workmen's compensation laws of that state. Death benefits provided for in the California statute were awarded to Mrs. Brown, making her loss a bit more bearable.[1]

If the above case seems ridiculous, it is because most citizens lack a complete understanding of the laws concerning workmen's compensation. Although the laws on this subject vary significantly from state to state, all were intended to expand the types of situations in which an injured party would be entitled to compensation from his employer. This chapter is designed to supply the information necessary to understand and take full advantage of the workmen's compensation law in Virginia, by explaining when one is covered under workmen's compensation, and how one files a claim for benefits. It is also necessary to

---

1. Wiseman v. IAC, 20 Cal. Comp. 306 (1956).

examine the philosophy behind the subject of workmen's compensation since it differs from other areas of the law in several important respects.

History of Workmen's Compensation Laws

At common law, lawsuits are generally instigated by a party who believes he has been "wronged" by someone. The case, when it comes to court, is an adversary contest aimed at righting the wrong claimed by one of the contestants. To win the contest, the party seeking recovery must be able to prove that the damage he suffered was due to the guilt or fault of the party he is suing. If the injured party is unable to establish guilt, or if the person at fault had a legal excuse for his conduct, there will be no recovery.

Before workmen's compensation laws were enacted, a successful lawsuit for a work-related injury depended entirely upon the injured worker's ability to establish negligence on the part of his employer. This was often an impossible task, since the employer enjoyed several important advantages in the courtroom. Often, the injured worker would not even bring a lawsuit against his employer since it was a costly venture with uncertain results. Regardless of the outcome of the lawsuit, the injured worker faced the probable loss of his job just for bringing the legal action against his employer. Fellow workers were reluctant to testify against their employer for the same reason.

For the employer successfully to defend himself against the accusation of negligence, three well-established defenses were available to him: (1) contributory negligence — the worker could not recover if he himself had been negligent in any degree, regardless of the extent of the employer's negligence; (2) the "fellow servant" doctrine — the employee could not recover if it could be shown that the injury had resulted from the negligence of a fellow worker; (3) assumption of risk — the injured worker could not recover if the injury was due to a "built-in hazard" of the job of which he had, or should have had, advance knowledge. Furthermore, only the injured worker himself had the right to bring the lawsuit. If he died, his survivors and dependents had no basis for legal action.[2]

In addition to these disadvantages, the common law remedies were inadequate from the employee's standpoint for one more important reason. Even if the injured worker managed to win the legal contest against his employer, several years often elapsed before he received his award. Long delays in bringing the case to trial and time-consuming appeals prevented the injured worker from receiving his settlement at the time it was needed most — immediately after his injury.

However unfair this situation might have seemed from the employee's standpoint, it must be kept in mind that these laws were the product of a set of values that were widely accepted by the lawmakers of the time. America was in the process of transforming itself from an agricultural to an industrial society and most people thought this transformation should be encouraged. By keeping the burdens on factory owners at a minimum, the goal of rapid industrialization could best be achieved. For these reasons, the lawmakers of the nineteenth century were reluctant to increase the scope of employer liability for work-related injuries.

Around the turn of the century, many people began to wonder if this goal was worth the cost. Industrial deaths and crippling injuries were rising at an alarming pace but the factory and mine owners were doing very little to improve safety and working conditions. Public opinion began to change in favor of the employee as information regarding the fearful accident and death toll in many industries became more widely known.[3] In 1908, Congress decided it was time for a reordering of priorities. The first American compensation law was enacted in that year, covering civil employees of the Federal Government.[4] By 1915, thirty states had passed their own workmen's compensation laws. On March 21, 1918, the Virginia legislature passed a law entitled "The Virginia

---

2. H. SOMERS, WORKMEN'S COMPENSATION 18 (1954).
3. See, *e.g.*, Hard, *Law of the Killed and Wounded*, EVERYBODY'S (Sept. 1908); C.H. Mark, *Our Murderous Industralism*, WORLD TODAY (Jan. 1907).
4. The Federal Employee's Liability Act, 45 U.S.C.A. § 51 *et seq.*

Workmen's Compensation Act." By 1949, workmen's compensation laws were enacted in every state in the Union.

OBJECTIVES OF WORKMEN'S COMPENSATION

The Virginia Workmen's Compensation Act, like every other workmen's compensation law, was enacted with one basic purpose in mind: to provide prompt and automatic compensation to workers and their dependents for injuries occurring in the course of their employment. To achieve this goal, it was necessary to abandon the requirement of proving fault in order to obtain recovery. The Virginia Act did away with the concept of the adversary contest and adopted an entirely new legal principle — liability without fault. The employer can on longer claim the defenses of contributory negligence, fellow servant doctrine or assumption of risk.

Adopting the concept of liability without fault served several purposes. Since it no longer matters who is at fault, the need for a full-blown trial is largely eliminated. The only questions that now need to be answered are: (1) Is the injured workman himself covered by the Act? and (2) What shall be the compensation for his injury (within the limits of the Act)?

In addition to eliminating much of the delay and large legal fees previously necessary to obtain a settlement, this principle shifted the financial risk of industrial accidents to the person most able to bear the burden — the employer. By adopting liability without fault, the lawmakers recognized that industrial injuries were an inevitable hazard of modern industry. The costs are therefore, a legitimate cost of production.[5] Since the employer is required to bear the financial burden for the injuries of his employees, he now has a greater interest in providing safer and more healthful working conditions.

---

5. The view that industrial injuries should be regarded as a necessary production expense was espoused in Humphrees v. Boxley Bros. Co., 146 Va. 91, 96, 135 S.E. 890 (1926), where the court said "[t]he damage resulting from an accident is treated as a part of the expense of the business and to be borne as such, as much as the expense of repairing a piece of machinery which has broken down."

Since the concept of fault was discarded in the Virginia Act, it was no longer logical to award settlements on the theory of punishing the "guilty" party. Before workmen's compensation laws were enacted, a sympathetic jury would occasionally award a huge sum of money to an injured worker to punish the employer for his wrongdoing. But since there are no "guilty" parties so far as workmen's compensation laws are concerned, settlements must be awarded on a different theory. The amount of compensation granted under the Virginia Act is determined by considering two factors: (1) the previous wages of the injured worker, and (2) the nature and extent of his disability. Continued medical attention and rehabilitation of the injured worker are also provided for in the Act. The payment of money awarded under the Workmen's Compensation Act is entirely different from the payment of welfare, and the two should not be confused. Injured employees are entitled to workmen's compensation payments as a matter of right. Payments are completely unrelated *to need* and are administered equally, regardless of the financial status of the employee.[6]

In addition to these primary objectives, workmen's compensation laws have the added benefit of reducing some of the causes of friction in the employer-employee relationship since they no longer need view each other as potential adversaries in the courtroom. Keeping the basic purpose of the Virginia Workmen's Compensation Act in mind, it is now time to examine the specific provisions of the Act.

WHO IS COVERED?

Workmen's compensation laws are designed to protect the employee. Under the provisions of the Virginia Act, employers are required to provide compensation to their employees or their dependents for job-related injuries and diseases. In order to understand to whom the Workmen's Compensation Act applies, it is necessary to know what is meant by the terms "employer" and "employee."

---
6. See, *e.g.,* Dillard v. Industrial Comm'n, 347 F. Supp. 71 (E.D. Va. 1972).

"Employer" is defined in the Virginia Act as including the State and any municipal corporation therein or political subdivision thereof and any individual, firm, association or corporation using the service of another for pay.[7] The term "employee" includes every person, including a minor, in the service of another under any contract of hire or apprenticeship, written or implied, except one whose employment is not in the usual course of the trade, business, occupation or profession of the employer.[8]

According to these definitions, a person will be considered an employee (and therefore covered under the Act) if three basic requirements are met. First, he or she must be working for an "employer" as defined by the Act. Providing one's service in exchange for pay by any of the above-named individuals, companies or political bodies will satisfy this requirement. The existence of a family relationship between employee and employer makes no difference, so long as the employee is being paid for his or her services.[9] In 1975, 1976 and 1977, the General Assembly made certain exceptions to the requirement that a person be paid for his services by providing that volunteer firefighters, volunteer lifesaving and rescue squad members, and auxiliary and reserve police, will be covered by the Act if the county or township agrees.[10]

The second requirement is that the person be working under "contract of hire or apprenticeship." This contract may be either expressed (in writing) or implied (presumed to exist under the circumstances). To meet this requirement, the relationship of master and servant must be found to exist.[11] Four elements will be considered in determining whether a master-servant

---

7. VA. CODE § 65.1-3.
8. *Id.* § 65.1-4.
9. In Glassco v. Glassco, 195 Va. 239, 241-42, 77 S.E.2d 843 (1953), the court said:
   These definitions [of employers and employee] are all inclusive and make no exception, as some of the [Workmen's Compensation] Acts do, because of family relationship between the employer and employee. . . . Nowhere in the statute do we find any basis for the claim that because the employer is the husband of the claimant the latter is to be barred from recovering death benefits payable to the dependents of a deceased employee.
10. VA. CODE § 65.1-4.1.
11. See Board of Supervisors v. Lucas, 142 Va. 84, 128 S.E. 574 (1925).

relationship exists: (1) the right to hire; (2) power of dismissal; (3) obligation to pay wages; and (4) power of control. If these elements are present, a master-servant relationship will exist and the second requirement will be satisfied.

Still, for the employment situation to come under the provisions of the Virginia Act, one more requirement must be satisfied, namely, the nature of the work itself must be in "the usual course of" the employer's trade, business or occupation. If the employment is usual and ordinary to the employer's business, it will be covered by the Act, even though the employee works on a nonpermanent or occasional basis. However, where the worker is engaged in employment that is not permanent or periodically regular, but occasional, or by chance *and* not in the usual course of the employer's trade or business, he will be classified as a casual employee not covered by workmen's compensation.[12]

It is easy to see that the question of whether or not an employment situation covered by the Virginia Act exists will often depend on the particular circumstances of each case.[13] The existence of a master-servant relationship is obvious in the case of a desk clerk working for a motel, but may be doubtful in cases where an *independent subcontractor* is engaged in the construction of an office building. Whether or not the type of work engaged in is in "the usual course of" the employer's business can often be determined only by examining the facts surrounding the individual case. For these reasons, it would be useless to attempt to classify all of the possible employment situations as to whether or not they are covered by the Act. Since this determination is crucial to the rights of the injured worker, it would be in his or her best interests to seek professional legal advice whenever there is doubt in this matter. For employees who are covered by workmen's compensation, the provisions of the Act are intended to be the exclusive remedy as between them and their employer.[14] This

---

12. Board of Supervisors v. Boaz, 176 Va. 126, 10 S.E.2d 498 (1940).

13. What constitutes an employee is a question of law, but whether the facts bring a person within the law's designation is usually a question of fact. Stonega Coke & Coal Co. v. Sutherland, 136 Va. 489, 118 S.E. 133 (1923).

14. VA. CODE § 65.1-40.

means that once it is determined that a worker is covered by workmen's compensation, he may not bring a lawsuit against his employer for damages resulting from the injury. However, several types of employment are specifically excluded from compulsory coverage under the Act. They are (1) employees of rail carriers, (2) casual employees (as previously defined), (3) domestic servants, (4) farm and horticultural laborers (unless the employer has a payroll of $15,000 per year or regularly employs more than four full-time employees), and (5) employees of any person, firm or private corporation, including a public service corporation, that regularly has fewer than three employees in service (this exemption does not apply to coal mine workers, however).[15] Employers of people in the excluded categories (casual employees, domestic servants, farm laborers and employees of companies with less than three employees) may *voluntarily* choose to be covered by the Act, but they cannot be forced to provide workmen's compensation benefits to their employees. If the employer elects to provide coverage under the Workmen's Compensation Act, he must notify his employees of his intention to do so.[16] Any of his employees then has the right to refuse coverage under the Act and may do so by notifying the Industrial Commission in Richmond. It should be noted that this is the only case where an employee has the right to reject coverage under the Act; in all other employment situations meeting the legal requirements previously discussed, the employee must accept coverage as provided in the Virginia Act.

At this point, one might wonder why any employee would want to refuse coverage under the Workmen's Compensation Act. This question can be answered by examining the legal remedies available to the injured worker who is not covered by the Act. Employees not covered by workmen's compensation include: (1)

---

15. *Id.* § 65.1-28.

16. Without giving notice of the voluntary coverage, the employer will be denied protection under the Act. In Dey v. Logan, 175 Va. 68, 7 S.E.2d 102 (1940), a farm laborer was allowed to bring a wrongful death action against his employer, who had taken out compensation insurance but had not notified his employees of the coverage. Failure to notify employees of coverage in cases where it is not compulsory effectively denies them the right to refuse coverage if they so choose.

employees in the five excluded employment situations where the employer chooses not to provide voluntary coverage; (2) employees in the five excluded employment situations who choose to reject the voluntary coverage provided by their employer, and (3) any other employee who, for some reason, does not meet all of the legal requirements necessary to come within the coverage of the Act. The legal remedies available to these people are the same as they were for employees before the Workmen's Compensation Act was passed. This means that they can bring a lawsuit against their employer in a court of law for damages suffered as a result of their injury. The adversary contest takes place in these situations, and the issue of fault again becomes crucial in the attempt to obtain a recovery. The common law defenses of contributory negligence, fellow servant doctrine and assumption of risk can be used by the employer in these cases in his effort to defeat the employee's claim. On the other hand, if the employee wins the case, his recovery will not be limited by the amounts specified in the Workmen's Compensation Act. A judge or jury may award the injured worker any amount supported by the evidence. The successful claimant in a lawsuit enjoys the added benefit of receiving his settlement in one lump sum, whereas workmen's compensation benefits, like income, are spread out over a longer period of time.

The workers who refuse voluntary coverage under the Act are taking a definite gamble. While the potential recovery in a lawsuit may be much greater than under the Workmen's Compensation Act, they could end up with nothing if they fail to prove a clear case of employer negligence. Since the decision to reject coverage under the Act must be made before any injury occurs, it should be made only after very careful consideration of the possible results.

Employees who are otherwise excluded from coverage under the Act are not refusing coverage by their own choice, but their recovery for a work-related injury or disease will still depend on their ability to prove employer negligence in a court of law. While their overall chances for recovery are lessened, resorting to a lawsuit may prove highly beneficial in some instances. For the domestic servant, farm or horticultural laborer (working for someone with a payroll of less than $15,000 per year and having four or fewer regular employees), or employee of any person or company hiring less than three regular employees, filing a lawsuit is the only chance to obtain a recovery for harm, since it is clear that they are not covered by the Act. If they are successful, their recovery will be limited only by the jury's decision and the evidence of damage.

For employees who have some doubt as to whether or not they are covered by the Workmen's Compensation Act, two alternatives are available. They can file a claim for workmen's compensation and attempt to prove that their employment situation is covered by the Act, or they can file a lawsuit for damages against their employer. To illustrate the possible results of choosing either alternative, a hypothetical case will be helpful.

Harold Badback was a maintenance man who occasionally did work for the XYZ Taxicab Company. Several times a year Harold would come to XYZ's headquarters and perform minor repair work on the building used to store the taxicabs not in use. While replacing a broken light fixture, Harold fell off a ladder and sprained his back. It was apparent that the fall was caused by a defective ladder supplied by the taxicab company. Harold consulted an attorney to determine his rights of recovery for the injury.

There is no doubt that the injury suffered by Harold was of a type intended to be covered by the Workmen's Compensation Act. It was clearly job-related. There was some doubt however, as to whether Harold was an "employee" covered by the Act. His work with XYZ was only occasional and it was difficult to determine if the nature of his work was "in the usual course of" the company's business.

Harold could choose to bring a lawsuit against the taxicab company in hopes of obtaining a recovery greater than would be possible under workmen's compensation. The taxicab company, in an effort to limit their liability, could challenge the lawsuit on the theory that Harold's employment was covered by the Workmen's Compensation Act and his only remedy was that provided by the Act. In this instance, *Harold would prevail only* if it is determined that his employment with XYZ was *not* covered by the Workmen's

Compensation Act. If it is determined that Harold's employment with XYZ was covered by workmen's compensation, he would be allowed to file a claim for benefits under the Act and the lawsuit would be dismissed.

But suppose Harold chose to file a claim for workmen's compensation in the first place. The taxicab company could attempt to challenge his claim on the theory that Harold's employment was not covered by the Act. It is in the company's best interests to avoid paying unnecessary claims under the Act. Furthermore, the company may feel certain that Harold would lose in a lawsuit against them. In this instance, Harold would be allowed to recover under the Workmen's Compensation Act *only* if it is determined that his employment with XYZ *was* covered by the Act. According to the provisions of the Act, the Industrial Commission will decide this question, based on the relevant facts. If it is determined that Harold was covered by the Act when his injury occurred, the commission will grant Harold's claim for compensation. If it is determined that the Act does not apply to Harold's employment with XYZ, no compensation will be awarded; however, Harold will then have the right to bring a lawsuit against the taxicab company.[17] His success will, of course, depend upon his ability to prove by a preponderance of the evidence a clear case of employer negligence.

If this hypothetical case seems complicated and confusing, then perhaps it has served its purpose. It was intended to show the importance of determining whether or not a given employment situation comes under the coverage of the Workmen's Compensation Act. Hopefully, it illustrates some of the elements to look for in answering this question as well as the uncertainties that often exist.

---

17. See, *e.g.*, Perrin v. Brunswick Corp., 333 F. Supp. 221 (W.D. Va. 1971), where the court held that "[i]f for any reason the statute is inapplicable to the case, the employee may have recourse to his common-law remedy."

WHAT TYPES OF INJURIES ARE COVERED?

Injury Defined

As previously stated, the Virginia Workmen's Compensation Act was designed to provide automatic coverage to employees for job-related injuries. Injury is defined under the Act and limited to "injury by accident, or occupational disease, arising out of and in the course of the employment . . . ." [18] According to this definition three elements must be proved for an injury to be covered by the Act: (1) that it was a result of an occupational disease or an accident; (2) that the injury arose "out of" the employment; and (3) that the injury occurred "in the course of" employment. From this, it can be seen that two distinct types of injuries were intended to be covered under the Act: injuries resulting from "accidents," and injuries resulting from "occupational diseases." Therefore, a separate discussion of each type would be appropriate.

(b) *Injuries Resulting From Accidents*

The word "accident" in its normal usage is thought of as being a specific event, such as a slip or fall. Since the Virginia Act does not define "accident," the courts have been given the job of determining the meaning of the word. They have given the term "accident" a somewhat different meaning than its ordinary use. In a landmark case,[19] the Virginia Supreme Court ruled that to constitute an injury by accident it is not necessary that there must be a slip, fall or other fortuitous circumstance, nor must there be an extraordinary occurrence in or about the work engaged in. The Virginia Supreme Court went on to define accident as an event happening through human agency, an event which under the circumstances is unusual and not expected by the person to whom it happens. Under this definition, there need be nothing unusual about the event itself; if an ordinary event produces an unexpected or unusual result, it will generally be termed an accident.

---

18. VA. CODE § 65.1-7.
19. Derby v. Swift & Co., 188 Va. 336, 49 S.E.2d 417 (1948).

Once it is shown that the injury resulted from an accident, it must also be established that the injury arose "out of" and "in the course of" the employment. These elements may sound very similar to each other, but they are in fact distinct.

The words "arising out of" refer to the origin or cause of the injury. An injury arises out of the employment when there appears to be a causal connection between the conditions under which the work is required to be performed and the resulting injury. The causative danger must be peculiar to the work and not common to the neighborhood. It need not have been foreseen or expected, but after the event it must appear to have had its origin in a risk connected with the employment and to have flowed from that source as a rational consequence.[20]

The words "in the course of" refer to the time, place and circumstances under which the injury occurred. An injury occurs in the course of the employment when it takes place within the period of employment, at a place where, from the nature of the work, the employee may reasonably be expected to be, and while he is reasonably fulfilling the duties of his employment or doing something which is reasonably incidental to his employment.

Stated in general terms, the phrase "arising out of and in the course of the employment" covers those injuries suffered by an employee while he is discharging some duty he is authorized to perform in furtherance of his employer's business, either directly or indirectly.[21] The Virginia courts have ruled that this phrase should be given a liberal interpretation in order to achieve the humane purposes of the Act.[22] The fact that the employee was not actually required to perform the act will not impair his or her right to compensation. A voluntary act of an employee which causes an injury will entitle him or her to compensation provided it is not an intentional self-inflicted injury, and provided the act is sufficiently

---

20. Southern Motor Lines v. Alvis, 200 Va. 168, 104 S.E.2d 735 (1958); Conner v. Bragg, 203 Va. 204, 123 S.E.2d 393 (1962).
21. Lucas v. Lucas, 212 Va. 561, 186 S.E.2d 63 (1972).
22. *Id.*

related to what the employee is required or authorized to do in fulfilling his or her duties of employment.[23]

This explanation of the elements required to be shown for an injury to be covered by the Act indicates that the ultimate question of whether the injury is covered will depend on the individual circumstances. Several illustrations showing how these requirements are applied in determining the question of coverage may be useful in understanding how they operate.

(1) *Accidents occurring outside of working hours*

Compensation is not limited to injuries occurring only during working hours. For example, an employee, while attending a lecture required by her employer, was struck on the head by a falling light fixture while waiting for the lecture to begin. The injury was covered under workmen's compensation, since the hazard was traceable to the employment and occurred at a place where the employee reasonably expected to be while she was reasonably fulfilling the duties of her employment.[24]

(2) *Injuries received while going to or from place of employment*

The general rule is that an employee going to or from his place of work is not engaged in any act growing out of and incidental to his employment.[25] There are three exceptions to this rule, however, and compensation will generally be awarded in either of the following cases: (a) where the means of transportation is provided by the employer or the time consumed in going to or from work is paid for by the employer; (b) where the route to and from the place of work is the only possible route available to the employee; or (c) where the employee on his way to or from work is still charged with some duty or task in connection with his employment.[26] Under this exception, an injury sustained by

---

23. *Id.*
24. Garris v. Peoples Drug Store, 162 Va. 428, 174 S.E. 665 (1934).
25. This rule was first stated in Virginia in Kent v. Virginia-Carolina Chem. Co., 143 Va. 62, 129 S.E. 330 (1925).
26. *Id.*

employee while performing an errand for his employer on his way home from work would be covered by the Act.[27]

(3) *Mysterious death*

Where an employee is found dead as the result of an apparent (but unproven) accident at his place of work or nearby, where his duties may have taken him during the hours of his work, the court or Industrial Commission will presume that the accident arose out of and in the course of employment. As such, the dependents of the employee will be entitled to workmen's compensation benefits, provided there is no evidence to indicate that the employee was not engaged in his master's business at the time. The case of Joe Brown, described at the beginning of this chapter illustrates the application of this principle.

There are many other examples of cases where employees have been awarded workmen's compensation benefits for injuries occurring under circumstances not generally recognized as being work related. In cases where there is any possibility that the injury may have arisen out of and in the course of employment, an employee can best protect his interests by notifying his employer of the injury and seeking professional legal advice on this question. There is nothing to lose and much to be gained by pursuing this course of action.

(c) *Injuries Resulting From Occupational Disease*

Under the Virginia Workmen's Compensation Act, any employee suffering from an occupational disease is entitled to workmen's compensation. Prior to 1966, the employee was entitled to benefits for this type of injury only after he became incapacitated from work because of it. Today, the employee becomes entitled to compensation in the form of medical benefits as soon as the diagnosis of the occupational disease is communicated to him.[28]

The term "occupational disease" means a disease arising out of and in the course of the employment. No ordinary disease of life to which the general public is exposed outside of the employment

---

27. Ferrell v. Beddow, 203 Va. 472, 125 S.E.2d 196 (1962).
28. VA. CODE § 65.1-49.

is compensable, except (1) when it follows as an incident of an occupational disease, or (2) when it is an infectious or contagious disease contracted in the course of employment in a hospital or sanitorium or public health laboratory.[29]

A disease can be said to arise out of the employment only if there is apparent to a rational mind after considering all the circumstances: (1) a direct causal connection between the conditions under which the work is performed and the occupational disease; (2) it followed as a natural incident of work as a result of the exposure caused from the nature of the employment; (3) it can be fairly traced to the employment as the proximate cause; (4) it does not come from a hazard to which the employee would have been equally exposed outside of the employment; (5) it is incidental to the character of the employer's business, and (6) it had its origin in a risk connected with the employment and flowed from that source as a natural consequence.[30]

Whether a disease is occupational must be determined by the particular characteristic of each employment, the type of work in which the employee is engaged and the effect it has on the *individual*.[31] Compensation for occupational disease is not limited to those types of employment which are regarded as being unhealthy to everyone, but includes employment situations from which the disease arises by reason of the particular claimant's susceptibility to the unhealthy conditions of the occupation.[32] However, an ordinary disease of life which is *aggravated* by working conditions is not covered as an occupational disease. For example, an employee previously suffering from asthma will not be covered under the Act if the conditions of his employment make the asthma worse.[33]

When an employee has an occupational disease covered by the Act, the employer for whom he was working when he was last injuriously exposed to the hazards of the disease shall be solely

---

29. *Id.* § 65.1-46.
30. *Id.*
31. Brisson v. Bateson Co., 42 O.I.C. 18 (1960).
32. Dowdy v. Black Constr. Co., 40 O.I.C. 44 (1958).
33. Sullins v. Southern States Coop., Inc., 49 O.I.C. 315 (1967).

responsible for providing compensation benefits. Injurious exposure means an exposure to the causative hazard of such disease which is reasonably calculated to bring on the disease in question.[34] In many cases, an employee will have been exposed to the disease-causing conditions while working for several different employers before he actually contracts the disease. Since it would be extremely difficult to determine the amount of responsibility that should be fairly borne by each employer, the "last injurious exposure rule" was designed as a matter of convenience in settling these claims and in the hope that the burdens would eventually "balance out" as between the employers.

There is a provision in the Virginia Workmen's Compensation Act that allows an employee who is affected by or susceptible to a specific occupational disease (because of previous exposures) to waive compensation for any aggravation of the condition resulting from subsequent injurious exposures.[35] Occupational diseases are the only area in which waivers are permitted and in any case, they may be used only with approval of the Industrial Commission. The theory behind the waivers is that they provide conditional employment to someone who may otherwise be unable to find an employer willing to hire him because of his susceptibility to an occupational disease.[36] While this theory may sound reasonable from the employer's standpoint, the fact remains that waiver provisions are available to the employer as a means of avoiding compensation payments to an employee who would otherwise deserve them. The waiver provisions under the Virginia Act are directly contrary to the recommendations of the National Commission on State Workmen's Compensation Laws. This commission was created to study the adequacy of state workmen's compensation laws and submit recommendations for improvement in the laws. The commission recommended that waivers not be permitted, as they run against the basic purpose of workmen's compensation.

---

34. VA. CODE § 65.1-52.
35. *Id.* § 65.1-53.
36. Jewell Ridge Coal Corp. v. Vance, 203 Va. 557, 125 S.E.2d 879 (1962).

Waivers in Virginia are most common in the coal mining and textile industries. Approximately ten percent of the workers in these industries have signed waivers for black lung disease and dermatitis. Many labor unions have been successful in banning the use of waivers as a condition for employment. Since the General Assembly has chosen not to comply with the recommendation that waivers be outlawed, the labor unions have remained the most effective force in dealing with this situation. Any employee (or prospective employee) who is asked to sign a waiver for an occupational disease should be fully aware of the consequences before doing so. Once the waiver is signed, the employee gives up all rights to compensation he may have against that employer for the disease covered.

Filing a Claim for Benefits

Certain procedural steps must be followed by the employee when he files a claim for benefits under the Virginia Workmen's Compensation Act. These requirements are very important and should be followed carefully to ensure that the rights of the employee will be protected.

Every injured employee or his representative is required by the Act to give written notice of the accident as soon after the accident as possible.[37] In any case, the maximum time limit for notifying the employer of the accident is 30 days. If notice is not given within this time, the employee will lose his right to compensation for the injury, unless he can show a reasonable excuse for not giving the notice and the employer has not been damaged by the failure to notify. Written notice will not be required in cases where a foreman or superior officer of the employer had actual knowledge of the occurrence of the accident.[38] The written notice must state the name and address of the employee and the time, place, nature and cause of the accident and of the resulting injury or death.[39] In

---

37. Va. Code § 65.1-85.
38. Actual knowledge of the accident by a foreman or superior officer of employee was held to be sufficient notice in Department of Game & Inland Fisheries v. Joyce, 147 Va. 89, 136 S.E. 651 (1927).
39. Va. Code § 65.1-86.

occupational disease cases, the employee must notify his employer within 60 days after learning he has the disease. The purpose of requiring the employee to notify his employer of the accident or disease is to enable the employer to investigate the facts and to furnish medical attention to minimize the injury. While there is a tendency not to require written notice whenever the employer has actual knowledge of the accident,[40] it is clearly in the employee's best interests to comply with this requirement.

As soon as the employer is notified of the accident or occupational disease, he is required to furnish a physician chosen by the employee from a panel of at least three physicians, selected by the employer, for as long as is necessary after the accident.[41] If the employer does not give the employee a choice from at least three physicians, the employee may choose any physician at the employer's expense. The employer must also furnish all necessary surgical and hospital service and supplies. In addition, the employer must also furnish at the direction of the Industrial Commission all reasonable and necessary vocational rehabilitation training services. The unjustified refusal of the employee to accept the medical service or vocational rehabilitation training provided by the employer shall *bar* the employee from further compensation until such refusal ceases. No compensation shall at any time be paid for the period during which the employee refused treatment, unless the Industrial Commission decides the refusal was justified.[42]

After the employee notifies his employer of the accident or occupational disease, it is the employer's duty to report this to the Industrial Commission. After receiving this report, the Industrial Commission will send an instruction sheet to the employee informing him of the steps that must yet be taken.

Of greatest importance is the requirement that the employee file a written claim with the Industrial Commission for compensation. This claim for compensation must be filed to enforce any rights the

---

40. 2 LARSON, WORKMEN'S COMPENSATION LAW § 78.31(a).
41. VA. CODE § 65.1-88.
42. *Id.*

employee may have to compensation for lost wages as well as to preserve his right to continued medical benefits. In cases of injury resulting from accident, the claim must be filed with the Commission within two years after the accident. If death results from the accident, the claim must be filed within one year after the time of death.[43]

In cases of injury caused by occupational disease, there are several time limitations that apply, depending on the type of disease. For coal worker's pneumoconiosis (black lung disease), the claim must be filed within three years after diagnosis of the disease is first communicated to the employee or within five years from the date of the last injurious exposure in employment, whichever comes first. For most other occupational diseases, (there are several specified diseases to which these time limits do not apply) the claim must be filed within two years after diagnosis of the disease is first communicated to the employee or within five years from the date of the last injurious exposure in employment, whichever comes first. If death results from any occupational disease during these time periods, the claim must be filed within three years after the date of death.[44]

The majority of claims are never contested, because in most cases there is no real dispute as to whether the employee is covered by the Act. In these cases, the claimant and the employer's insurance carrier usually submit a memorandum of agreement, on the basis of which compensation is ordered by the Industrial Commission. The memorandum of agreement, accompanied by the report of the attending physician, will state the circumstances surrounding the disability and the agreed amount of compensation to be paid. When the right to compensation has terminated, the claimant and the employer's insurance carrier generally sign and submit an agreed statement of fact stating the date on which the employee was able to return to work and the total amount of compensation paid. The employee does not have to sign the agreed statement of fact, however. If at this time the injured employee

---

43. *Id.* § 65.1-87.
44. *Id.* § 65.1-52.

believes he is not fit to begin work, he may refuse to return to his job. If the employer does nothing about this, the employee's right to receive benefits will continue. In most such cases, however, the employer will file an application for a hearing before the Industrial Commission to determine whether in fact the employee is fit to return to work. This hearing is conducted by one commissioner (or a deputy commissioner) [45] at or near the place where the injury occurred.[46] The claimant has the right to be represented by legal counsel at all such hearings.

If it is determined that the employee is not fit to return to work, his compensation will continue. If the commissioner finds that he is able to return to work, the employee's right to compensation will be terminated as of the date the employer filed the application for hearing. The employee has the right to appeal from this ruling. The application for review of the ruling must be made within fifteen days of the original ruling.[47] The full Commission will then review the findings and enter its judgment. Rulings of the full Commission may be appealed to the Supreme Court of Virginia if the petition for appeal is filed within thirty days. If the employee loses his appeal, he may nevertheless file an application for a hearing to review the award on the ground of a change in his condition. The limit for this request is two years from the date of the termination of the compensation awarded under the Act, except in cases of certain injuries and occupational diseases specified in the Act the employee shall have three years from the date of the termination of compensation to request the review. A change in condition is the only reason for which the review of an award, otherwise final, will be granted.[48] If the employee claims and is able to prove a change in condition of the original disability, he may be entitled to further benefits as determined by the Commission. The same appeal procedures will apply.

Sometimes the claimant and his employer (or insurance carrier) are unable to agree on the compensation amount from the start,

---

45. *Id.* § 65.1-96.
46. *Id.* § 65.1-94.
47. *Id.* § 65.1-97.
48. *Id.* § 65.1-99; see also *id.* § 65.1-56.

because the employer does not believe the worker is covered under the Act or because the parties cannot agree to the nature of the disability. In these cases, either party may file an application for a hearing before the Industrial Commission.[49] The hearing will be conducted in the same manner, with the same provisions for review and appeals, as previously stated. The only difference here is that the Commission must determine whether and in what amount the claimant is initially entitled to compensation benefits. As to whether the claimant is covered by the Act, the Commission will consider all of the elements previously mentioned in determining coverage. In determining the amount of compensation to be awarded, the Industrial Commission may consider all relevant facts and evidence, including reports and testimony furnished by the claimant's personal physician. Finally, it should be noted that the hearings are intended primarily to serve as a fact-finding procedure and not as an adversary contest. As such, many of the traditional courtroom rules have been relaxed in the effort to arrive at a fair and fully-informed decision.[50]

AMOUNT OF COMPENSATION

Several important changes in the Act were made by the 1975 General Assembly relating to the amount of compensation an injured employee is entitled to receive.

The types of disability resulting from accidents and occupational diseases are divided into four classes: (1) injuries which result in total incapacity; (2) injuries which result in partial incapacity; (3) certain specified injuries that are presumed to result in incapacity for periods specified in the Act; and (4) injuries which result in death. In addition to these categories, special provisions are set out in the Act for disability resulting from coal workers pneumoconiosis (black lung disease).

For *total incapacity* from all work-related injuries (arising either from accident or occupational disease), the specific dollar amount

---

49. *Id.* § 65.1-94.
50. For the complete scope of the Industrial Commission's power and rule-making authority, see VA. CODE §§ 65.1-10 to 65.1-22 and accompanying notes and cases.

the employee is entitled to receive each week is that amount equal to two-thirds of the employee's average weekly wage during the preceding year; however this amount may never total less than 25 percent nor more than 100 percent of the "average weekly wage of the Commonwealth." (For example, in 1975 the average weekly wage of the Commonwealth was found to equal $149.00. Therefore, in 1975 an injured employee was entitled to receive as weekly compensation two-thirds of his average weekly wage, up to $149 per week. His compensation could never be less than $37.25 per week, which is 25 percent of $149, the average weekly wage of the Commonwealth.) Compensation for total incapacity may be paid for up to 500 weeks. At the end of this time, the right to benefits will end.[51] An injured employee is entitled to total incapacity benefits even if his physical disability is only partial, if he can show an inability to market his remaining capacity for work.[52]

Compensation for *partial incapacity* (except for those cases coming under category 3, above) shall equal two-thirds of the difference between the employee's average weekly wage before the injury and the average weekly wage he is able to earn after his injury, but not more than 100 percent of the "average weekly wage of the Commonwealth." In these cases, the 500 week time limitation also applies. There is, however, no minimum amount of compensation he is entitled to receive.[53]

For *certain specific injuries,* incapacity is presumed to continue for a specified period of time, depending on the nature of the disability. Compensation payments are still based on two-thirds of the employee's past average weekly wage, with the same minimum and maximum limits used for total incapacity cases. For example, an employee who loses one leg as the result of a work-related injury is entitled to two-thirds of his average weekly wage, but not less than 25 percent nor more than 100 percent of the "average weekly wage of the Commonwealth," for a period of one hundred seventy-five weeks.[54]

---

51. VA. CODE § 65.1-54.
52. Island Creek Coal Co. v. Fletcher, 201 Va. 645, 112 S.E.2d 833 (1960).
53. VA. CODE § 65.1-55.
54. *Id.* § 65.1-56(15).

If *death* results from the accident within nine years, persons who were wholly dependent on the employee's earnings for support at the time of the injury shall be entitled to receive compensation equal to two-thirds of his past average weekly wages, but not less than 25 percent nor more than 100 percent of the "average weekly wage of the Commonwealth," for a period of 400 weeks. Wives and children under age 18 of the employee are entitled to these benefits for 500 weeks, plus $1,000.00 for burial expenses and reasonable transportation expenses for the deceased not exceeding $300.00. A husband of the employee (if actually dependent on her wages for support) will be entitled to these additional benefits.[55] These benefits shall be in addition to any compensation already received by the injured employee. Persons partially dependent on the employee at the time of injury will be entitled to a proportionate amount of these benefits.[56]

Third-Party Lawsuits

As previously stated, the Virginia Workmen's Compensation Act was designed to provide an exclusive remedy for parties sharing an "employment relationship" as defined by the Act. It has been determined that a person not meeting the legal requirements of an "employee" will not be covered. These people have the right to bring a lawsuit against the person for whom they were working for damages resulting from their work-related injury. In certain cases, an employee who is covered by the Act will also be allowed to bring a suit for damages against a negligent party even though he has already been compensated for his injury under the Act. The reason for allowing lawsuits in these cases is quite logical; however, the application of this rule to everyday work situations is not an easy task.

The whole theory behind workmen's compensation can be explained as a give and take process. The employer gives up his common law defenses of contributory negligence, fellow-servant doctrine and assumption of risk and receives the benefit of limited

---

55. *Id.* § 65.1-65.
56. *Id.*

liability for injuries suffered by his employees. The employee gives up his right to an unlimited recovery for his injuries in exchange for automatic and guaranteed compensation. In some instances, however, the injury will be caused by someone not intended to be protected by workmen's compensation. These persons are commonly referred to as third parties, or "other" parties to the employment. Since these people were not intended to take part in the give and take process, their legal rights and obligations are unchanged by the Workmen's Compensation Act. It would serve no logical purpose to allow these people to escape the consequences of their wrongful actions simply because the party to whom they caused injury was compensated for his loss by someone else. Neither would it be fair to force an employer to pay for the wrongful acts of someone not covered by the Act. For these reasons, a traditional lawsuit for damages by an employee will be permitted as against negligent third parties not protected under the Act.

It must be remembered that these third-party lawsuits are not an alternative to the right to receive workmen's compensation benefits. Rather, they are an additional remedy provided for the benefit of both employee and employer.[57] Any recovery obtained in these lawsuits will go first to the employer, to the extent that he has already paid compensation benefits to his employee. Any remaining proceeds go to the employee.[58] This method of dividing the lawsuit recovery serves two purposes. First, it reimburses the employer for the compensation he had to pay as a result of the third party's wrongful act. Secondly, it prevents the employee from receiving a double recovery for his injury. This is fair to everyone concerned: the employer, who, in a fault sense, is neutral, comes out even; the third person pays exactly the damages he would normally pay, which is correct, since to reduce his burden because of the Workmen's Compensation Act would be a windfall to him

---

57. *Id.* § 65.1-41. Under this section, an injured employee is no longer required to elect whether he shall accept an award of compensation from the employer, or procure a judgment in an action at law against the negligent third party. Stone v. George W. Helme Co., 184 Va. 1051, 37 S.E.2d 70 (1946).

58. VA. CODE § 65.1-42.

which he has done nothing to deserve; and the employee gets a full (but not a double) recovery for his injuries.[59]

If for any reason the Workmen's Compensation Act does not apply to a particular case, the employee can make use of his common law remedy of a suit for damages.[60] This rule has already been discussed from the standpoint of the injured worker who does not qualify as an "employee" under the Act. The other situation where the Act does not apply occurs when the employee, otherwise covered by the Act, suffers an injury caused by the negligence of someone not protected by the Act. Several categories of people are clearly "third parties" within the meaning of the Workmen's Compensation Act, but in many circumstances the question of whether or not an individual is a third party can only be decided by examining the specific employment relationship.

In cases where a person's status as a third party was put in issue, the Virginia courts have adopted the requirement that they be "strangers to the employment." [61] Thus, it has been decided that where an employee covered by the Act is injured by a fellow employee, his only right to recovery will be through the Workmen's Compensation Act.[62] The definition of "fellow employee" includes more than just employees working for the same employer. For example, when employees of two independent contractors (a painter and a plumber) are engaged in work which is part of the trade, business or occupation of the owner of the construction project, they will be classified as fellow employees.[63] Furthermore, the employee of a subcontractor engaged in the same trade, business or occupation as the general contractor cannot recover in a lawsuit against the general contractor for an injury arising out

---

59. LARSON, *supra* note 40, at § 71.20.
60. See note 17 *supra*.
61. Thus, an employee covered by the Virginia Workmen's Compensation Act has no right of action against another party for injuries received while engaged in the business of his employer unless that other party is a stranger to the business. Anderson v. Thorington Constr. Co., 201 Va. 266, 110 S.E.2d 396 (1959); Bristow v. Safway Steel Prods., 327 F.2d 608 (4th Cir. 1964).
62. See *e.g.*, Phillips v. Brinkley, 194 Va. 62, 72 S.E.2d 339 (1952).
63. Anderson v. Thorington Constr. Co., 201 Va. 266, 110 S.E.2d 396 (1959).

of and in the course of his employment.[64] Once again, the question of whether the independent or subcontractor is engaged in "the same trade, business or occupation" of the owner or general contractor is crucial in determining the rights of the injured employee. Professional legal advice should be sought whenever the answer to this question is in doubt.

Perhaps the clearest example of a third party against whom a lawsuit may be brought by the injured employee is the manufacturer of the machine or product that caused the injury. If it can be shown that the product (tool, machine, etc.) was somehow defective, the injured employee will be entitled to recover against the manufacturer in a third-party lawsuit.

Finally, it should be noted that a lawsuit against a third party may be brought by either the employee or the employer.[65] Since the employer is given the right to that part of the lawsuit recovery equal to the amount of workmen's compensation paid to the employee, he has a definite interest in seeing to it that all claims against negligent third parties are pursued. It is only logical then to allow him to pursue this course of action if for some reason the employee chooses not to. If the employer does recover from a third party, any amount in excess of what he has actually paid out in compensation benefits and legal fees must be given to the employee.[66]

---

64. Sykes v. Stone & Webster Eng'r Corp., 186 Va. 116, 41 S.E.2d 469 (1947).
65. VA. CODE § 65.1-41.
66. *Id.*

CHAPTER 12

Family Relationships

J. B. Hickox

IN GENERAL

Marriage, apart from its status as a private contractual relationship between the parties, is considered to be the foundation of society. The United States Supreme Court, in distinguishing marriage from other contracts, has stated:

> It is an institution, in the maintenance of which in its purity the public is deeply interested, for it is the foundation of the family and of society, without which there would be neither civilization nor progress.[1]

Due to its fundamental importance, marriage has always been subject to legislative control.[2] Today, every aspect of the marriage relationship — formation of the marriage bond, rights and obligations thereunder, dissolution of the marriage, and custody and maintenance of any children — is to some degree regulated by statute.

UNLAWFUL MARRIAGES

The state has the power to determine "who shall assume ... the matrimonial relationship within its borders."[3] In Virginia, the following marriages, among others, are prohibited by statute: a marriage entered into prior to the dissolution of an earlier marriage of one of the parties; a marriage between an ancestor and a descendant, or between a brother and sister; and a marriage between an uncle and a niece or between an aunt and a nephew.[4]

A prohibited marriage is void without judicial decree;[5] it confers

---

1. Maynard v. Hill, 125 U.S. 190, 211 (1888).
2. *Id.* at 205.
3. Toler v. Oakwood Smokeless Coal Corp., 173 Va. 425, 430, 4 S.E.2d 364 (1939).
4. VA. CODE § 20-38.1.
5. *Id.* § 20-45.1(a).

no legal rights, and it is as if no marriage had ever been performed.[6] But the fact that a marriage is void does not take away the power of a court to declare it invalid;[7] in fact, the court has stated that:

> ... it is often desirable and sometimes of highest importance both to individuals and to the community, that there should be a judicial decree in reference to a void marriage, for then the status of the parties and their children is set at rest, and the parties are justified in the eyes of the public in entering into a second marriage.[8]

Children born of a prohibited marriage are legitimate.[9] They are endowed with all the rights of legitimate issue, and are put on a level of equality with children born in lawful wedlock.[10]

Another impediment to lawful marriage is nonage. The minimum age at which persons may marry is sixteen.[11] Special procedures govern, however, if the female is pregnant and either of the parties is under the age of sixteen. Upon presentation of a doctor's certificate confirming the pregnancy, the clerk, with parental consent, must issue a marriage license; a marriage entered into under these circumstances is valid.[12] Parental consent is not required for the marriage of a person eighteen years of age or older, but it is a prerequisite to the valid marriage of a person between the ages of sixteen and eighteen.[13]

Traditionally, marriages of minors consummated without the required parental consent have been upheld as valid, the statutory provisions being viewed as merely directory.[14] However, this rule has been changed by a recent statute which provides that, absent

---

6. Chitwood v. Prudential Ins. Co. of America, 206 Va. 314, 317, 143 S.E.2d 915 (1965).
7. Henderson v. Henderson, 187 Va. 121, 126, 46 S.E.2d 10 (1948).
8. *Id.*
9. VA. CODE § 20-38.1.
10. Henderson v. Henderson, 187 Va. 121, 129, 46 S.E.2d 10 (1948).
11. VA. CODE § 20-48.
12. *Id.*
13. *Id.* § 20-49.
14. Needham v. Needham, 183 Va. 681, 687, 33 S.E.2d 288 (1945).

parental consent, all marriages solemnized when either or both of the parties are under the age of eighteen are void.[15]

The marriage of insane persons is also generally prohibited. However, the prohibition applies only to an insane woman under the age of forty-five years, or to an insane man who marries a woman under the age of forty-five years.[16] The purpose of the statute would seem to be not absolutely to prohibit the marriage of insane persons, but rather to prevent them from producing children. The prohibition would also seem to apply, at least by implication, to the mentally defective, for the statute prohibits the issuance of a marriage license to a feebleminded person.[17] Such marriages are void from the time so declared by a decree of divorce or nullity.[18] If no decree declaring the marriage void has been entered, it remains valid.[19]

The law of Virginia also prohibits marriages between persons of the same sex.[20]

FORMATION OF THE MARRIAGE

Every marriage in Virginia must be pursuant to a license and solemnized in the manner prescribed by statute.[21] This provision has been construed to be mandatory rather than merely directory. Thus, the so-called common law marriage is not recognized as valid in Virginia, for ". . . no marriage or attempted marriage, if it took place in this State, can be valid here, unless it has been shown to have been solemnized according to our statutes." [22]

The marriage license is issued by the clerk of the circuit court of the county or city in which the female or the male to be married usually resides.[23] The clerk may not issue a marriage license unless

---

15. VA. CODE § 20-45.1.
16. *Id.* § 20-46(2).
17. *Id.* § 20-46(4).
18. *Id.* § 20-45.1.
19. Cornwall v. Cornwall, 160 Va. 183, 191, 163 S.E. 439 (1933).
20. VA. CODE § 20-45.2.
21. *Id.* § 20-13.
22. Offield v. Davis, 100 Va. 250, 257, 40 S.E. 910 (1902).
23. VA. CODE § 20-14.

the parties first present a statement signed by a physician, that tests or examinations have been made to determine whether there is evidence of syphillis.[24] The purpose of the statute is not to prohibit the marriage of persons who have contracted venereal disease. However, in the event that evidence of syphillis is found, the physician must inform both parties, "... of the result of such test or tests, the nature of the disease and the possibilities of transmitting the disease to the marital partner ... and to their children...."[25] If the parties thereafter marry and remain in Virginia, they shall be deemed to have agreed to take whatever treatment is prescribed by the state health commissioner; failure to do so is punishable as a misdemeanor.[26]

Marriages may be solemnized by a minister of any religious denomination who has been duly authorized by order of any circuit court to celebrate marriages.[27] In the case of a religious society having no ordained minister, the marriage may be solemnized in the manner prescribed and authorized by the society.[28] The circuit court is also authorized to appoint one or more persons to celebrate marriages.[29]

A marriage license authorizes the marriage of the parties for a period of only sixty days; if this period elapses without the solemnization of a marriage, the license expires.[30] Even the fee to be charged for the celebration of a marriage is regulated by statute; the celebrant is permitted to charge a fee not to exceed twenty dollars.[31]

DESERTION AND NONSUPPORT

It has long been recognized that it is a father's legal and moral duty to support his dependent infant children.[32] Traditionally, a

---

24. *Id.* § 20-1.
25. *Id.* § 20-4.
26. *Id.* § 20-5.
27. *Id.* § 20-23.
28. *Id.* § 20-26.
29. *Id.* § 20-25.
30. *Id.* § 20-14.1.
31. *Id.* § 20-27.
32. Butler v. Commonwealth, 132 Va. 609, 613, 110 S.E. 868 (1922); Bruce v. Dean,

husband has also been liable for the support of his wife.[33] A recent statutory change imposes upon each spouse the duty to support the other and to support any dependent children if the child or spouse is in "necessitous circumstances." Failure to provide such support is a misdemeanor.[34] This change in statutory language has been construed as indicative of a legislative intent that the mother, as well as the father, of an infant dependent child or of an incapacitated child, shall also be accountable for the support of such child.[35] The statute also appears to indicate a legislative intent that a wife may be liable for the support of her husband.

Exclusive original jurisdiction of actions for desertion and nonsupport is vested in the juvenile and domestic relations district courts.[36] The offense is punishable by a fine of not more than five hundred dollars, or confinement in jail not to exceed twelve months, or both, or on work release employment for not less than ninety days nor more than twelve months.[37] In lieu of a fine or imprisonment, the court may direct the offender to pay a forfeiture of not more than one thousand dollars; the forfeiture may be directed by the court to be paid in whole or in part to the spouse or children.[38]

While in a technical sense the statutory provisions for desertion and nonsupport are criminal in nature, in their practical effect they are compensatory provisions. The court may direct periodic payments to be made for support, and may punish for contempt upon failure to do so.[39]

The father of a child born out of wedlock may also be held liable for the child's support, if he has voluntarily admitted paternity in writing, or if it is shown by other evidence beyond reasonable doubt

---

149 Va. 39, 47, 140 S.E. 277 (1927); Boaze v. Commonwealth, 165 Va. 786, 788, 183 S.E. 263 (1936).
33. Heflin v. Heflin, 177 Va. 385, 395, 14 S.E.2d 317 (1941).
34. VA. CODE § 20-61.
35. Commonwealth v. Shepard, 212 Va. 843, 845, 188 S.E.2d 99 (1972).
36. VA. CODE § 20-67.
37. *Id.* § 20-61.
38. *Id.*
39. Wright v. Wright, 164 Va. 245, 251, 178 S.E. 884 (1935).

that he is the father of the child and should be responsible for its support.[40]

A father's duty to support his children is based upon his right to their custody and control.[41] Where the child is living away from the parent, the question of the parent's liability for support depends upon the circumstances of the case. If the parent abandons the child, or drives him away from home, the parent is liable for support.[42] But a father cannot be said willfully to neglect and refuse to support his children where his wife, without reasonable excuse, keeps them from him.[43]

The law has no fixed standard to determine what constitutes necessitous circumstances. The amount of support "may vary with the conditions to which the parties have been accustomed. The necessaries of one person may be the luxuries of another, reared in and habituated to different surroundings."[44] Thus, what constitutes necessitous circumstances and the amount of support directed to be paid, will vary on a case to case basis according to the circumstances of the parties.

A support order of the juvenile and domestic relations district court becomes inoperative upon the entry of a decree of divorce if the divorce decree provides for the support and maintenance of the spouse and children.[45] Where the divorce decree is silent as to support, however, the support order of a juvenile and domestic relations district court continues in full force and effect.[46] Only a Virginia divorce decree will nullify a Virginia support order;[47] a

---

40. VA. CODE § 20-61.1. Evidence of paternity in this instance is limited to evidence of the following: that he cohabited openly with the mother during all of the ten months immediately prior to the birth of the child; that he gave consent that his name be used as the father of the child upon the birth records of the child; that he allowed the common use of his surname by the child; or that he claimed the child as his on any statement, tax return, or other document signed by him and filed with any local, state or federal government. *Id.*
41. Butler v. Commonwealth, 132 Va. 609, 614, 110 S.E. 868 (1922).
42. *Id.* at 613-14.
43. *Id.* at 613.
44. Burton v. Commonwealth, 109 Va. 800, 805, 63 S.E. 464 (1909).
45. VA. CODE § 20-79.
46. Werner v. Commonwealth, 212 Va. 623, 625, 186 S.E.2d 76 (1972).
47. Jones v. Richardson, 320 F. Supp. 929, 930 (W.D. Va. 1970).

foreign divorce decree is ineffective to nullify a support order of a Virginia court.

The Revised Uniform Reciprocal Enforcement of Support Act, recently enacted in Virginia, is a legislative attempt to provide an easy and accessible method for the enforcement of support orders in cases where the spouse who owes a duty of support is no longer resident in this State. Jurisdiction under this Act is vested in the juvenile and domestic relations district court,[48] notwithstanding the fact that there is pending in some other court an action for separation, annulment or divorce between the same parties.[49] The Act is also applicable where another court has already issued a support order and retained jurisdiction for its enforcement.[50]

Procedures under this Act are relatively simple and can be accomplished without the aid of an attorney. A verified petition is filed stating the name, address and circumstances of the dependents for whom support is sought, and, so far as is known to the petitioner, the name, address and circumstances of the deserting spouse.[51] The Virginia court must first determine whether the petition alleges facts from which it may find that a duty of support is owed.[52] Upon so finding, the Virginia court transmits this information to the proper court of the responding state (*i.e.*, the state in which the defaulting spouse is resident).[53]

If the responding court finds a duty of support, it may order the spouse to furnish support and subject his property to such order. Payments are made to the clerk of the court of the responding state,[54] who transmits them to the juvenile court in Virginia for disbursement.

Virginia, of course, also has duties as a responding state. The Commonwealth's attorney is charged with prosecution of cases in which Virginia is the responding state.[55] The Virginia court, if it

---

48. VA. CODE § 20-88.20:2.
49. *Id.* § 20-88.21.
50. *Id.*
51. *Id.*
52. *Id.* § 20-88.22.
53. *Id.*
54. *Id.* § 20-88.24.
55. *Id.* § 20-88.23.

finds a duty of support, will order payments to be made; failure to comply with its decree is punishable by proceedings for civil contempt.[56]

Although procedures under the Act are simple and can be accomplished by a layman without the aid of a private attorney, the efficacy of the Act as a means of enforcing support orders is questionable. A defaulting spouse can successfully evade prosecution so long as his whereabouts remain unknown. Additionally, prosecution of cases under the Act is the duty of the Commonwealth's attorney, who may not have the time, resources, or interest diligently to fulfill this duty.

ANNULMENT

Annulment rests within the inherent power of a court of equity; it is a power not conferred by statute but inherent with respect to all civil contracts voidable upon grounds recognized by equity.[57] This power is not lost because other grounds are specifically enumerated by statute.[58] If there is some impediment to a valid marriage contract a court of equity will declare the marriage void.[59]

The statute provides that either party may institute a suit for annulment when a marriage is alleged to be void or voidable for any of the following causes: the marriage was not solemnized under a license and in a manner authorized by statute; the marriage was entered into prior to the dissolution of an earlier marriage of one of the parties; the marriage is incestuous; one or both of the parties was under the age of eighteen and failed to comply with provisions for parental consent; either of the parties lacked capacity to consent due to mental incapacity or infirmity; or when the marriage is alleged to be void for reason of fraud or duress.[60]

The grounds for annulment must be clearly proven, for there is

---

56. *Id.* § 20-88.26.
57. Pretlow v. Pretlow, 177 Va. 524, 548, 14 S.E.2d 381 (1941).
58. *Id.*
59. *Id.*
60. VA. CODE § 20-89.1.

a presumption in favor of the validity of every marriage.[61] Annulment of an unconsummated marriage may be secured more readily than in a case where the parties have cohabited.[62]

The statute also enumerates certain additional instances in which a decree of annulment may be entered upon complaint of the party aggrieved: in the case of incurable impotency existing at the time of the marriage; where either party prior to the marriage, without knowledge of the other, had been convicted of a felony; where at the time of the marriage the wife, without knowledge of the husband, was pregnant by another man; where the husband, without knowledge of the wife, had fathered a child born to some other woman within ten months after the date of the marriage; or where either party has been a prostitute prior to the marriage, without knowledge of the other.[63]

Special rules govern in these additional instances. No annulment will be decreed if the aggrieved party has cohabited with the other after knowledge of the facts given rise to the grounds for annulment.[64] The guilty party is not permitted to institute suit. No annulment will be granted in these instances if the parties have been married for a period of two years prior to the institution of the suit.[65]

A decree of annulment ascertains that there has been no valid marriage between the parties.[66] Where a marriage is annulled, no alimony can be decreed.[67] However, the children of a marriage which is annulled are legitimate, and the court may make a further decree concerning the custody, care and maintenance of such children.[68]

---

61. 12 MICHIE'S JURISPRUDENCE *Marriage* § 13 (1950).
62. Pretlow v. Pretlow, 177 Va. 524, 539, 14 S.E.2d 381 (1941).
63. VA. CODE § 20-89.1. See Pretlow v. Pretlow, 177 Va. 524, 14 S.E.2d 381 (1941).
64. VA. CODE § 20-89.1.
65. *Id.*
66. 12 MICHIE'S JURISPRUDENCE *Marriage* § 16 (1950).
67. *Id.* at § 19.
68. Henderson v. Henderson, 187 Va. 121, 128, 46 S.E.2d 10 (1948).

DIVORCE

While annulment is an inherent equitable power of the court, divorce is not. Divorces may be granted only in such circumstances as the legislature prescribes.[69] In Virginia, a divorce from the bonds of matrimony may be granted for the following reasons: adultery; where either party subsequent to the marriage is convicted of a felony, sentenced to confinement for more than one year, and subsequently confined; where either party has been guilty of cruelty, abandonment or desertion, or has caused reasonable apprehension of bodily harm; and where the parties have lived separate and apart without interruption for a period of one year.[70]

The statute provides that a divorce will not be granted upon the uncorroborated testimony of either or both parties.[71] The purpose of this rule is to prevent the parties from obtaining a divorce by collusion.[72] The degree of corroboration required is a matter resting upon the facts of the particular case.[73] Where a particular fact is essential to complainant's case, some corroborative evidence is required; but where there is little possibility of collusion, the corroboration need only be slight.[74]

Adultery is "peculiarly a crime of darkness and secrecy"; it therefore may be established by circumstantial evidence.[75] The evidence must be such, however, "as to lead the guarded discretion of a reasonable and just man to the conclusion of the defendant's guilt." [76] Despite this evidentiary burden, the court has held that the allegation is sufficiently proved where the parties were together in a place where adultery would probably be committed.[77]

If the alleged adultery occurred more than five years prior to

---

69. Pretlow v. Pretlow, 177 Va. 524, 528, 14 S.E.2d 381 (1941).
70. VA. CODE § 20-91.
71. *Id.* § 20-99.
72. Raiford v. Raiford, 193 Va. 221, 228, 68 S.E.2d 888 (1952).
73. Graves v. Graves, 193 Va. 659, 661, 70 S.E.2d 339 (1952).
74. *Id.*
75. Musick v. Musick, 88 Va. 12, 15, 13 S.E. 302 (1891).
76. Throckmorton v. Throckmorton, 86 Va. 768, 772, 11 S.E. 289 (1890).
77. Musick v. Musick, 88 Va. 12, 15, 13 S.E. 302 (1891).

the institution of the suit for divorce, the divorce will not be granted.[78] Nor will a divorce be granted where the parties voluntarily cohabit after knowledge that adultery has been committed,[79] provided the offense is not repeated. In the former instance, the injured party is deemed to have condoned the act, and will not be heard to complain.[80] A single act of intercourse is sufficient to constitute condonation if it is voluntary and with knowledge of the offense.[81]

The principle of condonation is also applicable in cases of conviction of a felony. A divorce on this ground will be granted only if cohabitation has not been resumed after knowledge of the confinement.[82]

The desertion which will support a decree of divorce is composed of two elements: an actual breaking off of matrimonial cohabitation, and an intent to desert in the mind of the offender.[83] A separation by mutual consent is not a desertion by either party.[84] A separation commenced by mutual consent will be deemed to continue by mutual consent, unless one party can prove a good faith offer to resume cohabitation which was unjustifiably refused.[85]

In certain instances one spouse may be justified in leaving the other; the usual test is that the conduct of the other must be sufficient to establish the foundation for a divorce proceeding.[86] The actions of the deserting spouse will be deemed justifiable in instances of cruelty or reasonable apprehension of bodily harm.

It is generally recognized that the cruelty which constitutes grounds for divorce is that which "tends to bodily harm, and thus

---

78. VA. CODE § 20-94.
79. *Id.*
80. McKee v. McKee, 206 Va. 527, 532, 145 S.E.2d 163 (1965).
81. Tarr v. Tarr, 184 Va. 443, 448, 35 S.E.2d 401 (1945).
82. VA. CODE § 20-91.
83. Smith v. Smith, 202 Va. 104, 109, 116 S.E.2d 110 (1960); Graham v. Graham, 210 Va. 608, 610, 172 S.E.2d 724 (1970).
84. Smith v. Smith, 202 Va. 104, 109, 116 S.E.2d 110 (1960).
85. *Id.*
86. Stolfi v. Stolfi, 203 Va. 696, 701, 126 S.E.2d 923 (1962).

renders cohabitation unsafe; or that involves danger to life, limb, or health."[87]

A single act of cruelty usually is not sufficient to constitute grounds for divorce, unless it is so severe as to endanger life, or indicates an intention to do serious bodily harm.[88] Physical violence is not necessarily a prerequisite to the granting of a divorce on the ground of cruelty, for the court has recognized that:

> ... angry words, coarse and abusive language, humiliating insults, and annoyances in all the forms that malice can suggest, may as effectually endanger life or health as personal violence, and afford grounds of relief to the injured spouse ....[89]

The principle of condonation is not applicable in cases of cruelty. Cruelty may be condoned and forgiven to a certain point, but this fact does not preclude bringing it forward when it has reached the point where it is no longer tolerable.[90]

In cases of desertion, cruelty or reasonable apprehension of bodily harm, a divorce from the bonds of matrimony may be granted to the innocent party after a period of one year from the date of such act.[91] Virginia now also permits a no-fault divorce, in cases where the parties have lived separate and apart for a period of one year. This provision is the result of a legislative recognition that the interests of society will be better served by the legal termination of marriages which no longer exist in fact.[92] Under this provision, even the party who was at fault in causing the initial separation may be granted a divorce.[93]

Virginia also provides for a divorce from bed and board, or legal separation, on the grounds of desertion or abandonment, cruelty, or reasonable apprehension of bodily harm.[94] It should be

---

87. DeMott v. DeMott, 198 Va. 22, 28, 92 S.E.2d 342 (1956). See also Latham v. Latham, 71 Va. (30 Gratt.) 307, 321 (1878); Upchurch v. Upchurch, 194 Va. 990, 999, 76 S.E.2d 170 (1953).
88. DeMott v. DeMott, 198 Va. 22, 28, 92 S.E.2d 342 (1956).
89. Sollie v. Sollie, 202 Va. 855, 860, 120 S.E.2d 281 (1961).
90. *Id.*
91. VA. CODE § 20-91.
92. Canavos v. Canavos, 205 Va. 744, 747, 139 S.E.2d 825 (1965).
93. *Id.* at 748.
94. VA. CODE § 20-95.

emphasized that the divorce from bed and board is not the same in its legal effect as a divorce from the bonds of matrimony. In essence, the divorce from bed and board gives the injured party the right to live separate and apart from his or her spouse. It is not a final decree of divorce and neither party is free to remarry.[95] A divorce from bed and board may be revoked where the parties have reconciled and jointly apply to the court for revocation of the decree.[96] If no reconciliation takes place, either party may apply to the court for merger of a divorce from bed and board into a divorce from the bonds of matrimony when one year has elapsed from the entry of the bed and board decree.[97]

A prior decree of divorce from bed and board is not a necessary preliminary to a divorce from the bonds of matrimony. If desertion or cruelty is the ground for divorce, the court may grant a divorce from the bonds of matrimony to the innocent spouse if one year has elapsed since the alleged desertion or act of cruelty.[98] The only problem is one of proof.

In any divorce, the parties are usually deeply concerned over the issue of support, and the care, custody, and control of any children of the marriage. While the divorce suit is pending, the court is authorized to make such decree concerning the support and maintenance of the parties, and the care and custody of the children, as it deems proper.[99] The court may order the defendant to pay to the petitioning spouse any sums necessary to enable him or her to carry on the suit,[100] and such order is enforceable *via* contempt proceedings.[101] Interlocutory orders as to support, custody, and suit money are matters within the discretion of the

---

95. 6A MICHIE'S JURISPRUDENCE *Divorce and Alimony* § 4 (1976).
96. VA. CODE § 20-120.
97. *Id.* § 20-121. Although either party may apply for a merger, provisions for notice differ. The innocent party may apply for a merger without giving notice to the guilty party. A guilty party who moves for a merger, however, must give ten days' notice to the innocent spouse. *Id.*
98. VA. CODE § 20-121.01.
99. *Id.* § 20-103.
100. *Id.*
101. Eddens v. Eddens, 188 Va. 511, 517, 50 S.E.2d 397 (1948).

court; such orders have neither the dignity nor the effect of a final decree upon the merits.[102]

In decreeing an annulment, divorce from bed and board or divorce from the bonds of matrimony, or upon finding that neither party is entitled to a divorce, the court is expressly authorized by statute to make such further decree as to the support and maintenance of the parties, and the care, custody and support of their minor children, as it deems necessary.[103]

Traditionally, where a wife has been held blameless for the breach of marital relations, the law has imposed upon the husband the duty to support her according to his financial ability and the standard of living established during the marriage. Even where the wife was possessed of a sizeable estate in her own right, this did not relieve or lessen the obligation of her former husband to support her.[104]

The statutes now recognize that each spouse has a duty of support to the other and to the children of the marriage.[105] The factors which the court shall consider in determining support and maintenance for the spouse and children have been specifically enumerated by the legislature. These factors are:

(1) the earning capacity, obligations and needs, and financial resources of the parties;

(2) the education and training of the parties and the ability and opportunity of the parties to secure such education and training;

(3) the standard of living established during the marriage;

(4) the duration of the marriage;

(5) the age, physical and mental condition of the parties;

(6) the contributions, monetary and nonmonetary, of each party to the well-being of the family;

(7) the property interests of the parties, both real and personal;

(8) such other factors as are necessary to consider the equities between the parties.[106]

---

102. Wilkerson v. Wilkerson, 214 Va. 395, 397, 200 S.E.2d 581 (1973).
103. VA. CODE § 20-107.
104. Klotz v. Klotz, 203 Va. 677, 680, 127 S.E.2d 104 (1962).
105. VA. CODE §§ 20-61, 20-107.
106. *Id.* § 20-107.

In addition to or in lieu of periodic payments for maintenance and support of a spouse, the court may, in its discretion, award a lump sum payment, based upon consideration of the property interests of the parties except those acquired by gift or inheritance during the marriage.

The clear implication of the statute is that under appropriate circumstances, the court could order a wife to support her former husband, as well as the reverse. It is also clear that the old rule that a wife's separate estate was not to be considered in determining the amount of support awarded to her is no longer valid.

Support under the new statute is still based upon a fault concept of divorce. The spouse in whose favor grounds for divorce exist cannot be compelled permanently to support or maintain the other, or to make a lum sum payment.[107] However, a party who is granted a no-fault divorce, on the grounds that the parties have lived separate and apart for the requisite period, is not relieved of the obligation to support his or her spouse, unless that party can show that the initial separation was caused by the fault or misconduct of the other.[108]

A decree of support may be increased, decreased, or terminated by the court upon the application of either party.[109] However, it is of utmost importance that the divorce decree make some provision for support if this is desired. The statute authorizing the court to increase, decrease or terminate support does not authorize the subsequent granting of support where none was decreed initially.[110]

Often the parties to a divorce will enter into a property settlement, which the court incorporates and makes part of the divorce decree. A property settlement is a private contractual agreement which differs in its legal effect from a support decree. A support decree, for example, ceases upon remarriage of the

---

107. *Id.*
108. Mason v. Mason, 209 Va. 528, 531, 165 S.E.2d 392 (1969); Guy v. Guy, 210 Va. 536, 539, 172 S.E.2d 735 (1970).
109. VA. CODE § 20-109.
110. Perry v. Perry, 202 Va. 849, 853, 120 S.E.2d 385 (1961).

former spouse, or upon the death of either party.[111] The court cannot order termination of support payments in the event of death or remarriage, however, if the property settlement specifically provides otherwise.[112] Generally, failure to comply with a support decree is enforceable by contempt proceedings.[113] But where a property settlement is confirmed by the court and made a part of the divorce decree, and the court does not expressly order compliance with the agreement, the court may not punish such noncompliance via contempt proceedings.[114] A party who fails to object to the terms of a property settlement prior to the entry of a divorce decree which confirms that settlement is precluded thereafter from petitioning the court to increase, decrease, or terminate support.[115]

The court in a divorce suit is without jurisdiction to enter a decree affecting property rights except for dower and curtesy.[116] Thus, the court in a divorce proceeding has been held to be without jurisdiction to award exclusive use of the jointly owned home to the wife as part of the award of alimony and child support,[117] or to decide the issue of ownership of furniture acquired by the parties during the marriage.[118] If the parties cannot agree between themselves as to a division of their jointly held property, a separate suit in equity must be filed.

In divorce proceedings, one of the most important areas of concern to the parties and to the court is the custody of any minor children of the marriage. Sometimes the parties can agree amicably between themselves as to which spouse shall have custody of the children. If they cannot agree, a bitter and divisive battle often results, with the court being called upon to adjudicate the matter.

---

111. VA. CODE §§ 20-109, 20-110; Durett v. Durett, 204 Va. 59, 62, 129 S.E.2d 50 (1963).
112. VA. CODE § 20-109.
113. Id. §§ 20-113, 20-115.
114. Martin v. Martin, 205 Va. 181, 184, 135 S.E.2d 815 (1964).
115. VA. CODE § 20-109.
116. Guy v. Guy, 210 Va. 536, 541, 172 S.E.2d 735 (1970).
117. Jackson v. Jackson, 211 Va. 718, 719, 180 S.E.2d 500 (1971).
118. Guy v. Guy, 210 Va. 536, 541, 172 S.E.2d 735 (1970).

FAMILY RELATIONSHIPS   245

That the court has the power to award custody of a minor child in a divorce proceeding is not disputed.[119] The overriding consideration in all controversies over custody is the welfare of the child.[120] The trial court is vested with wide discretion in determining custody matters, but in determining what will be in the best interests of the children, consideration should be given to

> ... the fitness of each parent as to age, adaptability to the task of caring for the children, ability to control and direct them, and the ages, sex and health of the children, their temporal and moral well-being, as well as the environment and circumstances in the proposed home, and influences likely to be exerted upon the children.[121]

The wishes of the children of a reasonable age are also to be given consideration, although they are not conclusive.[122]

The mother is generally recognized as the natural guardian of her children of tender years, and if the parents are otherwise equally qualified to care for them, she will be given their custody.[123] This is especially true if the children are girls.[124] This rule is applicable even when the mother is not the innocent party and a divorce has been granted to the father,[125] for custody is not to be given to one parent to punish the other.[126]

The court may also determine that neither parent is a fit and proper person to have custody of the children, and award custody to some third party. The welfare of the child is of paramount concern; thus, where the best interests of the child demand, the court may disregard the technical, legal rights of the parents.[127]

---

119. VA. CODE § 20-107; Gramelspacher v. Gramelspacher, 204 Va. 839, 842, 134 S.E.2d 285 (1964).
120. Campbell v. Campbell, 203 Va. 61, 64, 122 S.E.2d 658 (1961), Hall v. Hall, 210 Va. 668, 671, 173 S.E.2d 865 (1970); Rowlee v. Rowlee, 211 Va. 689, 690, 179 S.E.2d 461 (1971).
121. Hall v. Hall, 210 Va. 668, 671, 173 S.E.2d 865 (1970).
122. *Id.* at 672.
123. Rowlee v. Rowlee, 211 Va. 689, 690, 179 S.E.2d 461 (1971).
124. Campbell v. Campbell, 203 Va. 61, 63, 122 S.E.2d 658 (1961).
125. *Id.*
126. Rowlee v. Rowlee, 211 Va. 689, 690, 179 S.E.2d 461 (1971).
127. Forbes v. Haney, 204 Va. 712, 716, 133 S.E.2d 533 (1963).

A decree concerning custody is always subject to change. Either party may apply to the court for a revision or alteration of a decree concerning the care and custody of the children; the court may make whatever revision the circumstances of the parents and the welfare of the children require.[128]

PROCEDURE IN ACTIONS FOR DIVORCE OR ANNULMENT

Jurisdiction of suits for annulment and divorce is in the circuit courts.[129] The suit must be instituted in the city or county in which the parties last cohabited, or at the option of the complaining party, in the city or county in which the defendant resides.[130] If the defendant is not a resident of Virginia, the suit may be instituted in the city or county in which the plaintiff resides. No suit for divorce or annulment may be instituted unless one of the parties is domiciled in Virginia, and has been a bona fide resident of the state for a period of at least six months prior to the commencement of the suit.[131]

The fact that the defendant is a nonresident, or that his whereabouts are unknown, is not an impediment to a divorce action. The statutes provide that in this instance the complaining party may proceed *via* an order of publication against the defendant.[132] The party instituting the suit still has the burden, however, of providing corroborative evidence and persuading the court that, under the circumstances of the case, a divorce should be granted.

Suits for divorce are conducted as are other suits in equity.[133] This means that all pleadings must be in proper legal form, and the action must conform in all respects to the rules of civil procedure which govern suits in equity. These procedures may appear highly technical, complex and cumbersome to the layman, and indeed they are. Although many people would undoubtedly

---

128. VA. CODE § 20-108.
129. *Id.* § 20-96.
130. *Id.*
131. *Id.* § 20-97.
132. *Id.* § 20-104.
133. *Id.* § 20-99.

prefer to be able to obtain a divorce without the necessity of representation by an attorney, as a practical matter it is all but impossible for them to do so.

ADOPTION

Adoption is "the act by which a person takes the child of another into his family and treats him as his own . . . ."[134] Legal adoption divests the natural parents of all legal rights and obligations in respect to the child.[135] An adopted child is, for all intents and purposes, the child of the persons adopting him; he is entitled to all rights and privileges of a child born in lawful wedlock.[136]

Virginia does not recognize common law adoption. The artificial relationship of parent and child cannot be created by private contract, the prescribed statutory proceedings being essential to that relationship.[137] Prospective adoptive parents initiate the adoption proceedings by filing a petition with the circuit court.[138] The matter is then referred to the state commissioner of public welfare and the child-placing agency or the local superintendent of public welfare. The child-placing agency or the local superintendent must conduct a thorough investigation and forward a report to the court and the state commissioner within sixty days; after receipt of the agency report, the state commissioner has thirty days in which to review the report and notify the court of his approval or disapproval.[139] If the court is satisfied that adoption is in the best interests of the child and the petitioners, an interlocutory order of adoption is entered.[140] During the following six-month period the local department of social services must visit the child in the home of the petitioners at least three times, and report its findings to the court.[141] At the end of

---

134. 14 MICHIE'S JURISPRUDENCE *Parent and Child* § 27 (1951).
135. VA. CODE § 63.1-233.
136. *Id.*
137. Clarkson v. Bliley, 185 Va. 82, 38 S.E.2d 22 (1946).
138. VA. CODE § 63.1-221.
139. *Id.* § 63.1-223.
140. *Id.* § 63.1-226.
141. *Id.* § 63.1-228.

the probationary period, if the court is satisfied that adoption is in the best interests of the adopting parents and the child, a final order of adoption is entered.[142]

No petition for adoption may be granted unless the parents of the child have consented in writing to the proposed adoption.[143] Consent must be executed by the parents or surviving parent of a child born in lawful wedlock.[144] In the case of a child born out of wedlock, consent of both parents or of the surviving parent is also required.[145] However, consent of the father of a child born to an unmarried woman is not required if the identity of the father is unknown.[146] Consent of the father of an out-of-wedlock child is also not required if the father is given written notice of the adoption proceedings by registered or certified mail and fails to object to the proposed adoption.[147] Parental consent is not valid unless the child is at least ten days old at the time the consent is signed.[148] A parent who is under the age of eighteen is legally capable of consenting to the adoption of his or her child and is fully bound by such consent.[149] If a licensed child-placement agency or a local board of public welfare or social services has custody of the child with the right to place him for adoption (either through court commitment or parental consent), the consent of that agency is required.[150] When the child is fourteen years of age or older, the consent of the child is also required, unless the child's best interest would be served by not requiring such consent.[151]

The court may in certain circumstances grant the adoption without parental consent, if it finds that consent is being arbitrarily withheld against the child's best interests.[152] The rights of the

---

142. *Id.* § 63.1-230.
143. *Id.* § 63.1-225.
144. *Id.*
145. *Id.*
146. *Id.*
147. *Id.*
148. *Id.*
149. *Id.*
150. *Id.*
151. *Id.*
152. *Id.*

parent may not be lightly terminated, however, and must be respected if at all consonant with the best interests of the child.[153] Where the nonconsenting parent has not, by his conduct or by previous legal proceedings, lost his right to the child, it must be shown that to continue the parent-child relationship would be detrimental to the child.[154] It is difficult to articulate any general rule concerning the circumstances under which consent will be deemed to be arbitrarily withheld contrary to the child's best interest, for such a decision always rests upon the facts and circumstances of the particular case.

An interlocutory order of adoption is subject to revocation "for good cause shown,"[155] the purpose of the interlocutory order being to permit the court to inquire into and consider matters which have developed during the pendency of that order.[156] An interlocutory order may not be revoked simply because a parent who previously consented to the adoption has changed his or her mind, for consent which is freely and knowingly given cannot subsequently be arbitrarily revoked.[157] However, in one case an interlocutory order was revoked where the child himself, who was fifteen years old, was bitterly opposed to the adoption.[158]

The court is permitted to waive the interlocutory order and probationary period and enter a final order of adoption in certain instances. For example, this is permitted in parent-stepparent adoptions where one of the petitioners is already the legal parent of the child; it is a usual procedure for the court to waive the interlocutory order and enter a final order in this instance. Waiver is also permitted when the child was placed in the home of the petitioners by a child-placing agency, has lived in the home of the petitioners for at least six months prior to the filing of the petition, and has been visited by a representative of the agency at least three times during the six-month period.[159] This procedure is

---

153. Malpass v. Morgan, 213 Va. 393, 399, 192 S.E.2d 794 (1972).
154. *Id.*
155. VA. CODE § 63.1-227.
156. Newton v. Wilson, 199 Va. 864, 868, 102 S.E.2d 299 (1958).
157. Bidwell v. McSorley, 194 Va. 135, 140, 72 S.E.2d 245 (1952).
158. Newton v. Wilson, 201 Va. 1, 4, 109 S.E.2d 105 (1959).
159. VA. CODE § 63.1-229.

usually followed in agency placement, and a final order of adoption is entered. Also, if a child twelve years of age or older has resided in the home of the petitioner continuously for as much as five years immediately prior to the filing of the petition, the court may waive the interlocutory order and enter a final order of adoption.[160]

In a parent-stepparent adoption, if the nonadopting parent is deceased or, if living, has consented to the adoption, the court may waive the requirement of an investigation and report by the state commissioner or local board of public welfare.[161] Waiver of the investigation is a matter within the court's discretion. The petitioners in a parent-stepparent adoption frequently do not understand the necessity of an investigation and report, or of the thoroughness of that investigation, particularly in view of the fact that the child is already living in their home and will in all probability continue to do so, regardless of the outcome of the adoption proceedings. The state commissioner and local board of public welfare, however, are only fulfilling their statutory duty in making an investigation when requested to do so by the court. The purpose of the social worker's visits and the questions asked is not to harass the petitioners, to invade the privacy of their home, or to suggest that they are not suitable adoptive parents; it is merely to fulfill the requirements of the statute.

An adopted child is in all respects legally the child of the adoptive parents. From the time of the entry of an interlocutory order, an adopted child inherits, according to the statutes of descent and distribution, from his adoptive parents who die intestate.[162] Adopted children may also inherit from relatives of the adoptive parents who die intestate, for the purpose of the statute is to put an adopted child on the same footing as a natural child.[163] This includes the right to take by representation in cases of intestacy.[164]

This principle is not applicable to the construction of wills, however. If a testator dies, bequeathing property to "X and his

---

160. *Id.*
161. *Id.* § 63.1-231.
162. *Id.* § 63.1-234; Fletcher v. Flanary, 185 Va. 409, 412, 38 S.E.2d 433 (1946).
163. McFadden v. McNorton, 193 Va. 455, 462, 69 S.E.2d 445 (1952).
164. *Id.*

heirs," *X*'s adopted child may or may not be an heir within the meaning of the will. The term "heir," as used in a will, is subject to different meanings dependent upon the context of the will, and will be construed so as to give effect to the testator's intent.[165] The term "heir" when used in a will has at times been construed to mean "heirs of the body" or "issue," thereby excluding an adopted child.[166] This problem can be avoided by careful drafting of testamentary instruments which clearly define the status of an adopted child, thereby eliminating the necessity for judicial construction.

JUVENILE LAW

The juvenile and domestic relations district courts have jurisdiction over all offenses committed by minors.[167] The purpose of the juvenile court is not to punish the juvenile offender, but to rehabilitate him. Each case is to be given careful, compassionate and individualized treatment. This policy is embodied in the Virginia statute which provides,

> It is the intention of this law that in all proceedings the welfare of the child and the family is the paramount concern of the State . . . .[168]

In order to effectuate this purpose, juvenile court proceedings traditionally have been very informal; the juvenile judge was vested with wide discretion in dealing with juvenile offenders, unhampered by the rigidity and technicalities of the rules governing criminal proceedings in adult courts.

In 1966, the United States Supreme Court recognized that:

> The absence of substantive standards has not necessarily meant that children receive careful, compassionate, individualized treatment. The absence of procedural rules based upon constitutional principle has not always produced

---

165. Newsome v. Scott, 200 Va. 833, 837, 108 S.E.2d 369 (1959); Merson v. Wood, 202 Va. 485, 488, 117 S.E.2d 661 (1971).
166. Newsome v. Scott, 200 Va. 833, 838, 108 S.E.2d 369 (1959); Merson v. Wood, 202 Va. 485, 489, 117 S.E.2d 661 (1971).
167. VA. CODE § 16.1-241.
168. *Id.* § 16.1-227.

fair, efficient and effective procedures. Departures from established principles of due process have frequently resulted not in enlightened procedure, but in arbitrariness.[169]

Accordingly, the juvenile offender is now entitled to certain minimal elements of due process: notice of the charges against him; [170] the right to representation by counsel, and to have counsel appointed in cases of indigency; [171] the protection of the constitutional privilege against self-incrimination; [172] and the right to confront and cross-examine witnesses.[173]

Despite these changes, juvenile court proceedings still differ from adult court proceedings in many important respects. The general public is usually excluded from all juvenile court hearings, but a child charged with violation of the criminal law has a right to a public hearing unless this right is expressly waived.[174] Records of juvenile court proceedings are usually withheld from public inspection.[175] A juvenile court adjudication is not a conviction; it does not impose any of the disabilities usually imposed by conviction of a crime and does not operate to disqualify the child from civil service appointment or military enlistment.[176]

Where a child fifteen years of age or older is charged with an offense which, if committed by an adult, would be punishable by confinement in the penitentiary, the juvenile court may transfer the case to a circuit court.[177] The court must first conduct a hearing to determine whether transfer should be made, and must find: (1) that there is probable cause that the child committed the alleged delinquent act; (2) that the child is not amenable to treatment or rehabilitation as a juvenile (except when the alleged delinquent act is armed robbery, rape or murder, the court may certify the child without making this finding); (3) that the child is not mentally

---

169. *In re* Gault, 387 U.S. 1, 17 (1967).
170. *Id.* at 33.
171. *Id.* at 41.
172. *Id.* at 55.
173. *Id.* at 57.
174. VA. CODE § 16.1-302.
175. *Id.*
176. *Id.* § 16.1-308.
177. *Id.* § 16.1-269.

retarded or mentally ill; and, (4) that the interests of the community require that the child be placed under legal restraint.[178] The circuit court to which such a case is transferred may deal with the juvenile according to the criminal law or may in its discretion deal with him according to the provisions of the juvenile law.[179]

The juvenile court may elect to retain jurisdiction in certain instances and treat the child according to the provisions of the adult criminal law. This procedure is applicable where a child fifteen years of age or older is charged with an offense which would be a misdemeanor or felony if committed by an adult and the court finds the provisions of the juvenile law inadequate to control or correct the child.[180] The penalty imposed under this provision may not exceed twelve months in jail.[181]

A child over the age of fifteen who is charged with an offense which would be punishable by confinement in the penitentiary if committed by an adult may elect to waive the jurisdiction of the juvenile court.[182] Such waiver may be made only with the written consent of counsel.[183] In this instance the circuit court to which the case is transferred must deal with the case in the same manner as other criminal prosecutions.[184]

The juvenile court has wide discretion in disposing of cases coming before it. It may take custody of the child and place him on probation; leave the child in his own home under court supervision; or commit the child to the care of the local board of public welfare or social services, a private agency, or any proper person such as a foster parent.[185] The court may also commit the child to approved private facilities within the state or to the State Board of Corrections.[186] This provision does not apply to those children who have run away or are "beyond parental control" or

---

178. *Id.*
179. *Id.* § 16.1-272.
180. *Id.* § 16.1-284.
181. *Id.*
182. *Id.* § 16.1-270.
183. *Id.*
184. *Id.*
185. *Id.* § 16.1-279.
186. *Id.*

"incorrigible," but only to those who have violated the criminal law.[187]

Special provisions also govern the arrest and detention of juveniles. A juvenile may be taken into immediate custody under the following circumstances: (1) when the juvenile court has issued an arrest or detention order; (2) when in the presence of the arresting officer the child has violated the law; (3) when the officer finds the child in such surroundings that protective custody is necessary; (4) when there is good cause to believe the child has committed an offense which would be a felony if committed by an adult; or (5) when the child has escaped from the custody of some agency to which he has been previously committed.[188] Generally a juvenile may not be confined in a police station, prison, or jail.[189] Certain exceptions are made when the child is fifteen years of age or older, but even under these instances the child must be kept in a room or ward separate from adult criminals.[190]

The statutes provide for special detention facilities for juveniles.[191] However, the court cannot place any child in such a facility unless (1) the child has no parent, guardian, custodian or other suitable person able and willing to provide supervision and care for such child; or (2) the release of the child would constitute an unreasonable danger to the person or property of others where the child is alleged to be delinquent; or (3) the release of such child would present a clear and substantial threat of serious harm to such child's life or health.[192]

The juvenile court also has jurisdiction over the disposition of a child whose parents are unable or refuse to provide proper care, who is abandoned or without proper parental supervision, whose parents wish to be relieved of his custody, or whose situation is such that his welfare demands some adjudication as to his care and custody.[193] Again, the court has wide discretion in its disposition

---

187. *Id.*
188. *Id.* § 16.1-246.
189. *Id.* § 16.1-249.
190. *Id.*
191. *Id.*
192. *Id.* § 16.1-248.
193. *Id.* § 16.1-241.

of the case. This includes the power to order that the child be permanently separated from his parents and placed for adoption.[194]

By statute, physicians, nurses, social workers, probation officers, teachers or other persons employed in public or private schools, kindergartens or nursery schools, persons providing full- or part-time child care for pay on a regularly planned basis, duly accredited Christian Science practitioners, mental health professionals, and law enforcement officers, in their professional or official capacity, who have reason to suspect that a child is an abused or neglected child, are required to either report the matter immediately to the local department of public welfare or social services or immediately notify the person in charge of the institution where they are employed, who must report the matter immediately to the local department.[195] An investigation will subsequently be made to determine whether the child is in need of the court's protection.[196] The juvenile court also has jurisdiction over the prosecution and punishment of persons charged with abuse or neglect of children.[197]

Any party aggrieved by an order of the juvenile court may appeal to the circuit court; an appeal must be taken within ten days of the order.[198] The case is heard *de novo* or as an entirely new case which may modify, reverse, or uphold the juvenile court.

---

194. *Id.* § 16.1-279.
195. *Id.* § 63.1-248.3.
196. *Id.* § 63.1-248.6.
197. *Id.* § 16.1-241.
198. *Id.* §§ 16.1-296, 16.1-132.

CHAPTER 13

Civil Liberties: Constitutional Rights

E. K. Pirog

IN GENERAL

A Virginia citizen enjoys a broad range of civil rights in common with the citizens of other states. These rights originally spring from the benefits of national citizenship and the guarantees of the Bill of Rights of the United States Constitution, rather than from state citizenship, although Virginia has incorporated most of these guarantees into its Constitution. This chapter will emphasize the general rules set forth by the Supreme Court of the United States which apply in federal courts and, with a few exceptions, in state courts as well.

FIRST AMENDMENT RIGHTS

Every citizen is guaranteed the right to freedom of speech and of the press.[1] This guarantee includes the right to express "symbolic speech" by displaying flags, signs, or other items intended to communicate an opinion or belief, as well as by acting in a manner intended to be communicative in nature.[2] Private expression of opinion is protected regardless of its offensive or annoying content, including speech which protests government policies.[3]

However, while this right is jealously protected by the courts against the slightest infringement by the states, it is not absolute.

---

1. U.S. CONST. amend. I.
2. Tinker v. Des Moines School Dist., 393 U.S. 503 (1969) (wearing black armband in protest of Vietnam War); Shuttlesworth v. Birmingham, 394 U.S. 147 (1969) (picketing).
3. Terminiello v. Chicago, 337 U.S. 1 (1949); Bond v. Floyd, 385 U.S. 116 (1966).

Obscenity,[4] and malicious libel and slander [5] are not protected by the First Amendment, nor is insulting or abusive language which is directed toward others and which has a direct tendency to cause violence.[6] For instance, a citizen may protest the government's policy of integration of public schools, but may not threaten students in those schools with abusive or obscene language.

A state may also prohibit the free exercise of the right of speech and the press when such expression presents a clear and present danger that "serious and substantial evil" will result to an interest which the state has a compelling need to protect.[7] The state may not only prohibit speech which presents a serious threat to the existence of its government, but may also ban any form of expression which tends to result in violence or in substantial interference with the rights of others.[8] To protect its valid interest, a state has the authority to make these types of expression punishable as crimes.[9]

The First Amendment also guarantees to all citizens the right of peaceful assembly and the right to petition the government to express ideas and grievances.[10] These rights, as well as other First Amendment rights, are guaranteed to Virginia citizens by the state constitution.[11] The United States Supreme Court has also found implicit in the freedoms of speech, petition, and assembly a right

---

4. Roth v. United States, 354 U.S. 476 (1957); Goldstein v. Commonwealth, 200 Va. 25, 104 S.E.2d 66 (1958); Ginsberg v. New York, 390 U.S. 629 (1968). See also VA. CODE §§ 18.2-372 to 18.2-389, providing punishment for various obscene publications, films, and acts as misdemeanors and felonies.

5. New York Times Co. v. Sullivan, 376 U.S. 254 (1964). See also VA. CODE § 18.2-417, which provides that the expression of slanderous or libelous statements shall be punishable as a misdemeanor.

6. Chaplinsky v. New Hampshire, 315 U.S. 568 (1942); Mercer v. Winston, 214 Va. 281, 199 S.E.2d 724 (1973). See also VA. CODE § 18.2-416, which provides that the use of abusive language which directly tends to result in violence shall be punishable as a misdemeanor.

7. Schenck v. United States, 249 U.S. 47, 52 (1919). See also Owen v. Commonwealth, 211 Va. 633, 179 S.E.2d 477 (1971).

8. Tinker v. Des Moines School Dist., 393 U.S. 503 (1969); Healy v. James, 408 U.S. 169 (1972).

9. See notes 4 to 6 *supra*.

10. U.S. CONST. amend. I.

11. VA. CONST. art. I, §§ 12, 16.

to freedom of association, which the Fourteenth Amendment requires Virginia and all other states to grant to their citizens.[12] Every citizen has the right to associate with others regardless of the race, creed, or political or religious affiliation of the members of the group,[13] and every group has the right to use public parks and other facilities to express their views, regardless of the offensiveness or unpopularity of those opinions.[14]

Again, these rights are not absolute; however, they may be abridged only upon the showing by the state of a valid and compelling interest which must be protected.[15] No citizen may be compelled to reveal his membership in an organization when the object of the inquiry is the harassment of the members by the state or by individuals,[16] nor may any benefits or employment conferred by the state be denied on the basis of membership in a group, including the Communist Party, unless the group possesses unlawful aims and goals and the state can prove a specific present intent by that member to further the unlawful aims of the group.[17]

Every citizen also enjoys the right to the free exercise of religion.[18] No one may be prevented from practicing religion nor be required to follow the beliefs or practices of another group or individual. Further, the state may not require attendance of religious services or the belief in a particular religion as a condition to the grant of benefits or rights by the state. For instance, the state may not condition probation of juveniles or other offenders on the attendance of church services.[19] The state may not require a religious test [20] or even an expression of belief in a god as a condition to the taking of state office or state employment.[21]

---

12. Louisiana *ex rel.* Gremillion v. NAACP, 366 U.S. 293 (1961).
13. NAACP v. Button, 371 U.S. 415 (1963).
14. Collin v. Chicago Park Dist., 460 F.2d 746 (7th Cir. 1972); National Socialist White People's Party v. Ringers, 473 F.2d 1010 (4th Cir. 1973).
15. See notes 16 and 17 *infra.*
16. NAACP v. Alabama, 357 U.S. 449 (1958).
17. Keyishian v. Board of Regents, 385 U.S. 589 (1967).
18. U.S. CONST. amend. I.
19. Jones v. Commonwealth, 185 Va. 335, 38 S.E.2d 444 (1946). See also Lundeen v. Struminger, 209 Va. 548, 165 S.E.2d 285 (1969) (requirement in divorce decree that children be brought up in Jewish faith is unconstitutional).
20. U.S. CONST. amend. I.
21. Torcaso v. Watkins, 367 U.S. 488 (1961).

Fourth Amendment Right to Freedom From Unreasonable Search and Seizure

The Fourth Amendment of the United States Constitution protects all citizens against unreasonable searches and seizures.[22] While the Virginia Constitution merely forbids searches or seizures under a general warrant,[23] the Virginia Supreme Court has held that the protections of the Fourth Amendment are extended to Virginia citizens by section 19.2-54 of the Virginia Code.[24] Further, the federal rule that any evidence obtained as a result of an invalid search or seizure is inadmissible as evidence at trial[25] has been held to apply to illegally obtained evidence in state trials.[26]

As a general rule, searches made without a warrant are unreasonable, as are searches under an invalid warrant.[27] To be valid, a warrant must specifically describe the place to be searched and the items to be seized,[28] and must be issued by a neutral and detached magistrate [29] upon proof of sufficient probable cause to believe that a crime has been committed and that the evidence [30]

---

22. U.S. CONST. amend. IV.
23. VA. CONST. art. I, § 10.
24. Wiles v. Commonwealth, 209 Va. 282, 163 S.E.2d 595 (1968); Kirby v. Commonwealth, 209 Va. 806, 167 S.E.2d 411 (1969). VA. CODE § 19.2-54 prohibits the issuance of general warrants and requires that warrants specifically describe the places to be searched and the items to be seized.
25. Weeks v. United States, 232 U.S. 383 (1914) (federal courts).
26. Mapp v. Ohio, 367 U.S. 643 (1961).
27. Chimel v. California, 395 U.S. 752, 762 (1969); Coolidge v. New Hampshire, 403 U.S. 443, 469-71 (1971); Lugar v. Commonwealth, 214 Va. 609, 202 S.E.2d 894, 897 (1974).
28. U.S. CONST. amend. IV; VA. CODE § 19.2-54.
29. Coolidge v. New Hampshire, 403 U.S. 443, 453 (1971).
30. "Evidence" of a crime has been defined as the fruits or instrumentalities of a crime; that is, the weapons or objects used to commit the crime (*i.e.*, such instrumentalities as crowbars and explosives used in the commission of a bank robbery) and the objects obtained as a result of that crime (*i.e.*, such fruits of a crime as money and jewelry obtained in a bank robbery). The term also includes those items which are themselves unlawful, such as narcotics, and those which are "mere evidence" of a crime, such as the clothes worn by robbers when robbing a bank. The United States Supreme Court has said that there are no different requirements for the seizure of the fruits and instrumentalities of a crime and of the mere evidence of a crime. Warden v. Hayden, 387 U.S. 294 (1967).

of this crime is located in the place to be searched.[31] Generally, everyone has a right to see a search warrant before allowing a search, and has a right to know what places are named to be searched and what items are listed to be seized.

In certain limited situations, warrantless searches are valid. However, searches made under these exceptions are strictly limited in their scope, and are valid only if based on probable cause to believe that a search is authorized.[32]

The first exception to the warrant requirement is a search made incident to a valid arrest.[33] When an arrest is made, the person of the suspect and the area within his immediate control may be searched for weapons or the evidence of the crime for which he has been arrested to prevent destruction or concealment.[34] If during that search any illegal items not connected to that crime are discovered, they may still be seized and may furnish probable cause to arrest for another crime or to procure a valid search warrant.[35] For instance, a person arrested for a traffic violation may lawfully be searched for weapons, and if during that search drugs or other illegal items are found, that person may lawfully be prosecuted for possession of those items.[36]

The area within the immediate control of the suspect has been defined as the area into which he might reach to gain possession of a weapon or destructible evidence.[37] If a person is arrested while sitting at a desk in a room, the desk may be searched, but no other part of the room or of the house may be searched unless the police have a search warrant for those areas,[38] regardless of whether

---

31. Draper v. United States, 358 U.S. 307 (1959).
32. Warden v. Hayden, 387 U.S. 294 (1967); Chimel v. California, 395 U.S. 752 (1969).
33. Chimel v. California, 395 U.S. 752 (1969). See also Lugar v. Commonwealth, 214 Va. 609, 202 S.E.2d 894 (1974).
34. *Id.*
35. Warden v. Hayden, 387 U.S. 294 (1967).
36. United States v. Robinson, 404 U.S. 218 (1973); Gustafson v. Florida, 414 U.S. 260 (1973).
37. Chimel v. California, 395 U.S. 752, 763 (1969).
38. Vale v. Louisiana, 399 U.S. 30 (1970).

other persons are present who are able to dispose of any evidence before a warrant may be obtained.[39]

However, under the so-called "plain view" exception, any items which are in plain view and are discovered inadvertently during a valid search may be seized if there is probable cause to believe the items are illegal or the evidence of a crime.[40] This exception applies to both searches made with a warrant and to valid warrantless searches. The Virginia Supreme Court has upheld the plain view exception and has allowed drugs which were discovered in plain view in a house being searched for a suspect to be used as evidence for conviction on a drug charge.[41]

A valid warrantless search may also be based on consent.[42] However, no person need consent to a search made without a warrant, and a search is invalid if consent is coerced [43] or was given only after the official making the search claimed to possess a warrant which is later discovered to be invalid or nonexistent.[44] Generally, consent for a search may not be given by a person other than the person against whom the search is directed [45] or his agent.[46] However, consent may be given by a third person if that person has joint access to or control of the place to be searched or the item to be seized.[47] A manager or night clerk of a hotel cannot validly consent to a search of a guest's room, for instance. However, the Virginia Supreme Court has allowed a parent who owns the house in which illegal items belonging to his child were discovered to consent to a search and seizure of those items,[48] and

---

39. *Id.*
40. Coolidge v. New Hampshire, 403 U.S. 443 (1971); Fox v. Commonwealth, 213 Va. 97, 189 S.E.2d 367 (1972); Lugar v. Commonwealth, 214 Va. 609, 202 S.E.2d 894 (1974).
41. Lugar v. Commonwealth, 214 Va. 609, 202 S.E.2d 894 (1974).
42. Schneckloth v. Bustamonte, 412 U.S. 218 (1973); United States v. Matlock, 415 U.S. 164 (1974).
43. Bumper v. North Carolina, 391 U.S. 543 (1968).
44. *Id.*
45. The person may be a person against whom a search is directed either because he owns or has possession of the place searched or of the items seized.
46. Stoner v. California, 376 U.S. 483 (1964).
47. United States v. Matlock, 415 U.S. 164 (1974).
48. Rees v. Commonwealth, 203 Va. 850, 127 S.E.2d 406 (1962) (parents

has held that the owner of a car could validly consent to a search and seizure of items belonging to a passenger who was present at the time of the search.[49] Generally, the owner or possessor of a place or object may validly consent to a search, and any evidence discovered may be used against the person who placed it there.

A fourth exception to the warrant requirement is a search of a building made by the police while in "hot pursuit" of a suspect. However, only those items which the police have probable cause to believe are evidence of the crime may be seized, and the search must end once the suspect has been discovered and taken into custody.[50]

Finally, a "moving vehicle" exception to the warrant requirement has been developed to deal with cars and other moving objects which are easily hidden or removed from the jurisdiction.[51] In certain situations, a search of an entire vehicle is authorized in a search incident to an arrest, as being the area within the immediate control of the suspect.[52] However, the search must be based on probable cause to believe that the vehicle contained weapons or the evidence of a crime, before it can be valid.[53] For example, a person arrested for a traffic violation will not have committed a crime which furnishes probable cause that the auto contains evidence of that crime. However, if an arrest is made for driving under the influence of alcohol or drugs, the vehicle may be searched for the illegal items, and any other evidence discovered may furnish probable cause for an arrest on other charges.

It is likely that a person arrested while driving a car will be taken to the police station, and the car will be either impounded, taken

---

consented to a search of their house which uncovered items belonging to a son who no longer lived there); Ritter v. Commonwealth, 210 Va. 732, 173 S.E.2d 799 (1970) (mother consented to give the police mail addressed to her son who still lived with her).

49. Henry v. Commonwealth, 211 Va. 48, 175 S.E.2d 416 (1970).
50. Warden v. Hayden, 387 U.S. 294 (1967).
51. Carroll v. United States, 267 U.S. 132 (1925); Chambers v. Maroney, 399 U.S. 42 (1970).
52. Id.
53. Chambers v. Maroney, 399 U.S. 42 (1970); Almeida-Sanchez v. United States, 413 U.S. 266 (1973).

CIVIL LIBERTIES: CONSTITUTIONAL RIGHTS 263

to the station, or left on the street. If a police officer has a valid reason to open or check the car, such as to close windows and lock doors, any items found in plain view may be seized and may provide probable cause for a search of the entire vehicle.[54] A car being held by the police is often checked and its contents inventoried to prevent claims that items in the car were stolen while it was at the police station. Again, if illegal items are discovered during such inventory, they may be seized and the entire vehicle may be searched.[55]

Absent such authorization for a search of the car, once a car is taken to the police station, it may not be searched without a warrant, for there is no longer any danger that the car will be removed from the jurisdiction, or its contents destroyed.[56] However, as a general rule, broad discretion is given for a search of a moving vehicle, and any illegal items discovered in a car during an arrest may generally be introduced in evidence.

Any evidence obtained as a result of an unlawful search and seizure is inadmissible as evidence at trial.[57] Further, any evidence obtained from a lawful search and seizure which is based upon unlawfully obtained evidence or information is also inadmissible.[58] The Virginia Supreme Court has held that evidence obtained by a search with a valid warrant was inadmissible at trial when the warrant was based on evidence seized during an unlawful arrest.[59] However, this evidence is only inadmissible in a trial to determine guilt, and may be used to determine whether there is sufficient ground for an indictment.[60]

Furthermore, as a general rule, no one may challenge the use of illegally obtained evidence unless he is the person against whom

---

54. Carter v. Commonwealth, 209 Va. 317, 163 S.E.2d 589 (1968); Cady v. Dombrowski, 413 U.S. 433 (1973).
55. Cabbler v. Commonwealth, 212 Va. 520, 184 S.E.2d 781 (1971), *cert. denied*, 405 U.S. 1073 (1972).
56. Preston v. United States, 376 U.S. 364 (1964); Dyke v. Taylor Implement Mfg. Co., 391 U.S. 216 (1968).
57. See notes 25 and 26 *supra*.
58. Wong Sun v. United States, 371 U.S. 471 (1963).
59. Leatherwood v. Commonwealth, 215 Va. 161, 207 S.E.2d 845 (1974).
60. United States v. Calandra, 414 U.S. 338 (1974).

the search was directed, whether because he was the owner of the place searched or was the possessor of the seized items.[61] The Virginia Supreme Court allows a person to challenge an unlawful search if he owns or has a right to possess the place searched or the property seized, if he is present when the seizure occurs, or if he is a joint occupant of a room or house searched.[62] In most cases, however, the challenge is permitted and the question to be determined is whether the evidence is admissible at trial.

RIGHTS OF AN ACCUSED IN CRIMINAL PROCEEDINGS

The Fifth Amendment guarantees several important rights to an accused in a criminal proceeding.[63] It also guarantees that no person shall be deprived of life, liberty or property without due process of law. However, as this clause applies only to the federal government, the right to due process will be discussed with the Fourteenth Amendment.

RIGHT TO INDICTMENT

In federal felony cases,[64] the Fifth Amendment provides that no person shall be tried except upon presentment [65] or indictment [66] by a grand jury.[67] Virginia law provides the same guarantees for an accused in a felony trial.[68] However, this requirement is only statutory and may be waived by the defendant.[69] The Virginia

---

61. Jones v. United States, 362 U.S. 257 (1960).
62. Sullivan v. Commonwealth, 210 Va. 205, 169 S.E.2d 580 (1969), *cert. denied*, 397 U.S. 998 (1970).
63. U.S. CONST. amend. V.
64. In Virginia, a felony is defined as any crime which is punishable by death or by confinement in the penitentiary. VA. CODE § 18.2-8. Generally, felonies are crimes punishable by one year or more in jail.
65. A presentment is a formal accusation of a crime found by a grand jury upon information known by its members. WEBSTER'S THIRD NEW INTERNATIONAL DICTIONARY 1793 (1969).
66. An indictment is a formal written accusation of a crime found by a grand jury upon information brought to its attention by the prosecuting attorney. *Id.* at 1150.
67. U.S. CONST. amend. V.
68. VA. CODE § 19.2-217.
69. Henson v. Commonwealth, 208 Va. 120, 155 S.E.2d 346 (1967).

Supreme Court has held that an accused indicted for attempted robbery could be validly convicted of robbery,[70] and a defendant indicted for manslaughter could lawfully be convicted of murder.[71] It appears that an indictment is required, but a slight difference in the offense charged and the offense upon which the conviction was based is not fatal to the conviction. A misdemeanor [72] may be tried upon an information from the prosecutor, as well as on presentment or indictment.[74]

DOUBLE JEOPARDY

The Fifth Amendment provides that no person shall be twice put in jeopardy (in danger of conviction) for the same offense.[75] The United States Supreme Court has held this right to be so fundamental as to apply to criminal trials in state courts.[76] The Virginia Constitution also prohibits the state from trying an accused twice for the same crime.[77]

In determining whether an accused has been twice put in jeopardy for the same offense, it is the identity of the offense charged, not the act, which is important.[78] Double jeopardy is a bar to a prosecution only if the offenses charged are identical, or one of the offenses is necessarily included in the other. However, one criminal act may give rise to several separate and distinct offenses.[79] For example, an accused tried for robbery of one man, and who is acquitted of the offense, may not be tried again for the robbery of another man who was also a victim in the original

---

70. *Id.*
71. Cunningham v. Hayes, 204 Va. 851, 134 S.E.2d 271 (1964).
72. In Virginia, a misdemeanor is defined as any crime which is not a felony. VA. CODE § 18.2-8.
73. An information is a formal accusation of a crime made by a prosecuting attorney on information brought to his attention. WEBSTER'S THIRD NEW INTERNATIONAL DICTIONARY 1160 (1969).
74. Jones v. Commonwealth, 60 Va. (19 Gratt.) 478 (1868).
75. U.S. CONST. amend. V.
76. Benton v. Maryland, 395 U.S. 784 (1969).
77. VA. CONST. art. I, § 8.
78. Comer v. Commonwealth, 211 Va. 246, 176 S.E.2d 432 (1970).
79. *Id.*; Miles v. Commonwealth, 205 Va. 462, 138 S.E.2d 22 (1964).

crime.[80] However, an accused may be tried both for robbery and the unauthorized use of an automobile, even though both offenses took place in one continuous act.[81]

The dismissal of charges or the declaration of a mistrial is a bar to subsequent prosecution only if it occurs at a stage of the proceeding in which the accused was put in danger of conviction. The Virginia Supreme Court has held that once a jury is sworn or the first witness is sworn in a nonjury trial, dismissal of the case without the consent of the accused operates as an acquittal on those charges; therefore, retrial on the identical charges would be placing the defendant in double jeopardy.[82]

PROTECTION AGAINST SELF-INCRIMINATION

Another right guaranteed to an accused in a criminal proceeding is the right not to be compelled to testify against himself.[83] This fundamental right has been held by the United States Supreme Court to apply to the states,[84] and is expressly guaranteed by the Virginia Constitution.[85] The privilege against self-incrimination is given only to those who might be put in danger of criminal prosecution if forced to answer questions, and applies to statements made at trial and at all other stages of the criminal prosecution. The privilege may be claimed by an accused and by any other person called to testify at trial.[86] However, once a person is guaranteed immunity from prosecution, the privilege is waived, and he may be forced to testify or be punished for contempt of court.[87]

No person accused of any crime can be compelled to testify in his own criminal trial. An accused who chooses to testify, however,

---

80. Ashe v. Swenson, 397 U.S. 436 (1970).
81. Comer v. Commonwealth, 211 Va. 246, 176 S.E.2d 432 (1970).
82. Rosser v. Commonwealth, 159 Va. 1028, 167 S.E. 257 (1933). VA. CODE § 19.2-292 provides that an acquittal on the facts and merits of a case is a bar to a second prosecution for that offense.
83. U.S. CONST. amend. V.
84. Malloy v. Hogan, 378 U.S. 1 (1964).
85. VA. CONST. art. I, § 8.
86. Woody v. Commonwealth, 214 Va. 296, 199 S.E.2d 529 (1973).
87. Flanary v. Commonwealth, 113 Va. 775, 75 S.E. 289 (1912).

waives that privilege to a certain extent. Testimony as to a criminal activity waives the privilege as to the details of that event, and the witness may be compelled to testify to additional details and submit to cross-examination on that subject, but he does not waive the privilege as to other related activity.[88] Any statements made while serving as a witness in a criminal trial are admissible in later proceedings unless they were made when the witness was testifying in his own behalf.[89]

The protection of the privilege extends to other forms of communication, such as papers or records.[90] However, evidence which is not of a testimonial or communicative nature is not protected by the Fifth Amendment.[91] The state does not violate the privilege against self-incrimination by requiring the accused to take a blood test,[92] to submit to fingerprinting, photographing, or measurement,[93] or to demonstrate an activity for the court.[94] These tests are not considered to be confessions,[95] and therefore, are admissible at trial.

The exercise of the privilege against self-incrimination by an accused may not be commented on at trial by a judge or prosecutor.[95] Furthermore, no presumption of guilt may be based on the defendant's decision to remain silent.[96]

---

88. Reid v. Commonwealth, 213 Va. 790, 195 S.E.2d 866 (1973); Woody v. Commonwealth, 214 Va. 296, 199 S.E.2d 529 (1973).
89. Harbaugh v. Commonwealth, 209 Va. 695, 167 S.E.2d 329 (1969).
90. Boyd v. United States, 116 U.S. 616 (1886); Rees v. Commonwealth, 203 Va. 850, 127 S.E.2d 406 (1962).
91. Schmerber v. California, 384 U.S. 757 (1966).
92. *Id.*; Gardner v. Commonwealth, 195 Va. 945, 81 S.E.2d 614 (1954).
93. Schmerber v. California, 384 U.S. 757 (1966).
94. *Id.*; Holt v. United States, 218 U.S. 245 (1910) (accused required to put on shirt to see whether it fit him).
95. Griffin v. California, 380 U.S. 609 (1965); Dean v. Commonwealth, 209 Va. 666, 166 S.E.2d 228 (1969).
96. VA. CODE § 19.2-268. The Virginia Supreme Court has also held that the prosecution may not comment on an accused's refusal to submit to a lie detector test, Barber v. Commonwealth, 206 Va. 241, 142 S.E.2d 484 (1965), the results of which are inadmissible evidence at trial, Lee v. Commonwealth, 200 Va. 233, 105 S.E.2d 152 (1958).

DEFENDANTS' RIGHTS AT TRIAL

The Sixth Amendment and the Virginia Constitution guarantee a number of rights which are considered indispensible to a fair trial.[97] These rights include a right to be informed of the nature and cause of the charges, compulsory process for obtaining favorable witnesses, and confrontation with the prosecution's witnesses. The right to confront witnesses includes the right to be present at every stage of the trial in the courtroom[98] and to cross-examine all witnesses.[99] Note, however, that the right to be present at trial may be forfeited if the defendant engages in disruptive behavior.

RIGHT TO COUNSEL

The Sixth Amendment guarantee of the right to counsel in all criminal prosecutions applies to both federal and state proceedings.[100] A person accused of committing a felony is entitled to the assistance of counsel at trial, and if defendant is indigent, he may have counsel appointed for him by the court.[101] Since 1972, this right has been extended to include persons accused of any misdemeanor or petty crime which is punishable by imprisonment.[102] However, no right attaches to persons accused of crimes or violations punishable only by fine or forfeiture.

The right to counsel includes not only the trial itself, but also any stage of a criminal prosecution which is critical to the right

---

97. U.S. CONST. amend. VI; VA. CONST. art. I, § 8.
98. Lewis v. United States, 146 U.S. 370 (1892).
99. Pointer v. Texas, 380 U.S. 400 (1965), which held these rights to apply to the states.
100. Gideon v. Wainwright, 372 U.S. 335 (1963). While there is no specific provision in the Virginia Constitution guaranteeing the right to counsel, the Virginia Supreme Court has held that the right is a fundamental one necessary for the fair trial of an accused. Fitzgerald v. Smyth, 194 Va. 681, 74 S.E.2d 810 (1953); Whitley v. Cunningham, 205 Va. 251, 135 S.E.2d 823 (1964).
101. Gideon v. Wainwright, 372 U.S. 335 (1963).
102. Argersinger v. Hamlin, 407 U.S. 25 (1972). The Virginia Supreme Court has followed the *Argersinger* rule even in case of traffic violations punishable by a short jail sentence. White v. Commonwealth, 214 Va. 559, 203 S.E.2d 443 (1974) (30 days).

CIVIL LIBERTIES: CONSTITUTIONAL RIGHTS   269

of the accused to a fair trial.[103] The important question then is: At what point in a criminal prosecution does the guarantee become effective?

In general, the period after arrest and before arraignment is not considered to be a critical stage of the prosecution. An accused is not entitled to the assistance of counsel for such limited investigations as fingerprinting or the taking of a blood test after an arrest for drunken driving.[104] However, if an accused is subjected to interrogation by the police after arrest, he must be informed that he has a right to remain silent, that he has a right to the presence of an attorney during questioning, and that if he cannot afford a lawyer, one will be appointed for him.[105] Any statements made by an accused after he has indicated his intention to remain silent and before he has a chance to talk to his lawyer are inadmissible as evidence.[106] However, any statements made voluntarily or after a knowing and intelligent waiver of the right to counsel are admissible; furthermore, statements which would be inadmissible on direct evidence are admissible on cross-examination to discredit the testimony of the defendant.[107] In interpreting this rule, the Virginia Supreme Court has held that voluntary answers by a suspect to questions asked by other persons, although in the presence of the police, are admissible in evidence.[108] It appears that by voluntarily submitting to interrogation, an accused loses his claim to assistance of counsel.

An accused has the right to assistance of counsel when he must submit to a line-up for the purpose of being identified by

---

103. Powell v. Alabama, 287 U.S. 45 (1932); White v. Maryland, 373 U.S. 59 (1963); United States v. Wade, 388 U.S. 218 (1967).
104. Schmerber v. California, 384 U.S. 757 (1966); Deaner v. Commonwealth, 210 Va. 285, 170 S.E.2d 199 (1969); Law v. Danville, 212 Va. 702, 187 S.E.2d 197 (1972).
105. Miranda v. Arizona, 384 U.S. 436 (1966). See also Massiah v. United States, 377 U.S. 201 (1964); Escobedo v. Illinois, 378 U.S. 478 (1964).
106. Miranda v. Arizona, 384 U.S. 436, 444 (1966).
107. Harris v. New York, 401 U.S. 222 (1971).
108. Wansley v. Commonwealth, 210 Va. 462, 171 S.E.2d 678, *cert. denied*, 399 U.S. 931 (1970) (mother); Williams v. Commonwealth, 211 Va. 609, 179 S.E.2d 512 (1971); Jones v. Commonwealth, 214 Va. 723, 204 S.E.2d 247 (1974) (expert administering polygraph test).

witnesses.[109] However, this right does not attach to persons who are put in a line-up before indictment, because a critical stage of the prosecution is considered to occur only after the initiation of criminal proceedings.[110] This right also does not cover an accused who has been identified only by witnesses viewing photographs.[111] If an accused has been denied the right to counsel during a line-up, that identification cannot be made the basis for an admissible in-court identification by the viewing witnesses.[112]

A preliminary hearing is required by Virginia statute before a suspect may be indicted for committing a felony[113] unless an indictment has already been returned by a grand jury.[114] If a preliminary hearing is held, a suspect has the right to assistance of counsel at the hearing.[115] Since Virginia law also provides that the right to counsel attaches at any hearing and at all other stages of the prosecution in a felony case,[116] it appears that indictment by a grand jury may also be a critical stage of the prosecution entitling an accused to the assistance of counsel.

Virginia law provides that no arraignment is needed for misdemeanors. If the accused appears before a magistrate and pleads, he will be tried immediately unless he can show good cause for a continuance.[117] By statute, if the charge against the accused is a misdemeanor the penalty for which may be by confinement in jail, the court is under the duty to ascertain whether or not the accused desires to waive his right to counsel. If he does not waive his right to counsel and claims indigence, the court must appoint counsel to represent him in the same manner in which counsel is appointed in a felony prosecution.[118]

---

109. United States v. Wade, 388 U.S. 218 (1967).
110. Kirby v. Illinois, 406 U.S. 682 (1972).
111. Drewry v. Commonwealth, 213 Va. 186, 191 S.E.2d 178 (1972); United States v. Ash, 413 U.S. 300 (1973).
112. United States v. Wade, 388 U.S. 218, 241 (1967).
113. VA. CODE § 19.2-218.
114. Benson v. Commonwealth, 190 Va. 744, 58 S.E.2d 312 (1950).
115. Noe v. Cox, 320 F. Supp. 849 (W.D. Va. 1970); Grey v. Slayton, 345 F. Supp. 1278 (W.D. Va. 1972).
116. VA. CODE §§ 19.2-157, 19.2-159.
117. *Id.* § 19.2-237.
118. *Id.* §§ 19.2-159, 19.2-160.

After trial, an indigent defendant is entitled to have the assistance of counsel in making an appeal; to ensure effective representation, an indigent is also entitled to receive a free transcript of the record of his trial.[119]

When counsel is appointed for an indigent accused on a criminal charge, the counsel so appointed must be compensated for his services in an amount fixed by the court in which he appears in accordance with a schedule which is provided by statute. The court will order the payment of such reasonable expenses incurred by the court-appointed attorney as it deems appropriate under the circumstances of the case.[120]

RIGHT TO TRIAL BY JURY

The right to trial by jury in a criminal case is guaranteed by the Sixth Amendment,[121] and, to a certain extent, by Virginia's Constitution.[122] Virginia does not accord the right to trial by jury to those accused of petty offenses, such as the violation of a municipal ordinance, which are punishable by fines only, not imprisonment.[123] For these petty offenses and all other nonfelony crimes, the defendant may first be tried in a district court without a jury, though he will have an absolute right of appeal to the circuit court where he may have a jury trial.[124] The Virginia Supreme Court has held that this procedure satisfies the Sixth Amendment

---

119. Cabaniss v. Cunningham, 206 Va. 330, 143 S.E.2d 911 (1965); Thacker v. Peyton, 206 Va. 771, 146 S.E.2d 176 (1966).

120. VA. CODE § 19.2-163, which provides the following schedule: (1) In a court not of record, a sum not to exceed $75.00; (2) in a circuit court to defend a felony charge that may be punishable by death or by confinement in the penitentiary for a period of more than 20 years, a sum not to exceed $400.00; and to defend any other felony charge, a sum not to exceed $200.00; and to defend any misdemeanor charge punishable by confinement in jail, a sum not to exceed $100.00.

On appeal, an indigent defendant is required to pay the appeal costs only if he loses the appeal. VA. CODE § 19.2-326.

121. Duncan v. Louisiana, 391 U.S. 145 (1968).

122. Bowen v. Commonwealth, 132 Va. 598, 111 S.E. 131 (1922).

123. Ragsdale v. Danville, 116 Va. 484, 82 S.E. 77 (1914); Duncan v. Louisiana, 391 U.S. 145, 158 (1968).

124. VA. CONST. art. I, § 8.

right to jury trial.[125] In felony cases, however, an accused has the right to a jury trial in the first instance.

Trial by jury may be waived, and by statute, a guilty plea to a felony or misdemeanor is an automatic waiver in Virginia. If a defendant enters a plea of not guilty, trial by jury may be waived only with the consent of the court and the prosecutor.[126]

Five jurors are required for misdemeanor trials, and twelve for felony trials,[127] although the defendant may consent to trial by a smaller number of jurors.[128] No one may be convicted of a crime in Virginia unless the jury is unanimous in its decision on the question of guilt.[129] Further, the right to trial by jury includes the right to trial by an impartial jury.[130] The United States Supreme Court has held that an accused is entitled to a jury selected from a representative sample of the population in the particular jurisdiction; any systematic exclusion of persons from juries based on race or sex may deny the defendant a fair trial.[131]

RIGHT TO A SPEEDY TRIAL

The right to a speedy trial requires that a defendant be brought to trial in Virginia [132] within a reasonable time after he has been indicted for a crime.[133] However, this right applies only after indictment, since the right to protection against prosecution for stale crimes is given effect by the running of the statute of limitations. In Virginia, prosecution for a misdemeanor must in most cases be commenced within one year after the commission of the crime,[134] and no one may be indicted for a felony once the statute of limitations for that crime has run.

A person accused of a misdemeanor is entitled to an immediate

---

125. Manns v. Commonwealth, 213 Va. 322, 191 S.E.2d 810 (1972).
126. VA. CONST. art. I, § 8; VA. CODE §§ 19.2-257, 19.2-258.
127. VA. CODE § 19.2-262.
128. VA. CONST. art. I, § 8.
129. *Id.*
130. *Id.*; Durham v. Cox, 328 F. Supp. 1157 (W.D. Va. 1971).
131. Smith v. Texas, 311 U.S. 128 (1940); Taylor v. Louisiana, 419 U.S. 522 (1975).
132. Klopfer v. North Carolina, 386 U.S. 213 (1967).
133. United States v. Marion, 404 U.S. 307 (1971).
134. VA. CODE § 19.2-8.

CIVIL LIBERTIES: CONSTITUTIONAL RIGHTS 273

trial when he first appears and pleads to the charge, unless good cause is shown for a continuance.[135] In a felony prosecution, if the accused is held in custody, trial must be held within five calendar months from the date of the indictment, and if he is not held in custody, then trial must be held within nine calendar months from the date of the indictment, unless excused.[136] The right to a speedy trial may be waived, and at least one district court in Virginia has held that consent to a continuance is a waiver of this right.[137] Further, the right does not apply to an appellate proceeding.[138]

In determining whether the requirement for a speedy trial has been excused, the United States Supreme Court has stated that no affirmative claim of prejudice to a defendant need be shown to find that this right has been denied.[139] Rather, the court's decision must be based on a consideration of such factors as the length of delay, the reason for delay, and the possibility of prejudice to the defense. However, the Court indicated that a failure by a defendant to assert this right would make it difficult for him to prove that he had been denied the right to a speedy trial.[140] Therefore, a defendant who intends to claim a denial of this right must show that he had demanded the right to a speedy trial and protested delay, that he neither contributed to nor consented to delay, and that he has been prejudiced in his defense.

RIGHT TO DUE PROCESS AND EQUAL PROTECTION OF THE LAW

(a) *Generally*

The Fourteenth Amendment guarantees that all citizens may enjoy the right to due process of law before they are deprived of life, liberty, or property and that all citizens are entitled to equal protection of the law.[141] Unlike the Bill of Rights, which applies

---
135. *Id.* § 19.2-237.
136. *Id.* § 19.2-243.
137. Delph v. Slayton, 343 F. Supp. 449 (W.D. Va. 1972).
138. Newsom v. Commonwealth, 207 Va. 844, 153 S.E.2d 235, *cert. denied*, 388 U.S. 918 (1967).
139. Moore v. Arizona, 414 U.S. 25 (1973).
140. Barker v. Wingo, 407 U.S. 514 (1972).
141. U.S. CONST. amend. XIV.

only against the federal government, the Fourteenth Amendment's guarantees were intended to apply against the states, and this amendment has often been used to incorporate the rights guaranteed by the first ten amendments as rights also enjoyed by state citizens.[142]

(b) *Due Process of Law*

Due process of the law, as guaranteed by the Fourteenth Amendment and the Virginia Constitution,[143] is a concept which cannot be governed by strict rules; rather, it must be determined by considering all the facts and circumstances of a particular situation. In some cases, a denial of constitutional rights may, in and of itself, be a denial of due process. In others, it may merely raise a presumption that there has been a denial of due process, and the defendant must also prove that the denial of this right has been so fundamentally unfair that he could not have been accorded a fair trial. The United States Supreme Court has stated that while denial of the right to counsel is *per se* a denial of due process in terms of prejudice to an accused's defense, the denial of a speedy trial is not, and the courts must first determine whether an accused has suffered any harm from the delay.[144]

Procedures which are obviously shocking in a democratic society, such as the use of physical violence to obtain a confession, clearly establish a denial of due process, and a confession obtained by force is inadmissible as evidence.[145] In other cases, however, the line between permissible and impermissible action is less sharply drawn, and the question of whether due process has been denied is a question to be determined by the court.

---

142. For discussion of various theories of incorporation, see Adamson v. California, 332 U.S. 46 (1947), including the concurring opinion of Justice Frankfurter and the dissenting opinions of Justices Black and Murphy.

143. VA. CONST. art. I, § 11.

144. Barker v. Wingo, 407 U.S. 514, 521 (1972).

145. Brown v. Mississippi, 297 U.S. 278 (1936). See also Rochin v. California, 342 U.S. 165 (1952) (pumping stomach of accused to recover drug capsules violates due process).

(c) *Equal Protection of the Law*

The Fourteenth Amendment guarantee that all citizens shall receive equal protection under the laws is supplemented by the Virginia Constitution's provision that all citizens have the right to be free of any governmental discrimination based on religion, race, color, sex, or national origin.[146] This guarantee prohibits the state from practicing, permitting or encouraging discriminatory tactics by its agents or citizens, either directly or indirectly (as by allowing the use of state courts for the enforcement of private discriminatory covenants).[147] Further, laws or regulations which are not unconstitutional on their faces are prohibited if they become discriminatory as applied or enforced.[148]

There is no guarantee, however, of absolute equality of every citizen for every purpose; rather, all persons belonging to a particular class or status must be treated equally. For example, a state may not arbitrarily grant preference to men over women in the selection of an administrator of a decedent's estate without consideration of the applicant's qualifications.[149] A state *may* legislate differently for members of the same class if the classification bears a reasonable relation to a valid legislative objective, and the discrimination (if any) is the least burdensome method by which that object can be achieved. However, while states have broad power to set up classifications for persons differently situated in economic and regulatory legislation,[150] classifications based on race or sex are subjected to stricter scrutiny and have been increasingly invalidated by the courts. Women in the armed forces, for instance, must be given equal opportunity with men to declare their spouses as dependents.[151] States may not differentiate between married and unmarried women in providing access to birth control, regardless of the

---

146. VA. CONST. art. I, § 11.
147. Shelley v. Kraemer, 334 U.S. 1 (1948).
148. Yick Wo v. Hopkins, 118 U.S. 356 (1886).
149. Reed v. Reed, 404 U.S. 71 (1971).
150. Weber v. Aetna Casualty & Surety Co., 406 U.S. 164 (1972).
151. Frontiero v. Richardson, 411 U.S. 677 (1973).

state's intent to discourage premarital sex.[152] No discrimination is permitted against illegitimate children compared to the treatment accorded to those children born in wedlock.[153] Any classification based on sex, race, or status such as marriage is open to question and might be successfully challenged.

The Civil Rights Act of 1964 guarantees that every citizen has the right to full enjoyment of all benefits and services provided by any place of public accommodation,[154] public facility,[155] or educational facility.[156] Both section 1982 of the Act and the Virginia Fair Housing Law prohibit discriminatory practices in the sale, lease or other disposition of property, and in any terms, conditions, or provisions of services, including discriminatory treatment by individuals involved in the sale or rental of residential real estate. Furthermore, no bank or other financing institution may refuse to grant a mortgage or other loan on the basis of race, sex, religion, or national origin.[157] Title VII of the Act bars an employer from refusing to hire on these grounds, and from discriminating as to compensation or other privileges of employment.[158] Virginia law allows the recovery of damages in cases in which equal pay has been denied for equal work, to the extent of double the amount of compensation unlawfully withheld.[159]

Thus, a Virginia citizen enjoys a broad range of rights which often, when abridged, may be given up quietly for fear of the futility of "fighting city hall." But every citizen should realize that these rights will be protected by the courts, and should be enforced by all those who, in good faith, believe they have been treated unfairly.

---

152. Eisenstadt v. Baird, 405 U.S. 438 (1972).
153. Levy v. Louisiana, 391 U.S. 68 (1968); Weber v. Aetna Casualty & Sur. Co., 406 U.S. 164 (1972); Gomez v. Perez, 409 U.S. 535 (1973).
154. 42 U.S.C. §§ 2000a to 2000a-6.
155. 42 U.S.C. §§ 2000b to 2000b-3.
156. 42 U.S.C. §§ 2000c to 2000c-9.
157. 42 U.S.C. § 1982; VA. CODE §§ 36-86 to 36-96.
158. 42 U.S.C. §§ 2000e to 2000e-17.
159. VA. CODE § 40.1-28.6.

CHAPTER 14

Women and the Law

J. H. Bedno

IN GENERAL

The law differs for men and women for a number of reasons — historical, physical, societal, and emotional — and such differences are difficult to categorize coherently. Some decisions of the Supreme Court limit the ways in which women can be treated differently from men, and any law which is sexually discriminatory is subject to constitutional scrutiny. The primary limitation on discrimination is the clause of the Fourteenth Amendment to the United States Constitution granting all citizens the right to "equal protection of the laws." There are many areas where federal law, elaborating this clause, protects a woman from inequities in state law, particularly in relation to her education and employment. Another guideline is the constitutional right to privacy which the Supreme Court has held gives a woman certain rights concerning her own body including the right, under some circumstances, to abortion [1] and birth control.[2] Furthermore, if the Equal Rights Amendment to the Constitution is ratified by the required number of states, this action should result in many more basic changes in women's status.[3]

The Virginia Constitution requires "... that the right to be free from any governmental discrimination upon the basis of ... sex ... shall not be abridged," but allows "separate but equal" treatment of the sexes.[4] The Virginia General Assembly has made

---

1. Roe v. Wade, 410 U.S. 113 (1973); Doe v. Bolton, 410 U.S. 959 (1973).
2. Griswold v. Connecticut, 381 U.S. 479 (1965).
3. See CITIZENS ADVISORY COUNCIL ON THE STATUS OF WOMEN, INTERPRETATION OF THE EQUAL RIGHTS AMENDMENT IN ACCORDANCE WITH LEGISLATIVE HISTORY (1974); Brown, Ellinger, Falk & Freedman, *The Equal Rights Amendment, A Constitutional Basis for Equal Rights for Women*, 80 YALE L.J. 871 (1971).
4. VA. CONST. art. 1, § 11.

considerable effort to remove obviously "sexist" language from the Virginia Code and to change gross inequities, and this process will no doubt continue. Many of the legal decisions affecting women are not made strictly according to statute but at the discretion of the circuit court judges who determine divorce and custody matters and the judges who preside over the juvenile and domestic relations district courts and often deal with child support, custody, and other situations involving fathers, mothers, and their children.[5] Although these judges are licensed attorneys,[6] often they are not trained in sociology or psychology. In Virginia they are at the time of this writing, with only one exception, male. These men, for the most part, have been trained in law schools that were, until recently, almost entirely male. They are not necessarily familiar with or sympathetic to any rights or needs of women which differ from the traditional feminine stereotype. These judges, therefore, sometimes still treat girls who run away from home, or who deviate from parental rules, more harshly than boys.[7] They still often hold that the mother is the only "natural" custodian of the child,[8] and they still enforce the legal dogma that the husband and wife "merge" into one person and that one person is the husband.[9]

In the light of this background information, the law may be considered to fall into four broad categories:

---

5. VA. CODE §§ 16.1-227, 16.1-278.
"The general tenor of these provisions is to give the judge of the Juvenile and Domestic Relations District Court very broad statutory powers, which are more specifically provided for than the inherent powers of other persons holding judicial office." 1973-74 OPS. VA. ATT'Y GEN. 205.

6. Circuit court judges must have been admitted to the bar of the Commonwealth at least five years prior to their appointment or election. VA. CONST. art. VI, § 7. Judges of district courts and juvenile and domestic relations district courts must be licensed to practice law at the time of their appointment or election. VA. CODE §§ 16.1-69.15, 16.1-230.

7. Meda Chesney-Lind, *Juvenile Delinquency, The Sexualization of Female Crime*, PSYCHOLOGY TODAY, July 1974, at 43.

8. "[T]he controlling rule is that in the usual case the welfare of the young child will be promoted by awarding custody to the mother, if she is a fit person and other things are equal." White v. White, 215 Va. 765, 213 S.E.2d 766 (1975).

9. BLACKSTONE, COMMENTARIES 433.

(1) Personal law: rights regarding one's body, marital rights and duties, children;
(2) Property law: rights in case of divorce, rights to inheritance, the right to contract and do business, to acquire credit, and to rent and own property;
(3) Law regarding status: rights as a student and working woman;
(4) Law concerning governmental authority: rights and obligations concerning jury duty, imprisonment, taxation, and other miscellaneous rights and restrictions.

Personal Law

(a) *Rape*

According to its definition in the Virginia Code, rape can only be committed against a female.[10] Although a rape would seem similar to an assault,[11] in that anyone who is attacked should be deserving of legal protection, the law only penalizes rapists who use force (or at least the credible threat of physical force) against victims 13 years of age or over, and also penalizes rapists charged with offenses involving females under the age of thirteen even in the absence of the use of force.[12] Greater protection is given to women who are known by the rapist to be mentally ill hospital patients or patients or pupils of an institution for the mentally ill, mentally retarded, feeble-minded or epileptic persons.[13]

If a man has "carnal knowledge" of a child under 13 years of age, he is guilty of a felony whether or not she resists him.[14] If she is between 13 and 15 years of age, the rapist must have "known" her against her will or be at least three years older than she for the offense to be considered a felony.[15] At 14 years of age

---

10. Va. Code §§ 18.2-61, 18.2-63, 18.2-64.
11. *Id.* at § 18.2-51 defines assault: "If any person . . . by any means cause [any other person] bodily injury, with the intent to maim, disfigure, disable, or kill . . . ."
12. *Id.* at § 18.2-61 defines rape: "If any person carnally know a female of thirteen years of age or more against her will, by force, or carnally know a female child under that age . . . ."
13. *Id.* § 18.2-64.
14. *Id.* § 18.2-61.
15. *Id.* § 18.2-63.

or older, the child will not be considered to have been raped if the court or jury finds her "of bad moral repute and . . . a lewd female" and finds that she consented to "unlawful carnal knowledge."[16] These standards are not further defined, and are left to the court to determine. The man who "has knowledge" of a willing child over 14 may protect himself from prosecution by marrying her and supporting her until she reaches 16 years of age.[17] (The Code, however, would seem to bar the marriage of anyone under 16 except in the case of judicial approval where the female is pregnant.)

The court is allowed to inquire into the "moral character" of a rapist's victim,[18] but will not go into the record of the accused rapist, for fear he may be convicted on the basis of crimes other than that with which he is charged. The victim may be allowed to testify in private.[19] Moreover, a victim's proof of emission by the rapist will strengthen the case against him, but the victim may be required to pay for the hospital tests that she must have soon after being raped in order to establish this evidence. It is established law in Virginia that a victim's testimony alone, without other evidence supporting it, can convict a rapist,[20] but only if his guilt is believed beyond a reasonable doubt.[21]

(b) *Seduction*

A virgin who is seduced by means of a fraudulent promise of marriage, or by a man already married, is also protected under the Code, which makes seduction a felony.[22] Yet there are no penalties for a woman who seduces a man whatever her marital status. Both

---

16. *Id.* § 18.2-65.
17. *Id.* § 18.2-66.
18. *Id.* § 18.2-65.
19. *Id.* § 18.2-67.
20. Fogg v. Commonwealth, 208 Va. 541, 159 S.E.2d 616 (1968).
21. In this matter, Virginia's law is progressive. In New York, where corroboration was required, the state arrested 1,085 people for rape in 1971, but secured only 18 convictions. S. Ross, *The Rights of Women,* AMERICAN CIVIL LIBERTIES UNION HANDBOOK (1973).
22. VA. CODE §§ 18.2-68 to 18.2-70.

men and women are prohibited from taking indecent liberties with any child under 14 years of age.[23]

(c) *Slander*

A woman's reputation is protected from verbal assault by a law which makes it illegal to lie maliciously about her chastity or to insult her grossly.[24] This statute is another instance in which protection is extended only to women.

(d) *Abortion*

A woman may have an abortion legally in Virginia, but state law requires that it be performed by a licensed physician, and, if after the first trimester (twelfth week), in a hospital licensed by or under the control of the state.[25] It is illegal to try to self-induce an abortion or to perform an abortion without a physician in attendance.[26] However, in practice, a pregnant woman will have some difficulty finding a hospital that will perform a second trimester abortion and probably will not find a Virginia hospital that will perform one after the twentieth week of pregnancy. Medical personnel and hospital officials are allowed to refuse to perform abortions on the ground that the procedure offends their consciences.[27] In Virginia, the Code requires the consent of the husband or a parent or guardian for a female under 18 years of age or adjudged incompetent by a court.[28] This is not a requirement in some other jurisdictions, and a woman may legally leave the state to have an abortion performed elsewhere.[29]

(e) *Illegitimate Child*

A mother of an illegitimate child cannot force the natural father to help support it unless he has voluntarily admitted paternity or can be shown to be its father "beyond reasonable doubt." She must

---

23. *Id.* § 18.2-370.
24. *Id.* § 18.2-417.
25. *Id.* §§ 18.2-72 to 18.2-74.
26. *Id.* § 18.2-71.
27. *Id.* § 18.2-75.
28. *Id.* § 18.2-76.
29. Washington, D.C., for example, has no requirement that a patient under 18 years of age have consent from a husband, parent or guardian.

be able to show that she and the child's father have lived together continuously since before the child was born, or that he has given consent to the child using his name, or that he has claimed it as a tax exemption; and she may request the court to order a blood grouping test, the result of which may be admitted in evidence.[30] If, however, the mother wants to put the child up for adoption, she must secure the father's permission if he is known.[31]

(f) *Birth Control and Sterilization*

Birth control information is legally available, and parental permission is not necessary for a person under 18 years of age to obtain it.[32] A sterilization (salpingectomy) may be performed upon a patient who is 21 years of age or over, but no such surgical operation may be performed prior to thirty days from the date of the consent or request therefor on any person who has not had at least one child. If the female is married, the husband's consent will also be required.[33] Some physicians may have private guidelines based on age and number of children which they believe relevant to whether they should perform such operations, but these

---

30. VA. CODE §§ 20-61.1, 20-61.2.

31. A parent who is less than 18 years of age shall be deemed fully competent and shall have legal capacity to execute a valid entrustment agreement and to give consent to adoption. If the identity of the father is not reasonably ascertainable, or if the father is given notice of the entrustment agreement or the adoption proceeding by registered or certified mail to his last known address and he fails to object to the entrustment or the adoption proceeding within twenty-one days of the mailing of such notice, an affidavit of the mother that the identity of the father is not reasonably ascertainable shall be sufficient evidence of this fact, provided there is no other evidence before the court which would refute such affidavit. VA. CODE §§ 63.1-204, 63.1-225.

"[I]t is my conclusion that a court is required to give notice of custody, entrustment or adoption proceedings only to an unwed father whose identity is *known*, or whose identity is reasonably ascertainable, through whatever information is available to the court. On the other hand, if the identity of a putative father is not known or reasonably ascertainable, no notice to him is required. . . . Where the mother refuses to reveal the identity of the father and no other information concerning his identity is available to the court, the court may consider that the father's identity is not known and proceed without notice to him." 1972-73 OPS. VA. ATT'Y GEN. 7.

32. VA. CODE § 32-137(7).

33. *Id.* § 32-423.

WOMEN AND THE LAW 283

guidelines do not have the force of law and bind only physicians wishing to be so bound.

(g) *Marriage*

The Code does not generally specify the behavior expected of a husband and wife in marriage. However, a married woman still retains many of the rights and disabilities of a wife recognized in the early English and American common law, usually modified, but not completely changed.[34] Her permanent home (domicile, in legal terminology) is ordinarily presumed to be that of the husband, and she must follow him to a new home [35] unless his choice of domicile is unreasonable. Only if a husband deserts or is cruel so as to establish grounds for divorce does a wife have the unquestioned right to establish her own legal domicile.[36] If the husband is not a Virginian (for example, a member of the armed services temporarily assigned to Virginia), the wife still will be subject to many of the responsibilities of citizenship [37] but will fail to be accorded many of its benefits. She cannot acquire these benefits unless she is able to prove that she lives in Virginia and intends to make it her permanent home.[38]

---

34. When a state institution required the husband's signature as a condition precedent for the wife's application for in-state tuition privileges, the Attorney General stated: "The Common Law concept that the wife takes the domicile of her husband has not been changed by statutory law in the Commonwealth of Virginia. Accordingly, in determining the domicile of a wife, State institutions must adhere to this concept." 1972-73 OPS. VA. ATT'Y GEN. 82.

35. See Brinkley v. Brinkley, 147 W.Va. 557, 129 S.E.2d 436 (1963); Belcher v. Belcher, 151 W.Va. 274, 151 S.E.2d 635 (1966).

36. Where a husband told his wife to get out, with no misconduct on her part, and she left, there was no desertion (but no grounds for divorce in his constructive desertion). Rowland v. Rowland, 215 Va. 344, 210 S.E.2d 149 (1974).

37. For example, the civilian spouse of a nondomiciliary serviceman is required to get a county motor vehicle license. 1974 OPS. VA. ATT'Y GEN. 67.

38. Concerning the wives of military personnel, the Attorney General has stated: "[I]t may be presumed that a husband and wife share the same domicile.... [The] presumption ... is a rebuttable one, and it is therefore the case that a wife may establish a domicile different than that of her husband. In such a case, the wife has the burden of proving that she is domiciled in Virginia. This requires her to rebut the presumption that she and her husband intend to share the same permanent home. She would have to show that she is not residing in Virginia for a specified purpose and fixed period of time, such as her husband's tour of duty in Virginia." The Attorney General went on to say that residence for one year, voter registration,

Under the common law, the husband owes his wife support during their marriage.[39] Until recently, a wife would not have owed him support unless he became disabled. However, the 1975 revision of Title 20 (Domestic Relations) of the Code now makes both marital partners equally responsible for each other's support and for support of the children.[40] While married, a wife must support her husband if he is in "necessitous circumstances."[41] In a divorce, the court may order the wife to support her husband.[42]

A woman's contribution to the marriage as a housewife, being both time- and energy-consuming, is now considered to be of legal value. This change in the tradition which regarded the material fruits of the marriage as belonging to the husband if paid for with his earnings was enacted into law by the 1977 General Assembly.[43]

Both parents have equal rights to their children, and, if either parent dies, the survivor becomes the child's natural guardian.[44]

At present, in matters of marital responsibility, divorce, and child custody, the Code is almost entirely sexless in expression, applying the traditional rules to both sexes rather than to one or the other. It no longer offers any special protections to the wife who usually still earns less than her husband and frequently earns nothing, who

---

automobile registration, drivers' license, and payment of taxes would *not* be sufficient to show domicile for a woman in this situation. 1973-74 OPS. VA. ATT'Y GEN. 66-67.

One must be "present in Virginia with the unqualified intention of remaining permanently." *Id.* at 319.

39. "It is the duty of the husband to support his wife. This duty ... is independent of any estate the wife may possess, and remains unaffected by the married woman's act. The estate of the wife is not liable for debts incurred in her support." 9 MICHIE'S JURISPRUDENCE *Husband and Wife* § 21 (1950).

40. VA. CODE § 20-61.

41. *Id.*

42. *Id.* §§ 20-107, 20-109.

43. *Id.* § 20-107, as amended. House Resolution No. 35, passed in 1975, authorized "[A] study on the rights and responsibilities of spouses, and the necessity of and means of recognizing the contributions of both to marriage and society." One of the aims of the study was to consider "The recompense due marital property from separate property."

44. VA. CODE § 31-1. See, on guardianship, Jones v. Henson, 202 Va. 738, 120 S.E.2d 286 (1961).

is the partner most likely to be deserted by a spouse, and who more often has custody of the children either by desire or necessity. Uniform Reciprocal Support Acts now help a woman collect support from an ex-husband who has left the state,[45] but it is still difficult to enforce payment. If a wife has not divorced or legally separated from her husband who has deserted her, the law will punish him for failing to support her, but will not help her to recover or enforce support payments.[46]

(h) *A Woman's "Married" Name*

In Virginia, a woman does not have to assume her husband's surname when she marries.[47] Traditionally, her last name will be considered to change automatically to that of her husband.[48] If she uses her husband's surname at any point after the marriage, the law will consider her name to have changed to that of her husband.[49] She may, however, request the court to change it back to her maiden name, or any other name she chooses.[50] When a divorce is obtained, she may, if she wishes, resume her maiden name as part of the decree.[51] Whatever name the mother bears, the children of her marriage will continue to bear their father's last name unless name changes can be obtained for them by application to the courts.

---

45. VA. CODE §§ 20-88.12 to 20-88.31, Revised Uniform Reciprocal Enforcement of Support Act.

46. But the nonpaying spouse is subject to criminal contempt prosecution if he fails to support his family, and may be sentenced to up to 12 months at hard labor. *Lack of Due Process in Virginia Contempt Proceedings for Failure to Comply with Order for Support and Alimony,* 4 U. RICH. L. REV. 128 (1969).

47. 1972-73 OPS. VA. ATT'Y GEN. 182-83.

48. 41 C.J.S. *Husband and Wife* § 9, p. 399 (1944); 65 C.J.S. *Names* § 3, pp. 4-5 (1966).

49. 1972-73 OPS. VA. ATT'Y GEN. 183.

50. VA CODE § 8.01-217.

This statute is based on the common law rule that anyone may change their name at will, if there is no fraudulent intent, and one authority says "there is strong reason to believe ... that this rule has never in the past and would not now permit a married woman to adopt a surname other than her husband's if he should object." L. KANOWITZ, WOMEN AND THE LAW, THE UNFINISHED REVOLUTION 43 (1969).

51. VA. CODE §§ 20-107, 20-121.

(i) *Intra-Family Immunity*

Generally, a husband and wife do not have to testify against each other in court, and neither is allowed to do so if the other objects.[52] There are exceptions to this general rule, as, for example, a wife may testify against her husband if he assaults or beats her [53] or if he injures her (or his) child.[54] The general rule has the result that spouses normally cannot sue each other. The courts may allow such suits where one spouse is covered by insurance and the other seeks recovery essentially against the insurance company.[55] An example of this situation would be a car accident in which one spouse is the driver, the other an injured passenger. Suits between spouses are not yet generally permitted except for suits relating to property.[56]

PROPERTY LAW

(a) *Divorce*

If a husband and wife have not agreed to a division of property at the time of divorce, the court will divide it in a "partition suit" which is separate from the divorce.[57] Property is apportioned on the basis of contribution, *i.e.,* whose earnings paid for it. "Joint" ownership doesn't mean anything at this stage.[58] If real estate, personal possessions, bank and credit union accounts, and stocks and bonds are held in both husband's and wife's name and the wife has been a nonwage-earning housewife throughout the marriage, bringing no money into the family when she married, all these possessions will be assigned to the husband by the court since he paid for them. However, property that is in the wife's name alone

---

52. *Id.* §§ 8.01-398, 19.2-271.1, 19.2-271.2. See also Shiflett v. Commonwealth, 447 F.2d 50 (4th Cir. 1971).
53. VA. CODE § 19.2-271.2.
54. *Id.* See also *id.* § 63.1-248.11.
55. Surratt v. Thompson, 212 Va. 191, 183 S.E.2d 200 (1971). In accord, Fountain v. Fountain, 214 Va. 347, 200 S.E.2d 513 (1973), *cert. denied,* 416 U.S. 939 (1974); Jackson v. Jackson, 214 Va. 351, 200 S.E.2d 515 (1973).
56. Vigilant Ins. Co. v. Bennett, 197 Va. 216, 89 S.E.2d 69 (1955). Also, one spouse may recover from the other under the Workmen's Compensation Act. Glassco v. Glassco, 195 Va. 239, 77 S.E.2d 843 (1953).
57. VA CODE §§ 8.01-81 to 8.01-93.
58. *Id.* § 20-111.

will be considered to have been a gift from the husband and will therefore be assigned to her. Also, if a wife can show that she made financial contribution to the purchase of such possessions, she will be assigned a proportional share.

(b) *Inheritance*

Because the state will consider the owner of property in a marriage to be, generally speaking, the person who has paid for it (as discussed above) and because the average woman marries a man older than herself and outlives him, it is important to the married woman to make sure that her husband has a valid will.[59] If he dies without a will,[60] leaving descendants, she will only inherit a fraction of his property (property she may have assumed was owned jointly).[61] The wife will be allowed to claim one-third of the husband's personal property (which includes everything except real estate) [62] and a dower interest in the real estate.[63] Even if her husband does leave a will, a wife has the option of rejecting its provisions and electing to take her share of his estate as provided by statute if she chooses.[64]

(c) *Right to Contract and Do Business*

Under the common law, a single woman's right to make any form

---

59. A surviving spouse in the case of partial intestacy will receive only what the will specifically provides. VA. CODE § 64.1-16. See also Newton v. Newton, 199 Va. 785, 102 S.E.2d 312 (1958).

60. VA. CODE §§ 64.1-1, 64.1-11.

61. There are a number of statutes concerning personalty held in joint tenancy allowing deposits to pass to the survivor. These include VA. CODE §§ 13.1-435 (corporate securities), 6.1-208.2 (credit union shares), 6.1-195.26 (savings accounts in Virginia savings and loan associations), and 6.1-73 (bank and trust company deposits).

See also VA. CODE § 55-20, which concerns real property, and abolishes survivorship between joint tenants. It provides: "When any joint tenant shall die, ... his part shall descend to his heirs, or pass ... as if he had been a tenant in common." There is, however, an exception to this section which provides that it is not applicable where it is manifest from the tenor of the instrument that it is intended that the part of the one dying should then belong to the survivors. *Id.* § 55-21; see Roane v. Roane, 193 Va. 18, 67 S.E.2d 906 (1951).

62. VA. CODE §§ 64.1-11, 64.1-16. See also Alexandria Nat'l Bank v. Thomas, 215 Va. 620, 194 S.E.2d 723 (1973).

63. VA. CODE § 64.1-19.

64. *Id.* § 64.1-13.

of business arrangement was substantially the same as a man's, but such right was virtually eliminated by her marriage.[65] Statutes have removed almost all of these old limitations, and a wife now has the right to sign contracts by herself, to sue people (including her husband in certain situations), to manage a business, and to make her own financial and property decisions.[66] If she is under 18 years of age and married, she is "emancipated" from her parents' control in business matters, but if she inherits an estate the court will appoint someone to manage it until she reaches 18.[67] A woman may decide not to handle her own affairs, in which case she may appoint an attorney who has the power to sign documents for her and in her name. There are detailed legal regulations for the protection of the woman, and the attorney is held strictly accountable that anything done in such a capacity is performed for the woman's benefit.[68]

(d) *Credit*

The state formerly exercised no authority over credit and lending institutions who refused to serve women, but Congress has intervened in this inequitable situation by enacting the Consumer Credit Protection Act which prohibits any creditor from discriminating against any applicant on the basis of sex or marital status.[69] In the past, Virginia banks, mortgage lending institutions, and retail establishments have routinely discriminated against women, but the federal Act makes such action illegal.

---

65. KANOWITZ, *supra* note 50, at 35.
66. "[S]ince the disabilities of married women have been disposed of by statute, they have almost the same rights as single women." 9 MICHIE'S JURISPRUDENCE *Husband and Wife* § 19, p. 508 (1950). See also, as to property rights of married women, VA. CODE §§ 55-35 to 55-47.
67. VA. CODE § 55-44.
68. *Id.* § 55-43.
69. The Consumer Credit Protection Act, Public Law 90-321, Titles I to VI, (15 U.S.C. § 1601 et seq.), as amended by the addition of Title VII, Equal Credit Opportunity, Public Law 93-495 (15 U.S.C. § 1691 et seq.).
Title VII of the Act (15 U.S.C. § 1691) specifies that (a) it is unlawful for any creditor to discriminate against any applicant on the basis of sex or marital status with respect to any aspect of a credit transaction, and (b) an inquiry of marital status is allowable if it is not being used for discriminatory purposes.

Furthermore, a Virginia statute patterned on the federal Act[70] now requires the State Corporation Commission to adopt regulations to enforce the provisions of the Virginia statute, such regulations to conform to and be no broader in scope than the regulations adopted under the federal Act.

Under federal and state law, insurance companies may deny coverage or set rates which cover all individuals within a "class," but may not discriminate within any given classification.[71] It is, at the present time, an undecided question whether insurance companies may use sex as the basis of such classifications. If the courts ultimately determine that sex is a "suspect" classification like race,[72] then it will surely be difficult for insurance companies to find compelling reasons to justify such discrimination. However, at present (for example) an insurance company may still deny coverage to divorced women as a class while extending it to divorced men.

(e) *Right to Rent and Own Property*

The Code prohibits discrimination on the basis of sex in the sale, rental, leasing, control, construction or management of housing.[73] Complaints are made to the Attorney General, who has the power to institute proceedings to investigate and enforce the law. A landlord may be prevented from evicting a tenant if a complaint has been filed, or from renting a disputed residence to another tenant. A landlord may refuse to rent to a person with children even though the typical single adult with children is a woman, and this fact might be regarded as sexual discrimination. The Code

---

70. VA CODE §§ 59.1-21.19 to 59.1-21.28.

The Virginia Fair Housing Law also prohibits discrimination on the basis of sex by banks, savings and loan institutions, credit unions, insurance companies, etc., in lending money for mortgages, house improvements, repairs or maintenance. *Id.* § 36-90.

71. VA. CODE § 38.1-52(7).

72. A minority of the Supreme Court (4-5) held sex to be a suspect classification in Frontiero v. Richardson, 411 U.S. 677 (1973). But the Court recently upheld a Florida statute providing for a special tax exemption for widows, reiterating the majority stance that sex is *not* a suspect classification in Kahn v. Shevin, 416 U.S. 351 (1974).

73. VA. CODE §§ 36-86 to 36-89, Virginia Fair Housing Law.

allows counties, cities and towns to enact further ordinances on the subject, and several have extended anti-discriminatory provisions to tenants with children.

A married woman has a potential claim against any real estate her husband owns, as discussed under (b) "Inheritance," above, and he cannot sell or transfer it without her signature without the buyer's right to the land becoming subject to her claim.[74] A woman has the right to own property in her own right as a married woman ("separate equitable estate"), meaning that her husband's permission is not needed for her to transfer or sell it.[75]

LAW REGARDING STATUS

(a) *Rights as a Student*

Women students in Virginia have gained a great many rights in recent years through federal legislation [76] and judicial decisions.[77] Thus, some of the major problems of sex discrimination seem to be on their way to a solution. For example, denial of admission to almost any elementary or secondary programs on the basis of sex is against the law.[78] The State Board of Education should be informed, and they will investigate. The state is attempting to equalize all vocational education programs to comply with federal law, and new facilities are being built according to federal

---

74. *Id.* §§ 64.1-19, 64.1-44.
75. *Id.* §§ 55-35 to 55-47, 64.1-21.
But note that the Court has held that, notwithstanding § 55-35, the presumption prevails that the husband is the owner of all property, real and personal, of which the wife may be in possession during coverture, especially if they are living together as husband and wife; and to overcome this presumption, in a contest between the husband's creditors and the wife, she must show affirmatively that the property is her own, and that it was derived from a source other than her husband and in good faith, if he is insolvent. First Nat'l Bank v. House, 145 Va. 149, 133 S.E. 664 (1926). See also Childress v. Fidelity & Cas. Co., 194 Va. 191, 72 S.E.2d 349 (1952).
76. This includes Title IX of the Education Amendments of 1972 (20 U.S.C. § 1681 et seq.), prohibiting discrimination against students or others; Title VII, section 799A (42 U.S.C. § 295h-9) and Title VIII (42 U.S.C. § 296 et seq.) of the Public Health Service Act, as amended by the Comprehensive Health Manpower Act and the Nurse Training Amendments Act of 1971, prohibiting discrimination in admission of students and against some employees.
77. Kirstein v. Rector & Visitors of the Univ. of Va., 309 F. Supp. 184 (1970).
78. 42 U.S.C. § 2000c et seq.

requirements. Sexually discriminatory textbooks are at present beyond the purview of the law, but many school systems are responsive to citizen complaints.

Universities are not allowed to bar female applicants or to apply quotas to their admission.[79] The only higher educational institutions which are legally allowed to refuse entrance on the basis of sex are one-sex private undergraduate colleges, which may not, however, discriminate or apply quotas in admissions if they decide to admit *any* applicants of the opposite sex.[80] The statute specifically exempts certain military academies, including the Virginia Military Institute, from regulation on this point.[81]

Any complaints relating to sexual discrimination in these institutions should be addressed to the Director, Office of Civil Rights, U.S. Department of Health, Education and Welfare, 330 Independence Avenue, S.W., Washington, D.C. 20201.

As discussed above under the heading "Personal Law," (g) "Marriage," state law regarding domicile forces women whose husbands are not Virginia domiciliaries to pay out-of-state tuition at state-supported colleges and universities unless they can establish their own intention of remaining in Virginia permanently.[82] This law also denies them access to scholarships [83] and grants-in-aid [84] reserved for Virginia domiciliaries. An exception is made if a woman was a Virginia domiciliary at the time of her marriage to a nonresident and the couple do not establish a home elsewhere before she begins her education. In such a case, the wife may retain her domiciliary status for purposes of school attendance.[85] However, this special provision does not apply to lower-income senior citizens who have the right to attend college

---

79. Kirstein v. Rector & Visitors of the Univ. of Va., 309 F. Supp. 184 (1970).
80. Memorandum to Presidents of Institutions of Higher Education Participating in Federal Assistance Programs, Table G of Higher Education Guidelines, Executive Order 11246 (1972).
81. Title IX of the Education Amendments of 1972, *supra* note 76, at § 901(a)(4) (20 U.S.C. § 1681).
82. VA. CODE § 23-7.
83. *Id.* §§ 23-35.10, 23-36.2, 23-38.45, 23-38.46, 23-38.49.
84. *Id.* §§ 23-38.12, 23-38.15, 23-38.18.
85. *Id.* § 23-7.

classes without payment of tuition only if they have been legally domiciled in Virginia for over a year.[86]

(b) *Rights Regarding Employment*

Congress has enacted considerable legislation which has the result of prohibiting most forms of discrimination in employment.[87] Women must not be discriminated against in hiring, promotion, job assignments, salaries, fringe benefits, or age requirements, or on the basis of their parental or marital status. The laws cover all businesses employing over fifteen persons and conducting interstate activities (*e.g.,* buying or selling any products or services out of Virginia); all businesses with federal contracts or grants of over $10,000; and all institutions receiving federal funds (*e.g.,* hospitals, schools, etc.). The Equal Employment Opportunity Commission in Washington has issued guidelines which give details as to what situations and conditions are considered discriminatory.[88] To file a complaint, one should first discuss the situation with her employer (who may take action to correct the inequity voluntarily). Then contact E.E.O.C. which is listed in the telephone book under "United States Government" in a number of Virginia localities. The law provides that an employer may not punish an employee for filing a complaint, so do not be afraid of reprisals.

For further information about federal rules concerning discrimination in employment, the reader should consult one of the

---

86. *Id.* §§ 23-38.55, 23-38.56.

87. The most sweeping legislation prohibiting discrimination is Title VII of the Civil Rights Act of 1964, as amended by the Equal Employment Opportunity Act of 1972 (42 U.S.C. § 2000e et seq.).

Other orders and legislation relating to job discrimination include:

Executive Order 11246, as amended by 11375 (1968), prohibiting discrimination in employment, including hiring, upgrading, salaries, fringe benefits, training and other conditions of employment.

Title IX of the Education Amendments of 1972, *supra* note 76, prohibiting some job discrimination relating to education.

Title VII and Title VIII of the Public Health Service Act, *supra* note 76.

Equal Pay Act of 1963, as amended by the Education Amendments of 1972 (29 U.S.C. § 206), prohibiting discrimination in salaries and most fringe benefits.

88. These guidelines are available from local E.E.O.C. offices and are frequently revised.

handbooks that have recently been published on the rights of women. An excellent one is *The Rights of Women, An American Civil Liberties Union Handbook,* by Susan C. Ross, published by Avon Books.

The State of Virginia has an office to implement the E.E.O.C. guidelines in relation to state employment.[89] Complaints relating to discrimination by state agencies, including state colleges and universities, should be addressed to the State Coordinator for E.E.O.C., P.O. Box 654, Richmond, Virginia 23205.

The Virginia Code contains very few provisions relating to sex and employment. The "protective" laws which used to exist to limit women's working hours and specify certain working conditions generally have been eliminated.[90] The Code requires that women receive equal pay for equal work,[91] but the statute does not provide any penalty for noncompliance by employers. A woman may sue under this statute to recover the wages "lost" by discrimination, but often the suit would not be economically worth undertaking and there is no protection under the statute from reprisals by the employer.

The conflict of interest statute forbids a person from working under the direct supervision of his or her spouse in state employment when the annual salary of the subordinate is ten thousand dollars or more.[92] This usually affects women since the typical situation is that of a subordinate female employee who marries her supervisor or a woman teacher whose husband is promoted to a principalship. The law does not dictate which party must leave the job held, but the realistic assumption is that the lower-paid, lower-ranking employee will leave, and that spouse is typically the wife. Virginia law does *not* prohibit husband and wife from working at parallel levels within the same institution or in

---

89. Established by Governor Godwin's Executive Order No. 1 (1975).
90. The elimination of most of these laws was quite recent (in 1974) and many employers are unaware of their repeal.
91. VA CODE § 40.1-28.6. Other statutes protecting workers' rights carry much stronger penalties and protections for complainants exercising their rights. For example, see *id.* §§ 40.1-51.1 and 40.1-51.1:1.
92. *Id.* §§ 2.1-348, 2.1-349, 2.1-352.

positions that are not directly related, and any institution denying employment in this situation on grounds of "conflict of interest" or "nepotism" is acting illegally under the federal anti-discrimination guidelines.

LAW CONCERNING GOVERNMENTAL AUTHORITY

(a) *Jury Duty*

Women in Virginia are now called for jury duty, but are legally excused if they plead the responsibility of a child or children 16 years of age or younger or a person having a physical or mental impairment requiring continuous care by them during normal court hours.[93] The United States Supreme Court has recently held that women as a class cannot be excluded from jury service or given automatic exemptions based solely on sex if the consequence is that criminal jury venires are almost all male.[94]

(b) *The Penal System*

Criminal sentencing in Virginia is generally set by the jury, which decides on the length of punishment for felonies, but sentences must be approved and can even be modified by the judge. The rate of female crime in Virginia is far lower than that of men,[95] but juries appear to show a distaste for female criminality by fixing proportionately longer sentences for women. Once in prison, a woman does not have nearly the range of programs designed to train her for return to private life which is available to men.[96] The Code prescribes equal opportunities for both sexes within the penal system.[97] Yet in actuality, women can train for only a small group of traditionally "female" jobs and take courses for "personality" development, while male inmates are offered considerable scope for training and further education. They do, however, have the

---

93. *Id.* § 8.01-341.
94. Taylor v. Louisiana, 419 U.S. 522 (1975).
95. Commitments to County and City Jails and City Jail Farms, Commonwealth of Va., Dep't of Welfare and Institutions (years ending June, 1970 and June, 1971).
96. "Blueprint" for Action in Virginia Corrections, Div. of Corrections, Dep't of Welfare and Institutions (1974), at 30, 31.
97. VA. CODE §§ 53-128.2, 53-128.7.

physical advantage of a much more benign institutional setting than most male prisoners.[98]

The custody of children under 18 years of age may be assumed by the juvenile courts for incorrigibility,[99] habitual truancy, or habitual disobedience.[100] Such deviant behavior, particularly if there are sexual overtones, may be taken far more seriously in girls than in boys, and a girl may be confined by the courts for behavior that would be regarded as typically youthful in a boy.[101] If a girl is committed to an institution or assigned to the custody of another by the courts and subsequently runs away, she may be arrested and returned to the same or stricter custody [102] although she has committed no act which would, if she were over 18, be considered a crime. Moreover, the court retains some control over juveniles until they reach age 21 under current law.[103] In addition, the Code allows the imprisonment of "incorrigibles" in adult penal institutions if they are over age 15, although in practice such confinement would only occur in an emergency situation.[104]

(c) *Miscellaneous*

Virginia income taxes now follow the federal model and perpetuate any sexual inequities in that model. There are some specific provisions relating to women in the tax laws, but since tax law is complex and highly codified, a woman should consult a specialist in the area if she believes she has particular tax problems resulting from her female status.

Women are not barred from any professions or occupations on the basis of sex in Virginia at present. However, such restrictions

---

98. "Blueprint" for Action in Virginia Corrections, *supra* note 96, at 34-37, 44-45, 57. See also A.E. Dick Howard, Address to the Senate and House Committees on Privileges and Elections, General Assembly of Va. (1973).

99. A finding of incorrigibility must be supported by evidence obtained in an investigation. Norwood v. Richmond, 203 Va. 886, 128 S.E.2d 425 (1962).

100. As to arrest and detention, see VA. CODE § 16.1-246. As to jurisdiction of the court, see *id.* § 16.1-241.

101. Chesney-Lind, *supra* note 7, at 46.

102. VA. CODE § 16.1-246. *Id.* § 16.1-323 applies when juvenile is fugitive from another state.

103. *Id.* § 16.1-242. See also 1972-73 OPS. VA. ATT'Y GEN. 522-23, confirming that control is retained until age 21.

104. VA. CODE § 16.1-249.

probably would not be found illegal if they were established on the basis of a rational relationship between the sexual restriction and the ability to perform duties of the profession or occupation.

There are no provisions in the Virginia Code or in federal law making discrimination on the basis of sex in public accomodations illegal.[105] A restaurant or hotel may refuse service on the basis of sex if its management wishes to do so.

A final note: The Virginia Code, in its "Military and Emergency Laws," specifies that "The militia of the Commonwealth of Virginia shall consist of all able-bodied citizens of this Commonwealth...."[106] No mention is made of sex.

---

105. The 1964 Civil Rights Act does not bar discrimination in places of public accommodation on the basis of sex (it deals with race, color, religion, and national origin). 42 U.S.C. § 2000a. And Virginia's statute on accommodations bars discrimination on the basis of religion only. VA. CODE § 57-2.1.

106. VA. CODE § 44-1 et seq.

CHAPTER 15

The Criminal Justice Process

E. J. Grammer

IN GENERAL

To ensure an orderly society, there must be rules, and the rules must be enforced; this is the premise of criminal law. Unlike civil law, whose purpose is to make a wronged person whole again either through specific performance or monetary compensation by the wrongdoer, criminal law is intended to deter behavior deemed detrimental to society and to deal fairly with those who so misbehave. A crime is an offense against the state whose rules have been broken; thus the people, or the state, prosecute a criminal trial.

Criminal law is largely statutory. It is written down in the Code of Virginia, which is enacted by the General Assembly. A criminal statute must clearly define the crime, for if a reasonable person cannot tell whether or not he is violating a statute, the courts will strike down the statute as unconstitutionally vague. Courts must construe criminal statutes strictly against the state; a judge cannot interpret a criminal statute in such a way as to enlarge the definition of the crime. In addition, a person cannot be convicted *ex post facto*, that is, for something which was made a crime only after he did it. Although an individual is deemed to know the law, the government must do its part to give him notice of the law.

Furthermore, there are strict safeguards to protect the rights of the accused and to preserve the integrity of the criminal justice system. Constitutional rights are designed to shield a suspect from abuses in criminal justice administration. For example, one may not be forced to give evidence against himself or undergo unreasonable searches and seizures. In the pursuit of justice, criminal trials are supposed to be carefully conducted so as to safeguard the defendant from prejudicial publicity, untrustworthy evidence, and other factors tending to result in an unfair trial. Because juvenile defendants are deemed to require even more protection and aid than adults, there are special rules for minors accused of a crime.

At the onset, an understanding of the distinction between misdemeanors and felonies is necessary. Frequently, procedural and substantive rules turn on this point. In Virginia, a felony is any crime whose governing statute prescribes punishment by death or imprisonment in a penitentiary, that is, imprisonment for one year or more. Less serious than felonies, misdemeanors comprise all other crimes, for which the offender may be jailed up to one year or given fines or other minor penalties.[1]

CRIMINAL PROCEDURE

(a) *Arrest*

Arrest occurs when a suspect is taken into custody in a manner authorized by law for the purpose of charging him with a criminal offense.[2] The suspect must be given notice of the arrest; he must be told that he is under arrest and why he is being arrested. To effect an arrest, an officer may use reasonable force in self-defense, to prevent escape, or to overcome resistance. Peace officers who have observed a crime taking place, who have probable cause to believe that the suspect has committed a felony, or who have obtained an arrest warrant may make lawful arrests. Also, private citizens may arrest a "wanted" felon or a person they observe in the act of committing a felony.[3]

When there is an arrest with a warrant, the police have investigated, concluded that there are reasonable grounds for belief that the suspect has committed a crime, and obtained an arrest warrant from a magistrate. Before issuing a warrant, the magistrate examines the complainant (the person desiring that the warrant issue) and other witnesses. If he is satisfied that there is reasonable cause to believe that the suspect has committed a crime, the magistrate will issue a warrant for arrest. The warrant states

---

1. VA. CODE § 18.2-8.
2. *Id.* §§ 19.2-71 to 19.2-83; FRED E. INBAU & MARVIN E. ASPIN, CRIMINAL LAW FOR THE LAYMAN 109 (1970).
3. VA. CODE § 19.2-100; PAUL B. WESTON & KENNETH M. WELLS, THE ADMINISTRATION OF JUSTICE 41 (1973).

the offense with which the suspect is charged, the grounds for reasonable belief that the suspect has committed the offense, and an order that the officer requesting the warrant arrest the suspect.[4] It is important that the warrant be valid, for the courts may later void the arrest or make evidence obtained during the arrest inadmissible in court because of an improper warrant.

Arrest may be made without a warrant when the officer making the arrest has observed the commission of a crime, has "probable cause" to believe that the suspect has committed an offense, or recognizes the person to be arrested as a "wanted" felon. When arrest takes place without a warrant, the suspect must be taken immediately to a magistrate, who will issue a warrant on the same basis as he would an arrest warrant obtained prior to the arrest.[5] An illegal arrest without a warrant may also invalidate the arrest or render some of the evidence inadmissible.

(b) *Booking*

Usually after the arrest, the arresting officers take the suspect to the police station where they make a complete report of the incident. At this time, if not before, they inform the prisoner of the specific crime with which he is charged and explain his constitutional rights under the circumstances. Next, fingerprints and photographs of the suspect are taken. Copies of these are sent to the FBI's Crime Computer for permanent storage of the record and to ascertain whether the suspect is wanted for other crimes elsewhere. During the booking, the suspect has a right to contact his lawyer, his family, or some other person for counsel.[6]

The suspect may get an immediate trial after arrest in misdemeanor cases. The trial must be in a district court with the consent of both the defendant and the state.[7]

(c) *Preliminary Hearing*

If the offense charged is a felony, Virginia statutes give the accused a right to a preliminary hearing in a district court as soon

---

4. VA. CODE §§ 19.2-71 to 19.2-76.
5. *Id.* § 19.2-100.
6. Interview with the Williamsburg Police.
7. VA. CODE §§ 16.1-129.1, 19.2-82.

as possible after the arrest. The accused has a right to be present at this hearing with his attorney and to assert a defense. At the preliminary hearing, the lower court hears the evidence and decides if the criminal charge is sufficiently supported by the state's evidence to require the accused to stand trial. If a prima facie case for the state is established, the accused is jailed or released on bail. If the state cannot show "probable cause" both that an offense was committed and that the accused has committed the offense charged, he must be released.[8]

(d) *Bail*

Unless the accused is charged with a crime punishable by death or life imprisonment under the laws of the state in which the offense was committed, the Virginia Code permits a judge or magistrate to admit the person arrested to bail. Bail is essentially an agreement between the accused and the state by which the accused guarantees his presence at his trial by delivering sureties which will be forfeited if he fails to appear. Although the judge or magistrate setting bail generally uses a schedule listing crimes and appropriate amounts for bail, the sum is within judicial discretion. The judge or magistrate's determination of bail may be appealed to a circuit court, and that decision may be appealed to the Supreme Court of Virginia.

In some instances, the judge or magistrate may, in his discretion, find it appropriate to release the accused on his own recognizance, relying on the good character of the accused as adequate assurance that he will appear in court. It is also within the discretion of the judge or magistrate to deny bail to a person unlikely to appear at his trial or to keep out of harm's way. For lesser crimes, a cash amount rather that a bail bond may be used. Should the accused fail to appear at his trial, the bail may be forfeited to the state and the accused may be subject to immediate arrest.[9]

(e) *Indictment*

A person accused of a felony has a right to a grand jury

---

8. *Id.* § 19.2-186.
9. *Id.* §§ 19.2-119 to 19.2-152.

indictment in Virginia.[10] An indictment is a written accusation by the grand jury; it is not a conviction. The state must present its evidence so that the grand jury can determine whether or not there is a prima facie case. The defendant has no right to be present at the grand jury deliberations nor to present a defense. A grand jury may issue an indictment before the suspect has been arrested.[11] In such a case, the court issues a *capias,* or order, for the suspect's arrest.

Some variations in the procedure of finding probable cause are available. When the accused waives his right to a grand jury indictment, he may be tried on an "information" issued by the prosecution. The bill of "indictment" is an accusation by the prosecutor which is submitted to the grand jury. When the grand jury acts on its own initiative, it issues a "presentment." [12]

The grand jury in Virginia is composed of five to seven persons chosen from a list of sixty citizens of upstanding character selected annually by the judge of the court for which the grand jury sits. The grand jury meets to hear the state's evidence on the first day of each term of court. In order for an indictment or "true bill" to issue, at lease four jurors must concur.[13]

(f) *Pretrial Activity*

Even before the trial, the defendant may assert his defense in various ways. For instance, he may make a motion to quash or dismiss the indictment, claiming that the indictment is in some way not legally proper. Or he may make a motion for a change of venue, *i.e.,* place of trial, asserting that he cannot obtain a fair trial in this particular place.[14] The defendant's attorney may also meet with the Commonwealth's Attorney (the prosecutor) to try to reach a compromise, sometimes called a plea bargain. Pursuant to such a "bargain," the defendant may become state's witness against another defendant or plead guilty in return for a promise from the

---

10. *Id.* § 19.2-217.
11. *Id.* § 19.2-216.
12. *Id.*
13. *Id.* § 19.2-202.
14. INBAU & ASPIN, *supra* note 2, at 94-95.

prosecutor to reduce the charges or to recommend a lighter sentence to the judge. The judge is not bound to accept this recommendation, but if he does not accept it, the accused is entitled to withdraw his guilty plea.[15]

Investigation of the facts pertaining to the alleged crime also should take place before the trial. Attorneys for both sides collect the evidence with which to prepare their cases and may agree to stipulate facts about which there is no dispute.

It should be noted that an accused person has a right to a fair and speedy trial. In Virginia, statutes provide that every person against whom probable cause has been found in a preliminary hearing or grand jury proceeding must be given a trial within a certain number of months, or else that person is forever discharged from prosecution.[16]

(g) *Arraignment*

Just before a felony trial begins, the defendant is officially arraigned or called to the bar of the court to answer the accusation contained in the indictment, information, or presentment. At this time, the defendant stands before the court while the charge is read in full. The clerk of the court then asks, "How say you (naming the prisoner) are you guilty or not guilty?" to which the defendant must plead, or answer.[17]

(h) *Pleading*

According to Virginia statutes, the defendant must himself announce his plea; his lawyer cannot do it for him. If the defendant pleads guilty, he will be convicted and either sentenced then on the basis of recommendations of the prosecution and probation officer or sentenced at a later date after the judge has read a pre-sentencing report. If the defendant pleads not guilty, he in effect denies all essential allegations of the indictment, placing the burden of proof on the prosecution. A plea of not guilty sets the trial in motion.

---

15. WESTON & WELLS, *supra* note 3, at 80.
16. VA. CODE § 19.2-243.
17. 5 MICHIE'S JURISPRUDENCE *Criminal Procedure* § 29 (1949).

In special situations a plea of *nolo contendere*, meaning "I do not wish to contend," may be made. In Virginia such a plea can be accepted in misdemeanor cases only, not in felony cases. A plea of *nolo contendere* is similar to a plea of guilty, authorizing conviction and sentencing for the crime alleged. Nonetheless it does not operate as an admission of the truth of any facts the prosecution alleged and cannot be used against a defendant in subsequent civil cases.[18]

(i) *Trial*

Once a defendant has pleaded not guilty, he has the right to a fair trial by either a judge or a jury. Jury trials are available only in the circuit courts. There are twelve jurors for a felony trial and five jurors for a misdemeanor trial. Jury selection, presentation of the evidence, and general trial procedure follow the procedure in civil cases as much as possible.[19] In criminal trials, however, the rules protecting the defendant's rights must be strictly observed because the course of his life, not just his finances as in civil cases, is at stake. In criminal cases, the prosecution must prove "beyond a reasonable doubt" that the defendant is guilty. When the prosecution meets its burden of proof and the judge or jury finds the accused guilty, he is convicted of the crime. At this point, the prisoner may appeal to a higher court, asserting that there were prejudicial errors in his trial.

(j) *Sentencing*

After conviction comes sentencing, which completes the judgment of the court. If there has been a jury trial, Virginia law dictates that the jury should impose the sentence as well as render the verdict. When the judge alone hears the case, he decides the punishment. Often the judge will request a pre-sentencing report from the court's probation officer. This report, which contains information about the prisoner and a sentencing recommendation based on his record and circumstances, helps the judge determine

---

18. VA. CODE § 19.2-254.
19. *Id.* §§ 19.2-260 to 19.2-264. See also 5 MICHIE'S JURISPRUDENCE *Criminal Procedure* §§ 9-12 (1949).

fair terms of punishment. Other factors influencing the sentencing decision are the prosecution's sentencing recommendation and the defendant's mitigating evidence. Both judge and jury, in determining the sentence, must follow the minimum and maximum time periods set out in the statute governing the crime.[20] A prisoner may have the time he spent in jail awaiting trial deducted from his sentence.

Punishment is supposed to be tailored to fit the particular circumstances of each crime. In some cases it might be decided that a suspended sentence would best serve justice. Unlike a pardon, which completely excuses the prisoner, a suspended sentence is merely a reprieve. The person receiving a suspended sentence is released under supervision. This freedom is based on good behavior; therefore it is within the discretion of the court to revoke the suspended sentence in a judicial hearing if the defendant is found to have misbehaved at any time during the period of suspended sentence or probation.[21]

Finally, a person who has served time in prison may be released early on parole. The procedure and requirements for parole are much like those governing the suspended sentence, since they are based on the prisoner's good behavior while in confinement. The Virginia Board of Probation and Parole determines paroles.

CRIMES

(a) *Principals and Accessories; Conspiracies and Attempts*

One need not be the actual perpetrator of a crime to be subject to criminal liability. The very act of aiding someone else in the commission of an offense is itself a crime. Thus a principal in the second degree, who is present at the scene of the crime aiding the perpetrator, or an accessory before the fact, who aids the perpetrator in the preparations for the offense, may be punished as if he were the principal in the first degree, that is, the perpetrator, except that in the case of a killing for hire an accessory

---

[20]. VA. CODE § 19.2-295; as to classification of criminal offenses and punishment therefor, see *id.* §§ 18.2-8 to 18.2-17. See also 5 MICHIE'S JURISPRUDENCE *Criminal Procedure* §§ 70-75 (1949).

[21]. VA. CODE §§ 19.2-303, 19.2-306. See also 5 MICHIE'S JURISPRUDENCE *Criminal Procedure* §§ 76, 77 (1949).

before the fact or principal in the second degree to a capital murder shall be punished as though the offense were murder in the first degree. It is a misdemeanor to act as an accessory after the fact, i.e., to aid the perpetrator after the offense has been committed.[22]

Furthermore, conspiring or urging another (soliciting) to commit a felony can be a felony. The punishment for conspiracy can be as great as the punishment for the crime itself. An attempt to commit an offense generally may be assigned the same punishment as the crime itself.[23]

(b) *Crimes Against the Person*
(1) *Homicide*

The killing of one human being by another is homicide. However, it should be noted that if a killing is justified or excused by law, it is not a crime. The gravest form of homicide is the felony of murder, which by definition must involve the element of malice. Murder, other than capital murder, by poison, lying in wait, imprisonment, starving, or by any willful, deliberate and premeditated killing are declared by statute to be first degree murder. Also, first degree murder includes killing in the commission of, or attempt to commit, arson, rape, robbery, burglary, or abduction, except when these offenses constitute capital murder.[24] Capital murder, for which the death penalty or imprisonment for life is prescribed, is the willful, deliberate and premediated killing of any person by another in an abduction with intent to extort money or a pecuniary benefit, or the willful, deliberate and premeditated killing of any person by another for hire, or the willful, deliberate and premeditated killing of any person by an inmate in a penal institution or while in the custody of an employee thereof, or the willful, deliberate and premeditated killing of any person in the commission of robbery while armed with a deadly weapon, or the willful, deliberate and premeditated killing of a person during the commission of, or subsequent to, rape, or the willful, deliberate and premeditated killing of a

---

22. VA. CODE §§ 18.2-18 to 18.2-21.
23. *Id.* §§ 18.2-22 to 18.2-29.
24. *Id.* § 18.2-32.

law-enforcement officer when such killing is for the purpose of interfering with the performance of his official duties.[25] All murder other than capital murder and murder in the first degree is murder of the second degree.

Manslaughter does not involve malice, but it is not justified or excused by law. Voluntary manslaughter, a felony, is an unlawful killing without malice in the sudden heat of passion or with provocation.[26] Involuntary manslaughter is accidental killing, contrary to the intention of the persons involved, in an unlawful but not felonious act. It is the least serious form of homicide.[27]

(2) *Rape*

The felony of rape is the carnal knowledge of a woman without her consent. Consent is presumed not given when the victim is under 13 years of age or is incompetent. Elements of the crime of rape include force and penetration by the offender and lack of consent by the victim.[28]

(3) *Assault and battery; maiming*

It is unlawful to do bodily harm to another without legal excuse. The unlawful use of force on another is battery; putting another in fear of a battery is an assault. A simple assault or assault and battery is a misdemeanor. A more aggravated form of battery is maiming. In Virginia, it is a felony to shoot or stab someone with malice and the intent to maim, disfigure or kill; the same act committed without malice is classified by statute as a less severe felony. A battery may be classified as an attempt at another crime, such as rape or murder.[29]

(4) *Driving while intoxicated*

Because the practice of driving while intoxicated has great potential for doing harm to others as well as the drunken driver, such action has been made a misdemeanor resulting in the forfeiture of the perpetrator's driver's license in addition to other

---

25. *Id.* § 18.2-31.
26. *Id.* § 18.2-35.
27. *Id.* § 18.2-36.
28. *Id.* §§ 18.2-61 to 18.2-67.
29. *Id.* §§ 18.2-51 to 18.2-57.

penalties. The penalty for drunken driving increases with repetition of the offense.[30]

(c) *Crimes Against Property*

(1) *Theft*

Historically, larceny involved a trespass resulting in a taking and carrying away of personal property of another with the intent of depriving the true owner of his goods permanently. Embezzlement was the conversion to the offender's own use of property with which he was entrusted by virtue of his employment or trust. Taking by false pretenses occurred when one wrongfully obtained title to the property of another through misrepresentations of the perpetrator.[31]

Nowadays in Virginia as elsewhere, the historically rigid requirements for larceny have been relaxed. Embezzlement and taking by false pretenses, as well as receiving stolen goods with knowledge that they are stolen, are statutorily declared to constitute larceny and are punishable as such.[32]

The Virginia Code defines the felony of grand larceny as the taking of property worth $5.00 or more from the person of the theft victim, or worth $100.00 or more if not from the person of the victim. All other larceny is petit larceny, a misdemeanor.[33] Robbery may be loosely defined as larceny plus violence. Use of violence or putting the theft victim in fear concurrent to or before the taking converts larceny into the felony of robbery.[34]

(2) *Burglary*

Like the definition of larceny, the former rigid definition of burglary has been relaxed by statute. Burglary now encompasses the breaking and entering of the dwelling, shop, warehouse, bank, office, etc., of another with the intent to commit a felony or larceny therein. The crime lies in the breaking and entering with felonious intent; one may be convicted of burglary even though no theft

---

30. *Id.* §§ 18.2-266 to 18.2-273.
31. BERTHA R. WHITE, CRIMES AND PENALTIES 22-29 (1970).
32. VA. CODE §§ 18.2-108, 18.2-111.
33. *Id.* §§ 18.2-95, 18.2-96.
34. *Id.* § 18.2-58.

occurs. Both burglary and the possession of burglary tools are felonies in Virginia.[35]

(3) *Arson*

Arson, the malicious burning of a building or structure, is a felony. The penalties vary with the circumstances. For example, it is a greater offense to burn a building with knowledge that someone is within.[36]

(4) *Forgery; counterfeiting*

One who makes a false writing which would have legal effect if genuine commits the felony of forgery. It is a separate crime to "utter," or attempt to employ the document as genuine with knowledge of its invalidity. Counterfeiting, or making false money, notes, tickets, and the like is a related felony, as are crimes involving fraud and misrepresentation.[37]

(d) *Crimes Against the State Policy*

(1) *Generally*

Some criminal statutes are directory rather than prohibitory, attempting to direct behavior toward certain desired goals. For instance, it has been made a crime for those responsible to neglect to obtain medical aid for a sick child. Laws making it a crime to misuse telephones are another example. Other criminal statutes are designed to protect the sovereignty of the state. Thus it is unlawful to commit treason against the state, to bribe a public official, to commit perjury, or to obstruct justice.[38] There are also regulatory statutes, such as parking regulations, which more closely resemble civil law and usually carry the maximum penalty of a fine.

"Victimless" crimes, or crimes supposedly reflecting the state's social policy, have been the subject of much debate. It has often been argued that such laws do not adequately reflect changes in the social attitudes of today's society. Furthermore, enforcement of these laws dealing with persons' lifestyles has

---

35. *Id.* §§ 18.2-89 to 18.2-94.
36. *Id.* §§ 18.2-77 to 18.2-88.
37. *Id.* §§ 18.2-168 to 18.2-246.
38. *Id.* §§ 18.2-434 to 18.2-485.

proven difficult. Such offenses include consensual sodomy and other acts to which neither party objects, as well as acts which affect the perpetrator alone, such as use of drugs.

(2) *Gambling*

Except for authorized raffles, bingo games, and similar legalized betting, gambling is currently prohibited in Virginia. Although bills to legalize race track betting are regularly discussed in the General Assembly, with the listed exceptions, it is still a misdemeanor to wager or play at any game for money or anything of value.[39]

(3) *Sex offenses*

Crimes against nature, such as buggery or sodomy, are felonies in Virginia. Adultery, *i.e.*, voluntary sexual intercourse by a married person with a person not his or her spouse, and fornication, *i.e.*, voluntary sexual intercourse between persons not married, are misdemeanors. It is also a misdemeanor to engage in prostitution, that is, adultery or fornication for gain, or to further prostitution or to keep or frequent a "bawdy house."[40]

(4) *Drugs*

The Virginia Code contains schedules of controlled drugs, which comprise prescription drugs and illegal narcotics such as heroin and marijuana. Marijuana, like heroin, is classified among those drugs most subject to abuse. One who commits an offense using such Schedule I drugs is subject to the greatest penalties. It is unlawful to possess, make, sell, or distribute controlled drugs except as authorized by law. However, there is a provision in the Code granting the trial court discretion to discharge or place on probation first time offenders.[41]

---

39. *Id.* §§ 18.2-325 to 18.2-340.
40. *Id.* §§ 18.2-344 to 18.2-371.
41. *Id.* §§ 18.2-247 to 18.2-265; 54-524.84:1 to 54-524.84:13.

CHAPTER 16

Procedure in Civil Suits

L. G. Gonella

In General

Unlike most of the other chapters in this book, which deal with *substantive* law (legal content), this chapter will concern itself with *procedural* law (legal processes used for the maintenance of litigation) as applied to civil suits. Civil suits generally are cases involving actions brought by individuals seeking redress from other individuals or the state. (Criminal procedure was discussed *supra* in Chapter 15.)

Virginia has recently undergone a judicial reorganization. By 1980 every court will have a full-time judge who will be prohibited from practicing law privately. Virginia's new court structure resembles a pyramid. The state has been carved into a number of judicial areas containing one district and one circuit. In each district there is one General District Court and one Juvenile and Domestic Relations District Court. Both are referred to as courts *not* of record. Appeals from these courts are to the Circuit Court of that particular area. All appeals from Circuit Courts are to the Supreme Court of Virginia. Both the Circuit Courts and the Supreme Court are referred to as courts of record.

This chapter will begin its discussion with the courts not of record and then take a brief look at the courts of record. By statute, all Virginia courts have both legal and equitable power, and can, with some limitations in the District Courts, dispense either type of remedy depending upon the party's request or the judge's discretion as to which is more appropriate. "Plaintiff" refers to the person bringing the action and "defendant" refers to the person who is being sued. This chapter is designed to acquaint the reader generally with the court procedures, not to enable him to conduct his own case. If one wishes to file suit, or has a suit filed against him, he is advised to consult an attorney. The lawyer will know the proper method of proceeding in any particular situation.

GENERAL DISTRICT COURT

In civil cases the General District Court has exclusive jurisdiction (sole legal control) over all civil litigation where the amount being sued for is less than $500, and shares jurisdiction with the Circuit Court when the amount is between $500 and $5,000.

Before initiating a case, the party seeking the trial should consider the question of venue. Venue is an important legal factor in any case, since it determines in what judicial district a suit may be filed. Usually, a case is tried in the judicial district where the defendant resides; however, venue is a tricky legal problem which an attorney is best suited to handle. The reader should simply be aware of it.

Assuming that the determination of the district in which to file the suit has been made, the plaintiff or his attorney begins the suit by obtaining a civil warrant. This warrant is prepared by a magistrate of the district, whose name is supplied by the clerk's office, upon furnishing to him the following information: (1) name and address of the plaintiff and defendant, (2) the amount and nature of the claim, and (3) the trial date (check with the court for this). The fee for acquiring this warrant is $5.00. The suit is said to have commenced once the warrant has been issued by the clerk, the fee has been paid, and the defendant has been properly served with the warrant.

The civil warrant is given to the sheriff of the judicial district. It is the duty of this officer to "serve" the defendant. In Virginia, proper "service of process" (*i.e.*, notice that a case is being filed against him) can be accomplished in a number of ways. One method is to hand the defendant the notice in person. Another is to deliver it to a member of his family, provided such a person is over sixteen years old and lives with the defendant. If the officer cannot find the defendant or any member of his family at home, he can post the notice on the front door of the defendant's residence. An officer may "serve process" in his judicial district only; any attempt by him to act outside of his district is usually void.

Once the defendant (or defendants) have been so "served," he should appear in court on the date set out in the warrant. Failure to do so will result in a default judgment against the party. There is no need for a "response" (*i.e.*, answer to the charges). The party need just appear in court if he wishes to dispute the claim. If the defendant wishes to admit liability, he need not appear at all.

Once the plaintiff has secured judgment, he can enforce it if necessary. See the discussion of enforcement of judgments, *infra* in this chapter under the heading "Miscellaneous," subheading (c).

If the defendant has a claim against the plaintiff, he can inform the plaintiff by filing a counterclaim, or the defendant can file his own warrant using the same procedures outlined above. Once this has been done, the parties are ready for the subpoena of witnesses and documents.

If a party wishes to examine an opposing party's papers or books, he must fill out an affidavit describing what he wants, who has it, and why he wants it. The information must be stated in reasonably certain terms. The affidavit is then presented to the judge; if he feels the information desired is relevant to the suit, he will issue a subpoena ordering the opposing party to give the documents to the party requesting them. Failure to comply with the subpoena can result in a fine or imprisonment for contempt of court. This punishment may be appealed to a higher court if the appeal is made promptly.

If a party wishes to subpoena a witness (or witnesses), to compel his testimony at trial, the party must go before the clerk of the court where the case is to be tried and request that a subpoena be issued. A service fee will be charged. The party must tell the clerk whom he wishes subpoenaed, who wants him, when he is wanted, and for what case his testimony is required. The clerk will include all of this information in the subpoena and it will be delivered to the sheriff of the district. The officer who serves the subpoena generally follows the same procedures as for the service of process described earlier. It must be remembered that an officer has the power to serve someone in his judicial district only. Attempts to serve outside the proper district will usually result in an invalid service. This subpoena procedure is followed in the Circuit Court as well.

Prior to a trial, the judge, at his discretion, may call a pretrial conference (this usually occurs only at the Circuit Court level) at which attorneys for the parties will meet with the judge. Each side reveals what evidence he will present and what he intends to prove. The attorneys also exchange other information. The purpose of this conference is to enable the parties to know what law and issues are to be contested, what documents are to be presented, and what witnesses are to be called. Exchanging this information prior to trial results in a smoother and speedier trial by preventing most unfair surprises and resulting delay. All agreements in the conference on the issues of fact and law, and on the evidence and witnesses to be presented at trial, are generally binding on both parties.

These preliminary steps having been taken, the trial begins. It is important to note that all trials in the General District Court and Juvenile and Domestic Relations District Court are conducted without a jury. Juries are available only at the Circuit Court level.

The plaintiff begins the trial process by presenting his side of the controversy through testimony of witnesses, exhibits of documents, and any other pertinent evidence which will prove his point. It is the job of the opposing counsel to object to any evidence which he feels is irrelevant to the controversy or contrary to a rule of evidence established by a state law. In the Circuit Court, such arguments supporting these objections are usually made outside the hearing of the jury; since there is no jury at the District Court level, the lawyers are not required to "approach the bench" so as to make their arguments away from the jury box. At the conclusion of this process, the defendant begins his suit by presenting his evidence and countering objections made, if any, by plaintiff or his counsel. When this is completed, the judge renders a decision (final judgment).

The losing party has the right to appeal to the Circuit Court if the amount in dispute in the case was over $50, or if the case involved the constitutionality or validity of a statute or ordinance.

This appeal must be noted and a bond posted within ten days after final judgment, or the right of appeal will be lost.

The winning party either collects his award of damages, or, if the loser fails to pay, follows the procedures for enforcement of judgment, discussed *infra*.

Trials at the General District Court level are usually less formal than the procedures outlined above. Although the procedures outlined will help one to understand what occurs before, during and after trial, they will not enable the layman to try his own case.

JUVENILE AND DOMESTIC RELATIONS DISTRICT COURT

The Juvenile and Domestic Relations District Court handles all intra-family cases involving noncriminal matters, including custody and child support suits where the Circuit Court has not granted a divorce to the parties or otherwise ruled on these matters. It also has jurisdiction over all offenses committed by or against juveniles (including traffic offenses).

The Juvenile and Domestic Relations District Court has jurisdiction over all juveniles (children under eighteen who are physically or legally residing in its judicial district). Hearings may be started either by detention or arrest, or by petition. Most hearings arise by petition; arrest or detention rarely occurs. The process for a hearing usually begins when an "Intake Officer" (usually a social worker or probation officer) either hears a complaint or witnesses certain conduct. On the basis of this information, the officer decides whether the court should be petitioned for a hearing. The "Intake Officer" is given great discretion in this area, though the decision whether or not to petition for a hearing usually comes after a conference with interested parties (parents, the juvenile, complaining parties, and attorneys, if any — and it is best to have one there). If the officer feels a hearing is needed, he will petition the court for an official solution to the problem. Should the hearing not be deemed necessary, the officer and the parties involved can work out some other solution. Once a formal hearing is sought, the court sends a notice of the hearing to those who have legal custody of the juvenile.

The hearing itself resembles a very informal trial. The results may vary depending upon the reasons for the hearing. Appeals from any final judgment of this court are taken to the Circuit Court. All juveniles who come before the Juvenile and Domestic Relations District Court have an absolute right to appeal their case. There are two important features of the juvenile court system: (1) Juveniles convicted of a crime in a Juvenile and Domestic Relations District Court are not placed in a criminal status, meaning that, unlike an adult criminal, a juvenile would not be hindered in seeking a professional career, entering civil service or seeking entrance to military academies; and (2) after a specified time period, all records of the trial are destroyed and the juvenile's record is "wiped clean."

CIRCUIT COURT

The Circuit Court for a judicial circuit is composed of one or more judges who hear appeals from courts not of record. The Circuit Court also has exclusive jurisdiction over all divorce cases, criminal cases, contests over wills, and civil cases involving an amount in controversy over $5,000, and all cases for which a removal [1] has been filed by the defendant.

The court hears all cases *de novo* (as if the case had never been heard in another court) and offers the parties involved the advantage of a jury trial. If the amount involved in the suit is less than $1,000, a jury of five is provided; if the amount is $1,000 or more, seven jurymen are provided.

The process of selecting a jury takes place before trial. When a jury trial is to take place, it is important that the people who serve on the jury act in an impartial manner. This impartiality is achieved through a process called *voir dire*, in which the judge, using his own questions and those submitted by attorneys for both sides,

---

1. If the amount involved in a case is over $500, the defendant, before the trial date in the District Court, may file for the removal of the case to the Circuit Court provided the trial has not commenced or a judgment has not been rendered in another court. There is a service fee, a writ tax, a deposit, and a court cost payment, and the defendant must show that he has a substantial defense to the plaintiff's charges.

examines potential jurors to weed out persons who may be biased in favor of one side or the other. If one of the lawyers, or the judge himself, feels that a person is prejudiced against, or partial towards, one party, the potential juror may be "challenged." Each side is permitted a certain number of peremptory challenges (meaning that they can object to a person serving on the jury without explaining why). When peremptory challenges have been exhausted, the parties must explain to the judge why a person should not serve on the jury for the case. If the judge agrees with the reasons of the challenging party, he will exclude the person being challenged from sitting on the jury for that particular trial.

Once the civil trial begins, the procedures regarding presentation of evidence are similar to, though more formal than, those employed in the General District Court. However, besides objecting, there are a number of tactics either party can employ to advantage during trial:

1. *Motion for Summary Judgment*

When either party ends the presentation of the evidence, the opposing party can "move for summary judgment," claiming that the other party has either failed to prove his charges or has presented evidence which backs up the opposing party's defense.

2. *Demurrer/Motion to Strike Evidence*

If the court overrules the opposing party's motion for summary judgment, the opposing party can choose to demur to that party's case. A demurrer to the evidence may be referred to as a legal way of saying "so what?" When a party demurs, he says to the court, "Even if the opposing party's evidence is looked upon in the most favorable light and all doubts are resolved in his favor, that party still has not presented a set of facts which provide a legal basis for a case for him." A party can make this motion only twice during trial — once at the end of the opposing party's presentation of evidence, and then after the presentation of all the evidence. A party who demurs must retract all the evidence he has presented which conflicts with the evidence put forth by the other side. If this motion is made in Circuit Court, the jury must retire and let the judge render a verdict. If the judge grants the motion for demurrer, the party so moving wins the case. If the motion is denied, the moving party loses the case. A safer course is for the attorney to make a motion to strike the opposing side's evidence, in effect asking the judge to declare that evidence insufficient to support the claim or defense asserted. If this motion is granted, judgment is given for the moving party; but if it is denied, the trial continues without detriment to the moving party.

3. *Voluntary Nonsuit*

This motion is filed by the plaintiff prior to a final decision or the granting of a demurrer/motion to strike if he sees that there is a good chance he may lose the case. This enables the plaintiff to seek a voluntary dismissal of his case. The effect is as if no case had ever been brought, and the plaintiff may re-file his suit later, after correcting any mistakes he may have made in his preparation.

If the trial has not been concluded by any of these motions, at the end of the presentation of all the evidence each party summarizes his case. After this summation, the judge instructs the jury on the law being applied in the trial. This instruction is written after a consultation with the lawyers for each side in the suit. The consultation may take place at the pretrial conference.

Each party has the right to object to the judge's instruction. Once the jury has been instructed, they retire and upon return deliver a verdict. Each side has the right to request that each juror announce his decision. This is called "polling the jury."

When the verdict is given, the losing party has the option of filing one of the following motions:

1. *Motion for a New Trial*

A motion charging error by judge or jury, misconduct of the other party, unfair surprise, excessive damages.

2. *Motion to Set Aside the Verdict*

A motion charging that the verdict is contrary to the evidence presented.

3. *Motion in Arrest of Judgment*
A motion charging errors which are apparent just by looking at the transcript of the case.

Each side presents an argument on the motion filed (whichever motion the lawyer chooses). If the party making the motion loses his argument, a final judgment at law or a final decree in equity is rendered by the court. Should the party win his argument, a new trial usually results.

When final judgment has been obtained, the winning party can enforce it if necessary. See the discussion of enforcement of judgments, *infra* in this chapter under the heading "Miscellaneous," subheading (c).

SUPREME COURT OF VIRGINIA

The Supreme Court is composed of seven justices. There is generally no appeal as a matter of right to this body, as the court has complete discretion as to what cases it will hear. A discussion of procedures here would be futile since each case is handled by lawyers and the parties rarely appear before the court.

MISCELLANEOUS

(a) *Magistrates*
Virginia formerly had justices of the peace. This office survives now under the new name of "magistrate." The magistrates, who can be found in the various judicial districts, are empowered to issue warrants of arrest for civil and criminal cases upon a showing of probable cause. They also issue civil warrants. The clerk's office will provide any person seeking a warrant with the name of a magistrate in his district. A person who is served with a warrant should be certain that a member of his family or a friend contacts a lawyer if he is unable to do so himself.

(b) *Discovery*
The term discovery refers to a series of Virginia procedural rules which permit either party to secure depositions, admissions, interrogatories (written questions), physical examinations of

opposing parties and production of written evidence (books, records, sales slips, etc.) prior to the beginning of trial before the Circuit Court. These rules set out what methods are to be used and the various protections for individuals against whom they are being used (*e.g.,* protective orders). A person who is subject to a request for a deposition or any of the discovery devices should contact his lawyer to ensure that his rights will be protected.

(c) *Enforcement of Judgments*

Unfortunately, in some cases a final judgment by a court in favor of a party does not ensure that he will receive the damages he has been awarded. If the losing side does not satisfy the judgment, the winning party must seek judicial enforcement of his judgment. Property, both real (*e.g.,* land) and personal (*e.g.,* furniture) can be subject to judicial seizure and sold at public auction to satisfy judgment debts.

It is important to note the following: (1) If a person receives notice that his property is being levied on to satisfy a debt and tries to carry away this property or sell it, he is subject to a criminal charge; and (2) Title 34 of the Virginia Code lists what property is exempt from levy (judicial seizure and/or execution).

In those situations in which the judge and the creditor are unsure what real estate or other tangible or intangible property is owned by the losing side, resort must be had to a process referred to as an "Interrogatory to a Debtor." The first step is to go to the clerk of the court where the judgment was obtained and have him issue an interrogatory subpoena, which costs $5.00. The subpoena requires the person against whom judgment was rendered to attend a hearing where the judgment creditor may question him as to what property he owns and its value. Once that party learns what property the judgment debtor has, the presiding judge is asked to order that person to hand over the real estate deed or the tangible property itself to the sheriff or the sergeant for sale. If the debtor has been served or given notice of the subpoena and fails to appear, he is subject to an arrest warrant.

CHAPTER 17

Federal Assistance

M. E. Hopkins

L. M. Williams

In General

> We the People of the United States, in Order to form a more perfect Union, establish Justice, insure domestic Tranquility, provide for the common Defense, promote the general Welfare, and secure the Blessings of Liberty to ourselves and our Posterity, do ordain and establish this Constitution for the United States of America.

The Preamble to the Constitution of the United States in theory guarantees that the Nation exists for all people and that the well-being of all the people — including the poor — is within the legitimate objectives of society. To fulfill those objectives, or at least to lessen the disparity between the poor and the affluent, the Federal Domestic Assistance Programs were created. Some of the major programs available to individuals or families needing assistance include Food Stamps, Supplemental Security Income, Aid to Families with Dependent Children, and Medicaid.

Public assistance programs are created to help people in genuine need, and the degree of need must be verified by information, which is usually provided by the applicant. Any personal information that may be necessary to establish eligibility is confidential and is not open to public display.

A prime human concern is hunger and inadequate nutrition. Any discussion of assistance programs should rightly begin with an examination of the Food Stamp Program — a measure designed to alleviate these conditions.

Food Stamp Program

The Food Stamp Program created by the Food Stamp Act of 1964, and amended by Public Law 91-671, is a measure designed to lessen the cost of food by issuing stamps to low-income households. These stamps allow the purchase of food at a significantly lower price than retail value. Food stamps are not free; one must first pay a minimal sum (determined by family size and income) to obtain stamps. The purchasing power of the stamps is, however, far greater than the initial cash amount expended for them. The use of food stamps is an attempt to help a family improve its diet without spending all of its income on nondurable goods.

After purchasing food stamps, the recipient uses them to purchase groceries, usually at a participating retail food store. Food stamps cannot be used at fast food outlets or other restaurants.

Federal responsibility for the direction of the food stamp program lies with the Department of Agriculture. The actual distribution of the food stamps to participants is the responsiblity of the state welfare department. Such administration is subdelegated to local welfare agencies.

A potential recipient's qualifications are determined by national eligibility standards that examine household income, affiliation of household members, and work registration. Certain deductions are allowed to establish household income eligibility: income taxes (local, state, and federal); social security taxes; retirement payments; union dues; and shelter expenditures in excess of thirty percent of household income, such as utility payments, rent, mortgage payments on an owned home, real estate taxes, and medical costs in excess of $10 per month. Tuition and required educational costs are also deductible.

A household is defined as an association of people related through blood, kinship or legal communion recognized by state law who share the same household and kitchen and who buy food together or otherwise reside as one economic entity. Any individual 60 years of age or older is considered a family for food stamp purposes.

In the event of a change in the status of a household, the alteration in size, income, or the relationship of the household members must be disclosed to the local welfare or food stamp office. Failure to disclose significant information may cause a household to receive less aid than it is legally entitled to, because a decrease in income or an increase in household size would necessarily decrease the funds expended for food stamps and increase the allotment of food stamps. There are also certain legal penalties for a recipient's failure to reveal a change in household status which would result in a decreased allotment. The household may even be eliminated from the food stamp program for concealment of such information. In addition, the misuse of food stamps may lead to legal penalties. Any use of food stamps inconsistent with the provisions of the Food Stamp Act is a misdemeanor if the stamps are valued at less than $100. If the value of the stamps is $100 or more, the violator will be charged with a felony. Furthermore, food stamps may not be obtained through barter, sale, or any other manner contrary to food stamp provisions and regulations.

Should an applicant or a food stamp recipient believe that he is being improperly denied the benefits of the program, that individual has the right to a hearing before a higher authority designated by the state welfare agency. The applicant has the right to challenge the local agency when he believes that undue delay has occurred in the processing or consideration of his application. The recipient has the right to present arguments and witnesses on his behalf and the state agency has the responsibility to aid the recipient in formulating the appeal. Any failure to process food stamp applications within the mandatory 30-day period is a violation of the Act.

SUPPLEMENTAL SECURITY INCOME PROGRAM

Besides the Food Stamp Program, the Department of Health, Education, and Welfare administers a financial assistance plan which aids individuals whose income may be inadequate or nonexistent. The Supplemental Security Income Program (SSI), which became effective on January 1, 1974, is designed to supplement the income of the aged, the blind, and the permanently and totally disabled. An individual who is over 65 years old, blind, (visual impairment of 20/200 or less in the best eye even with the use of a corrective lens), or disabled, and who can demonstate need based on examination of income, is eligible for SSI payments.

A disabled person is one who is not capable of working due to a physical or mental condition. Such a disability must be one which has been in existence for at least 12 months or one that may result in death. A minor may qualify for benefits if it can be shown medically that the impairment is of adequate gravity. Finally, those who were considered permanently or totally disabled under Title XVI of the Social Security Act of 1972 and who were eligible under that plan retain that eligibility. Since the SSI payments are different for individuals and couples, in order to qualify as an eligible spouse it must be shown that the husband or wife is aged, blind, or disabled and has not been residing independently from his or her spouse who is similarly incapacitated. Lastly, the applicant must be a United States citizen or alien resident intending to live permanently in the United States.

Upon meeting eligibility requirements, an individual is entitled to payments of $146 per month if his income is less than $1,500 a year. Couples are paid $219 monthly if their combined income is less than $2,250 a year.

Besides the individuals mentioned above, others may qualify for SSI payments. An "essential person" is within this catagory, which includes individuals who are not normally eligible for SSI payments in their own right, but who reside with a qualified individual who is not a husband or wife, *e.g.,* a grandparent. Finally, alcoholics and drug addicts are entitled to SSI benefits, if they undergo treatment. If immediate relief is needed and an applicant seems likely to fulfill the eligibility requirements, an advance payment not in excess of $100 may be granted.

No applicant may be denied consideration because of discrimination or prejudice based upon race, color, or national origin. It is the responsibility of state welfare or public assistance officers to make available information concerning eligibility requirements and application procedures to those seeking such aid and information. If an agency expresses a reluctance to reveal such information, the applicant should seek legal aid or help from a welfare rights organization whose main function is to assist applicants or recipients. Generally, information that affects the public must be made available for examination during the regular office hours of the agency or office.

If an individual feels that he has been deprived of his rights in some way, or if the agency has been unduly tardy in the consideration of an application, or if payments have been decreased or stopped for no apparent reason, he may request a review or hearing in which the agency must explain its actions. At this time the applicant or recipient may tell the hearing officer (if it is a local dispute) what injury or wrong has been committed. If the review of the decision rendered by the hearing officer is unsatisfactory, the individual has the right to request a review by the State Board of Welfare. Ultimately, the Secretary of Health, Education, and Welfare may review the dispute if it cannot be resolved at a lower level. As with the Food Stamp Program, there are penalties for giving false information in order to receive payments. If an applicant or recipient is found to have lied in representing his eligibility, there is a penalty of up to $1,000 and/or a year in prison.

MISCELLANEOUS PROGRAMS

In addition to the provisions of the Supplemental Security Income Program, there are many other programs which involve medical services and benefits for children. There are several programs of which the public is often unaware or misinformed. They are:

1. *Cuban Refugee Program*

    This program is available in any locality in the state to assist Cuban refugees under specified conditions. It is administered by the local welfare departments but is funded entirely by the federal government.

2. *Preventive and Remedial Medical Services*

    These services are available to parents in an effort to establish paternity for children born out of wedlock and to secure support from those parents who have deserted their children.

3. *Services to Aged and Disabled Adults*
The services in this category consist of assisting with arrangements for homemaking, special care at home, and counseling in personal problems.

The local welfare department should be contacted if one feels that he qualifies for any of the programs outlined above. The local department will advise applicants as to their eligibility for these programs.

Medicaid

The medical assistance program commonly called Medicaid became effective in 1965 under the provisions of Public Law 89-97. It is a program designed to provide medical care for poor persons. The federal and state governments share the cost of the Virginia Title XIX Medical Assistance Program. The amount of federal funds available to each state depends upon the average per capita income in the state.

Medicaid provides financial assistance for certain health care expenses for categorically needy persons and category related-medically needy persons. Category related-medically needy persons are individuals and families who meet all eligibility requirements except for income and financial resources for welfare payments. Persons in this cateogry are able to provide their own clothing, shelter, and food, but they do not have sufficient funds to pay for medical expenses. In addition, a medically needy person must also be either blind, totally disabled, age 65 or older, or a "dependent child."

Categorically needy persons are recipients of welfare funds or are persons eligible to receive money under one of the following programs: Old Age Assistance, Aid to the Blind, Aid to Permanently and Totally Disabled, and Aid to Families with Dependent Children.

Financial eligibility is important in determining eligibility for Medicaid. A maximum income of $1,900 per year is allowed for one person, $2,500 for two people, plus an additional $400 for each dependent. Persons with incomes in excess of the established amounts may be eligible for medical assistance if the excess is insufficient to meet the total cost of medical care. Coverage for this group is limited to six months for each application.

Those who are disabled or age 65 or older may qualify for Aid to the Permanently and Totally Disabled or for Old Age Assistance. There are several requirements that one must meet to be eligible for these programs. They are:

A. *Aid to the Permanently and Totally Disabled*
1. *Age.* The year of birth must be established. The applicant must be age 18 through 65.
2. *Residence.* The applicant must be a Virginia resident. A person is considered a resident of Virginia if he is living in the state voluntarily and not for a temporary purpose. One cannot qualify if he is a resident in a public institution or a patient in a private or public institution for victims of mental disease or tuberculosis.
3. *Continuing Eligibility.* An individual meets the residence requirements as long as he is making his home in Virginia.
4. *Property Transfer.* An individual cannot assign or transfer property in order to become eligible for APTD at any time within two years immediately prior to application.
5. *Need.* A person must be in need of public assistance.

B. *Old Age Assistance*

In the Old Age Assistance category, the applicant must be age 65 or older. He must be a resident of Virginia and in need of public assistance. If any transfer of property is made by the applicant, consideration must be given to the circumstances, such as whether payment was made for the property and, if so, whether it approximated the fair market value of the property. Applications for Aid to the Permanently Totally Disabled or for Old Age Assistance should be made at the department of public welfare in the county or city where the applicant lives.

C. *Aid to Families with Dependent Children*

Aid to Families with Dependent Children is a money payment in the form of a check for needy children living in the home of a parent or other relative. State and federal funds are used to finance this program. In order to receive benefits from this program the applicant must meet the following eligibility requirements in Virginia:

1. He must under 16 years of age, or under 21 years old if regularly attending school; or be 16 or 17 years of age with an incapacity which prevents him from attending school or from making effective use of school attendence or for whom there is no appropriate program of education or training available;
2. He must be a resident of Virginia;
3. He must be in need of public assistance;
4. He must be deprived of parental support or care by reason of death, continued absence of the parent from home, or the physical or mental incapacity or unemployment of a parent.
5. He must be living in the home of a parent, or of certain specified relatives, or in foster care.

In Virginia assistance may not be denied an otherwise eligible child who is obviously under 12 years old, but cannot prove his birthdate. Otherwise, birthdates must be established.

The amount of the monthly payment is the budgetary deficiency adjusted to the nearest dollar. An amount deemed sufficient for basic necessities is subtracted from the applicant's income, and the grant is the difference between the two amounts. The grant will adjust according to the fluctuations in the family's income. Under Emergency Assistance to Needy Families with Children, the total payment which may be granted to a family must not exceed $750 during any period of less than thirty consecutive days within a twelve month period.

All earned and unearned income which is actually available to members of an assisted family for current use on a regular basis must be reported. Only income actually available for current use can be counted in determining eligibility on the basis of need. All income must be verified, and it is the responsibility of the recipient to report any changes in his regular income within ten days after they occur. Income from property when the individual is not actively employed or when no managerial responsibilities are involved is not considered earned income. Self-employment is defined as a business, farming, or commercial enterprise from which the individual receives income earned through his own efforts, including his active management of property. Regular income earnings are those received from permanent, full- or part-time employment on a planned basis. Those earnings received from seasonal employment must also be accounted for.

Certain income must be disregarded in determining the need of the assistance unit and the amount of the assistance. No inquiry can be made regarding the amount of earnings of an eligible child who is under the age of 14 years. All earned income of each eligible child age 14 or older who is either a full- or part-time student must be disregarded. If the parent is receiving SSI, none of his income can be counted as available to the AFDC assistance unit.

Some property is an allowable reserve. An applicant may own his home, which is defined as a lot including adjoining land used for a vegetable garden or for outbuildings essential to the dwelling. Furnishings and equipment used in the operations of the home and one motor vehicle are allowable. Cash on hand may not exceed $400. If the applicant has life or retirement insurance, it should not exceed $1,000 in face value.

Under federal requirements, a child may not be denied AFDC either initially or subsequently because of conditions in the home unless provision is otherwise made pursuant to the state law for adequate care and assistance with respect to the child. This suitable home policy is a device that may be used by state welfare agencies to regulate or control the moral conduct of adult beneficiaries. However, a state regulation that made cohabitation with a man other than a husband a disqualifing factor has been invalidated.

Any home visits by welfare officials to check on the status of an applicant must be made during working hours. If someone is living in the home of an AFDC recipient and has not been reported to the welfare agency, the agency may seek the aid of the local police department to discover the nature of that person's presence in the AFDC home and to ensure that he is not reaping unauthorized benefits from the AFDC program.

The Parent Locator Service may be utilized to discover the whereabouts of any absent parent. The purpose is to enforce the parent's obligation to supply support payments. AFDC state programs must provide for the development and implementation of a program under which the state agency would undertake, in the case of a child born out of wedlock who is receiving AFDC, to establish the paternity of the child and to help secure support for him. Virginia law requires that a parent provide support for his or her children who are under the age of 18. Law enforcement officials are allowed to review welfare case records. However, there must be a written agreement between the agency and the law enforcement officials that such information is only to be used in the detection and prosecution of welfare fraud, the location of deserting parents, and the establishment of paternity in order to secure support, or in support of the AFDC program.

A child may not be denied AFDC benefits because a parent fails to identify the father of a child born out of wedlock. A state welfare regulation that required the mother to name the father of her child prior to qualification was invalidated. Nor should the mother's refusal to participate in a paternity suit against the father affect the child's receipt of benefits.

The locality responsible for the AFDC payment is that jurisdiction in which the applicant resides. When a recipient of AFDC benefits moves from one locality to another, he is entitled to receive uninterrupted assistance if there is no other change in his circumstances which would render him ineligible.

D. *Coverage*

Many medical expenses are covered by the AFDC program and Medicaid. They include:

1. *In-Patient Hospital Services*

    No limitation has been placed on the number of days of in-patient care which are covered. The duration of care is based on the physician's certification as to medical necessity.

2. *Out-Patient Hospital Services*
   These services must be furnished by a physician or a doctor of dental surgery in his office.
3. *Laboratory and X-ray Services*
   Laboratory work-ups may be ordered by a physician in his office, or they may be performed by an independent laboratory.
4. *Nursing Home Care*
   The State Health Department must classify the home as a skilled or intermediate care facility. There is no limitation on the number of nursing home days for which payment will be made, but periodic review of the patient's condition is necessary to determine the continuous need for assistance.
5. *Physicians' Services*
   The physician must be licensed. Psychiatric treatment will be provided if a psychological evaluation reveals that a recipient is in need of such a service.
6. *Home Health Services*
   These services include all services provided for a recipient under the authorization of a physician.
7. *Clinical Services*
   Therapeutic services can be furnished to an out-patient under a physician's instructions in a certified facility which is operated to provide medical care to out-patients.
8. *Pharmaceutical Services*
   Certain drugs will be provided when authorized by a physician. They include:
   a. antacids
   b. cough and cold preparations
   c. dermatologicals
   d. hemorrhoid preparations
   e. internal analgesics
   f. laxatives
   g. vitamins
   h. family planning supplies
   i. anti-nauseants

j. eye preparations
k. anti-diarrheals

The above-named drugs are in the category of nonlegend drugs. Legend drugs, which require a prescription, are also provided.

9. *Prosthetic Devices*

Prosthetic devices (artificial limbs) must be preauthorized by the local department of health.

10. *Optometry Services*

Refractions and eyeglasses must be preauthorized by the appropriate local health department. Services in this category must be rendered by a licensed practitioner.

11. *Podiatry (Foot Ailment) Services*

Services available in this area of specialization are any of those that a licensed practitioner is legally authorized to provide. Such services must be prescribed by a physician licensed to practice medicine.

12. *Dental Services*

Eligibles under age 21 may receive all services needed. Certain specific services such as bridgework or any other dental work must be preauthorized by the Director of Dental Services of the Medical Assistance Program at the request of the person providing the dental services.

13. *Family Planning Services*

Drugs, supplies, and devices provided in this area of specialization must be under the supervision of a physician.

14. *Transportation*

Ambulance services are provided only when the recipient's physical condition is such that no other method of transportation would be feasible. Nonemergency transportation by common carrier must be preauthorized by the local health center.

Medicaid is an extensive program under close scrutiny by the local welfare agencies. Persons giving the agency fraudulent information are subject to prosecution. Information given to the local agency is kept confidential. The Medicaid program's future depends upon the cooperation of the recipients in giving truthful information and using the services in the prescribed manner. When applying for Medicaid, some individuals may become discouraged because of the red tape involved; certain facts must be verified before the applicant can be considered as eligible, but this procedure is intended only to protect the public from fraudulent claims.

Persons who feel that they are in need of Medicaid should contact their local welfare department for a determination as to whether they meet the eligibility requirements, since they are subject to change. Recipients who are displeased with a decision regarding their grant have the right to appeal to the State Health Department. Individuals who have been denied assistance have the same right of appeal.

Conclusion

Although this chapter is by no means an exhaustive discussion of the available means to obtain federal assistance, a knowledge of the programs outlined may be of benefit to the individual or family in need of help. It is hoped that the information outlined here will provide the necessary encouragement for a needy person to seek the benefits from the financial and social programs currently being offered.

Index

A

ABORTION, p. 281.

ACCESSORIES TO CRIME, pp. 304, 305.

ACCIDENTS.
Industrial accidents.
  Workmen's compensation.
    Injuries resulting from accidents covered, pp. 213 to 216.
Insurance.
  See INSURANCE.
Motor vehicles.
  Negligence, pp. 192, 193.
  See MOTOR VEHICLES.
Negligence.
  See NEGLIGENCE.
Workmen's compensation.
  Injuries resulting from accidents covered, pp. 213 to 216.

ACTIONS AT LAW.
Civil procedure.
  See CIVIL PROCEDURE.
Divorce or annulment.
  Procedure, pp. 246, 247.
Landlord and tenant.
  Rent escrow, pp. 71 to 73.
  Rights of landlord, p. 79.
  Virginia residential landlord and tenant act, p. 82.
Procedure.
  See CIVIL PROCEDURE.
Workmen's compensation.
  Third-party law suits, pp. 225 to 228.

ADOPTION, pp. 247 to 250.
Common law adoption.
  Virginia does not recognize, p. 247.
Consent requirement, pp. 248, 249.
Defined, p. 247.
Effect, pp. 250, 251.
Intestate succession.
  Status of adopted children, p. 113.
Procedure, pp. 247, 248.

ADULTERY.
  Divorce.
    Ground for divorce, pp. 238, 239.
    Misdemeanor, p. 309.

AGED PERSONS.
  Federal aid.
    Medicaid, pp. 325 to 322.
    Services to aged and disabled adults, p. 325.

AGENTS.
  Insurance agents.
    See INSURANCE.

ALCOHOLIC BEVERAGES.
  Motor vehicles.
    Driving under the influence.
      Tests, p. 186.
      Unlawful, pp. 306, 307.

ANNULMENT OF MARRIAGE, pp. 236, 237.

APPEALS.
  Juvenile and domestic relations district courts, pp. 215, 315.

ARRAIGNMENT, p. 302.

ARREST, pp. 298, 299.
  Juveniles, p. 254.
  Warrants, pp. 298, 299.

ARSON, p. 308.

ARTICLES OF CONFEDERATION, p. 8.

ASSAULT.
  Tort liability, pp. 196, 197.
  Unlawful, p. 306.

ATTEMPTS TO COMMIT CRIME, p. 305.

ATTORNEYS AT LAW.
  Bar examination, pp. 13, 14.
  Clients.
    Lawyer-client relationship, pp. 18 to 21.
    Responsibilities of attorney to client, pp. 17 to 22.
    Responsibilities of client to attorney, pp. 22, 23.
  Code of professional responsibility, pp. 17, 18.
  Constitution of the United States.
    Right to counsel, pp. 268 to 271.

ATTORNEYS AT LAW—Cont'd
  Contingent fees, pp. 25, 26.
  Disciplinary proceedings, pp. 21, 22.
  Education, pp. 12 to 14.
  Ethics.
    Code of professional responsibility, pp. 17, 18.
    Violations.
      Disciplinary proceedings, pp. 21, 22.
  Fees, pp. 23 to 29.
    Client liable, p. 23.
    Contingent fees, pp. 25, 26.
    Landlord and tenant.
      Recovery of reasonable attorney's fees, p. 82.
    Liability of client, p. 23.
  Group legal service plans, pp. 28, 29.
  Landlord and tenant.
    Recovery of reasonable attorney's fees, p. 82.
  Lawyer referral service, p. 16.
  Legal aid societies, p. 27.
  Officers of the court, p. 15.
  Out-of-state attorneys, p. 14.
  "Paralegals," pp. 27, 28.
  Qualifications, pp. 12 to 14.
  Real estate transfers.
    Contract of sale, pp. 49, 50.
    Representation of both buyer and seller, p. 57.
  Right to counsel, pp. 268 to 271.
  Selection of an attorney, pp. 14 to 17.
  Students.
    Third-year practice, p. 27.
  Training, pp. 12 to 14.

AUTOMOBILES.
  General provisions.
    See MOTOR VEHICLES.

AVIATION.
  Insurance.
    Airline single-trip accidental death insurance, pp. 159, 160.

B

BAIL, p. 300.

BANKS AND BANKING.
  Husband and wife.
    Joint accounts.
      Rights of surviving spouse, pp. 125, 126.

BAR EXAMINATION, pp. 13, 14.

BATTERY.
Tort liability, pp. 197, 198.
Unlawful, p. 306.

BIRTH CONTROL, pp. 282, 283.

BONDS, SURETY.
Executors and administrators, pp. 129, 130.
Landlord and tenant.
Forthcoming bond, pp. 76, 77.

BUGGERY.
Felony, p. 309.

BURGLARY, pp. 307, 308.

C

CHAIN LETTERS.
Pyramid contracts unenforceable, pp. 36, 37.

CHILD ABUSE.
Reporting, p. 255.

CIRCUIT COURTS.
Civil procedure, pp. 315 to 318.
Jurisdiction, p. 315.

CIVIL LIBERTIES.
Constitutional rights generally.
See CONSTITUTION OF THE UNITED STATES.

CIVIL PROCEDURE, pp. 310 to 319.
Circuit courts, pp. 315 to 318.
Demurrer, p. 316.
Discovery, pp. 318, 319.
General district court, pp. 311 to 314.
Judgments.
See JUDGMENTS.
Jury.
Circuit court, pp. 315, 316.
Juvenile and domestic relations district court, pp. 314, 315.
Motions.
Arrest of judgment, p. 318.
New trial, p. 317.
Setting aside evidence, p. 317.
Striking evidence, p. 316.
Summary judgment, p. 316.

CIVIL PROCEDURE—Cont'd
Motions—Cont'd
Voluntary nonsuit, p. 317.
Nonsuit.
Voluntary nonsuit, p. 317.
Supreme court of Virginia, p. 318.

CLERGYMEN.
Marriage.
Solemnization of marriage, p. 232.

COLONIAL LAW.
American colonial law generally, pp. 6, 7.
Virginia colonial law, pp. 10, 11.

COMMERCIAL CODE.
See UNIFORM COMMERCIAL CODE.

COMMON LAW.
Anglo-Saxon influence, pp. 3, 4.
Colonial America, p. 6.
Evolution, pp. 2 to 6.
History, pp. 2 to 6.
Norman influence, p. 4.

CONSPIRACY, p. 305.

CONSTITUTION OF THE UNITED STATES.
Attorneys at law.
Right to counsel, pp. 268 to 271.
Double jeopardy, pp. 265, 266.
Due process of law.
Fourteenth amendment, p. 274.
Equal protection of the law.
Fourteenth amendment, pp. 275, 276.
Fifth amendment rights, pp. 264 to 267.
First amendment rights, pp. 256 to 258.
Fourteenth amendment rights, pp. 273 to 276.
Fourth amendment.
Right to freedom from unreasonable search and seizure, pp. 259 to 264.
Freedom of speech, pp. 256 to 258.
Freedom of the press, pp. 256 to 258.
Historical background, pp. 8 to 10.
Indictments.
Right to indictment, pp. 264, 265.
Jury.
Right to trial by jury, pp. 271, 272.
Searches and seizures.
Right to freedom from unreasonable search and seizure, pp. 259 to 264.

CONSTITUTION OF THE UNITED STATES—Cont'd
   Self-incrimination, pp. 266, 267.
   Sixth amendment rights, pp. 268 to 272.
   Trial.
      Defendant's rights at trial, pp. 268 to 272.
   Witnesses.
      Self-incrimination, pp. 266, 267.

CONSTITUTION OF VIRGINIA.
   Historical background, pp. 10, 11.

CONSUMERS.
   Contracts.
      How consumers can legally break contracts, pp. 37 to 40.
      Warranties, pp. 41 to 44.
   Credit.
      Women, pp. 288, 289.
   Warranties.
      Uniform commercial code, pp. 41 to 44.

CONTRACTS.
   Ability to contract, p. 32.
   Acceptance, pp. 33, 34.
      Uniform commercial code, p. 41.
   Capacity to contract. p. 32.
   Chain letters.
      Pyramid contracts unenforceable, pp. 36, 37.
   Consideration, p. 34.
   Consumers.
      How consumers can legally break contracts, pp. 37 to 40.
      Warranties, pp. 41 to 44.
   Defined, p. 30.
   Elements, pp. 33, 34.
   Express contracts, p. 31.
   Gambling contracts.
      Unenforceable, pp. 35 to 36.
   Governmental protection on modification, pp. 35 to 37.
   Implied contracts, p. 31.
   Insurance contracts.
      See INSURANCE.
   Minors.
      Ability to contract, p. 32.
   Offer, p. 33.
      Uniform commercial code, p. 41.
   Oral contracts, p. 30.
   Procedures for contracting, pp. 33, 34.
   Pyramid contracts.
      Unenforceable, pp. 36, 37.

CONTRACTS—Cont'd
  Real estate transfers.
    Contract of sale, pp. 49 to 51.
    Listing contract, pp. 47 to 49.
  Statute of frauds, p. 35.
  Types of contracts, pp. 30, 31.
  Unconscionable contract.
    Unenforceable, p. 37.
  Uniform commercial code.
    Sale of goods, pp. 40 to 44.
  Women.
    Right to contract and do business, pp. 287, 288.
  Written contracts, pp. 30, 31.
    Required when, pp. 34, 35.

CORPORATIONS.
  Taxation.
    Federal income tax.
      Returns.
        Filing, p. 86.
    Virginia state income tax.
      Declaration of estimated taxes, p. 97.
      Returns.
        Filing, p. 96.

COUNTERFEITING, p. 308.

COURTS.
  Circuit court.
    Civil procedure, pp. 315 to 318.
    Jurisdiction, p. 315.
  General district court.
    Civil procedure, pp. 311 to 314.
    Jurisdiction, p. 311.
  Juvenile and domestic relations district court.
    See JUVENILE AND DOMESTIC RELATIONS DISTRICT COURT.
  Supreme court of Virginia.
    Civil procedure, p. 318.

CRIMES.
  Accessories, pp. 304, 305.
  Adultery, p. 309.
  Arson, p. 308.
  Assault and battery, p. 306.
  Attempts to commit crime, p. 305.
  Buggery, p. 309.
  Burglary, pp. 307, 308.

CRIMES—Cont'd
  Conspiracy, p. 305.
  Counterfeiting, p. 308.
  Driving while intoxicated, pp. 306, 307.
  Drugs, p. 309.
  Forgery, p. 308.
  Gambling, p. 309.
  Homicide, pp. 305, 306.
  Larceny, p. 307.
  Maiming, p. 306.
  Manslaughter, p. 306.
  Murder, pp. 305, 306.
  Principals and accessories, pp. 304, 305.
  Prostitution, p. 309.
  Rape, p. 306.
  Robbery, p. 307.
  Sex offenses, p. 309.
  Sodomy, p. 309.
  Theft, p. 307.

CRIMINAL PROCEDURE, pp. 297 to 304.
  Arraignment, p. 302.
  Arrest, pp. 298, 299.
  Bail, p. 300.
  Booking, p. 299.
  Indictment, pp. 300, 301.
  Pleading, pp. 302, 303.
  Preliminary hearing, pp. 299, 300.
  Pretrial activity, pp. 301, 302.
  Rights of accused.
    Constitutional rights generally.
      See CONSTITUTION OF THE UNITED STATES.
  Sentencing, pp. 303, 304.
  Trial, p. 303.

CURTESY, pp. 122, 123.

D

DEATH.
  Workmen's compensation.
    Amount of compensation, p. 225.
    Mysterious death covered, p. 216.

DEBTORS AND CREDITORS.
  Executors and administrators.
    Payment of deceased's debts, p. 131.
  Homestead allowance, p. 124.

INDEX

DECEDENTS' ESTATES, pp. 111 to 132.
  Executors and administrators.
    See EXECUTORS AND ADMINISTRATORS.
  Intestate succession.
    See INTESTATE SUCCESSION.
  Taxation.
    Federal estate tax, pp. 98, 99.
    Virginia inheritance tax, pp. 99, 100.
  Wills.
    See WILLS.

DEFAMATION.
  Tort liability, pp. 198, 199.
  Women, p. 281.

DEMURRER, p. 316.

DESERTION AND NONSUPPORT, pp. 232 to 236.
  Divorce.
    Abandonment or desertion as ground for divorce, pp. 238, 239.
  Juvenile and domestic relations district courts.
    Jurisdiction, pp. 254, 255.
  Revised uniform reciprocal enforcement of support act, pp. 235, 236.

DEVELOPMENT OF THE LAW.
  See HISTORY OF THE LAW.

DISCOVERY.
  Civil cases, pp. 318, 319.

DISEASES.
  Workmen's compensation.
    Coverage of injuries resulting from occupational disease, pp. 216 to 219.
      Filing of claim for benefits, p. 221.

DISTRESS FOR RENT, pp. 74 to 79.

DIVORCE, pp. 238 to 246.
  Actions for divorce or annulment.
    Procedure, pp. 246, 247.
  Adultery.
    Ground for divorce, pp. 238, 239.
  Annulment of marriage, pp. 236, 237.
  Child custody, pp. 244 to 246.
  Cruelty.
    Ground for divorce, pp. 238 to 240.
  Desertion.
    Ground for divorce, pp. 238, 239.
  Divorce from bed and board, pp. 240, 241.

DIVORCE—Cont'd
  Grounds, pp. 238 to 241.
  Procedure in actions for divorce, pp. 246, 247.
  Property.
    Court without jurisdiction to enter decree affecting property rights, p. 244.
    Partition, pp. 286, 287.
  Support and maintenance, pp. 241 to 243.
  Wills.
    Revocation of will, pp. 120, 121.

DOUBLE JEOPARDY.
  Constitution of the United States, pp. 265, 266.

DOWER, pp. 122, 123.

DRIVER IMPROVEMENT ACT, pp. 180 to 182.

DRUGS.
  Criminal offenses, p. 309.

E

EDUCATION.
  Women.
    Rights as student, pp. 290 to 292.

EMPLOYER AND EMPLOYEE.
  Negligence.
    Liability for negligence, p. 194.
  Taxation.
    Federal income tax.
      Withholding tax, p. 94.
    Social security taxes, pp. 97, 98.
  Women.
    Rights regarding employment, pp. 292 to 294.
  Workmen's compensation.
    General provisions.
      See WORKMEN'S COMPENSATION.

EMPLOYMENT AGENCIES.
  Prohibited act, pp. 39, 40.

ENGLISH COMMON LAW.
  See COMMON LAW.

ESTATES.
  Decedents' estates.
    See DECEDENTS' ESTATES.

EVIDENCE.
  Exclusionary rule, p. 263.
    Illegal arrest without warrant, p. 299.

EVIDENCE—Cont'd
    Motion to strike evidence, pp. 316, 317.

EXECUTORS AND ADMINISTRATORS, pp. 128 to 132.
    Accounting for assets, pp. 131, 132.
    Appointment, pp. 128, 129.
    Bonds, surety, pp. 129, 130.
    Debtors and creditors.
        Payment of deceased's debts, p. 131.
    Expenses.
        Reimbursement, p. 131.
    Powers and duties, pp. 129 to 132.
    Probate tax, p. 130.
    Reimbursement for expenses, p. 131.
    Taxation.
        Probate tax, p. 130.

F

FALSE IMPRISONMENT.
    Tort liability, p. 198.

FEDERAL ASSISTANCE, pp. 320 to 332.
    Aid to families with dependent children, pp. 327 to 329.
        Coverage, pp. 329 to 332.
    Cuban refugee program, p. 324.
    Food stamp program, pp. 320 to 322.
    Medicaid, pp. 325 to 332.
        Coverage, pp. 329 to 332.
    Preventive and remedial medical services, p. 324.
    Services to aged and disabled adults, p. 325.
    Supplemental security income program, pp. 322 to 324.

FEDERAL INCOME TAX.
    See TAXATION.

FEES.
    Attorneys at law, pp. 23 to 29.
        Contingent fees, pp. 25, 26.
        Landlord and tenant.
            Recovery of reasonable attorney's fees, p. 82.
    Drivers' licenses, p. 177.
    Real estate transfers, p. 58.

FIRE PREVENTION.
    Landlord and tenant.
        Right of tenant to install devices, p. 67.

FOOD STAMP PROGRAM, pp. 320 to 322.

FORGERY, p. 308.

FRAUD.
  Wills, p. 118.

G

GAMBLING.
  Contracts.
    Gambling contracts unenforceable, pp. 35, 36.
  Prohibited, p. 309.

GARBAGE AND TRASH.
  Landlord and tenant.
    Tenant to remove and dispose, pp. 65, 66.

GENERAL DISTRICT COURTS.
  Civil procedure, pp. 311 to 314.
  Jurisdiction, p. 311.

GIFTS.
  Taxation.
    Federal gift tax, pp. 100, 101.
    Virginia gift tax, p. 101.

H

HISTORY OF THE LAW, pp. 1 to 11.
  Articles of confederation, p. 8.
  Colonial American law, pp. 6, 7.
  Common law, pp. 2 to 6.
  Constitution of the United States, pp. 8 to 10.
  English common law, pp. 2 to 6.
  Magna Carta, p. 5.
  Origins, pp. 1, 2.
  Virginia law, pp. 10, 11.
  Workmen's compensation laws, pp. 203 to 205.

HOME SOLICITATION SALES ACT, pp. 37 to 39.

HOMICIDE, pp. 305, 306.

HUSBAND AND WIFE.
  Banks and banking.
    Joint accounts.
      Rights of surviving spouse, pp. 125, 126.
  Curtesy, pp. 122, 123.
  Desertion and nonsupport, pp. 232 to 236.
  Divorce.
    See DIVORCE.

HUSBAND AND WIFE—Cont'd
  Dower, pp. 122, 123.
  Intestate succession.
    Interest of surviving spouse, pp. 123, 124.
    Surviving spouse.
      Rights, p. 287.
  Intra-family immunity, p. 286.
  Marriage.
    See MARRIAGE.
  Motor vehicles.
    Surviving spouse.
      Obtaining title to family automobile, pp. 124, 125.
  Tenancy by the entirety.
    Real estate, p. 55.
  Wills.
    Interest of surviving spouse, pp. 122 to 126.
    Surviving spouse.
      Rights, p. 287.

I

ILLEGITIMATE CHILDREN.
  Intestate succession, pp. 113, 114.
  Rights of mother, pp. 281, 282.
  Support.
    Liability of father, pp. 233, 234.

INCOME TAX.
  Federal income tax, pp. 85 to 95.
    See TAXATION.
  Virginia state income tax, pp. 95 to 97.
    See TAXATION.

INDICTMENTS, pp. 300, 301.
  Constitution of the United States.
    Right to indictment, pp. 264, 265.

INFANT.
  See MINORS.

INHERITANCE.
  Intestate succession generally.
    See INTESTATE SUCCESSION.

INJURIES.
  Negligence.
    See NEGLIGENCE.

INSANE PERSONS.
  Marriage.
    Prohibited, p. 231.

INSURANCE, pp. 133 to 136.
   Accident and sickness insurance, pp. 155 to 160.
      Airline single-trip accidental death insurance, pp. 159, 160.
      Definition of "accident," p. 158.
      Group health insurance, p. 159.
   Agents.
      Authority, pp. 137 to 139.
      Defined, pp. 136, 137.
   Airline single-trip accidental death insurance, pp. 159, 160.
   Automobile insurance, pp. 160 to 165.
      Conditions in policy, pp. 164, 165.
      Coverage, pp. 160, 161.
      Exclusions in policy, pp. 164, 165.
      Motor vehicle registration.
         Requirements, pp. 171, 172.
      Omnibus clause, pp. 162, 163.
      Uninsured motorist coverage, p. 163.
      Unknown motorist coverage, pp. 163, 164.
   Contracts.
      Insurable interest, pp. 139 to 141.
      Life insurance, pp. 147, 148.
         Rights and duties under contract, pp. 152, 153.
      Mandatory provisions, p. 141.
   Defined, p. 133.
   Fire insurance, pp. 143 to 147.
   Group health insurance, p. 159.
   Group life insurance, pp. 153 to 155.
   Insurable interest, pp. 139 to 141.
   Kinds of insurance companies, p. 134.
   Licenses.
      Agents, p. 137.
      Insurance companies, p. 136.
   Life insurance, pp. 147 to 155.
      Annuities, pp. 148, 149.
      Application, pp. 149, 150.
      Contracts.
         Mandatory policy provisions, pp. 150, 151.
         Prohibited policy provisions, pp. 151, 152.
      Definitions, pp. 147 to 149.
      Group life insurance, pp. 153 to 155.
      Procurement, pp. 149, 150.
      Settlement options, p. 149.
   Motor vehicles.
     Automobile insurance. See within this heading, "Automobile insurance."
   Mutual companies, pp. 134, 135.

INSURANCE—Cont'd
Property insurance.
Application, pp. 141 to 143.
Regulation of insurance companies, pp. 134 to 136.
State corporation commission.
Regulation, supervision and inspection of insurers, pp. 135, 136.
Stock companies, pp. 134, 135.
Title insurance, pp. 165, 166.

INTEREST.
Landlord and tenant.
Obligations of landlord, pp. 63, 64.

INTESTATE SUCCESSION, pp. 111 to 116.
Adoption.
Status of adopted children, p. 113.
Advancements, pp. 115, 116.
Husband and wife.
Interest of surviving spouse, pp. 123, 124.
Surviving spouse.
Rights, p. 287.
Illegitimate children, pp. 113, 114.
Murder.
Bar to inheritance, p. 116.
Per capita, p. 115.
Personal property.
Statute of distributions, pp. 112, 113.
Per stirpes, p. 115.
Real estate.
Statute of descent, p. 112.

J

JOINT TENANTS AND TENANTS IN COMMON.
Real estate, p. 55.

JUDGMENTS.
Enforcement, p. 319.
Motion in arrest of judgment, p. 318.

JURY.
Constitution of the United States.
Right to trial by jury, pp. 271, 272.
Number of jurors, p. 272.
Right to trial by jury, pp. 271, 272.
Waiver, p. 272.
Selection.
Circuit court, pp. 315, 316.

JURY—Cont'd
  Women.
    Jury duty, p. 294.

JUVENILE AND DOMESTIC RELATIONS DISTRICT COURTS, pp. 251 to 255.
  Appeals, pp. 254, 315.
  Arrest and detention of juveniles, p. 254.
  Child abuse.
    Jurisdiction, p. 255.
  Civil procedure, pp. 314, 315.
  Desertion and nonsupport.
    Generally, pp. 232 to 236.
    Jurisdiction, pp. 254, 255.
  Hearings, pp. 314, 315.
  Intake officer, p. 314.
  Jurisdiction, pp. 251 to 255, 314.
    Transfer or waiver of jurisdiction, pp. 252, 253.
  Procedure, pp. 314, 315.
  Transfer of jurisdiction, pp. 252, 253.
  Waiver of jurisdiction, p. 253.

L

LAND.
  Real estate.
    See REAL ESTATE.

LANDLORD AND TENANT.
  Abandoned dwelling unit.
    New rental terminates old lease, pp. 79, 80.
  Absence by tenant.
    Landlord's remedy for tenant's failure to give required notice, p. 79.
  Access to premises.
    Injunctive relief to compel, p. 81.
    Obligation of tenant to grant to landlord, p. 67.
    Unlawful entry.
      Tenant's remedies, p. 81.
  Actions at law.
    Rent escrow, pp. 71 to 73.
    Rights of landlord, p. 79.
    Virginia residential landlord and tenant act, p. 82.
  Attorneys at law.
    Recovery of reasonable attorney's fees, p. 82.
  Bonds, surety.
    Forthcoming bond, pp. 76, 77.
  Burglary-prevention devices.
    Right of tenant to install, p. 67.

LANDLORD AND TENANT—Cont'd
Common areas.
Obligations of landlord, pp. 64, 65.
Responsibility of landlord to maintain, p. 196.
Damage or destruction of premises.
Obligations of tenant, p. 66.
Right of tenant to vacate, pp. 70, 71.
Disclosure of information.
Obligations of landlord, p. 64.
Distress for rent, pp. 74 to 79.
Duties.
Landlord, pp. 62 to 65.
Tenant, pp. 65 to 68.
Fire prevention.
Right of tenant to install devices, p. 67.
Forthcoming bond, pp. 76, 77.
Garbage and trash.
Tenant to remove and dispose, pp. 65, 66.
Holdover tenants.
Remedies of new tenant, pp. 68 to 70.
Interest.
Obligations of landlord, pp. 63, 64.
Landlord's obligations, pp. 62 to 65.
Lease, pp. 60 to 62.
Breaches by landlord.
Tenant's remedies, pp. 68 to 73.
Breaches by tenant.
Landlord's remedies, pp. 73 to 82.
Prohibited provisions, pp. 61, 62.
Statute of frauds, p. 62.
Term, p. 61.
Termination, pp. 79 to 81.
Maintenance of premises.
Obligations of landlord, pp. 64, 65.
Remedies of landlord for tenant's failure to maintain, p. 79.
Negligence.
Liability for negligence, pp. 195, 196.
Possession of premises.
Landlord's duty to deliver right to possession, pp. 68, 69.
Tenant's remedies, pp. 69, 70.
Remedies for wrongful act.
Landlord, pp. 73 to 82.
Tenant, pp. 68 to 73.
Rent.
Default.
Remedies of landlord, pp. 74 to 79.

LANDLORD AND TENANT—Cont'd
  Rent—Cont'd
    Default—Cont'd
      Waiver of right to terminate tenancy of defaulting tenant by acceptance of periodic rent payments, p. 80.
    Retaliatory increases.
      Prohibited, pp. 81, 82.
    Termination of rental agreement.
      Recovery of back rent, p. 80.
  Rent escrow, pp. 71 to 73.
  Retaliatory action against complaining tenant.
    Prohibited, pp. 81, 82.
  Right of entry.
    Injunctive relief to compel access, p. 81.
    Obligation of tenant to grant to landlord, p. 67.
    Unlawful entry.
      Tenant's remedies, p. 81.
  Rules and regulations.
    Obligation of tenant to obey, pp. 66, 67.
  Security deposit.
    Obligations of landlord, pp. 62, 63.
  Services.
    Failure by landlord to supply essential services.
      Remedies of tenant, p. 70.
    Landlord may not recover or take possession of dwelling unit by willfully interrupting services, p. 80.
    Willful diminution of essential services by landlord.
      Tenant's remedies, p. 71.
  Sheriffs.
    Distress for rent, pp. 74 to 79.
  Tenant's obligations, pp. 65 to 68.
  Termination of tenancy, p. 61.
  Vacation of premises.
    Damage or destruction of premises.
      When tenant may vacate, pp. 70, 71.
    Notice to vacate, p. 65.
    Obligations of tenant, pp. 67, 68.
  Virginia residential landlord and tenant act, pp. 59, 60.

LARCENY, p. 307.

LAW STUDENTS.
  Legal education generally, pp. 12 to 14.
  Third-year practice, p. 27.

LAWYER REFERRAL SERVICE, p. 16.

LAWYERS.
  See ATTORNEYS AT LAW.

LEASE, pp. 60 to 62.
  Breaches by landlord.
    Tenant's remedies, pp. 68 to 73.
  Breaches by tenant.
    Landlord's remedies, pp. 73 to 82.
  Prohibited provisions, pp. 61, 62.
  Statute of frauds, p. 62.
  Term, p. 61.
  Termination, pp. 79 to 81.

LEGAL HISTORY.
  See HISTORY OF THE LAW.

LIBEL AND SLANDER.
  Tort liability, pp. 198, 199.
  Women, p. 281.

LICENSES.
  Drivers' licenses. See within this heading, "Motor vehicles."
  Insurance agents, p. 137.
  Insurance companies, p. 136.
  Motor vehicles.
    Driver's license, pp. 174 to 182.
      Drunk driving.
        Suspension of license for failure to submit to tests, p. 186.
      Exemptions, p. 176.
      Expiration periods, p. 177.
      Fees, p. 177.
      Loss of licenses.
        Violations of motor vehicle code, pp. 178 to 182.
      Point system, pp. 180 to 182.
      Renewal, pp. 177, 178.
      Types, pp. 174, 175.
      Violations of motor vehicle code.
        Driver improvement act, pp. 180 to 182.
        Loss of license, pp. 178 to 182.
    Plates, pp. 173, 174.

LOANS.
  Real estate transfers.
    Financing, p. 56.

M

MAGISTRATES, p. 318.

MAGNA CARTA, p. 5.

MAIMING, p. 306.

MANSLAUGHTER, p. 306.

MARIJUANA.
Controlled drug, p. 309.

MARRIAGE, pp. 229 to 247.
Age.
Requirements, pp. 230, 231.
Annulment, pp. 236, 237.
Procedure in actions for annulment, pp. 246, 247.
Clergymen.
Solemnization of marriage, p. 232.
Common law marriage.
Invalid in Virginia, p. 231.
Divorce.
See DIVORCE.
Husband and wife generally.
See HUSBAND AND WIFE.
Incest.
Prohibited marriage, pp. 229, 330.
Insane persons.
Prohibited, p. 231.
Minors, pp. 230, 231.
Solemnization, pp. 231, 232.
Unlawful marriages, pp. 229 to 231.
Women.
Married name, p. 285.
Status of married women, pp. 283, 285.

MEDICAID, pp. 325 to 332.
Coverage, pp. 329 to 332.

MINORS.
Contracts.
Ability to contract, p. 32.
Marriage, pp. 230, 231.

MOTIONS.
See CIVIL PROCEDURE.

MOTOR VEHICLES, pp. 167 to 186.
Accidents, pp. 183 to 185.
Negligence, pp. 192, 193.
Reports, p. 184.
Alcoholic beverages.
Driving under the influence.
Tests, p. 186.

MOTOR VEHICLES—Cont'd
Alcoholic beverages—Cont'd
Driving under the influence—Cont'd
Unlawful, pp. 306, 307.
Certificate of title, pp. 168 to 171.
Citations, pp. 185, 186.
Driver improvement act, pp. 180 to 182.
Driver's license. See within this heading, "Licenses."
Drunk driving.
Tests, p. 186.
Husband and wife.
Surviving spouse.
Obtaining title to family automobile, pp. 124, 125.
Inspection, pp. 172, 173.
Insurance.
Automobile insurance.
See INSURANCE.
Registration.
Insurance requirements, pp. 171, 172.
Licenses.
Driver's license, pp. 174 to 182.
Drunk driving.
Suspension of license for failure to submit to tests, p. 186.
Exemptions, p. 176.
Expiration periods, p. 177.
Fees, p. 177.
Loss of licenses.
Violations of motor vehicle code, pp. 178 to 182.
Point system, pp. 180 to 182.
Renewal, pp. 177, 178.
Types, pp. 174, 175.
Violations of motor vehicle code.
Driver improvement act, pp. 180 to 182.
Loss of license, pp. 178 to 182.
Plates, pp. 173, 174.
Negligence.
Automobile accidents, pp. 192, 193.
Liability for negligence, pp. 193, 194.
Registration.
Inspection.
Requirements, pp. 172, 173.
Insurance.
Requirements, pp. 171, 172.
License plates, pp. 173, 174.
Title certificate, pp. 168 to 171.

MOTOR VEHICLES—Cont'd
  Title.
    Certificate, pp. 168 to 171.
  Traffic citations, pp. 185, 186.
  Violations of motor vehicle code.
    Citations, pp. 185, 186.
    Driver improvement act, pp. 180 to 182.
    Loss of driver's license, pp. 178 to 182.
    Point system, pp. 180 to 182.

MURDER, pp. 305, 306.
  Intestate succession.
    Bar to inheritance, p. 116.

N

NEGLIGENCE, pp. 187 to 196.
  Automobile accidents, pp. 192, 193.
  Causation.
    Negligent act must cause injury, pp. 190, 191.
  Contributory negligence, p. 191.
  Damages.
    Requirement of injury, pp. 190, 191.
  Defective products, p. 200.
  Defined, p. 188.
  Duty owed to others, pp. 188, 189.
  Employer and employee.
    Liability for negligence, p. 194.
  Injury.
    Negligent act must cause injury, pp. 190, 191.
  Landlord and tenant.
    Liability for negligence, pp. 195, 196.
  Liability.
    Exceptions, pp. 193, 194.
    Generally, pp. 193, 194.
    Landlords and tenants, pp. 195, 196.
    Real estate.
      Owners and operators, pp. 194, 195.
  Motor vehicles.
    Automobile accidents, pp. 192, 193.
    Liability for negligence, pp. 193, 194.
  Real estate.
    Liability of owners and occupiers, pp. 194, 195.
  Standard of care, p. 189.
  Victim's wrongful conduct.
    Effect, p. 191.

O

OCCUPATIONAL DISEASES.
  Workmen's compensation.
    Coverage of injuries resulting from occupational disease, pp. 216 to 219.
    Filing of claim for benefits, p. 221.

P

PARENT AND CHILD.
  Adoption.
    See ADOPTION.
  Desertion and nonsupport, pp. 232 to 236.
  Divorce.
    Child custody, pp. 244 to 246.

PARTNERSHIPS.
  Taxation.
    Federal income tax.
      Returns.
        Filing, pp. 85, 86.
    Virginia state income tax.
      Returns.
        Filing, p. 96.

PERSONAL PROPERTY.
  Intestate succession.
    Statute of distributions, pp. 112, 113.
  Taxation.
    Intangible personal property, pp. 104, 105.
    Tangible personal property, p. 104.

PLEADING.
  Criminal procedure, pp. 302, 303.

PRISONS AND PRISONERS.
  Women, pp. 294, 295.

PRIVACY.
  Invasion of privacy.
    Tort liability, pp. 199, 200.

PROBATE, pp. 126 to 128.
  Tax, p. 130.

PROFESSIONS AND OCCUPATIONS.
  Women.
    Restrictions, pp. 295, 296.

PROPERTY.
  Divorce.
    Court without jurisdiction to enter decree affecting property rights, p. 244.

PROPERTY—Cont'd
  Divorce—Cont'd
    Partition, pp. 286, 287.
  Insurance.
    See INSURANCE.
  Personal property.
    See PERSONAL PROPERTY.
  Real estate.
    See REAL ESTATE.
  Taxation, pp. 102 to 106.
    Intangible personal property, pp. 104, 105.
    Liability of taxpayer for taxes, pp. 105, 106.
    Real estate taxes, pp. 103, 104.
    Tangible personal property, p. 104.
  Women.
    Right to rent and own, pp. 289, 290.

PROSTITUTION.
  Misdemeanor, p. 309.

R

RAPE, pp. 279, 280, 306.

REAL ESTATE.
  Closing, pp. 57, 58.
  Intestate succession.
    Statute of descent, p. 112.
  Joint tenancy, p. 55.
  Landlord and tenant.
    See LANDLORD AND TENANT.
  Negligence.
    Liability of owners and occupiers, pp. 194, 195.
  Ownerships.
    Types of ownership, pp. 54, 55.
  Rental.
    Landlord and tenant law generally.
      See LANDLORD AND TENANT.
  Sale. See within this heading, "Transfers."
  Taxation, pp. 103, 104.
  Tenancy by the entirety, p. 55.
  Tenancy in common, p. 55.
  Title insurance, pp. 165, 166.
  Title search, pp. 51 to 54.
  Transfers, pp. 45 to 58.
    Assumption of loan, p. 56.
    Attorneys at law.
      Contract of sale, pp. 49, 50.

REAL ESTATE—Cont'd
  Transfers—Cont'd
    Attorneys at law—Cont'd
      Representation of both buyer and seller, p. 57.
    Closing, pp. 57, 58.
    Contracts.
      Contract of sale, pp. 49 to 51.
      Listing contract, pp. 47 to 49.
    Deed.
      Recordation, p. 58.
    Fees and costs, p. 58.
    Financing, p. 56.
    Title insurance, pp. 165, 166.
    Title search, pp. 51 to 54.

RECORDATION.
  Deeds, p. 58.

RECORDS.
  Taxation.
    Requirement of recordkeeping for IRS recognition, p. 84.

RENT.
  Landlord and tenant.
    See LANDLORD AND TENANT.

REPORTS.
  Motor vehicle accidents, p. 184.

RIGHT OF ENTRY.
  Landlord and tenant.
    Injunctive relief to compel access, p. 81.
    Obligation of tenant to grant to landlord, p. 67.
    Unlawful entry.
      Tenant's remedies, p. 81.

ROBBERY, p. 307.

S

SALES.
  Defective products.
    Tort liability, pp. 200, 201.
  Goods, pp. 40 to 44.
  Misrepresentation.
    Tort liability, pp. 200, 201.
  Real estate transfers.
    See REAL ESTATE.
  Tax, pp. 101, 102.

SALES—Cont'd
　Uniform commercial code.
　　Sale of goods, pp. 40 to 44.
　　Warranties.
　　　Breach of warranty.
　　　　Tort liability, pp. 200, 201.

SEARCHES AND SEIZURES.
　Constitution of the United States.
　　Right to freedom from unreasonable search and seizure, pp. 259 to 264.
　Exclusionary rule, p. 263.
　Search warrants.
　　Required, pp. 259, 260.
　　　Exceptions, pp. 260 to 263.

SEDUCTION, pp. 280, 281.

SENTENCING.
　Criminal procedure, pp. 303, 304.

SEX OFFENSES, p. 309.
　Rape.
　　See RAPE.

SHERIFFS.
　Landlord and tenant.
　　Distress for rent, pp. 74 to 79.

SOCIAL SECURITY.
　Taxation, pp. 97, 98.

SODOMY.
　Felony, p. 309.

SOLICITORS.
　Home solicitation sales act, pp. 37 to 39.

STARE DECISIS.
　Historical background, pp. 4, 5.

STATE CORPORATION COMMISSION.
　Insurance.
　　Regulation, supervision and inspection of insurers, pp. 135, 136.

STATUTE OF FRAUDS, p. 35.
　Lease, p. 62.

STERILIZATION.
　Women, pp. 282, 283.

SUMMARY JUDGMENT.
　Motion, p. 316.

INDEX 359

SUPREME COURT OF VIRGINIA.
  Civil procedure, p. 318.

T

TAXATION, pp. 83 to 110.
  Corporations.
    Federal income tax.
      Returns.
        Filing, p. 86.
    Virginia state income tax.
      Declaration of estimated taxes, p. 97.
      Returns.
        Filing, p. 96.
  Decedents' estates.
    Federal estate tax, pp. 98, 99.
  Deductions.
    Federal income tax. See within this heading, "Federal income tax."
  Employer and employee.
    Federal income tax.
      Withholding tax, p. 94.
  Estate taxes.
  Federal estate tax, pp. 98, 99.
    Virginia inheritance tax, pp. 99, 100.
  Executors and administrators.
    Probate tax, p. 130.
  Federal estate tax, pp. 98, 99.
  Federal gift tax, pp. 100, 101.
  Federal income tax.
    Accumulative earnings tax, p. 95.
    Adjusted gross income, pp. 87, 88.
    Capital gains and losses, pp. 91 to 93.
    Computation of taxable income, pp. 86 to 93.
    Corporations.
      Filing of returns, p. 86.
    Credits, pp. 90, 91.
    Deductions.
      Itemized deductions, pp. 89, 90.
      Standard deduction, pp. 89, 90.
      Trade and business deductions, pp. 88, 89.
    Exempt income, p. 87.
    Exemptions.
      Personal exemptions, p. 90.
    Gross income, pp. 86, 87.
    Income averaging, pp. 93, 94.
    Minimum tax, p. 95.
    Partnerships.
      Filing of returns, p. 86.

TAXATION—Cont'd
  Federal income tax—Cont'd
    Personal exemptions, p. 90.
    Personal holding company tax, p. 95.
    Returns.
      Filing.
        Corporations, p. 86.
        Partnerships, pp. 85, 86.
        When to file, p. 85.
        Who must file, p. 85.
      Preparation.
        Assistance, p. 83.
    Taxable income, p. 88.
      Computation, pp. 86 to 93.
    Withholding tax, pp. 94, 95.
  Gift taxes.
    Federal gift tax, pp. 100, 101.
    Virginia gift tax, p. 101.
  Income tax.
    Federal income tax. See within this heading, "Federal income tax."
    Virginia state income tax. See within this heading, "Virginia state income tax."
  Inheritance tax, pp. 99, 100.
  Intangible personal property, pp. 104, 105.
  Partnerships.
    Federal income tax.
      Returns.
        Filing, pp. 85, 86.
    Virginia state income tax.
      Returns.
        Filing, p. 96.
  Personal property.
    Intangible personal property, pp. 104, 105.
    Tangible personal property, p. 104.
  Probate tax, p. 130.
  Property taxes, pp. 102 to 106.
    Intangible personal property, pp. 104, 105.
    Liability of taxpayer for taxes, pp. 105, 106.
    Real estate taxes, pp. 103, 104.
    Tangible personal property, p. 104.
  Real estate taxes, pp. 103, 104.
  Records.
    Requirement of recordkeeping for IRS recognition, p. 84.
  Returns.
    Federal income tax. See within this heading, "Federal income tax."

TAXATION—Cont'd
Returns—Cont'd
Preparation.
Assistance, p. 83.
Virginia state income tax.
Filing, p. 96.
Sales and use tax, pp. 101, 102.
Social security taxes, pp. 97, 98.
Tangible personal property, p. 104.
Tax planning, p. 106.
Virginia state income tax, pp. 95 to 97.
Declaration of estimated income, p. 97.
Deductions, p. 96.
Exemptions, p. 96.
Internal revenue code.
Incorporation by reference, pp. 95, 96.
Out-of-state taxes.
Credit, p. 96.
Wills.
Probate tax, p. 130.

TENANTS.
General provisions.
See LANDLORD AND TENANT.

THEFT, p. 307.

TITLE INSURANCE, pp. 165, 166.

TITLE SEARCH, pp. 51 to 54.

TORTS.
Assault, pp. 196, 197.
Battery, pp. 197, 198.
Defamation, pp. 198, 199.
Defined, p. 187.
False imprisonment, p. 198.
Intentional torts, pp. 196 to 200.
Libel and slander, pp. 198, 199.
Negligence.
See NEGLIGENCE.
Privacy.
Invasion of privacy, pp. 199, 200.

TRASH.
See GARBAGE AND TRASH.

TRIAL.
Civil procedure.
See CIVIL PROCEDURE.

TRIAL—Cont'd
  Constitution of the United States.
    Defendant's rights at trial, pp. 268 to 272.
  Criminal procedure, p. 303.
  Jury.
    Right to trial by jury, pp. 271, 272.
  New trial.
    Motion for new trial, p. 317.
  Speedy trial.
    Right to speedy trial, pp. 272, 273.

U

UNIFORM COMMERCIAL CODE.
  Sale of goods, pp. 40 to 44.
  Warranties, pp. 41 to 44.

V

VERDICT.
  Motion to set aside verdict, p. 317.

VIRGINIA STATE BAR.
  Attorneys at law generally.
    See ATTORNEYS AT LAW.

W

WARRANTIES.
  Breach of warranty.
    Tort liability, pp. 200, 201.
  Uniform commerical code, pp. 41 to 44.

WARRANTS.
  Arrest warrants, pp. 298, 299.
  Search warrants.
    See SEARCHES AND SEIZURES.

WELFARE.
  Federal assistance.
    See FEDERAL ASSISTANCE.

WILLS, pp. 116 to 126.
  Curtesy, pp. 122, 123.
  Definitions of terms, p. 116.
  Divorce.
    Revocation of will, pp. 120, 121.
  Dower, pp. 122, 123.
  Fraud, p. 118.
  Handwritten wills.
    Holographic wills, p. 119.

WILLS—Cont'd
  Holographic wills, p. 119.
  Husband and wife.
    Interest of surviving spouse, pp. 122 to 126.
    Surviving spouse.
      Rights, p. 287.
  Lapse, p. 121.
  Mistakes, p. 118.
  Pretermitted heirs, pp. 121, 122.
  Probate, pp. 126 to 128.
  Requirements for effective will, p. 116.
  Revocation, pp. 120, 121.
    Revival or republication, p. 121.
  Surviving spouse.
    Interests, pp. 122 to 126.
  Taxation.
    Probate tax, p. 130.
  Testamentary capacity, pp. 116, 117.
  Testamentary intent, pp. 117, 118.
  Types of wills, pp. 118, 119.
  Undue influence, pp. 117, 118.
  Witnesses.
    Requirements, pp. 119, 120.

WITNESSES.
  Constitution of the United States.
    Self-incrimination, pp. 266, 267.
  Wills.
    Requirements, pp. 119, 120.

WOMEN, pp. 277 to 296.
  Abortion, p. 281.
  Birth control, pp. 282, 283.
  Contracts.
    Right to contract and do business, pp. 287, 288.
  Credit, pp. 288, 289.
  Divorce.
    General provisions.
      See DIVORCE.
  Education.
    Rights as student, pp. 290 to 292.
  Employer and employee.
    Rights regarding employment, pp. 292 to 294.
  Husband and wife.
    General provisions.
      See HUSBAND AND WIFE.

WOMEN—Cont'd
Illegitimate children.
Rights of mother, pp. 281, 282.
Inheritance, p. 287.
Jury duty, p. 294.
Marriage.
Married name, p. 285.
Status of married women, pp. 283, 285.
Prisons and prisoners, pp. 294, 295.
Professions and occupations.
Restrictions, pp. 295, 296.
Property.
Right to rent and own, pp. 289, 290.
Rape, pp. 279, 280.
Seduction, pp. 280, 281.
Slander, p. 281.
Sterilization, pp. 282, 283.

WORKMEN'S COMPENSATION, pp. 202 to 228.
Accidents.
Injuries resulting from accidents covered, pp. 213 to 216.
Actions at law.
Third-party law suits, pp. 225 to 228.
Amount of compensation, pp. 223 to 225.
Claim for benefits.
Filing, pp. 219 to 223.
Coverage.
Injuries covered. See within this heading, "Injuries covered."
Who is covered, pp. 206 to 212.
Death.
Amount of compensation, p. 225.
Mysterious death covered, p. 216.
Diseases.
Coverage of injuries resulting from occupational disease, pp. 216 to 219.
Filing of claim for benefits, p. 221.
Historical background, pp. 203 to 205.
Injuries covered, pp. 213 to 219.
Definition of "injury," p. 213.
Injuries resulting from accidents, pp. 213 to 216.
Injuries resulting from occupational disease, pp. 216 to 219.
Objectives, pp. 205, 206.
Occupational diseases.
Coverage of injuries resulting from occupational disease, pp. 216 to 219.
Filing of claim for benefits, p. 221.
Partial incapacity.
Amount of compensation, p. 224.

WORKMEN'S COMPENSATION—Cont'd
Third-party law suits, pp. 225 to 228.
Total incapacity.
Amount of compensation, pp. 223, 224.